# THE VOICE OF THE LAW IN TRANSITION

VERHANDELINGEN
VAN HET KONINKLIJK INSTITUUT
VOOR TAAL-, LAND- EN VOLKENKUNDE

235

AB MASSIER

# THE VOICE OF THE LAW IN TRANSITION
## Indonesian jurists and their languages 1915-2000

Translated from the Dutch by
Michaela Wouters

KITLV Press
Leiden
2008

*Published by:*
KITLV Press
Koninklijk Instituut voor Taal-, Land- en Volkenkunde
(Royal Netherlands Institute of Southeast Asian and Caribbean Studies)
P.O. Box 9515
2300 RA Leiden
The Netherlands
website: www.kitlv.nl
e-mail: kitlvpress@kitlv.nl

KITLV is an institute of the Royal Netherlands Academy of Arts and Sciences (KNAW)

This book is a translation of Ab Massier's PhD thesis *Van recht naar hukum; Indonesische juristen en hun taal, 1915-2000* (Leiden, 2003)

The research undertaken for this book was made possible, in part, by study trip grants supplied by the Nederlandse Organisatie voor Wetenschappelijk Onderzoek (NWO, Netherlands Organization for Scientific Research)

The translation was funded by the Nederlandse Organisatie voor Wetenschapelijk Onderzoek (NWO)

*Cover:* Creja ontwerpen, Leiderdorp

ISBN 978 90 6718 271 3

# Contents

# Abbreviations

| | |
|---|---|
| AB | Algemeene Bepalingen van Wetgeving voor Nederlandsch-Indië |
| AMS | Algemeene Middelbare School |
| a.t.b. | ambtenaar ter beschikking |
| *Bb.* | *Bijblad op het Staatsblad van Nederlandsch-Indië* |
| BPHN | Badan Pembinaan Hukum Nasional |
| BW | Burgerlijk Wetboek voor Nederlandsch-Indië |
| DPR | Dewan Perwakilan Rakyat |
| DPRD | Dewan Perwakilan Rakyat Daerah |
| Gama | Universitas Gadjah Mada |
| HBS | Hoogere Burger School |
| HIR | Herziene Inlandsch (later: Indonesisch) Reglement |
| IR | Inlandsch Reglement |
| Kepmen | keputusan menteri |
| Kepmenkeh | keputusan menteri kehakiman |
| Keppres | keputusan presiden |
| *LN* | *Lembaran Negara* |
| LPHN | Lembaga Pembinaan Hukum Nasional |
| Menkeh | Menteri Kehakiman |
| Ned. Stb. | Nederlands Staatsblad |
| NJV | Nederlandsche Juristen-Vereeniging |
| OSVIA | Opleidingsschool voor Inlandsche Ambtenaren |
| PKI | Partai Komunis Indonesia |
| PNI | Partai Nasional Indonesia |
| PP | peraturan pemerintah |
| PPPI | Perhimpoenan Peladjar-Peladjar Indonesia |
| RBg | Rechtsreglement Buitengewesten |
| RIS | Republik Indonesia Serikat |
| *RNI* | *Regt in Nederlandsch-Indië* |
| RO | Reglement op de regterlijke organisatie en het beleid der justitie in Nederlandsch-Indië |
| Rv | Reglement op de burgerlijke rechtsvordering |
| SK | surat keputusan |
| *Stb.* | *Staatsblad van Nederlandsch-Indië* |
| STOVIA | School tot Opleiding van Inlandsche Artsen |
| Sv | Reglement op de strafvordering |
| UI | Universitas Indonesia |

| | |
|---|---|
| UNAIR | Universitas Airlangga |
| UNDIP | Universitas Diponegoro |
| UNHAS | Universitas Hasanuddin |
| UNPAD | Universitas Padjadjaran |
| USU | Universitas Sumatera Utara |
| UU | undang-undang |
| UUDS | Undang-undang Dasar Sementara |
| WvK | Wetboek van Koophandel van Nederlandsch-Indië |
| WvS | Wetboek van Strafrecht voor Nederlandsch-Indië |

# Preface

This is the English version of *Van 'recht' naar 'hukum'; Indonesische juristen en hun taal, 1915-2000*, the PhD thesis I defended at Leiden University in September 2003. Apart from minor corrections and deletions, the original Dutch text has been followed. Although the number of footnotes has been reduced – mainly by moving references into the body of the text – many remain. This is partly because this book aims at a rather heterogeneous readership, including Indonesian law specialists, legal sociologists, linguists and historians. The footnotes help fill the gaps for one category of readers or another, without interrupting the argument in the main text. The second reason for so many footnotes is that the history told in this book, of the Indonesian legal community and its languages, is based not only on theories of law and language, but also on 'facts' and memories collected from a variety of books, magazine articles and interviews. As most people are not aware of how they speak, and do not often write about how they speak, I had to make do with all sorts of 'contextual evidence'. Where I found this evidence is indicated in the footnotes.

Whereas the Dutch version of this book gave examples of Dutch legal terms and expressions used in Dutch and Netherlands Indies law, most of these have been omitted in the English version. Because the Anglo-Saxon/English system of law is fundamentally different from the continental/Dutch legal system, many of the English terms that have been used to translate Dutch legal terms will unavoidably sound peculiar.

During the last century, the spelling rules of Indonesian changed several times. In this book, Indonesian terms are spelt according to the rules that have been applied since 1972 (*undang-undang*),[1] unless indicated otherwise (*mèster-bamboe*). Geographical names are written with their current spelling (Yogyakarta). Capitalized names of government institutions are spelt according to the rules applicable in the days of their foundation (Panitia Penghaloes Bahasa), unless the institution has survived under this name (Mahkamah Agung). For clarity's sake, personal names are written with their original

1 The Ejaan Yang Disempurnakan (EYD) or 'Perfected Spelling'.

spellings (Iwa Koesoema Soemantri). However, in references to literature, the spelling used on the title page is followed (Iwa Kusuma Sumantri 2002).

Many people have contributed to the making of this book. First of all, I gratefully seize the opportunity to thank those whom Leiden University custom didn't allow me to thank in my thesis. I am indebted to professors Ton van Haaften, Nick Huls, Hein Steinhauer and Willem Witteveen for their willingness to read my thesis critically and to be on the supervisory committee. To four other members of this committee I wish to pay special tribute.

Mardjono Reksodiputro, professor of criminology, practising lawyer, and member of a number of boards and commissions including the Komisi Hukum Nasional (National Law Commission) , helped and encouraged me during my research, in Indonesia, in the Netherlands, and by email. I am grateful for his willingness to make time for me on several occasions.

Dr. Adriaan Bedner was a wonderful colleague and a great support, in particular during the years I worked at Rapenburg 33 in Leiden, where the Van Vollenhoven Institute for Law, Governance and Development was then located. Adriaan's broad interests and unremitting enthusiasm have been an inspiration to me.

Professor Jan Michiel Otto, Director of the Van Vollenhoven Institute of the Leiden Faculty of Law and one of my supervisors, gave me the opportunity to work at Leiden University. I have greatly appreciated his trust, friendship and support over the years, and his attention to practical issues such as arranging grant extensions and planning for my professional future. He made me realize the importance of transforming plans and ideas into action.

Finally, professor Henk Maier, presently working at the University of California at Riverside, became my 'guru' while I was preparing my Master's thesis at the Department of Languages and Cultures of Southeast Asia and Oceania, at Leiden University. I very much enjoyed the many talks we had in his office, filled with books, piles of paper and pipe tobacco. I have come to regard the period I worked on my PhD thesis as a stage in growing up. Over the years, I have become more self-confident. I learned to write my own story, in more than just the literal sense. Henk Maier was an important catalyst in this process, combining a ceaseless stream of questions with a warm interest in my research and in other aspects of my life. I will always be grateful for that.

This brings me to the translator. Writing my thesis has made me keenly aware of the challenges of translation. As anyone who has mastered a foreign language beyond the initial phase will have experienced, learning a language that is not one's own is not about simply transposing a message in one's mother tongue into the foreign language. It is, rather, learning what to say and what not to say in that language. Correspondences or bridges between words or phrases in one language to words or phrases in another are treacherous: translation is like leaping from one shore to the opposite shore, plunging into a world in which nothing means what it seems to mean. Michaela Wouters, MA, a native speaker of both Dutch and English and an experienced translator, has produced a translation of my book which demonstrates this insight. I thank her for having ploughed through the long, complex and sometimes vague language of my thesis, turning it into powerful and easily readable English. A large part of whatever appreciation this book may receive is to her credit. Any imperfections that remain are my own.

I owe the Koninklijk Instituut voor Taal-, Land- en Volkenkunde (Royal Netherlands Institute of Southeast Asian and Caribbean Studies, KITLV) for generously allowing me to lard my book with photographs from its rich collection. I thank my former colleagues at KITLV Press for their care with editing this book. I am particularly grateful to Ms Rita DeCoursey, who graciously helped me out with the English in parts of the text, and Ms Marjan Groen, who skillfully yet in a record time managed to transform my manuscript into a book.

After I completed my PhD thesis in 2003, a number of people who contributed to my research have deceased. It is with great respect that I commemorate professor Daniel Lev, professor Koesnadi Hardjasoemantri and Purwoto Gandasubrata S.H.[2]

I would like to end with a few words about Han Bing Siong, LL.M.[3] Having abandoned his post of senior lecturer in criminal law at the Universitas Indonesia, Jakarta, in the 1960s to embark on PhD research in the Netherlands, the 1965-1966 coup made his temporary stay in the Netherlands a permanent one. Han's professional career was spent at the Ministry of Education and Sciences. On the side, he became one of the world's leading experts on Japanese swords, an interest sparked by his boyhood experiences during the Japanese occupation of the archipelago. Later in life he published several extensive articles on this period in *Bijdragen tot de Taal-, Land- en Volkenkunde*. Drawing on both Western and Japanese-language sources, he provides a remarkably balanced picture of the Japanese administration in the Indonesian archipelago. Over the years, I came to know him as a man of high standards, both as a scholar and as a human being. Han Bing Siong died unexpectedly in March 2005, only a year and a half after the sudden death

2 The Indonesian academic degree of 'Sarjana Hukum' (S.H., literally 'legal expert/scholar') is comparable to the LL.B degree.

3 Until the early 1960s, the law course in Indonesia, modelled on that in The Netherlands, knew one major degree – known as the *doctoraal* - before the doctorate. Graduates with a *doctoraal* law degree were and are entitled to the academic title of *meester* (Mr. or Mr). This book substitutes 'LL.M' for the Dutch 'Mr.' as the latter might be confused with the English abbreviation of 'mister'.

Han Bing Siong, LL.M, 1932-2005 (courtesy of Kirsten Storm)

of Vonny, his wife for almost fifty years. I am grateful that he was willing to publish a review of my thesis (Han Bing Siong 2004), and a few points he mentioned there I incorporated in this book. Above all, I feel honoured to have known him and hope this book may help commemorate him.

# Preface to the original (Dutch) version

A long road was travelled before this book came into being. Although my interest in language dates back to my childhood, the idea for this research only germinated between 1988 and 1991. Lecturing in Legal Indonesian, appointed by the Nederlands Onderzoekscentrum voor het Recht van Zuidoost-Azië en het Caraïbisch Gebied (NORZOAC, Dutch Research Centre for Law in Southeast Asia and the Caribbean – now the Van Vollenhoven Institute for Law, Governance and Development) of the Leiden Faculty of Law, aroused my interest in the language used in Indonesian law. My next post was a traineeship at the Centrum voor Niet-Westerse Studies (CNWS, Centre for Non-Western Studies) but this did not result in a PhD thesis either. During my collaboration on the Indonesian-Dutch Legal Dictionary Project (1993-2000) and in the period thereafter, however, the research for my thesis was continued and completed from home.

It goes without saying that it was not plain sailing all the way. PhD research tends to severely try the family life of the would-be Doctor and my endeavours were no exception to that rule. Equally, the researcher himself is sorely tested, the path of research and writing being strewn with obstacles and pitfalls and leading into numerous cul-de-sacs, forcing one to try yet another approach. When weighing up the good against the bad, though, the scales invariably tip into the positive. Research and writing are fun. Gathering the pieces of the jigsaw, discovering new associations, creating order from chaos – these are the stuff of life for a doctoral student. Above all, writing a thesis represents the development – so eloquently described by Mikhail Bakhtin – from 'another's word' towards 'one's own word'. You set out following scrupulously the ideas of revered, or not so revered as the case may be, authorities in the field, become impassioned with certain views which in their turn you put into perspective and finally you arrive, slowly and painstakingly, at a piece of writing you are entitled to call your own.

The research undertaken for this book may largely have been carried out single-handedly, it could not have been brought to fruition without the support of many people. Those who provided me with information for my research were joined by all those enquiring with interest into my progress, those who were prepared to read or proof my texts or help me in any other way over the last few years. Should I list them all (in so far as the custom of Leiden University permits), this thesis would be substantially more voluminous! Needs must I abridge the credits.

The interviews I held in both Indonesia and Holland (see Bibliography) were an important source of data for my research. The answers to many of the questions in the forefront of my mind were not to be found in literary sources, rather they were embedded in the memories of those who had first hand experience of the episode in question themselves. I would like to take this opportunity to express my thanks to all those who spared me the time for an interview and for the more than hospitable reception that frequently accompanied it. I had more extensive exchanges with several people, whom I would like to mention individually (in alphabetical order): professors Anton Moeliono, Ph.M. Hadjon and Koesnadi Hardjasoemantri; Ms. Lamya Moeljatno S.H.; Purwoto Gandasubrata S.H.; professor J.E. Sahetapy; Ms. Soerastri Isminingsih Djojodipoero S.H.; professors R. Soetojo Prawirohamidjojo, Sudikno Mertokusumo and C.F.G. Sunaryati Hartono. I am grateful to Ms. Retnowulan Sutantio S.H. for both the large amount of time she placed at my disposal and her assistance in obtaining a visa extension. I gained enormous understanding from my discussions with professors G.J. Resink, St. Takdir Alisjahbana and Hamid Attamimi. Regrettably, this thesis can no longer be presented to them.

I am greatly indebted to Han Bing Siong, LL.M and to professor Ko Swan Sik, who, on the one hand, were able to recollect a veritable wealth of information about the Indonesian legal education in the 1950s and, on the other, were prepared to comment in detail on the drafts of various chapters. I am grateful to professor Daniel Lev for the stream of data he sent my way over the years and for his never-ending interest in my work. Greg Churchill JD, Albert Dekker, LL.M, dr. Nicole Kansil-Niessen, drs. Jerry Mager, dr. Harold Munneke, drs. Jan van Olden, dr. Barbara Oomen, professor Brian Tamanaha, dr. Marjanne Termorshuizen-Arts and dr. Gerard Termorshuizen I thank for reading (and, at times, commenting on) parts of the thesis and its initial versions. The positive feedback about the texts they and others supplied formed an important stimulus in completing this book.

Several libraries will regain their usual stock levels soon – in direct proportion to the clear up of our house! I would like to thank Albert Dekker, LL.M, Sylvia Holverda-Winterink and Cora de Waaij-Vosters, LL.M of the Van Vollenhoven Institute's library, as well as Rini Hogewoning, Josephine Schrama and drs. Sven Aalten of the library of the Koninklijk Instituut voor Taal-, Land- en Volkenkunde. I am equally grateful to professor A. Teeuw for the many documents supplied.

Kari van Weeren is much appreciated for taking care of all of the red tape surrounding a promotion on my behalf. Thanks also to dr. Susi Moeiman for the Indonesian summary and to drs. Thea Meinema and Rosemary Robson-McKillop, BA (Hons) for the English one. My gratitude is extended to Lam Ngo for his promptness in providing the cover photograph.

A special thanks goes to dr. Bas Pompe for the support given and the confidence shown from the earliest days of my academic career and for all that I have learnt from him, not only at the Van Vollenhoven Institute but also on the badminton court, be it with less successful results.

Since my very first university appointment, Nel de Jong, in her capacity of colleague, child minder, 'tante-oma' Nel and, above all, friend, has closely followed the developments in my research and in our domestic ups and downs. It gives me enormous pleasure that she has agreed to assist me in defending my thesis.

The credits, too, now have reached the private sphere. A word of thanks to Barbara Floris-Meulenberg and Mattanja Latuhihin-Van der Wielen for creating much research time for me by taking the children off my hands. In the same vein, I am grateful to Nel Klompenhouwer-Emondt Fauël who was always there when most needed.

I thank my parents for their support and the interest they showed during my studies and for always allowing me to choose my own path in life.

Hanna, Naziha and Elias – I want to address a separate word to you three. I am glad that you so often, and so delicately, reminded me that life is not just about PhD theses. In the years to come, you deserve a Dad who is more patient and more pleasant and more attentive to boot. I promise I will try my hardest.

Finally, I mention the person on whom the last few years have undoubtedly taken the heaviest toll. Sharing your life with a doctoral student in the process of writing a thesis clearly comes under the heading of having all of the trouble and none of the fun. It requires great reserves of tolerance and endurance but above all, love. For that reason, Hanneke, I dedicate this book to you.

# Introduction

> [A]n ordering such as that of the law is unimaginable without language. Impossible to have law without formulation, it is juris*diction*, the *speaking* of law, that is required: a decision on the law expressed in words, which decision rests on general formulae in turn cast into words. (Paul Scholten, *Mr. C. Asser's handleiding tot de beoefening van het Nederlandsch burgerlijk recht; Algemeen deel*, 1931, p. 41.)

It is generally recognized that the legal profession is one in which language plays an important role. Drafting legislation, deeds or court decisions, addressing the court with a legal argument – writing, speaking and, less tangibly present, reading and listening, are at all times at the heart of legal work. It is language that earns jurists their living. The law degree course and the various stages of training that follow it prepare the future jurist, judge or notary for working in and with a specialized language and its corresponding terminology. One could say that a thorough command of that language and terminology constitutes a jurist's most important tool. From this perspective, the severity of the impact on the legal establishment of the implementation of a new national language and thus, also of a new legal language – such as took place in Indonesia – will be self-evident. Letting go of the former language and terminology and effecting the transition to the new ones entails a long and arduous process. This book aims to cast light upon part of that process.

For the above purpose, the criticism of their language usage that Indonesian jurists have been voicing, particularly since 1974, when the first national congress dedicated to the theme of 'legal language' was held, is taken up (Chapter I). The main issues are the lack of uniformity of language and terminology, the deviation from the official standard and the unintelligibility – to jurists themselves, even – of legal Indonesian. The inaccessibility of legal language to laymen may be a near-universal source of complaint, enduring criticism by jurists of their own professional language is far less common – *working in* and *with* a language is a far cry from talking *about* it, so the registers of legal handbooks and journals do not normally list 'language' as a keyword.

In response to the complaints, the Indonesian government did take several measures but these failed to quell the criticism. In the first chapter, this is ascribed partly to the relatively minor *extent* of the measures and partly to their *nature*. I doubt whether the people and institutions involved assessed correctly what had caused the identified defects of legal language. For example, the transformation of the legal system from one primarily in the Dutch language to one primarily in Indonesian seems to have played a far more important role than is evident from either the literature on legal language or the measures implemented. At the heart of this, apart from a political motive – the government wished to distance itself from the legacy of the colonial days – seems to be the theoretical approach to language that is taken, usually implicitly. The dominant metaphor applied to the phenomenon of 'language' is that of an *instrument* – language is available to the jurist as a tool with which to ply his trade. Language is placed in isolation, as it were, in this way of thinking, and is separated from both user and context. Thus, the very antecedent (in the Dutch language) of Indonesian law and the Indonesian legal language itself are demoted to second place.

Chapters II, III and IV explore why 'language' has become an issue among jurists and where the causes of the shortcomings identified are to be found. In Chapter II, an approach to language is outlined that, instead of taking it to be an instrument, highlights it as a form of human action – *languaging* (Becker 1992). 'Doing law' thus is redefined from acting by *means* of language into a *lingual activity* based on and resulting in text. From this new perspective, the history of the Indonesian legal community as well as its language and texts are sketched, at first during the era of the Netherlands East Indies (Chapter III), then under the Republik Indonesia (Chapter IV). Chapter V contains the conclusions and a summary of developments since 1974. The year 1915, figuring in the subtitle of this work, was selected as the starting point because the first cohorts of *rechtskundigen* (jurists) had by then graduated from the Rechtsschool (Law School) in Batavia. The year 2000 serves as the cut-off point as a first evaluation of the years since Suharto was ousted could then be drawn up.

This story of language and law is about the jurists, about those engaged in the world of national, state law following several years of training, who, in carrying out their profession, express themselves verbally and in writing. It is about what Brian Tamanaha (1993) terms the intersubjective legal community. Placing the focus thus, various themes that might otherwise be eminently suited to a lingual approach of the law are left out of consideration. For example, this work does not include an analysis of legal language usage over the years from a linguistic perspective, for instance, nor from that of argumentation theory.[4] Neither is the degree of impact the transition from Dutch to Indonesian had on the development of theory within the different areas of law explored here. Also omitted is language usage in contexts other than the sphere of state law, such as those in which the rules applied derive from religion or tradition. Although it is generally fair to say that the role of state law is on the increase across the globe, in Indonesia and many another former colony, heterogeneity continues to be a feature of the law in practice.[5] Finally, no attempt is made to address the questions of whether Indonesians seeking justice were aware of the language transition process and of whether the law became more accessible to the layman as time went by. These are interesting questions, however, if only because they tie in, to an extent, with an essay by the remarkable title of 'Indonesische rechtstaal' ('Indonesian legal language') that was published as far back as 1922. It was written by the celebrated Leiden professor and 'explorer' of adat law C. van Vollenhoven, who urged Indonesian jurists to develop a 'national Indonesian legal language' in which to express adat law, comprising words and descriptions such that 'the common Indonesian, to whom one addresses these words in his own language, may experience them as his own instead of as the inventions of a mandarin tongue'.[6]

The above are some of the issues and themes that deserve to be investigated in future studies. In the research into the law and its development in Indonesia, a lingual approach has not as yet been undertaken. Inexplicably so, as one could justifiably argue that for Indonesian jurists, it was precisely the switch to another language that constituted the most fundamental (though perhaps barely perceived) change to their oral and written communication. Research from a lingual perspective may cast light on the blind spots of other angles. Moreover, the insights gained may be used to better map the development of the law elsewhere, past or present. To cite some examples, Sri Lanka has also switched to using indigenous languages for formal legal purposes;[7] Malaysian jurists have somewhat apprehensively been moving

4 In the handbook by Van Eemeren, Grootendorst and Snoeck Henkemans, 'argumentation' is defined as a 'verbal, social and rational activity aimed at persuading a person reasonably qualified to assess the acceptability of a particular stance by using a constellation of propositions to justify or disprove the proposition expressed in the stance' (Van Eemeren, Grootendorst and Snoeck Henkemans 1997:5).

5 Otto 1992:99-106. Because of the overlap in the jurisdictions of the different courts (state courts, religious courts, institutions dispensing traditional or village law), sometimes a litigant may choose his venue. The term 'forum shopping' has been applied to this phenomenon (Von Benda-Beckmann 1984:37).

6 Van Vollenhoven 1922:18. To set the record straight, the author did not have Indonesian or, in the words of that time, Malay legalese, in mind. Rather, he advocated an 'Indonesian language' at a more abstract level, as a collective term for the adat law registers of the various regional languages.

7 For comprehensive treatment of this subject, see Cooray 1985.

away from English towards Malaysian (*bahasa Malaysia*) since 1990;[8] South Africa now sees a large number of African languages being used as formal legal languages, side by side with the existing ones (Afrikaans and English);[9] and in numerous other countries – the republics of the Commonwealth of Independent States (the former USSR) and the People's Republic of China among them – different areas of the law (private law, in the case of the examples given) are being cast into a new language for the first time. And let's not overlook the fact that Dutch law itself underwent several changeovers to a new legal language in the course of its history. It is therefore not before time to express the hope that future research into law development will allow the lingual perspective to come into its own.

8 See Abdul Hamid Bin Omar 1991.

9 For more on this process, see Olivier 1994.

## CHAPTER I

# Legal language in the limelight

*Introduction*

In November 1974 a conference entitled 'Bahasa dan Hukum' (Language and Law) was held in the northern Sumatran towns of Medan and Prapat.[1] Its theme was the language of the law (*bahasa hukum*) in the sense of the use of the Indonesian language in legislation, in practising and teaching law, and in the literature on the subject.[2] The conference particularly focussed on the questions of how to enhance the uniformity of the language and terminology wielded in the field of law and how to improve lawyers'[3] command of Indonesian (*Simposium Bahasa dan Hukum* 1976:5, 7). The organizers were the Badan Pembinaan Hukum Nasional (BPHN, National Law Development Centre) of the Ministry of Justice and the Law Faculty of the Universitas Sumatera Utara (USU, University of North Sumatra). The latter also hosted the event.

This conference was the first nation-wide gathering devoted to the subject of legal language,[4] as well as the first event organized by the recently founded

1 The presentations held at this conference, which took place from 25-27 November, were published in *Simposium Bahasa dan Hukum* 1976.

2 *Simposium Bahasa dan Hukum* 1976:5. From the presentations and conclusions of the conference it may be deducted that Indonesian (*bahasa Indonesia*) was meant. For example, the first definition arrived at at the conference was that Indonesian legal language is Indonesian applied in the field of law. Other languages besides Indonesian that jurists used to use (and to some extent still do) for these purposes could also be classed as legal language. There is Dutch, the official language of countless decrees and bylaws dating back to the Dutch colonial era that were still in force (many still are). Then there is English, from the 1960s onwards increasingly the language of the literature used in teaching law, as well as the language of internationally oriented law practices.

3 In this book the terms 'lawyer' and 'jurist' (Dutch: 'jurist') are used indiscriminately, somewhat in deviation from normal Anglo-Saxon usage, to denote any person with a law degree, whether or not working as a legal practitioner. The Dutch 'advocaat' and the Indonesian 'advokat' or 'pengacara', who fulfil roles similar to those performed by the British 'barrister' and 'solicitor', are referred to as 'advocates'.

4 Though at the second Kongres Bahasa Indonesia (Indonesian Language Conference), held in Medan in 1954, a working party had investigated the use of the Indonesian language in legisla-

BPHN.[5] The then Minister of Justice Mochtar Kusumaatmadja opened the conference in person and stayed on to attend the entire three day event (*Simposium Bahasa dan Hukum* 1976:5), which was chaired by the Medan professor of law and former judge Mahadi. Presentations were held by both lawyers and linguists. Apart from Mahadi, the field of jurisprudence[6] supplied professor Soetan Mohamad Sjah, who had been publishing on legal language since the 1950s.[7] The practice of the law was represented by J.N. Siregar, (civil law) notary (*notaris*) at Jakarta and head of the course in notarial law at the Universitas Indonesia (UI), also in the capital, and by Busthanul Arifin, Mahkamah Agung (Supreme Court) judge. Emissaries from the domain of linguistics and language policy were the renowned St. Takdir Alisjahbana, Anton M. Moeliono, Sabaruddin Ahmad and S.W. Rudjiati Muljadi, the latter being head of the Lembaga Bahasa Nasional (LBN, National Language Institute).

It was no coincidence that the language of the law should be the subject of a 1974 BPHN conference. First of all, it was a 'hot' topic among legal circles. In his opening speech, the Minister of Justice referred to the third Seminar Hukum Nasional (National Law Seminar) that had taken place in Surabaya earlier in the year.[8] On that occasion, legal language had been debated both in connection with the teaching of law and within the framework of legislation and the administration of justice, one advocated solution being that of uniformity of language and terminology.[9]

Language was an important issue in legal circles at that time because of the transition the law and those involved in it were undergoing. In terms of their numbers and influence, the cohorts of jurists educated in the Dutch language had gradually been overtaken by those who had no command of

---

tion and public administration (see footnote 23 and Chapter IV).

5 The BPHN was created in August 1974 to succeed the Lembaga Pembinaan Hukum Nasional (LPHN, National Law Development Institute). The establishment of the BPHN was enacted in Keppres no. 45/1974 dated 28-8-1974, while its positioning, remit, functions and organizational structure were determined in Kepmenkeh no. JS. 4/3/5 of 1975.

6 For clarity's sake, the term 'jurisprudence' in this book is used to denote the theory or philosophy of the law. The Dutch 'jurisprudentie', which normally means 'the body of precedents', is here referred to as 'judicial decisions' or 'court decisions'.

7 Sjah produced many a publication on legal terminology in the 1950s and 1960s. See, for instance, Soetan Mohamad Sjah 1960 and his contributions to *Hukum dan Masjarakat* 1961, 3-4:46-9 and 1964, 3-4:105-8.

8 *Simposium Bahasa dan Hukum* 1976:7; compare SK Menkeh no. J.S. 1/11/6 dated 8-11-1974 (concerning the commission that was to organize the conference). The conclusions of this seminar, having been held by the nearly defunct LPHN (see footnote 5), are contained in *Kesimpulan Seminar Hukum Nasional ke III* 1974.

9 See *Kesimpulan Seminar Hukum Nasional ke III* 1974, the paragraph 'Pembaharuan pendidikan hukum dalam rangka pembinaan dan pembaharuan nasional' on p. 4, the paragraph 'Perundang-undangan, pembinaan hukum dan pembangunan nasional' on p. 3 and the paragraph 'Peranan peradilan dalam pembinaan dan pembaharuan hukum nasional' on p. 2.

Dutch. Tension thus ensued between the advocates of Dutch as the primary language of the law (in the sense of the language actually representing the 'basis' of Indonesian law) and those in favour of Indonesian performing that role. In his speech, Mochtar pointed out that the older jurists in particular were dismissive of the quality of legal literature in Indonesian and generally considered the Indonesian language to be insufficiently developed to express legal concepts.[10] Moreover, the gradual decline of the Dutch language in Indonesia posed a real problem due to a substantial number of laws formulated in Dutch, dating back to the colonial era, still being in force at that time.[11] This legacy was viewed increasingly as an alien element within the growing body of legislation in the Indonesian language.[12]

A second factor contributing to lawyers' heightened awareness of the language aspects of law in the early 1970s was the emphasis placed on and the attention paid to the development of a national system of law in those years. The second Rencana Pembangunan Lima Tahun (Repelita, Five Year Strategy for National Development), covering the years 1974-1979, contained a long paragraph on law and, partly because the Indonesian economy was now in better shape, developing the law was financed to a considerably greater extent than in the previous period.[13]

In January 1974 Mochtar Kusumaatmadja was appointed Minister of Justice and was charged with the realization of the plans. His had been a carefully considered appointment – the former advocate and senior lecturer in International Law at the Bandung Universitas Padjadjaran (UNPAD), in his capacity of dean, had been closely involved with the research into law innova-

10 For this reason, the examination of legal issues ought to be based on foreign-language literature, particularly Dutch (*Simposium Bahasa dan Hukum* 1976:12). Sunaryati Hartono (1979:29-30), lecturer at the Bandung Universitas Padjadjaran (UNPAD) and head of the BPHN since the 1980s, reports the resistance encountered by education innovators from the camp of the jurists wanting to safeguard the use of the Dutch language and of literature in that language.

11 See Churchill 1992:2, 8-10, Pompe 1994:18, 1996:340-2. The declining command of Dutch is also evident from several legal dictionaries published in this transitional epoch, which clarify Dutch terms in particular in the Indonesian language: *Pembahasan hukum; Pendjelasan-pendjelasan istilah-istilah hukum Belanda-Indonesia untuk studie dan praktijk* by Martias gelar Imam Radjo Mulano, member of the *pengadilan tinggi* (court of appeal) of Medan (Medan: Pertjetakan dan Toko Buku, 1969); *Kamus hukum* by R. Subekti and R. Tjitrosoedibio (Djakarta: Pradnja Paramita, 1969); *Istilah-istilah hukum dalam Bahasa Belanda; Terjemahannya, arti sehari-hari dan arti sebagai istilah hukum* by Paulus Moeljadi Dwidjodarmo (Bandung: Vicanata, 1972) and *Kamus hukum* by J.C.T. Simorangkir, Rudy T. Erwin and J.T. Prasetyo (Djakarta: Madjapahit, 1972).

12 At the seminar in Surabaya, translation into Indonesian of the laws in Dutch and 'assimilation' of the Indonesian passages into the laws in Indonesian had been suggested (the seminar compilation contains 'kesejajaran', 'alignment') (*Kesimpulan Seminar Hukum Nasional ke III* 1974, section 'Perundang-undangan, pembinaan hukum dan pembangunan nasional', p. 3).

13 Pompe 1996:148. During the period 1974-79, the sum of 30 billion rupiah was allocated specifically to the development of the law.

tion being conducted by the university, as well as with the development of a new curriculum. The Faculty of Law had therefore officially been granted the status of pioneer (*fakultas hukum perintis*) (Sunaryati Hartono 1979:28-9). To the devoted minister, the future of the law of Indonesia could not but be in the Indonesian language, the application of which, in his opinion, was quintessential to the development of a national system of law. While involved in establishing a new curriculum for law faculties, in developing teaching materials in Indonesian and in setting up a court decision reference system at the UNPAD, he is bound to have come across heterogeneous and poor Indonesian on a daily basis. The shortcomings, though, were part and parcel to him of the very need to use Indonesian, which could, after all, only be improved through use.[14]

Thirdly, lawyers were not alone in their preoccupation with the Indonesian language, which was a subject of debate and concern in much wider circles. The unbridled borrowing of foreign words, English ones in particular, irked many people.[15] The heterogeneity of language usage and terminology, in spelling and terminology as well as in grammar, and the general disregard for Indonesian were also focussed on.[16] During gatherings such as the symposium on language and literature of 1966, the Seminar Bahasa Indonesia (Indonesian Language Seminar) of March 1972 and the Seminar Politik Bahasa Nasional (National Language Policy Seminar) of 1975, standardization and uniformity, key terms at the conference on legal language at a later date, were the buzzwords of the day.[17] Nor was the debate about language restricted to academ-

14 *Simposium Bahasa dan Hukum* 1976:12; compare with Busthanul Arifin 1976. Mochtar here referred to his preface to Damian and Hornick 1972 (the source is the second edition of 1974). Several details relating to the organization of the conference were supplied by professor Mardjono Reksodiputro (interview dated 1-6-2001). Mardjono, responsible for the Pusat Dokumentasi Hukum (Law Documentation Centre) at the Universitas Indonesia, had been approached by Mochtar Kusumaatmadja with a view to setting up a national documentation system. Mardjono gave a presentation on this subject at the 1974 Seminar Hukum Nasional.

15 The borrowing was due to the greatly increased and still growing number of foreign experts, tourists and others visiting Indonesia from the beginning of the Orde Baru (New Order) onwards and bringing with them all manner of imports (international academic jargon, Western dress, magazines, music, English) (Jones 1976:195-7; Steinhauer 1981:12). The Governor of Jakarta, Ali Sadikin, issued an edict in 1974 ordering signs carrying foreign names and adverts to be replaced with signs in Indonesian (Jones 1976:204).

16 Mochtar Lubis 1972:64-9; Johannes 1972:94, 98; Harimurti Kridalaksana 1975:46; Simandjuntak 1972:24-5; Andi Hakim Nasoetion 1972:41-2; Awaloedin Djamin 1972:49. It should be borne in mind that relatively few Indonesians had any command of the national language in those days. Ricklefs (1993:305) claims that in 1971 40.8% of Indonesians knew Indonesian, whereas in 1980 the figure had risen to 61.4%. In the census held in 1990 15.5% of Indonesians over the age of five listed Indonesian as their first language (Steinhauer 2002:11).

17 See Mochtar Lubis 1972:69, Johannes 1972:98, Amran Halim 1972:146, Harsja W. Bachtiar 1972:237-8, *Politik bahasa nasional* 1975:177, Harimurti Kridalaksana 1975:44-6, 49-50, A. Moeliono 1975:33-8 and Steinhauer 1981:13.

ics. The press generally showed enormous interest in conferences dedicated to language,[18] Anton Moeliono wrote a column for the prestigious daily *Kompas* from the 1960s onwards (see A. Moeliono 1984) and the Bandung professor J.S. Badudu explained the snares and pitfalls of Indonesian to the general public in a programme on national television (Steinhauer 1981:12). From 1974 to 1975 official policy relating to language benefitted from major investment, in terms of both finance and infrastructure.[19]

In accordance with the aims laid down in the second Five Year Strategy, a seminar on language policy was organized, preceded by a large preparatory meeting, large-scale national projects on language and literature were initiated and the Pusat Pembinaan dan Pengembangan Bahasa (Centre for the Cultivation and Development of Language, Pusat Bahasa or Language Centre in short) was founded and given a much stronger position than its predecessor, the aforementioned Lembaga Bahasa Nasional.[20]

A possible fourth reason for the choice of legal language as the conference topic lay in its relative political neutrality, even though some aspects of this subject were quite sensitive (the generation gap, for instance). The importance of a neutral topic should not be underestimated. The legal world was

18 The conference book appends the reports of ten newspapers, carrying headlines such as 'Escape from the language jungle' (*Suara Karya*) and 'Immediate standardization of Indonesian required to beat back chaos' (*Kompas*) (Djajanto Supra and Lake 1972:311, 278). Also see Maier 1997:689.

19 'National language policy' was defined as the national policy for tackling all manner of language questions, consisting of a plan, guidelines and rules (*Politik bahasa nasional* 1975:172).

20 Keppres no. 45/1974. The position of the Pusat Bahasa was formulated in Kepmendikbud no. 079/0/1975 and amended by Kepmendikbud no. 0222g/O/1980. The institution was charged with putting into practice the policy for language research and development and, contrary to its predecessor, came directly under the Minister of Education and Culture (Effendi 1974:1; A. Moeliono 1981:18; Rudjiati Muljadi 1975:5). The areas of activity of the Pusat Bahasa encompassed Indonesian and the regional languages, the Indonesian and regional bodies of literature, lexicology and terminology, and the development of language and literature (*Pusat Pembinaan dan Pengembangan Bahasa* 1991:11-4). Developing the language had to be stepped up, according to the second Five Year Strategy, in order to 'effect competence among a wide social audience in the use of as high as possible a quality of Indonesian as the national Indonesian interpersonal communication tool' (Repelita II, cited by Effendi 1974:6). The Seminar Politik Bahasa Nasional was held in Jakarta in February 1975 with the preparatory meeting (Praseminar Politik Bahasa Nasional) taking place from 29/31-10-1974. New funding for language policy was allocated to the Lembaga Bahasa Nasional via research and development projects on the Indonesian language and literature and on the regional languages and bodies of literature (Proyek Penelitian/ Pengembangan Bahasa dan Sastra Indonesia dan Daerah). Apart from implementing an effective national language policy, its aims were to set up an information centre dealing with language, to create a technical staff, to develop language and literature, to promote collaboration on language matters, to develop the Indonesian language through the mass media and to instigate initiatives in the areas of writing, translating and publishing (Rudjiati Muljadi 1974; compare Effendi 1974:6-9).

still licking its wounds after the painful conclusion of the power struggle over the independence of the judiciary. The political powers that be had been victorious – the Judiciary Act passed in 1970 (UU no. 14) provided the Executive with far-reaching control over the functioning of the judicial apparatus.[21] Legal language as the topic of the first BPHN conference therefore allowed the fledgeling institute a – politically speaking – fairly unencumbered start in life.

Leaving aside the above four factors, the conference on language and law in Medan and Prapat came about due to certain people in certain posts. In addition to Mochtar Kusumaatmadja as Minister of Justice, there was the Head of the BPHN, J.C.T. Simorangkir, as well as the Head of the BPHN's Pusat Penelitian dan Pengembangan (Puslitbang, Research and Development Centre), T.M. Radhie. Simorangkir had already demonstrated his interest in language, for example by publishing a legal dictionary some years previously (see footnote 11). Radhie's reputation for languages dated back to his student days and he was also a close acquaintance of Mahadi's, who was said to speak very good Indonesian and who had chaired the second Kongres Bahasa Indonesia (Indonesian Language Conference), also held in Medan, as early as 1954.[22] Being a man of both law and language, Mahadi was eminently suited to the task of chairing the conference. Furthermore, the location of 'his' University of North Sumatra close to the cradle of the Malay language may have helped to persuade the organizers to opt for Medan.

### *Topics and conclusions of the Simposium Bahasa dan Hukum*

The Minister of Justice considered the conference to be the turning point in the evolution of the Indonesian legal language. It heralded the end of a period in which legal jargon had mostly been allowed to develop unchecked and the

21 The new act maintained the Ministry of Justice's responsibility for the administration of *pengadilan negeri* (courts of dirst instance) and *pengadilan tinggi* (courts of appeal), which also included the authority to transfer judges (art. 11 clause 1; compare with Lev 1978:53-8 and Pompe 1996:85-8). What little independence the judiciary managed to exercise from 1970 onwards was put paid to by the politics of patronage of the then Minister of Justice Oemar Seno Adji. The retirement, in 1974, of Supreme Court president R. Subekti, whose office had been the judiciary's last stronghold in the struggle for its independence, is sometimes seen as the tentative last curtain of the drama. Subekti was succeeded by Seno Adji himself, while the next Minister of Justice, Mochtar Kusumaatmadja, maintained his Department's iron grip on the Supreme Court and the judiciary (Pompe 1996:89-103).

22 Interview with Mardjono Reksodiputro dated 1-6-2001. Mardjono mentioned the BPHN's Daud Syah in the same breath. The obituary published in the judiciary's journal, *Varia Peradilan*, on the occasion of Mahadi's death draws attention to his outstanding language usage in correspondence, pleadings and other court documents, court decisions and academic writings alike, as well as to his aversion to the use of foreign words (Amarullah Salim 1989:161).

dawn of a deliberate, planned approach (Mochtar Kusumaatmadja 1976:8; Busthanul Arifin 1976:77-8). Come what may, the poor quality and heterogeneity of language usage by jurists, previously under discussion at the 1954 conference mentioned above, would be addressed.[23]

As is the case with all professions, over the centuries specialist language developed amongst jurists, too. Lawyers' formulations differ from those employed by people not trained in law. Not only do they use specific terms, they also use normal terms in specific meanings. Unlike other professionals, however, jurists, in choosing their words, must give a degree of consideration to the layman. After all, they produce texts, certain types of which, such as laws and judicial decisions, have a bearing on large sections of the general public.

Whether or not the tendency on the part of lawyers to use language aimed at colleagues only ought to be curbed by the duty to consider 'the common man' was a matter of widely diverging opinions amongst Indonesian jurists and linguists. At one end of the spectrum, jurists supported the view that the language of the law fell entirely outside of the sphere of influence of Indonesian grammar, whereas at the other, linguists (predominantly) were opposed to the very concept of 'bahasa hukum' (legal language) in that the language used by jurists did not constitute an independent *language*. Rather, it represented a *register* of Indonesian and thus ought to satisfy the basic rules of that language.[24]

23 Mochtar Kusumaatmadja 1976:8-9. The preliminary recommendations on language made by A.G. Pringgodigdo and Kuntjoro Purbopranoto had served as the introduction to Section B of the 1954 conference, which dealt with language usage in legislation and public administration. The first conclusion drawn by this section was the need to establish a government committee, consisting of jurists, linguists and experts in the fields of adat, religion and religious law, charged with correcting the Indonesian used to formulate *undang-undang* (acts) and other central government legislation (*peraturan2 negara*), with checking the language usage in the drafts of emergency acts and other central government legislation prior to their being passed and with ensuring that legal terms were set, clear and not subject to change before giving them the committee's seal of approval. The examples given of legislative terms in need of being replaced were the term 'kebutuhan' (having an undesirable connotation in some regional languages) and a long list of foreign words ('retributie' (retribution), 'rel' (riot), 'legaliseer' (legalize) and so on). Another conclusion stipulated that experts in religious law be added to the so-called Seksi Hukum (Law Section) of the national Komisi Istilah (Terms Committee). In respect of uniformity, the discrepancy was pointed out between the legal terms applied in higher law education on the one hand and in legislation on the other ('atas kuasa Undang2' versus 'berdasarkan Undang2', for instance), as well as in spelling ('diubah' versus 'dirubah' and 'dirobah'). The section also concurred with the conclusions arrived at by Kuntjoro Purbopranoto towards the end of his preliminary recommendations, including his positioning of legal language as distinct from 'common' language usage (*Pusat Pembinaan dan Pengembangan Bahasa* 1991:46-8).

24 *Simposium Bahasa dan Hukum* 1976:9. According to Moeliono, there was no such thing as 'legal *language*' ('*bahasa* hukum') – at best one could speak of a 'legal language *register*' ('*laras* bahasa hukum') (interview dated 26-2-1994 and A. Moeliono 1981:124; compare with Sabaruddin

Mochtar Kusumaatmadja saw the conference primarily as an opportunity for bridge building between the camps and advocated middle ground. Legal language inevitably possessed particular features, he claimed, but to allow it, therefore, to deviate from the first principles and ground rules of Indonesian was going too far. The language of the law, too, constituted part of the Indonesian language and should not become unintelligible to the general public.[25]

The closing statement of the conference – the starting point for several measures – adopted Mochtar's formula more or less verbatim. This statement defined Indonesian legal language as Indonesian applied in the field of law and, because of its function, possessing a distinct terminology, composition and style.[26] Therefore its use in a legal context, too, would have to comply with the gen-

---

Ahmad 1976:96-7). At the Seminar Politik Bahasa Nasional of 1975, Harimurti Kridalaksana (1975:49-50) argued that standard Indonesian was required for official communications (official and civil service correspondence, announcements by government agencies, legislation and the like), professional treatises (official reports and academic writings), public speaking (presentations, lectures and sermons, for example) and for conversing with people commanding one's respect.

25 *Simposium Bahasa dan Hukum* 1976:9. Mochtar's convenient point of departure here is that texts complying with the rules of grammar can be understood by the public at large, an assumption that does not hold much water. Even disregarding the barriers imposed by the specialized terminology, comprehension of an average legal text, with its very formal writing style, requires a level of proficiency that simply is not within everyone's reach. The specific demands placed on legal texts almost compel lawyers to a language usage that is incomprehensible to the layman (also see Takdir Alisjahbana 1976:31). That everyone should be able to understand the law is a view with a long history – see G. van den Bergh 1979:47-8.

26 Notary Siregar's contribution (1976:63-76) touches on the reason for using particular formulae in legal texts. He elaborated on the set phrases that occur in notarial documents. Dealing with each section of a deed in turn, he examined the requirements the deed had to satisfy in accordance with the 1860 Reglement op het notaris-ambt (Regulations governing the office of notary) (*Staatsblad van Nederlandsch-Indië* – hereafter *Stb.* – 1860, no. 3). Failure to comply with requirements specifically prescribed by the Reglement meant either that the notary incurred a fine or that the deed forfeited its authenticity (relating to special status of deeds under the law of evidence and execution]). Siregar's first example was the exordium of a deed: 'Pada hari ini, hari Senin tanggal duapuluh lima Nopember seribu ratus tujuh puluh empat (25-11-1974); Hadir dihadapan saya, Salim, Sarjana Hukum, notaris di Jakarta, dengan dihadiri saksi-saksi yang nama-namanya akan disebut pada akhir akta ini'. This fragment was translated into Indonesian from the Dutch formula – for many years, Indonesian notaries commonly used model books providing a Dutch text for each type of deed with a more or less literal translation in Indonesian alongside – 'Heden, ..., verschenen voor mij, ..., notaris te ..., in aanwezigheid van getuigen wier namen aan het slot van deze akte worden genoemd [...]'. (Translated into English, the formula reads 'Today, being Monday the Twenty-Fifth Day of November in the Year of our Lord Nineteen Hundred and Seventy-Four, appeared before me, Salim S.H., Notary at Jakarta, in the presence of witnesses whose names are given in the concluding part of this deed [...]'.) This particular formula, hardly a diamond of literary style, has its origins in the requirements laid down in art. 22 and 25 of the above Regulations, to wit that the notary's full name and place of office and the place, the day, the date and the year of drawing up the deed be stated, and that said drawing up takes place in the presence of two witnesses (Siregar 1976:64-5).

eral requirements and rules applicable to the Indonesian language.[27] A formulation was thus arrived at that was entirely in keeping with the aspirations of that time, in all sectors of society, to improve the usage of the Indonesian language. Also, explicitly stating *Indonesian* to be the language of the law sent an unmistakable message to those still wishing to adhere to Dutch.

Most of the conclusions and recommendations of the conference relate to the shortcomings of the language of the law (as identified in the contributions and during the discussions) and to the ways in which these shortcomings might be remedied, the ultimate aim being to strengthen the position of the law.[28] Prior to examining in more detail in which respects the conference considered the language of the law to be below par, the requirements imposed on it should be given. In the first place, as touched upon above, legal Indonesian had to comply with the rules of 'common' Indonesian.[29] Its usage had to be set, clear, unambiguous and stylish though above all, it had to be effective – legal formulation needed to embody the essence of the train of thought and be as efficacious as possible.[30] Most of these characteristics, previously advocated in the presentations, require no elaboration.[31] The call for stylishness, however, is also encoun-

27 '1. Bahasa Hukum Indonesia adalah bahasa Indonesia yang dipergunakan dalam bidang hukum, yang mengingat fungsinya mempunyai karakteristik tersendiri; oleh karena itu bahasa hukum Indonesia haruslah memenuhi syarat-syarat dan kaedah-kaedah bahasa Indonesia. 2. Karakteristik Bahasa Hukum terletak pada kekhususan istilahnya, komposisinya serta gayanya.' (*Simposium Bahasa dan Hukum* 1976:106 sub 1; compare Takdir Alisjahbana 1976:23, 30-1 and Sabaruddin Ahmad 1976:95-7.) Elsewhere in the conclusions it was claimed that legal language was not the exclusive domain of jurists but belonged to the whole of society (*Simposium Bahasa dan Hukum* 1976:108). The formulation of the conclusions and recommendations of the conference was to be carried out by two committees, one of which (Committee I) concerned itself with legal language in general, whereas the other (Committee II) focussed principally on legal terminology. (Committee II nevertheless also came up with recommendations for the language of the law.) Committee I was presided over by the specialist in legislation A. Hamid S. Attamimi of the Sekretariat Negara (Secretariat of State). Its conclusions were based primarily on the preliminary recommendations made by the three speakers from the linguistics camp, namely Anton Moeliono, Takdir Alisjahbana and Sabaruddin Ahmad. Committee II was chaired by the jurist Hasan Wargakusumah (*Simposium Bahasa dan Hukum* 1976:106-10).

28 The first recommendation issued by Committee I reads: 'the function of the law in the era of nation-building [...] be reinforced, as determined in the Garis-garis Besar Haluan Negara (Broad Outlines of State Policy)' (*Simposium Bahasa dan Hukum* 1976:107).

29 Also see A. Moeliono 1976:14-8 and Sabaruddin Ahmad 1976:95-7, 101-2.

30 'Bahasa Hukum Indonesia sebagai bagian bahasa Indonesia merupakan bahasa moderen yang penggunaannya harus tetap, terang, monosemantik dan harus memenuhi syarat estetika' (*Simposium Bahasa dan Hukum* 1976:106-7 sub A.3).

31 Anton Moeliono (1976:15), for example, expressed the opinion that the language of the law should meet the same standards as scientific language, in that it should be businesslike, precise, objective, concise and restrained, and its terminology should be more set and stable than in any other field. Alisjahbana argued for simple and easily accessible language and syntax, Sabaruddin Ahmad for clear, set, accurate language with regular grammar and fixed, unambiguous terms (Takdir Alisjahbana 1976:30-1; Sabaruddin Ahmad 1976:95-9). Clarity and the absence of ambi-

tered in Busthanul Arifin's contribution, aimed predominantly at the language used by judges. Arifin underlined the trinity of truth, justice and beauty and argued that only a just, beautifully formulated and articulated judgement could command respect.[32]

Some of the features put forward during the conference as being desirable for legal language were not explicitly present in the conclusions. A theme raised in several contributions, albeit in varying contexts, was the quest for and expression of a uniquely Indonesian quality, an Indonesian authenticity (*keaslian*) in law and in its language. This theme was not altogether new; Kuntjoro Purbopranoto had argued some twenty years earlier for legal language that would draw primarily on the terms and concepts of indigenous law and language (see footnote 23 and Chapter IV).

There was also the general drive, characteristic of the 1970s, towards cleansing the Indonesian language of foreign words. In addition to an influx of English terms, legal language in particular was exposed to the influence of Dutch, as a substantial body of legislation in the Dutch language was still in force. Sabaruddin Ahmad therefore proposed that in developing legal terminology, Indonesian, regional and other Austronesian languages be drawn on first, and that foreign (Western, that is) languages serve as a last resort. After all, nothing could reflect more accurately original Indonesian values than our 'own' languages and words, according to Ahmad.[33] Equally, Mahadi suggested that the adat law maxims and sayings of the different adat law areas (*adatrechtskringen*) be consulted to attempt to arrive at wholly Indonesian values on which to base a national Indonesian system of law.[34]

A line of reasoning more or less in keeping with that of Ahmad and Mahadi was put forward by Busthanul Arifin. To his mind, Indonesian legal

---

guity were also noted as desirable features by Busthanul Arifin and Siregar (Busthanul Arifin 1976:85; Siregar 1976:63-4).

32 Making unsuitable any judge who, due to a physical defect, was incapable of pronouncing judgement in an eloquent fashion, as this would detract from the sanctity of the hearing (Busthanul Arifin 1976:85).

33 Sabaruddin Ahmad 1976:98-101, 103. In his presentation, language builder Anton Moeliono (1976:15) argued that the attempt to incorporate Indonesian authenticity in the language of the law should not be at the expense of its systematic and consistent development (in connection with the morphology, for example). The requirement for system and consistency also applied to the Indonesian policy in respect of the development and standardization of academic terminologies, taking as their basis the classification of the various sciences (see *Panduan penyusunan kamus bidang ilmu* 1993).

34 Mahadi 1976:39, 49-50. A very different song was sung by Alisjahbana when speaking out against the view that the law 'was merely the product of the historical development of a society' (Takdir Alisjahbana 1976:34, 33). He placed more weight on the creative powers of the law: 'Law is the twin of Education: each helps the other to shape the new society and its culture' (Takdir Alisjahbana 1976:34). See Chapter IV.

language had, up until then, been sorely neglected and its development had been left to whoever happened to be drafting legislation or teaching law. The language usage in the field of law therefore consisted mainly of translations from Dutch and, subsequently, English (Busthanul Arifin 1976:77-8). The clarity of the Indonesian text suffered as a result – some 1950s texts were said to be intelligible only alongside a virtually parallel Dutch text (either from the Netherlands or from the Netherlands East Indies past). Moreover, no two translators produced the same text, which was particularly problematic to young jurists no longer trained in Dutch.[35] Arifin's main objection to the continued influence of foreign languages, however, was that this would impede the development of the Indonesian law along the 'furrows of Indonesian authenticity'.[36] For this very reason, the study of Dutch should not be reintroduced into the curricula of law faculties, nor should too much emphasis be placed on mastering English. The development of a system of law that would reflect a quality peculiar to Indonesia might best be promoted by (for example) rephrasing in Indonesian the sense of justice (*rasa hukum*) existing in regional adat law communities, which used instead of Indonesian the relevant regional language as their main communication tool.[37]

The conference conclusions do not explicitly state whether or not lawyers would commonly translate or had commonly translated from Dutch. Generally speaking, the defects of the legal language are hardly enumerated at all. It is simply noted that the legal language has shortcomings, to be found particularly in the semantics of the words, the morphology and the syntax.[38] Only those relating to the word 'semantics' are defined more closely, namely as the heterogeneity (*ketidakseragaman*) of legal terms and expressions (*Simposium Bahasa dan Hukum* 1976:108). The presentations held by Rudjiati Muljadi and St. Mohamad Sjah stood out in pursuing the nature and causes of this problem, which was far from new (see footnote 23). As early as October 1942 (when Dutch as the official language had mostly fallen by the

35 Busthanul Arifin 1976:77-8, 83-4. Arifin quoted the acts relating to the Mahkamah Agung (the Supreme Court; UU no. 1/1950) and misdemeanours of an economic nature (Undang-undang Darurat no. 7/1955) as examples.

36 'Politik pintu terbuka terhadap dunia luar, di bidang hukum mengandung bahaya menciutnya perhatian akan bahasa hukum Indonesia, yang sekaligus berarti menciutnya perkembangan pembangunan hukum menurut alur-alur keaslian' (Busthanul Arifin 1976:78).

37 Busthanul Arifin 1976:79, 83, 85-6. If judges in the regions concerned were to put this into practice, the result would be both an expansion of the legal literature available and an improvement in the judges' proficiency (Busthanul Arifin 1976:85-6).

38 'Simposium melihat adanya kekurangsempurnaan dalam Bahasa Hukum yang sekarang dipergunakan, khususnya dalam semantik kata, bentuk dan komposisi kalimat' (*Simposium Bahasa dan Hukum* 1976:107 sub A.4). There are three ways at least of interpreting (and therefore translating) this Indonesian sentence. According to dr. Ewald Ebing of KITLV, the interpretation given is the most plausible one.

wayside), an official body had been founded to determine which Indonesian terms might be appropriate to replace the Dutch ones. However, neither the dictionaries and glossaries published by this Komisi Bahasa Indonesia (Indonesian Language Committee), nor those of subsequent Komisi Istilah (Terms Committees) managed to curb the rank proliferation of terms (legal ones amongst them) (see Chapter IV). Institutions such as government departments and courts, joined by the authors of law books and the lecturers at law faculties, felt at liberty to use or, if necessary, invent Indonesian legal terms.[39]

Listing current terms and publishing new lists thus continued to be an important aspect of the remit of successive institutions concerned with legal terminology. But state committees were not the only ones engaged in this activity. Other institutions – faculties, for example – also spent time and energy in this area, meaning that, over the years, the rampant growth of the number of terms in turn resulted in a prolific increase in the number of glossaries and lists. With the cessation of the official bodies' activities in the period 1966-1972, due to a lack of funds, this process got completely out of hand.[40]

From the above, one might be tempted to think that only the terminology was heterogeneous, but the fixed components of certain legal texts, too, displayed little uniformity.[41] Alisjahbana took the view that these were but aspects of a bigger problem with which the Indonesian language had to contend. He put it that Indonesian 'lacked suitable words, was chaotic, disorderly and unstable, and subject to aimless, continual change' – ultimately having a disastrous effect on the formulation of the law.[42] What springs to mind

39 Some examples provided by Sjah were 'mengingat' and 'memperhatikan', used by the legislator and the Supreme Court respectively in the sense of 'bearing in mind that', and the no less than seven Indonesian terms for 'natuurlijke verbintenis' ('natural obligation', an obligation (Dutch 'verbintenis') which is not enforceable by law but which has the same legal effects as an 'ordinary' obligation) he had found – including a term he himself had proposed in 1960 (Mohamad Sjah 1976:51-3).

40 According to Muljadi (1976:58-9), the Seksi Ilmu Hukum (Jurisprudence Section) of the Komisi Istilah had by then collected 6,081 law terms, of which 4,264 had been listed in draft form and 1,650 were published in 1958.

41 Siregar (1976:71-3) quoted six different versions of the phrase 'opgemaakt in minuut en verleden te ...' (drawn up in a single copy and executed at ...) (at the end of a deed) and an incredible twelve translations of the phrase 'waarvan akte' (for the record). Siregar (1976:74-5) concluded his presentation with a model for the heading and ending of a deed, which in his view complied with the requirements of the Reglement op het notaris-ambt (Regulations governing the office of notary) and (to as great an extent as possible) possessed the qualities desirable from the perspective of linguistic style. Compare with Mohamad Sjah's comment on the terms of 'mengingat' and 'memperhatikan' in legislation and judicial decisions (see footnote 39).

42 '[B]ahasa Indonesia kekurangan kata-kata yang diperlukan, kacau, tak beraturan, labil, berubah-ubah tak berketentuan' (Takdir Alisjahbana 1976:34).

is the image of a stray bullet, incessantly influenced by external forces and lacking 'weight', a fixed 'base' or 'core' of its own.

The perception of the shortcomings of the language of the law in 'the semantics of morphology and syntax' is evident from several presentations given at the symposium. Much attention was devoted to the frequency with which long and complicated, 'un-Indonesian' sentences occurred. In so far as translations of Dutch legislation were at issue, Moeliono pointed the finger at translators working too literally.[43] Regarding the morphology, sloppy punctuation was taken to task, while Alisjahbana's presentation drew attention to the aspect of spelling.[44] Moeliono's argument highlighted the deficient command of the Indonesian lan-

43 A. Moeliono 1976:16, 19. The example given by Moeliono relates to art. 282 clause 1 of the Wetboek van Strafrecht (Criminal Code). The official text reads: 'Hij die eenig geschrift waarvan hij den inhoud kent of eenige hem bekende afbeelding of voorwerp, aanstootelijk voor de eerbaarheid, hetzij verspreidt, openlijk ten toon stelt of aanslaat, hetzij om verspreid, openlijk tentoongesteld of aangeslagen te worden, vervaardigt, invoert, doorvoert, uitvoert of in voorraad heeft, hetzij openlijk, of door verspreiding van eenig geschrift ongevraagd, aanbiedt of als verkrijgbaar aanwijst, wordt gestraft met gevangenisstraf van ten hoogste een jaar en vier maanden of geldboete van ten hoogste drie duizend gulden' (He who [I] either distributes, exhibits publicly or displays, [II] produces, imports, transports, exports or stocks with a view to distributing, exhibiting publicly or displaying, or [III] either openly or by unsolicited circulation supplies or declares available any writing with the content of which he is familiar or any illustration or object offending public decency, shall be punished with a term of imprisonment not exceeding one year and four months or a fine not exceeding three thousand guilders).
The translation found by Moeliono reads as follows (following in Moeliono's footsteps, the constituents of the sentence representing its basic structure are given in italics): '*Barang-siapa jang menjiarkan*, mempertundjukkan kepada umum, menempelkan, atau untuk disiarkan, dipertundjukkan kepada umum atau ditempelkan, membuat, memasukkan kedalam negeri, mengirim terus didalam negeri, mengeluarkan dari negeri atau menjimpan, atau dengan terang-terangan atau dengan menjiarkan tulisan menawarkan tidak atas permintaan orang, atau menundjukkan bahwa boleh didapat: *tulisan* jang diketahuinya isinya, atau gambar atau barang jang dikenalnja melanggar kesusilaan, *dihukum* dengan hukuman pendjara selama-lamanja satu tahun empat bulan atau denda sebanjak-banjaknya tiga ribu rupiah.' This translation proposed by Moeliono arranges in an orderly fashion the complex subject of the principal clause (in English 'he who' accompanied by a string of relative clauses describing the unlawful acts) ('barangsiapa yang [...]; barangsiapa [...]; barangsiapa [...]'), followed by a brief repetition of the subject (as 'ia', meaning 'he') and the remainder of the principal clause (with the indication of the punishment: 'maka ia dihukum (dipidana) dengan hukuman [...]' or '*he* shall be punished with [...]').

44 A. Moeliono 1976:19; Takdir Alisjahbana 1976:24-30. Awareness of the structural peculiarities of Indonesian, too, was thought to contribute to greater precision in the use of language, resulting in turn in a higher degree of clarity. Alisjahbana, for example, drew attention to a flaw in Indonesian, namely that it is not clear from the form of an adjective to which noun in the sentence it refers. 'Lembaga Bahasa Nasional' can therefore mean either 'institute for the national language' or 'national institute for language', and 'politik bahasa nasional' can mean both 'policy relating to the national language' and 'national policy for language' (also relating to languages other than the national one). Alisjahbana proposed the use of hyphens in case of doubt ('Lembaga-Bahasa Nasional' and 'politik-bahasa nasional'), which, incidentally, is not in keeping with the 1972 spelling rules (Takdir Alisjahbana 1976:30).

guage by large sections of society in general (A. Moeliono 1976:14).

The points on which the Indonesian legal language was found wanting during the Simposium Bahasa dan Hukum have now been reviewed. The causes of the deficiencies identified during the conference have also been mentioned – the want of an institution with the means and the authority to counter the proliferation of legal terms and expressions (provoking heterogeneity in language and terminology); the inadequate command of the Indonesian language on the part of jurists (obviously affecting the quality of the texts they produced); and the continued omnipresence of Dutch sources of law (necessitating the continuation of the practice of translating, often too literally).

How to tackle the heterogeneity of legal terms was a dominant subject of the recommendations put forward at the close of the conference. It was advised that interdisciplinary collaboration be initiated for the purpose of large-scale stocktaking of legal terms.[45] Previously compiled lists and inventories, too, would need to be catalogued. In addition, measures were proposed for the standardization of current legal terms and for the creation of new ones.[46] The presentations had also raised the issue of the existing standard lexicons requiring amendment – the prevailing method of coining new Indonesian terms had consisted of translating single Dutch terms, without any regard for the viability of the terms thus created in the day-to-day practice of the law. Many terms proposed had never been adopted into common usage (Mochtar Kusumaatmadja 1976:9; Rudjiati Muljadi 1976:62). Also, a set of guidelines for creating terms had been called for, to be referred to when undertaking activities in the area of legal terminology.[47] One speaker had highlighted the government's special duty of care – it would be required to wield uniform, unambiguous legal terminology. Moreover, to promote the uniformity of the vocabulary applied in teaching law and in drafting legislation, law professors and jurists involved in legislating would need to meet on a regular basis. Finally, the spelling of legal terms would need to be consistent (Sabaruddin Ahmad 1976:102-3). The plea for deriving terms and 'building blocks' from the indigenous languages has been touched upon above.

Another area of heterogeneity to be tackled was that of legal theory.

45 *Simposium Bahasa dan Hukum* 1976:107 sub B.2 and B.6. In addition to the input of lawyers and linguists, the recommendations also envisaged the help of experts in adat law and in religious matters (Sabaruddin Ahmad 1976:102). Muljadi, in her capacity of head of the Lembaga Bahasa Nasional, assumed a role of modesty – the terminology of the law was the concern of lawyers, and linguists could merely assist (Rudjiati Muljadi 1976:62).

46 *Simposium Bahasa dan Hukum* 1976:107 sub B.9, 108; compare Mochtar Kusumaatmadja 1976:9-10, Rudjiati Muljadi 1976:62 and Mohamad Sjah 1976:52.

47 Mochtar Kusumaatmadja 1976:10-1. Also see A. Moeliono's remark about the importance of a systematic and consistent approach (see footnote 33).

One of the recommendations of the conference read that 'the consensus amongst jurists about certain legal matters and their views on particular questions had to be recorded immediately'.[48] This tied in neatly with the aim of a fully-fledged body of legal literature in the Indonesian language. Mochtar Kusumaatmadja expounded on the impossibility of developing a truly national legal system while law books were written in a language that was inaccessible to the common man – everyone should be able to gain full understanding of the subject matter (Damian and Hornick 1974:v). In so far as lawyers could be said to have common convictions, these were phrased and written in Dutch. With the command of Dutch waning over the years, recording those common convictions had become a matter of urgency. In other words, rather than in the uniformity of legal language, the issue here lay in constructing a solid foundation, a common point of departure for a system of law in the Indonesian language.[49]

To improve the proficiency of (future) jurists, it was suggested that Indonesian be added to the law faculties' curricula.[50] For the subject of command of language (*penguasaan bahasa*), it was recommended that specific emphasis be placed on the command of *legal* language.[51] With regard to legislation in Dutch that was still in force, there were calls for an official translation produced through a joint effort of lawyers and linguists. This recommendation (concerning only the *fashion* in which translation was to take place) took a much more modest approach than Busthanul Arifin's proposal, which, pending new legislation in the Indonesian language, advocated official translation of *all* colonial laws still in force (*Simposium Bahasa dan Hukum* 1976:107 sub B.7; Busthanul Arifin 1976:86). Anton Moeliono had taken a stance, as already mentioned, against overly-literal translation.

A number of proposals was put forward to introduce measures in respect of Indonesian legal language in general. A new agency was called for, to be established by the BPHN and the Lembaga Bahasa Nasional, which was to be charged specifically with the implementation of measures in respect of

48 'Perlunya membukukan dengan segera kesepakatan ahli-ahli hukum dalam berbagai masalah hukum dan pendapat ahli-ahli hukum tentang hal-hal tertentu' (*Simposium Bahasa dan Hukum* 1976:107 sub B.10).

49 Compare Arifin's argument for the Indonesification of adat law.

50 *Simposium Bahasa dan Hukum* 1976:107 sub B.3. By decree of the Minister of Education and Culture, the subject of 'pengetahuan bahasa' ('knowledge of language') had previously been included in the minimum requirements for law curricula (Padmo Wahjono in Mahadi 1975:31). The decree resulted partly from a recommendation made by the Jurisprudence Subconsortium.

51 *Simposium Bahasa dan Hukum* 1976:108. It is not clear whether this is the same subject as the course in Indonesian mentioned above. Alisjahbana (1976:34), too, had highlighted the importance of a sound command of the Indonesian language, one of the pillars of the new Indonesian society.

legal language.[52] It was thought advisable to hold workshops dedicated to the problems with legal language as they applied to particular areas of law. To make the issues and the approaches to their remedies more widely known, the setting up of a publication was recommended (*Simposium Bahasa dan Hukum* 1976:107 sub B.11, 108). Moeliono's case for a systematic and consistent process reverberates in the suggestion of letting the development of the legal language be guided by the structure of the law applicable to its different areas (*Simposium Bahasa dan Hukum* 1976:107 sub B.5). Finally, it was recommended that experts in the Indonesian language henceforward be involved in the drafting of new legislation.[53]

### *Measures implemented since 1974*

Some of the recommendations put forward at the Simposium Bahasa dan Hukum were acted upon in the years to follow. With respect to the legal terminology, in 1975 the Sub-Konsorsium Ilmu Hukum (Jurisprudence Subconsortium)[54] and the BPHN had catalogued prior initiatives aimed at standardization, along with their results.[55] In the survey conducted to this effect, which was aimed primarily at government departments and faculties

52 *Simposium Bahasa dan Hukum* 1976:108. Arifin, too, had declared himself in favour of collaboration between the Supreme Court/Ministry of Justice on the one hand and the National Language Institute on the other (Busthanul Arifin 1976:85-6; compare with Mochtar Kusumaatmadja 1976:10). At the meeting in preparation of the Seminar Politik Bahasa Nasional, Rudjiati Muljadi had argued generally for nationwide collaboration on the issue of language development, to be participated in by the Institute and the different departments, educational institutions, professional organizations and society at large (Rudjiati Muljadi 1974:2; compare Effendi 1974:6-9).

53 *Simposium Bahasa dan Hukum* 1976:107 sub B.8; compare with Busthanul Arifin 1976:85. Ahmad had also argued for examining and, if necessary, correcting legislation already in force. To achieve this aim, a state committee would have to be formed which would have to ensure the use of set, clear and unambiguous terminology (Sabaruddin Ahmad 1976:102-3).

54 The Sub-Konsorsium Ilmu Hukum was founded in 1969 as part of the Konsorsium Ilmu-ilmu Sosial dan Budaja (Social and Cultural Studies Consortium) of the Ministry of Education and Culture (Soetandyo Wignjosoebroto 1994:233; Konsorsium Ilmu Hukum 1991:1). Its members were the deans of the most prominent faculties of law; its remit was that of a thinktank of the Directorate-General for Higher Education of the government department mentioned above. In 1982 the Sub-Konsorsium was renamed the Konsorsium Ilmu Hukum (Jurisprudence Consortium).

55 The summary report of this survey may be found in Husein and Sunggingsari 1980. The report was based on data collected from 36 respondents from within government departments (64% of those approached) and 99 respondents from the law faculties (36% of those approached). The report also considered the collections of terms that had been gathered by the Department for Labour, Transmigration and Cooperatives, the Badan Pembina Pasar Uang dan Modal (Centre for the Development of the Money and Capital markets), the Komisi Istilah of the Ministry for Education and Culture (1955-58), the Pusat Bahasa (1973), the Law Faculty of the Universitas Hasanuddin and various individuals (Yunus Husein and Retno Sunggingsari 1980:533).

of law, many respondents proved to be in favour of standardizing the meanings of existing legal terms.[56] The survey report made a case for follow-up research, to be conducted by means of interviews, into the problems encountered in this standardization process and into the behavioural patterns of the respondents in their usage of (legal) language. Concrete measures would need to be taken as soon as possible in order to effect uniformity in the use of legal terms. Special standardization bodies would need to be set up within government institutions such as departments and faculties of law. It was also recommended that workshops and seminars be organized to support the standardization process (Yunus Husein and Retno Sunggingsari 1980:534-6).

From the 1980s onwards, lexicons were produced (Dutch-Indonesian and English-Indonesian), dictionaries were composed and a legal thesaurus was compiled (Budiarto 2000; Wiratmo Dianggoro 1996:50), all under the auspices of the BPHN and all aimed at the desired standardization of legal terms. The first dictionary, issued in 1985, covered criminal law and the rules governing criminal procedure. It was followed successively by parts dealing with the law of persons (*hukum perorangan*), patrimonial law/law of property (*hukum kebendaan*), contract law (*hukum perikatan*), the law on evidence and prescription/limitation (*hukum pembuktian dan daluarsa*), commercial law (*hukum ekonomi*) and constitutional law (*hukum tata negara*), the series being concluded with a general edition (1999).[57] The standardization lists also included terms

56 The questionnaires had been sent to the upper echelons of the civil service, especially departments, and to the law faculties of the state universities. The majority of the respondents from within government departments indicated that they were in favour of such standardization, as per the above. Moreover, the standardization, in their view, ought to take place in close collaboration with other departments, the scope of which overlapped their own.

57 Budiarto 2000:10-1. The criminal law dictionary (*Kamus hukum pidana*) was completed under the direction of team chairmen T.M. Daud Syah and M. Budiarto, respectively, both of them jurists. The Pusat Bahasa was represented by Anton Moeliono in the role of vice chairman/editor. He filled the same position in the case of both of the private law publications (Badan Pembinaan Hukum Nasional 1989-90, 1990-91), under the chairmanship of the female advocate Hajati Suroredjo. The criminal law team also comprised a group of 'formulators' or 'definers' (*perumus*) in variable formation (namely Estiana Hermina, Sri Budiarti, Budiarti, Nayla Widharma Tadjudin, Wijaya Tejalaksana, Ani Chairani Sumantri and Andi Hamzah), as well as a team of advisors (*penimbang*). The remit of the latter team, the formation of which varied, too, was to evaluate the terms and definitions suggested and, where necessary, to correct them or come up with alternative solutions. This team consisted of members of widely diverse branches of the legal profession, these being T.M. Radhie (BPHN), M. Hasan Wargakusumah (BPHN), H. Adi Andojo Sutjipto (Mahkamah Agung), A. Karim Nasution (Kejaksaan Agung, Prosecution Servcie), Sri Sukesi Adiwimarta (Pusat Bahasa), Asis Safioeddin (Universitas Airlangga, Surabaya), M. Saleh Baharis (BPHN), Lamya Moeljatno (Universitas Gadjah Mada, Yogyakarta), Wahjono Darmabrata (Pusat Dokumentasi Hukum, UI) and R. Soegondo Kertanegara (Pengadilan Tinggi Yogyakarta), who had deceased prior to completion of the project. With the exception of the vice chairman, the private law team was made up exclusively of jurists – Woerjati Martosewojo, Rusminah, Wienarsih Imam Subekti, Fred A. Tumbuan and Marjam Sutjiati Hadi Iman. The editorial team employed

relating to, for instance, international law and agrarian law.[58] The dictionaries contain definitions in Indonesian of Indonesian entries, here and there a reference to a relevant legal clause and, in the case of a translation in Indonesian of an existing foreign language term, the original Dutch or English.[59]

As to the size of the dictionaries, the criminal law volume contains an estimated 850 entries, the patrimonial law/property law volume just over 200 and the general legal dictionary some 1,200. Some overlap occurred between the terms entered in the general dictionary and those contained in the earlier volumes.[60] By contrast, the English-Indonesian dictionary covering economic law (Erawaty and Badudu 1996) was substantially more voluminous. This edition had, in actual fact, not been produced under the aegis of the BPHN but under that of the ELIPS I project sponsored by USAID.[61] Sunaryati Hartono, Head of the BPHN, was closely involved, in a personal capacity, in

on the general dictionary was led by A.F. Elly Erawaty, with Agus Anwar as the secretary and Alma Evita Almanar (the only non-jurist, presumably a linguist), Husaini Kadir, Sumarni Alam, Ida Padmanegara, Made Sudiarsih, Suharyono and Enny Nurillah as ordinary members.

58 Budiarto 2000:9-10. The standardization lists are exemplified by Badan Pembinaan Hukum Nasional 1994-95, 1995-96. These lists (the ones cited here being English-Indonesian) contain keywords from the domain of 'economic law' ('hukum ekonomi', 'hukum bisnis' – an area of law with a considerably wider scope than the traditional concept of 'hukum dagang' (commercial law) loaned from the Dutch (*handelsrecht*), which also encompasses subjects such as tax law and employment law). The terms relate to an array of legal topics, from banking law, contract law, transport law and intellectual property law to taxation law, employment law, insurance law, capital gains law, IT law, company law, maritime and aviation law governing transport and residential law. The very first decision mentioned in the lists, that of appointing a Legal Terms Standardization Team, is Kepmenkeh no. G-49.PR.09.03 dated 1989. The teams charged with the production of the lists were managed by the successive heads of the BPHN, Sunaryati Hartono and H.A.S. Natabaya. The members of the teams were jurists but, in the case of the second list, included two linguists, namely J.S. Badudu and Sri Sukesi Adiwimarta.

59 The criminal law dictionary included a Dutch-Indonesian lexicon, the Indonesian terms of which in turn formed entries in the glossary part of the work. For example, the lexicon contains the Dutch word 'misdrijf' (criminal offence) and gives the Indonesian 'kejahatan' alongside. 'Kejahatan' is an entry in the actual dictionary part, which in turn supplies the original Dutch term with a definition in Indonesian. The two private law dictionaries lack the bilingual lexicon but are otherwise organized in the same way, albeit with the 1989 publication arranged according to the Dutch entries.

60 By way of comparison, the *Indonesisch-Nederlands woordenboek privaatrecht* (Indonesian-Dutch private law dictionary) published in 2000 (Massier and Termorshuizen-Arts 2000) contains close to 10,000 entries, including synonyms, deviant spellings and the like.

61 The Economic Law and Improved Procurement Systems Project (ELIPS I) ran from 1992 to 2001. This dictionary contains terms in connection with the subjects of national and international commercial law, banking law, insurance law, transport law, investment law, the law governing the financial market and securities, company law, contract law and competition law (Erawaty and Badudu 1996:v). Its method of referencing is similar to that of the dictionaries elaborated upon above, the main difference lying in the former's point of departure being English terms instead of the Dutch ones of the latter.

the production of this dictionary.[62]

The BPHN initially worked together with the Pusat Bahasa but a difference of opinion between Sunaryati Hartono and Anton Moeliono of the Pusat Bahasa put paid to the collaboration. One bone of contention was the old division between lawyers and linguists over the degree of compliance with the rules of standard Indonesian. In other words, should lawyers grant linguists a say in the language used in the execution of their profession and if so, to what extent? The stance that legal language merely represented a register of the Indonesian language and should comply quite simply with the general rules, was felt to be too rigid at the BPHN. After all, there were times when jurists really had no choice but to abandon those rules.[63] Moeliono's position was filled by professor Yus Badudu from Bandung, a man well-known due to the TV programme he presented. This epoch saw the production of a dictionary for each area of law being abandoned – following the dictionaries for constitutional law (1994-1995) and economic law, published in the framework of the ELIPS project, a general legal dictionary integrating the subject dictionaries already completed was the new objective.

It was Sunaryati's intention to create an Indonesian system of law accompanied by its own legal language. This standardization project neatly tied in with another BPHN project, called Ganti Baju (something like 'changing clothes'), which aimed to accelerate the pace of replacing legislation carried over from the colonial era (estimated in 1994 to consist of approximately 400 regulations) with laws in the Indonesian language. The new legislation was to be couched in the Indonesian terms determined through the standardization project, thus creating an opening for an important contribution towards the uniformity of Indonesian legal terminology.[64]

A book on the language of the law, also included in the conference recommendations, was indeed published. In 1979 the conference speakers from USU, Mahadi and Sabaruddin Ahmad, jointly published *Pembinaan bahasa*

62 Erawaty, J.S. Badudu and Sunaryati all emerged from Bandung academia.

63 Interview with Sunaryati Hartono, Agus Anwar and Made Sudiarsih dated 29-1-1994. The Kitab Undang-undang Hukum Acara Pidana (KUHAP, Criminal Procedure Code) promulgated in 1981, too, caused a heated discussion between Anton Moeliono and several lawyers over the terminology employed in the book. Particularly controversial was the use of the term *pengadilan* to mean 'court'. Adhering to the customary function of derivations with the affix *peN-...–an*, the term 'peng-adil-an' ought to indicate something like 'trying'. Moeliono therefore argued that the terms 'badan pengadilan' (something like 'body for trying') or 'mahkamah' ought to be used for 'court' (sources: report contained in *Hukum dan Pembangunan* 18 (1988):71 of the Seminar Bahasa Indonesia Hukum, held at the Universitas Indonesia on 13-2-1988, and interviews with A. Moeliono and Mardjono Reksodiputro on 13-4-1994 and 2-5-1994).

64 Interview with Sunaryati Hartono, Agus Anwar and Made Sudiarsih dated 29-1-1994. The BPHN played a considerable part in the process of developing new legislation. The centre produced the so-called 'academic drafts', academically sound law proposals.

*hukum Indonesia* (The construction of Indonesian legal language).[65] This book provided a historical, linguistic and sociological framework for the problems surrounding the language of the law and was intended as a guide for everything related to improving the usage of Indonesian in the legal world (Mahadi and Sabaruddin Ahmad 1979:vii). The book's leitmotiv is that language plays a crucial role both in the law and for jurists: 'however good and perfect the law may be, without language it cannot be upheld in society' (Mahadi and Sabaruddin Ahmad 1979:18). That language, moreover, should be systematic and grammatical (the linguistic perspective) as well as rational, in the sense that the use made of the language should concur with the ideas or intentions one meant to express (sociological perspective) (Mahadi and Sabaruddin Ahmad 1979:19). The irregularities in morphology, syntax and spelling characteristic of many a legal text should therefore be done away with, as should the heterogeneity of legal terminology and its resultant chaos. The book made the case for establishing a national committee of jurists, linguists, theologians and experts in adat law and other subjects, to be charged with improving the use of language in legislation and other legal texts and with ensuring that the terms used were set, clear and unambiguous (Mahadi and Sabaruddin Ahmad 1979:54-73).

The book on legal language and the standardization of legal terms having emanated from the recommendations of the Simposium Bahasa dan Hukum, the translation of legislation in the Dutch language was also tackled. As mentioned above, the conclusions had referred merely to the manner of translating and had altogether avoided the issue of that entire body of legislation requiring translation. At the 1979 Seminar Hukum Nasional IV (National Law Seminar), the need for a wholesale translation had been put forward – in so far as that legislation was thought to have continued relevance.[66] 1983 thus saw the publication, by the BPHN, of a translation, dubbed official (*resmi*), of the Wetboek van Strafrecht/Kitab Undang-undang Hukum Pidana (Criminal Code).[67] This translation was based on a painstaking evaluation of existing

65 Mahadi and Sabaruddin Ahmad 1979. The book was published under the auspices of the BPHN.

66 *Kitab Undang-undang Hukum Pidana* 1983:7; compare *Hasil Seminar Hukum Nasional Keempat* 1980:50 sub 3d. On this occasion, it was also recommended to use translations in Indonesian of legal literature in Dutch or other foreign languages to support law research and teaching (p. 50 sub 3c).

67 In addition to BPHN Head J.C.T. Simorangkir, the team of translators consisted of the lawyers R. Sudarto (Universitas Diponegoro, Semarang), Mahadi, J.E. Sahetapy (Universitas Airlangga, Surabaya) and Sardjono (secretary) and the linguist Amran Halim. For more on the history, from independence onwards, of the Wetboek van Strafrecht, originally promulgated in the *Staatsblad* in 1915 (*Stb*. no. 732), see Han Bing Siong 1959-60 in particular. Of the major codes of the colonial era, the Wetboek van Strafrecht is the only one to have been given an official (in the sense of statutory) *Indonesian* designation (UU no. 1/1946 art. VI) – Kitab Undang-undang

translations. Because the text was published by not just any government agency but by a department of the Ministry of Justice, the BPHN hoped to bestow on it a certain official status and, inherently, added authority (*Kitab Undang-undang Hukum Pidana* 1983:8).

The BPHN's decision to issue a translation of the Wetboek van Strafrecht, of all the laws to choose from, may be explained by the fact that this code, unlike the Burgerlijk Wetboek (BW, Civil Code) and the Wetboek van Koophandel (WvK, Commercial Code), applied to *all* Indonesians (Dekker and Van Katwijk 1993:17). Moreover, criminal law had been of particular concern to the government since the days of colonial domination, not in the least in terms of making available translations.[68] The Wetboek van Strafrecht ended up as the most prolifically translated text by far (into Malay and Indonesian, respectively) through private initiative and therefore required a standard translation more urgently than any other text.[69]

---

Hukum Pidana. However, no Indonesian translation of this text was ever promulgated in the *Lembaran Negara* (State Gazette), that is, obtained the formal status of an act (*undang-undang*). The only official version of the code, from the point of view of being legally binding, still is the Dutch original as promulgated in 1915 and subsequently amended.

68 This may be deduced from the nineteenth-century translations of Netherlands East Indies legislation into Malay, Javanese and other archipelago languages still extant. A translation dubbed 'official' of the Wetboek van Strafregt voor Inlanders in Nederlandsch-Indië (Criminal Code for Natives in the Netherlands East Indies) (*Stb.* 1872, no. 85) was issued as early as a year following the Code becoming law, in Latin script and bearing the title *Boekoe kaädilan hoekoeman atas bangsa Djawa dan sebrang di India-Nederland; Menoeroet salinan jang telah di oendang-oendangken oleeh kangd-jeng Goebernement, dengen di pindahken kapada hoeroef Ollanda/Wetboek van Strafregt voor Inlanders in Nederlandsch-Indië; Volgens de officieele vertaling* (Semarang: Van Dorp). Two years later an edition was published in Arabic script (*djawi*) (Batavia: Landsdrukkerij). Both this criminal code and the Wetboek van Strafregt voor Europeanen (Criminal Code for Europeans) (*Stb.* 1866, no. 55) were published in translations carried out privately in 1872 (D.E. van den Berg, *Boekoe Wet perkara hoe-koemannja orang bangsa Djawa dan lain bangsa, jang di samaken dengen bangsa Djawa di India-Nederland*, Soerabaja: Thieme, and L. Wolfe and C. Schreutelkamp, *Oendang-oendang di atas hak hoekoeman boeat Hindia-Nederland; Kitab boeat orang-orang Wolanda*, Batavia: Ogilvie, respectively). From the 1920s onwards, translations were published under the auspices of the Balai Poestaka/Volkslectuur (People's Literature) of the new Wetboek van Strafrecht that pertained to all population groups (*Stb.* 1915, no. 732 in conjunction with 1917, no. 645), until the 18th edition was issued in 1960, which was edited by A.W. Djumena. By contrast, translation of the Indische Burgerlijk Wetboek (Netherlands East Indies Civil Code) (*Stb.* 1847, no. 23) and the Wetboek van Koophandel (Commercial Code) (*Stb.* 1847, no. 23) was left to private initiative. Also see Chapter III.

69 Fifteen translations at least were produced during the period 1915-83 (the year in which the BPHN translation was published). Apart from the texts mentioned explicitly in the preface and introduction to the BPHN issue – being those by Moeljatno ([Yogyakarta]: n.n., 1959) and Soesilo (Bogor: Politeia, around 1959) as well as the Engelbrecht legislation readers from the 1950s and 1960s (see footnote 78) – translations were produced or published by J.L.T. Rhemrev (Semarang: Van Dorp, 1919), Balai Poestaka/Volkslectuur (Weltevreden, 1921; 18th edition edited by A.W. Djumena in 1960), the Staf Umum Angkatan Udara (General Air Force Staff) at Yogyakarta (1948), Jusuf Ismail and Mangkuningrat (Bogor: Oranje, 1948, tenth edition 1952), H. Soerjanatamihardja (Djakarta: Van Dorp, 1952), Seno Soeharjo (Bogor: Politeia, 1955), K.H.

Measures were also taken to adapt the teaching of law. Following the Simposium Bahasa dan Hukum, held towards the end of 1974, where it had been suggested that the subject of Indonesian be added to the curriculum and that that of language command be tailored to usage in a legal context, another conference took place in 1975 which focussed on the innovation of law teaching and of vocational training in law.[70] One proposal raised at that conference was to train law students in drafting legislation, in constructing contracts and in writing academic treatises. In the years to follow, the lecturer and subsequent criminology professor Mardjono Reksodiputro (see footnote 14) was to cast himself as a fervent proponent of including language and related subjects in the curricula of the law faculties. From the mid-1970s onwards, he held the key positions of assistant dean (1975-1980) and dean (1984-1990) of the Law Faculty of the UI of Jakarta and that of secretary of the national Konsorsium Ilmu Hukum (Jurisprudence Consortium) (from 1989 onwards). According to Mardjono, jurists failed in the very aspect where they ought to demonstrate their expertise, namely in their skilled use of the spoken and written word.[71]

His efforts to make language part of the courses in law were, however, met with fierce resistance from the Consortium and the law faculties.[72]

---

Husin (compiler and translator/author of the trilogy *Kitab himpunan perundang-undangan Negara Republik Indonesia*, Djakarta: Kementerian Penerangan, [1957]-1960), Dali Mutiara (Djakarta: Bintang Indonesia, around 1960, 14th edition 1962), Budiarto and K. Wantjik Saleh ([Jakarta]: Ghalia Indonesia, 1979), Sugandhi (Surabaya: Usaha Nasional, 1981), Soenarto Soerodibroto (Jakarta: Soenarto, 1982) and by the publishers Pradnya Paramita at Jakarta (1983).

70 The conference was entitled Simposium Pembaharuan Pendidikan Hukum dan Pembinaan Profesi Hukum (*Seminar Evaluasi Pembaharuan Pendidikan Hukum* 1982:50-1).

71 Mardjono Reksodiputro 1995b:73. Mardjono's stance derived from the language usage in the many dissertations that had crossed his desk. In a conversation at the UI, Mardjono described the language usage encountered in dissertations as 'telegram style', 'bureaucratic', 'formal'. The students cited all manner of legislation to their hearts' content (prompting reactions from M. like 'you strike me as a newspaper typesetter, plagiarizing other people's work!'), but seemingly failed to understand that the reader had to be grabbed by the story. Mardjono linked this to language teaching in secondary school. He had noticed that his children were required to learn vast amounts of theory, rules and definitions by rote and gained the impression that teachers who had been trained at the Institut Keguruan dan Ilmu Pendidikan (IKIP, Institute of Teacher Training and Pedagogy) in particular turned language lessons into a highly theoretical affair. Perhaps language teachers worked on the false assumption that knowing the rules was tantamount to being able to apply them, Mardjono said. He detected the same fondness of rules in instilling the Pancasila (the official philosophical foundation of the Indonesian state, comprising five principles – see Chapter IV). He had had to teach his children himself how to write a flowing, logically constructed paper. Mardjono extended his observations to recent court decisions, which displayed a noticeable lack of judicial considerations, in the sense of the elaboration of the judge's reasoning in arriving at his judgement. It might be that the judges were simply incapable of performing the reasoning process, Mardjono thought, or else they could reason but not commit their argument to paper (interview dated 2-5-1994).

72 Interview dated 2-5-1994. Mardjono said that university colleagues did not consider Indonesian and other languages to be appropriate subjects for a law curriculum. The students'

Indonesian as a subject was indeed mandatory for a short spell in the 1980s but later became optional, though the subject of 'Writing for law' (*Penulisan hukum*), crowned with a dissertation, is compulsory throughout the country.[73] During Mardjono's deanery, the 1988 Seminar Bahasa Indonesia Hukum (Seminar on Legal Indonesian) was held at the UI, with Anton Moeliono as the sole speaker.[74]

In addition to Indonesian, Mardjono felt that English and Dutch also belonged to the mandatory curriculum subjects. They were the keys to an externalizing perspective, one aimed at other systems of law, which was crucial as long as little literature on foreign law systems was available in Indonesian. Knowledge of Dutch was indispensable in constructing a national, Indonesian system of law – prior to replacing the old system with a new one, a thorough understanding was necessary in order to establish exactly what was to be replaced. As a rule, however, law students had a very poor command of foreign languages (Mardjono Reksodiputro 1989:543, 1995a:7). As with arguing the case for education in the Indonesian language, Mardjono proposed a team effort by the law and arts faculties, as well as collaboration with the Netherlands in respect of the subject of Dutch (interview dated 2-5-1994). Accordingly, in 1988 and 1989, the course 'Nederlands als bronnentaal/Dutch as a source language' was offered to Indonesian lecturers in Dutch at the law faculties of the Indonesian state universities.[75]

---

inability to write a decent paper either escaped their attention or they applied much lower standards, according to Mardjono. The Student Council, too, challenged him to justify his decision to implement language teaching. Dutch especially went against the grain but Indonesian did not get a favourable reception either. The typical reaction, according to Mardjono, was 'Why should I, an Indonesian, take classes in Indonesian?' (interview dated 2-5-1994). Incidentally, in the teaching of law in Indonesia in particular, language classes had long been customary – the subjects of Malay and Javanese (as well as Latin, briefly) had been mandatory at the (Dutch-language) Rechtshoogeschool (Law College) (compare with Chapter III).

73 Interview dated 2-5-1994, also see Mardjono Reksodiputro 1995b:73, 1995c:79. A teaching manual for the subject of 'Penulisan hukum' was issued in 1993 (Agus Brotosusilo et al., *Penulisan hukum; Buku pegangan dosen*, Jakarta: Konsorsium Ilmu Hukum, Departemen Pendidikan dan Kebudayaan in collaboration with the Yayasan Asia). In 1997 the internal publication *Bahasa hukum Indonesia; Bahasa Indonesia untuk bidang hukum* was produced by Panuti Sudjiman, lecturer in legal Indonesian at the Universitas Atmajaya of Jakarta. Sudjiman pointed out that, notwithstanding the 1974 recommendation of emphasizing *legal* language in the teaching of law, the content was by and large identical to that used in teaching the subject of Indonesian Language (pp. iv, 12). The course book contains a number of texts taken from various types of legislation, which form the basis for questions testing one's comprehension and for clarifying the special features of the text (such as composition, syntax and style). The texts are accompanied by assignments which provide the student with the opportunity to practise the application of Indonesian grammar.

74 The seminar, held on 13-2-1988, is discussed briefly in *Hukum dan Pembangunan* 18 (1988):71.

75 These lecturers (selected to attend the course) taught law students at S1 level (equivalent

Within the framework of Dutch-Indonesian legal cooperation during the period 1985-1992, too, attention was paid to Dutch as a source language for Indonesian jurists.[76] Part of one of the cooperation programmes aimed to develop the law libraries in Indonesia and improve access to the sources of law, which entailed making available in Indonesian judicial decisions and articles in law journals (in the Dutch language) dating from the colonial era.[77] A translation was published of the well-known general part of the Asser series on private law, written by Paul Scholten, the celebrated Amsterdam professor (and founding father of the Rechtshoogeschool (Law College) – see Chapter III), and a new edition of the Engelbrecht legislation reader was financed, now providing Indonesian translations of the most important colonial legislation still in force.[78]

---

to an undergraduate degree course). The objective of the project was to upgrade their skills so as to enable them, on the one hand, to teach law students at S2 level (equivalent to postgraduate studies) themselves and, on the other, to guide and coordinate S1 courses. A shortage of lecturers in Dutch for S1 level meant that the objective could not be attained, however (source: report on course 'Dutch as a source language' appended to a letter by J.W. de Vries dated 20-12-1988 and addressed to the Dutch Ministry of Education). Eleven and five lecturers, respectively, participated in the two courses held in 1988 and 1989, of which three came from the state university of Jakarta, two from each of the universities of Bandung, Yogyakarta, Semarang, Surabaya, Ujung Pandang and Medan and one from Denpasar. The programme involved four months at the Faculty of Arts of the Universitas Indonesia, followed by more than three months in Leiden and Amsterdam. The author, then engaged by the Nederlands Onderzoekscentrum voor Recht in Zuidoost-Azië en het Caraïbisch gebied (Dutch Research Centre for Law in Southeast Asia and the Caribbean, Norzoac for short, later the Van Vollenhoven Institute for Law, Governance and Development) in Leiden, led the subject of 'Reading and translating Dutch legal texts'.

76 On the Dutch side, there was the Nederlandse Raad voor Juridische Samenwerking met Indonesië (Netherlands Council for Cooperation with Indonesia in Legal Matters), while the Indonesian participants in the programme were the Badan Perencanaan Pembangunan Nasional (National Development Planning Agency or Bappenas), the Mahkamah Agung, the Ministry of Justice (the BPHN, among others) and the Ministry of Education and Culture (the Konsorsium Ilmu Hukum and others). Over time, the cooperation programme came to consist of five components, to wit a programme involving the law faculties, a programme to enhance Indonesia's legislative capacity, a programme aimed at the judiciary, a course for prosecutors and a reinforcement programme (*ondersteunend programma*) (also see *Law reform in Indonesia* 1997:58, 70).

77 See Dekker and Van Katwijk 1992 and 1993b. These schemes formed part of the reinforcement programme.

78 *Himpunan Engelbrecht* 1989. According to L. Pasmans, director of the publishing company Ichtiar Baru-Van Hoeve, 40,000 copies of the compilation were sold, the majority to private enterprises such as law and accountancy firms but some also to courts of law (interview dated 10-5-1994). Since independence, new editions of the Engelbrecht reader had already been issued, containing not only the original Dutch and Indonesian texts but also several translations in Indonesian (for example, the Wetboek van Strafrecht) and in Dutch (such as UU no. 1/1950 in respect of the Mahkamah Agung). The last edition was published in 1960 (*Kitab2 undang2 Republik Indonesia* 1960), the last reprint of which was issued in 1971. Scholten's *Algemeen deel* (General Part, original edition 1931), translated by Siti Soemarti Hartono and edited by Sudikno Mertokusumo, was published in Indonesian in 1992, bearing the title of *Mr. C. Asser penuntun*

Moreover, when Dutch development aid was cancelled by the Indonesian government, in 1992, putting a rather abrupt stop to the juridical cooperation, a project proposal was being prepared to produce an Indonesian-Dutch and a Dutch-Indonesian legal dictionary. A fairly recent scion of this proposal was the *Indonesisch-Nederlands woordenboek privaatrecht* (Indonesian-Dutch private law dictionary), which came into being in 2000 (Massier and Termorshuizen-Arts 2000). With respect to the cooperation, finally it should be mentioned that courses in Dutch were provided, for example to Indonesian jurists engaged in drafting legislation.[79]

### *Failing measures*

Notwithstanding the array of measures, the quality of the legal language used seems to have improved little since 1974. From that year on, lawyers' language and terminology have been dealt with in innumerable books and articles,[80] and the quinquennial Kongres Bahasa Indonesia has continued

---

*dalam mempelajari hukum perdata Belanda; Bagian umum* (Yogyakarta: Gadjah Mada University Press).

79 Konsorsium Ilmu Hukum 1991:75-7; 'Legal cooperation between Indonesia and the Netherlands 1985-1992' (memo Centre for International Legal Cooperation dated December 1994); Bongenaar 1992:5-7.

80 A random dip into the wealth of literature since 1974: Kamal Firdaus, 'Bahasa dalam sidang pengadilan' (*Keadilan* 5-3 (1978):15); Sujatmo Martosuhardjo, *Bahasa Belanda hukum* (Jakarta: Program Pendidikan Pasca Sarjana, Universitas Indonesia, 1982); Mahadi, 'Bahasa hukum adat dalam peta bumi bahasa hukum nasional' (*Hukum dan Pembangunan* 13 (1983):214-22); Padmo Wahjono, 'Beberapa permasalahan bahasa hukum di Indonesia' (*Hukum dan Pembangunan* 13 (1983):201-13); Yus Badudu, 'Masalah pengembangan bahasa Indonesia sebagai bahasa hukum' (*Hukum dan Pembangunan* 13 (1983):223-32); Purnadi Purbacaraka and Soerjono Soekanto, 'Pendidikan hukum dan bahasa hukum' (*Hukum dan Pembangunan* 13 (1983):233-9); Soetan Mohamad Syah, 'Permainan bahasa' (*Hukum dan Pembangunan* 13 (1983):240-2); Hilman Hadikusuma, *Bahasa hukum Indonesia* (Bandung: Alumni, 1984); J.C.T. Simorangkir, 'Bahasa dan istilah hukum Indonesia' (*Suara Pembaruan*, 9-6-1987); Asis Safioedin, 'Perkembangan bahasa Indonesia dalam karya hukum' (*Yuridika* 3 (1988):301-9); Anton Moeliono, 'Bahasa Indonesia dalam akta notaris' (*Media Notariat* 4 (1989):239-48); F.A. Tumbuan, 'Pembahasan terhadap makalah Prof. Dr. Anton Moeliono "Bahasa Indonesia dalam akta notaris"' (*Media Notariat* 4 (1989):249-54); Slamet Djabarudi, 'Bahasan untuk "Bahasa Indonesia dalam akta notaris"' (*Media Notariat* 4 (1989):255-6) and 'Bahasa hukum' (*Forum Keadilan* 14-5-1992, pp. 62-3); 'Bila bahasa hukum tidak jelas' (*Berita Yudha*, 31-8-1989); 'Bahasa hukum perlu disederhanakan' (*Neraca*, 22-10-1992); Hernadi Affandi, 'Persoalan bahasa hukum dan perkembangannya di Indonesia' (*Bisnis Indonesia*, 28-10-1994); 'Bahasa notaris berbelit dan ketinggalan zaman' (*Kompas*, 12-12-1994); Ismail Saleh, 'Bahasa hukum' (*Kompas*, 6-6-1995); 'Bahasa hukum yang berbelit perlu disederhanakan' (*Kompas*, 25-7-1996); H.A.S. Natabaya, 'Kerancuan bahasa hukum refleksi bahasa Indonesia' (*Kompas*, 26-7-1996); Satya Arinanto, 'Bahasa hukum' (*Kompas*, 5-8-1996); Busthanul Arifin, 'Bahasa hukum kita' (*Mimbar Hukum* 31 (1997):68-70); 'Eufemisme dalam bahasa hukum kurang tepat' (*Kompas Online*, 16-10-1997); 'Bahasa hukum harus lugas' (*Kompas*

with its standard theme of legal language, inviting many a prominent figure from the legal world (in 1983 and 1988 the then ministers of Justice) onto the stage.[81] The tone of the lectures, articles and books is often critical in the extreme. The aspects at which the criticism is directed have remained the same. A 1996 BPHN publication evaluating 25 years of legal language points out the heterogeneity of language and terminology, the irregularity of word forms and sentence structures and the sloppiness of spelling and punctuation.[82] Other publications also vent their frustration in this respect.[83] Well-known additional points of criticism are that the language used in legal contexts is incomprehensible to the layman or is unintelligible per se[84] and contains word-for-word translations from Dutch or English.[85]

---

*Online*, 1-11-1997); Panuti Sudjiman, *Bahasa hukum Indonesia; Bahasa Indonesia untuk bidang hukum* ([Jakarta: n.n.], 1997); Bahder Johan Nasution, *Bahasa Indonesia hukum* (Bandung: Citra Aditya Bakti, 1998); Soetandyo Wignjosoebroto, 'Hukum dan pemaknaannya menurut pengalaman kebahasaan para penggunanya; Sebuah pengantar ke arah "kajian hukum dengan pendekatan semiotik"' (*Jentera* 2002, 1:5-20); Anom Surya Putra, 'Bahasa hukum yang pharmacon; Keluar dari Logos' (*Jentera* 2002, 1:21-36); Gregory Churchill, 'Badai bahasa; Tanda-tanda arah perubahan dari kosa-kata hukum' (*Jentera* 2002, 1:49-67); B. Arief Sidharta, 'Bahasa hukum Indonesia; Krisis bahasa di antara pakem dan frase' (*Jentera* 2002, 1:80-8); Marsillam Simanjuntak, 'Marsillam; "Bahasa hukum sering memperkosa kaidah tata bahasa"' (*Jentera* 2002, 1:89-94); Irma Hidayana, 'Bahasa hukumku melambung tinggi' (*Jentera* 2002, 1:96-104); Agus Priyanto, 'Membumikan bahasa hukum' (*Jentera* 2002, 1:106-14); 'Bahasa hukum sering membingungkan' (*Kompas Online*, 23-8-2002).

81 The speakers at the conferences of 1978, 1983, 1988, 1993 and 1998 (Kongres Bahasa Indonesia III-VII), in succession, were Mahadi ('Menuju bahasa hukum dan bahasa administrasi yang lebih mudah dipahami'; Jakarta: Pusat Pembinaan dan Pengembangan Bahasa, 1978); Minister of Justice Ali Said ('Bahasa hukum sebagai obyek dan subyek pembangunan nasional'; Jakarta: Pusat Pembinaan dan Pengembangan Bahasa, 1983); Minister of Justice Ismail Saleh ('Bahasa Indonesia sebagai sarana untuk menciptakan tertib hukum dalam masyarakat', *Varia Peradilan* 41 (1989):136-45); legislation expert A. Hamid S. Attamimi, senior lecturer in constitutional law at the UI and employed at the Sekretariat Negara ('Bahasa Indonesia dalam perundang-undangan'); and the Head of the BPHN, H.A.S. Natabaya ('Bahasa Indonesia dalam wacana hukum', in: Hasan Alwi et al. 2000:301-8).

82 Badudu 1996:3, 21-2. The team had been established by virtue of the 1994 Kepmenkeh G-112.PR.09.03. Apart from Badudu, the team members were Yunan Hilmy (BPHN, secretary), Din Muhammad (Ikatan Hakim Indonesia, Indonesian Society of Judges), Hasan Alwi (Pusat Bahasa), Sutarso (Faculty of Law of the Universitas Pancasila, Jakarta), H. Abu Jusuf (Ikatan Notaris Indonesia, Indonesian Society of Notaries Public), H. Bagir Manan (Perhimpunan Perancang Peraturan Perundang-undangan Indonesia, Indonesian Society of Legislative Drafters), Wiratmo Dianggoro (BPHN) and Lindawati Ginting (BPHN). The text is based on an evaluation of laws, court decisions, deeds, legal handbooks and a dissertation.

83 Yus Badudu 1983; Ismail Saleh 1989; Slamet Djabarudi 1992; Marsillam Simanjuntak 2002.

84 Mahadi 1979; Ismail Saleh 1989; Hernadi Affandi 1994; Badudu 1996; *Bahasa hukum harus lugas* 1997; Arief Sidharta 2002; Marsillam Simanjuntak 2002; Irma Hidayana 2002.

85 Padmo Wahjono 1983; Yus Badudu 1983; A. Moeliono 1989; Slamet Djabarudi 1992; Irma Hidayana 2002. Also pinpointed are the frequent use of euphemisms (*Eufemisme dalam bahasa hukum* 1997), the transcription of inadequacies linked to the original Dutch terms (Purnadi

Without entering into the different points of criticism and their mutual compatibility here, one may already conclude that, up until the present day, the measures derived from the Simposium Bahasa dan Hukum seemingly have failed to deliver their objective. A possible cause of this failure might be the *scope* of the measures taken. For example, the number of terms included in the BPHN dictionaries and lexicons to date is rather limited. More importantly, as with government bodies in general, the BPHN encountered considerable difficulty in effecting any large-scale distribution of its publications (and continues to do so). In accordance with current legislation, the proprietary rights on the publications of such an institution remain with the state and are not to be sold on. The dictionaries, already in limited editions due to the humble budget available for these projects, were distributed to a small number of individuals and failed to reach the retail outlets. Any civilian interested in the subject matter who happens to be aware of the existence of the dictionaries, may apply in writing to the BPHN and order a copy. It goes without saying that this distribution method precludes the BPHN publications from attaining any sizeable reach (and therefore effect) (Churchill 1992:14-5; Hasan Alwi et al. 2000:311). The market for legal dictionaries thus is the domain, by and large, of private publishing houses. And a substantial market it is, too – not counting the reprints of the Subekti, Martias, Simorangkir and Moeljadi dictionaries (see footnote 11), at least fourteen new legal dictionaries reached the shelves between 1975 and 1999.[86] Any impetus towards uniformity the

Purbacaraka and Soerjono Soekanto 1983; Arief Sidharta 2002) and the application to one and the same Dutch term of various Indonesian designations, none of which accurately hit the mark (Purnadi Purbacaraka and Soerjono Soekanto 1983).

86 In 1986 the ninth edition of Subekti's dictionary was issued (Jakarta: Pradnya Paramita); in 1982 the second of Martias's (Jakarta: Ghalia Indonesia); in 2000 the sixth of Simorangkir's (Jakarta: Sinar Grafika) and in 1980 the second of Moeljadi's (Jakarta: Karya Nusantara) (see footnote 11). New dictionaries were *Kamus Hukum; Bahasa Belanda, Indonesia, Inggeris* by Yan Pramadya Puspa (Semarang: Aneka, around 1977); *Kamus hukum adat* by Soerjono Soekanto (Bandung: Alumni, 1978); *Istilah dan peribahasa hukum bahasa Latin* by Andi Hamzah (Bandung: Alumni, 1985); *Kamus istilah hukum Fockema Andreae; Belanda-Indonesia* ([Bandung]: Binacipta, 1983), a translation by Saleh Adiwinata, A. Teloeki and H. Boerhanoeddin St. Batoeah of the famous Dutch concise jurisprudence dictionary by Fockema Andreae (1977 edition); *Kamus yurisprudensi dan beberapa pengertian tentang hukum (acara) perdata* by Andi Tahir Hamid (Surabaya: Bina Ilmu, 1984); *Kamus hukum* by Andi Hamzah (Jakarta: Ghalia Indonesia, 1986); *Rechtstermen; Istilah2 hukum bahasa Belanda* by Anak Agung Gede Djelantik (Denpasar: Kayumas, 1987); *Kamus tata hukum Indonesia* by Padmo Wahjono (Jakarta: Ind. Hill, 1987); *Kamus istilah hukum Belanda-Indonesia* by Sulaeman Binol (Jakarta: Dian Rakyat, 1990); *Kamus hukum* by Sudarsono (Jakarta: Rineka Cipta, 1992); *Bahasa hukum Belanda-Indonesia* by Saleh Adiwinata (Bandung: Alumni, 1992); *Kamus umum; Khusus bidang hukum dan politik* by Zainul Bahri (Bandung: Angkasa, 1996); *Kamus istilah menurut peraturan perundang-undangan Republik Indonesia 1945-1998 [...]* by the Tim Redaksi Tatanusa (Jakarta: Tatanusa, 1999, along with the 2000 and 2002 supplements); and *Kamus istilah aneka hukum* by C.S.T. Kansil (Jakarta: Pustaka Sinar Harapan, 2000).

BPHN dictionaries may provide probably is counteracted, if only partially, by these private publications.[87] Finally, these small-scale stabs at the standardization of legal terminology are no match for the deep-rooted student habit of adopting the terms used by their lecturers (Padmo Wahjono 1983:212; Sutarso 1996:34; see also Chapter IV).

With regard to carrying out translations of legislation, it is noted that to date only a single translation has been produced and published under the auspices of the BPHN, namely of the Wetboek van Strafrecht. But, even though this work was published by a government body and could, therefore, be considered to be 'official', from a legal point of view it has no status to set it apart from any other translation privately undertaken and published.[88] It follows that, since 1983, the market for such private productions seems to have declined very little. Reprints of Moeljatno's and Soesilo's translations were issued,[89] for instance, as was a new translation of Andi Hamzah as well as one in the Engelbrecht legislation reader of 1989.[90] In this instance, too, the BPHN has to compete with the ingrained habit on the part of (senior) lecturers to impose a particular translation on their students (see Chapter IV).

Further research should be undertaken into the effect to date on lawyers' linguistic ability of the incorporation of language classes into the study of law. It is clear that the language used by students in their dissertations, papers and the like continues to attract scathing criticism.[91] The 1996 BPHN

87 Naturally, factors such as the identity of the composer, the type of dictionary and the number of copies printed have an effect. The privately published issues are widely divergent in nature and size. Some are lists of headwords and their translations, others contain definitions or references to relevant legislation. Several publications deal extensively, or chiefly, with adat law terminology. There are reference dictionaries in Indonesian or in two or sometimes three languages. Apart from providing Indonesian keywords, the greater share of the books consist mostly of Dutch entries. The size of the publications ranges from tens of pages to many hundreds. The translation by Saleh Adiwinata et al. of *Fockema Andreae's Rechtsgeleerd handwoordenboek* (1977 edition) deserves a special mention. Where the legislative clauses referred to in the original book were found to have an exact counterpart in the Indonesian legislation (for example when articles were cited from the (old) Dutch Burgerlijk Wetboek or Wetboek van Koophandel), the Dutch clauses were replaced with the corresponding Indonesian ones.

88 See Churchill 1992:33. The BPHN translation was used as an aid in drafting the Indonesian criminal code, which remains to be implemented (interview with Mardjono Reksodiputro dated 2-5-1994). Reprints of the translation have been included in Soenarto Soerodibroto, *KUHP dan KUHAP dilengkapi yurisprudensi MA dan HR* (fourth edition, second printing, Jakarta: Raja Grafindo Persada, 1994), and in *KUHAP dan KUHP* (compiled by Redaksi Sinar Grafika, Jakarta: Sinar Grafika, [1998]).

89 The 20th (edited) edition of Moeljatno's translation was published in 1999 by Bumi Aksara in Jakarta. The tenth printing of Soesilo's was issued in 1989 by Politeia in Bogor.

90 See footnote 78. Andi Hamzah's translation, entitled *KUHP, Kitab Undang-Undang Hukum Pidana yang telah disesuaikan dengan undang-undang baru* and edited by Oemar Seno Adji et al., was published in 1986 by Ghalia Indonesia in Jakarta.

91 Sutarso 1996:16-7, 35; interviews with Koesnadi Hardjasoemantri (5-5-1994) and with

research partially blamed the sources on which students drew for their work, mainly legal literature written in or translated into very poor Indonesian, whether or not originating with their own lecturers. It was recommended that the subject of Indonesian be made compulsory for some time to come, either for the duration of the course or, in any event, for the last few years (Sutarso 1996:16-7, 35). The lectures in Dutch are of limited benefit to the majority of law students, who merely take the subject for one or two semesters.[92]

It has been argued above that the inadequate scope of the measures taken may have undermined their effect. The *nature* of the measures may also have played a role, however. For comparison's sake, it might be useful here to examine the activities of the Nederlandsche Juristen-Vereeniging (NJV, Dutch Jurists' Society) at the outset of the twentieth century. By order of this society, in 1912 a committee was appointed to report 'with respect to the shortcomings of Dutch legal language and the means to improve it' (Drucker 1916, I:I). From the 1840s in particular, critical articles had been written calling into question the 'purity', specifically, of the Dutch language of the law (G. van den Bergh 1979:4, 1994a:xlii-xliii). The efforts of the committee, comprising six lawyers and one linguist, resulted in the publication of two volumes in 1916.[93] The first part contained the actual report, made up of historical comments on Dutch legal language in general and on the language, style and form of laws, court decisions, other procedural documents and deeds in particular. The second part listed Latin and other non-Dutch expressions along with their possible substitutes in Dutch. Mahadi was familiar with this report, as is evident from his contribution to the 1974 conference, for example (Mahadi 1976:39; Mahadi and Sabaruddin Ahmad 1979:36).

Several similarities may be detected between the Dutch report and the literature on Indonesian legal language, both in terms of the desirable changes to be introduced into the language of the law of either nation and of the faults found with its usage. For example, according to the Dutch committee, the phraseology of bills should above all be fixed and uniform, the style of their formulation should be cogent, frugal and plain and the writing should be grammatically correct and, if possible, polished. Texts should be written in such a way that any party needing to take note of their contents, should be able to gain an easy understanding (Drucker 1916, I:34-5). Court decisions, too, should be formulated in good Dutch and be phrased in plain language of a sober, serious and dignified style (Drucker 1916, I:110-3). Anyone and

---

Mardjono Reksodiputro (2-3-1994).

92 Interviews with Frieda Husni Hasbullah (10-2-1993), Hafni Sjahruddin (29-2-1994) and with Lamya Moeljatno and Soerastri Isminingsih Djojodipoero (23-2-1993); Pompe 1996:342.

93 Drucker 1916. The lawyers were H.L. Drucker (chairman), S.J. Fockema Andreae, C. Bake, B.C.J. Loder, C.W. Star Busmann and J. van Kuyk. The linguist was Marcellus Emants.

everyone should be able to understand the decisions, even more so than the law (Drucker 1916, I:110-2, 146).

The criticism the report levelled at the prevalent language usage in legislation and judicial decisions generally relates to the many 'foreign elements', especially Latin ones, which over the centuries have spawned a 'barbarian' and 'deformed' legal language.[94] A large number of examples are quoted, mainly from legislation, to demonstrate the perceived lack of uniformity ('fixed, constant, stringently applied language') – synonymous terms, expressions and other formulae, as well as expressions bearing more than one meaning (homonyms) (Drucker 1916, I:37-51). Yet another issue is the use of very long and complicated sentences (Drucker 1916, I:78, 126-32). A solution proposed with a view to improving jurists' language is to establish a separate body, entrusted with the form of laws (Drucker 1916, I:105-8). Besides expressing the hope that legislator and judges be eminently conscious of the importance of good language, the committee specifically appeals to the authors of legal textbooks and handbooks. Although the language they choose to use cannot be prescribed, it is argued, they have a particular responsibility – after all, their books contribute substantially to the linguistic development of jurists-to-be, and continue to exert influence afterwards, too, when consulted in the practice of the law.[95]

The analogies between the literature on the Dutch language of the law of the early twentieth century and that on its Indonesian counterpart from the 1970s onwards can hardly be missed. The heterogeneous terminology, the deviation from the language norm, the frequent use of foreign words and the incomprehensibility of legal language to the public at large are the key issues of both. The similarities are less interesting than the differences, however. In the Netherlands, the literature devoted to legal language was for a long time confined to 'occasional, anecdotal comment' (G. van den Bergh 1979:5-6), whereas in Indonesia, legal language has grown into a theme that has preoccupied linguists and lawyers alike for decades now and that has, in a sense, managed to achieve the status of policy theme. Comparing the conclusions and recommendations of the Indonesian conference, at this juncture, with those put forward by the Dutch committee and leaving aside the infinitely

94 Drucker 1916, I:iv, vii, 16-7, 54-9, 117. The excessive use of 'posh' or 'ceremonious' words, and of redundant ones, is also pointed out (Drucker 1916, I:59-71).

95 'Not only are these [handbooks and textbooks] used continually in studies and court rooms as oracles of the practical application of the law, they also control the education and the moulding of the jurist. Upon first becoming acquainted with the law, the student will adopt his masters' manner of speaking, of which he will form a habit to remain with him for the rest of his days, changing which costs effort and exertion.' (Drucker 1916, I:v.) The following pages cite a great many Latin terms and expressions erroneously (in the opinion of the committee) used in the handbooks (Drucker 1916, I:vi-vii).

more far-reaching measures for the improvement of the language of the law recommended at Medan, two elements shine in their absence from the Dutch report. The first is the recommendation relating to translation, the second that of recording jurists' consensus. Both of these touch on the roots of the Indonesian legal system in the Dutch language and on the winding up of the legacy of that past.

When reviewing the report on the 1974 conference and the steps subsequently taken, one wonders whether in relation to the issue of legal language, this winding up of the colonial past was judged at its true value. The matter was certainly taken into consideration several times and in several ways. In his opening speech at the conference, Mochtar mentioned the transition of the primary language of the law from Dutch to Indonesian. Busthanul Arifin, in his presentation, drew attention to the dangers of the continuing impact of Dutch, among other languages, on the development of Indonesian law and argued for translation of legislation in the Dutch language into Indonesian. The question also came to the fore at the conference in an implied fashion – a large proportion of the concrete examples provided in the contributions concerned the trickiness of translating from Dutch.[96]

Later books and articles, too, occasionally relate the problems surrounding the language of the law to the colonial legacy.[97] As recently as 1997 Arifin ruled out the standardization of the legal language as long as jurists in Indonesia insist on *translating*, from Dutch, English or Arabic (for those areas subject to Islamic law).[98] However, the historical aspects of the issue of legal language have become swamped by measures aimed at the language of the law itself, that is, the standardization of the terminology, dictionaries, language lectures and the establishment of all manner of bodies to monitor and improve the quality of legal texts such as pieces of legislation. 'Developing an Indonesian legal language' has become the central theme of a host of meas-

96 This holds true for Anton Moeliono's example of the Wetboek van Strafrecht article, for the passages of deeds cited by the notary Siregar, for the texts provided by Mohamad Sjah and for Arifin's position that the Indonesian legal language consisted substantially of translations from the Dutch. It further applies to Rudjiati Muljadi's contribution, examining the organizations that produced Indonesian legal terms to substitute the Dutch ones.

97 The 1996 BPHN survey mentioned the continued application of Dutch-language legislation as one of the factors counteracting the homogeneity of language and terminology (Badudu 1996:3). Padmo Wahjono, Sutarso and Busthanul Arifin all argued in favour of producing official translations of Dutch-language legislation, specifically with a view to enhancing the uniformity of the language used in law (Padmo Wahjono 1983:207; Sutarso 1996:33-4; Busthanul Arifin 1997:69). Also see Churchill 1992:32-3, *Jentera* 2002, 1:3, Arief Sidharta 2002:82 and Marsillam Simanjuntak 2002:91.

98 Standardization could only be attained, according to Arifin (1997:68-70), once a solid foundation had been lain in the shape of a national system of law, to replace the patchwork quilt of yore with its randomly stitched on ad-hoc pieces of legislation.

ures; yet the unfinished business of the Dutch-language legacy, possibly the main cause of the predicament in which the Indonesian language of the law finds itself, has to vie for attention with a plethora of other topics.[99]

The low priority allotted to digesting the Dutch-language past was at least partly a deliberate choice. The 1970s designers of law policy, under the direction of Mochtar Kusumaatmadja, focussed specifically on the prospect of a new, national system of law. Issuing or promulgating official translations of colonial legislation, the BPHN translation of the Wetboek van Strafrecht, for instance, required retrospection. The influential Sunaryati Hartono, of Mochtar's 'school of thought', therefore unequivocally declared herself opposed to any such measures – only from a historical viewpoint could translation be of any value.[100] Leaving aside the political climate, a role may have been played by the practical consideration that selecting translations that might gain the approval of all the jurists prominent in the area of law in question would be a herculean if not impossible task. The umpteen translations of, for example, the Wetboek van Strafrecht and the overabundance of synonyms in the legal terminology provide just as many examples of this conundrum.

The limited attention paid to the past may also be ascribed in part to the theoretical and mostly implicitly acknowledged presumptions about language that emerge from the Indonesian literature on legal language. One metaphor in particular is rife in that literature, namely that of language as an *instrument*. To jurists, legal language is a means to be used in the formulation and transmission of legal concepts, a means subservient to the execution of that which is at stake, being the law.[101] Inherent in the metaphor, which is usually implied rather than stated,[102] is the notion that the language of law-

99 Of the 17 recommendations made by the two conference committees, only two are devoted to the Dutch language legacy (either specifically or implied) (*Simposium Bahasa dan Hukum* 1976:107-8).

100 Sunaryati Hartono 1979:33. Compare with Bongenaar (1992:23): '[B]y publishing official translations, the Government would have officially recognized the continued validity of a great amount of colonial legislation'. It would be much more pertinent, in Sunaryati's view, to translate *recent* Dutch legislation, court decisions and literature. Those texts could then serve the dual purpose of being both reference and source (though not exclusively so) for Indonesian law reformers. By contrast, the advocate and author Suardi Tasrif (1975:15) was extremely sceptical with regard to the much more ambitious plan of issuing new legislation, particularly because no official translations had been produced as yet of the old codes.

101 See Mahadi and Sabaruddin Ahmad 1979:35-6, Busthanul Arifin 1976:78, Ismail Saleh 1989:137 and Natabaya 2000:307, for example. Natabaya distinguishes between the preparation of the legal materials and their 'casting into language' ('penuangannya ke dalam bahasa').

102 Consider the doctrine approved at the close of the conference that legal language is 'Indonesian used in the field of the law'. Also see A. Moeliono's argument (1976:15) for developing hand in glove the jurisprudence and the accompanying legal language; Arifin's view that the language of the law had been neglected (even though the law had been practised) (Arifin 1976:77-8)

yers is separable from its usage context, the world of the law. In actual fact, the very expression of 'legal language' ('bahasa hukum') or 'language of the law' implies a condition of distinctness.[103] Seen from this perspective, 'developing the legal language' should be the mainstay of any policy aiming at solving problems related to the use of legal language.[104] The nature of those problems, along with their history, is thus shifted into second place. Language becomes acontextual – incidentally banishing the historical context, too.

In the legal sphere, the instrument metaphor goes a fair way back,[105] though it has long been disproved in linguistic circles and in other walks of life. More recent theories have in common the supposition that language and thinking are inseparable and that, although we may have a command of language in certain respects, language also has a command of *us* in significant other respects.[106] Diametrically opposed to the attempts to construct an 'effective instrument', an exact and unambiguous legal language, that is, it has been argued that multiplicity of meaning is quintessentially characteristic of natural languages (G. van den Bergh 1979:36; Mellinkoff 1990:393), placing particular emphasis on the inalienability of utterances from their concrete

---

and the concern for the 'efficacy' of the legal language, a measure typically applied to instruments (compare with *Simposium Bahasa dan Hukum* 1976:107 sub B.4 and Mahadi and Sabaruddin Ahmad 1979:35-6).

103 See Broekman 1979:81-2. The metaphor also fits in with the traditional distinction between 'language' ('bahasa') and 'language usage' ('penggunaan bahasa') (see BPHN 1976:106 sub A.1, 3, 107 sub A.4, B.3, 108, for example). Compare with Mahadi and Sabaruddin Ahmad (1979:1), who state as the first problem that 'the condition and the use of Indonesian are not yet stable'.

104 In the words of Mahadi and Sabaruddin Ahmad (1979:78), language, rather than being instinctively generated, is created, consciously *made* by man.

105 G.C.J.J. van den Bergh ascribes the traditional popularity of the instrumental or instrumentalistic concept of language amongst jurists in part to the potent impact mathematical-scientific logic has had on legal reasoning since the seventeenth century. The influential *Pandektenwissenschaft* ('pandects' science') or *Begriffsjurisprudenz* of the last century, a movement counting F.C. von Savigny (oft-cited in Indonesian legal literature) among its members, strove 'to apply far-reaching concept analysis to arrive at the definition of purely formal, analytical concepts, allowing the logical construction of the law, in a mathematical fashion' (G. van den Bergh 1994b:112). The law was primarily viewed as the collective of 'law situations' to be obtained, maintained, surrendered or forfeited by the individual (G. van den Bergh 1979:49). Rational argumentation and formal logic, interpretation and definition continue to play a pivotal role in legal reasoning, which is stated in terms of 'propositions' and 'concepts'. These are expressed in descriptive sentences and words or terms, respectively, which also refer to reality (namely states of affairs and objects or persons, respectively) (Loth 1984:70-1; compare with White 1990:29-32). In a context in which logic, an autonomous, 'self-generating' discourse (something *follows logically from* something else), is the guiding principle, language is relegated to an inferior position – just like the symbols used to give expression to mathematics, language, here, ought to be a non-normative and exact instrument that allows the rationally constructed arguments to be expressed with maximum lucidity (G. van den Bergh 1979:16, 38).

106 See G. van den Bergh (1979:39): 'There is no higher or deeper meaning than that which we are able to phrase'.

contexts and thus on the relevance of context to the meaning of those utterances. The notion of language as a tool at the disposal of the speaker/writer has increasingly given way to the perception of language as a form of behaviour, a repertory of manners.[107]

Such ideas have, of course, also been discussed in the Indonesian literature on the law.[108] Yet the instrumental approach remains the dominant perspective by far. The instrument metaphor, though rarely formulated explicitly, may in theory be called the leitmotiv coursing through the successive measures. Chapter II will explore a more modern view of the nature of language and law and of their interrelationship. From this new perspective, the history of the Indonesian legal community and its language usage will be examined in chapters III and IV. This history begins in the days of the Netherlands East Indies, with Dutch as the official language of the law and all that surrounded it; it continues with the banishment of Dutch during the Japanese occupation and finally follows the gradual, actual substitution of Dutch with the Indonesian language up until the starting point of this book, the 1974 Simposium Bahasa dan Hukum. Chapter V, then, will seek to answer the questions of why Indonesian lawyers have now been concerned with their language usage for more than a quarter of a century, of where the real shortcomings of that usage are to be found and of what their causes have been.

107 An interesting counterpart to these critical comments on the discourse on Indonesian legal language is to be found in the critique by the jurist Jacob Israël de Haan in respect of the notions about language amongst jurists in general and of the NJV committee's report in particular – see Chapter II. De Haan (1994:69-72, 108-28) rebuked the NJV committee for merely evaluating the superficial traits of legal language usage and overlooking the essence of the language; for merely inspecting the paintwork on the ship and omitting the mechanisms of propulsion.

108 In his contribution to the conference, Alisjahbana quoted O. Gierke to oppose the divorce of language and law – language does not simply cloak the law, it constitutes the actual *corpus* of the law (Takdir Alisjahbana 1976:32, borrowed from Leo Weisgerber, *Die Muttersprache im Aufbau unserer Kultur*, Düsseldorf: Schwann, 1957, pp. 178-9). Moreover, he scrutinizes terms such as (Dutch) 'rechts*praak*' (juris*diction*), (German) 'rechts*prechen*' (*pronouncing* judgement), (German) 'Rechts*pruch*' (legal *adage*) and (English) 'sentence' (Takdir Alisjahbana 1976:31). Also see Mohamad Sjah 1974:13, Padmo Wahjono 1983:201 and Arief Sidharta 2002:84.

## CHAPTER II

# The language of the law

### *A living impulse*

> Discourse lives, as it were, beyond itself, in a living impulse [...] toward the object; if we detach ourselves completely from this impulse all we have left is the naked corpse of the word, from which we can learn nothing at all about the social situation or the fate of a given word in life (Bakhtin 1996a:292).[1]

In Chapter I it has been argued that the principal metaphor for the phenomenon of language we encounter in the Indonesian literature on the language of the law, whether implied or explicit, is that of an instrument.[2] Language is a tool to aid the lawyer in the practice of his profession of jurisprudence. Seen from this perspective, which is also embedded in other, often commonly applied metaphors and expressions (like language 'usage'), three more or less separate entities may be distinguished – the jurist, the language and the law. The instrument metaphor has a bearing on the interpretation of the problems surrounding the Indonesian legal language and on the measures taken to deal with them.[3] Metaphors related to a complex manifestation such as language can actually have a certain elucidative effect, especially when offset by other metaphors. That which remains out of sight from one angle, may be highlighted from another. Though by applying a single metaphor virtually all of the time, one runs the risk of allowing the blind spots implied by that one metaphor to become ingrained.

1 Rather than speaking in terms of 'language', 'language usage' and small units such as 'sentences', Bakhtin refers to 'discourse' (*slovo*), the base unit of which is the 'utterance' (*vyskazivanie*) (Clark and Holquist 1984:10).

2 In linguistics a distinction is made between language as a type of human *act* (language usage), in which framework 'language utterances' are studied, and language as an *instrument* applied by people, in which framework 'language structures' are examined (Dik and Kooij 1979:20-1). The near exclusive attention paid in the field of linguistics, over many decades, to language constructions or, in other words, the instrumental approach, seems to have left its mark on the Indonesian literature on the language of the law.

3 See Chapter I. A second well-known metaphor is that of language as a code, used to convey messages or concepts. Terms such as 'coding' and 'decoding' are used in this connection.

The instrument metaphor obscures several important aspects of the nature of language in daily practice. For example, the notion of the instrument (or code) suggests a certain space between the language and its 'user' (the speaker or writer or lawyer, whatever the case may be). It creates the illusion that the speaker or writer, prior to embarking on the act of speaking or writing, has the opportunity to scrutinize the instrument and, if necessary, to fine-tune it to the task at hand. In day-to-day reality, however, speakers, writers and their audiences rarely are conscious of an object called 'language' placed before them awaiting some form of use. Instead of 'using language', they *speak, write, understand* or *answer*. In other words, they act more or less automatically (compare Bakhtin 1996a:259, Morson and Emerson 1990:145). The speaker or writer responds to something (questions, texts, thoughts) which, as cogently put by Mikhail Bakhtin in the above quote, goes accompanied, as it were, by the language in a 'living impulse'. Instead of applying the compound noun phrase 'language usage', a simple verb, the term 'languaging' as coined by Alton Becker, for example, would be much more apt (Becker 1992:118-9).

Taking an utterance to constitute a response to and within a concrete situation, the comprehension of that concrete situation, the context of the utterance, that is, becomes crucially important in penetrating the nature and form of the utterance itself. In other words, the context is not a variable to be added once language has been described in the abstract, but a factor to be examined in order to understand why it is that people speak (listen) and write (read) in a particular way, to understand the essence of language in daily practice. In the case of 'languaging', people continuously tune in, so to speak, to a perpetually changing context.[4] Restricting oneself by and large to the analysis of fragments of unrelated legal texts and their systematic abstractions (grammar and lexicon, to name but two), one overlooks the quintessential explanation of why it says what it says – not only in the texts analysed but in all future ones, too.[5]

[4] Becker 1992:118-9. Compare with Morson and Emerson 1990:40 and Peter Winch, who proposes that language has developed *between* people. He rejects the notion that there must have been a single person who *first* used language (Winch 1990:36-7, 43-4). Also see Romaine in the closing sentence of her introduction into sociolinguistics (deliberately entitled 'Language *in* society' rather than 'Language *and* society'), in which she exposes the fundamental barrier between traditional linguistics and sociolinguistics: '[T]here is little point in trying to formulate a satisfying social theory of language by attempting to graft a sociolinguistic methodology onto a mainstream linguistics which seems determined to remain basically asocial with its fundamental distinction between knowledge of language (i.e. competence) and its use (i.e. performance)' (Romaine 2000:247, compare with pp. ix-x).

[5] See Bakhtin (1996a:292): 'To study the word as such, ignoring the impulse that reaches beyond it, is just as senseless as to study psychological experience outside the context of that real life toward which it was directed and by which it is determined'. Traditional linguistics are concerned, as it were, with the (dead) 'traces' left behind by living organisms, the 'sclerotic deposits

The context (or contexts) in which utterances are made is (are) extremely complex, fluid and transitory.[6] Only part is located physically 'outside' of the speaker (writer) – of primary importance are the memories and attitudes of the speaker (writer) himself. The context supports the utterance in some respects but contradicts it in others. Though only some aspects of the context form part of the discursive (that which can be verbalized) consciousness[7] of the speaker (writer), it does determine the processes of conception and reception of the utterances, the verbal communication. One might say that both utterances and their interpretation stem from what Bakhtin defines as a continuous *dialogue* between the various options presented by the context.[8]

As pointed out above, the context that influences utterances is multifaceted. Leaving aside the facets attached to the preceding utterance of a partner in conversation, which may be responded to,[9] as well as other concrete events occurring in the environment of the speaker (writer), several internal-dia-

---

of an intentional process, signs left behind on the path of the real living project of an intention, of the particular way it imparts meaning to general linguistic norms' (Bakhtin 1996a:292). The image that springs to mind here is that of research into coral, that is, into colonies of floral polyps in their natural, submarine habitat. In this metaphor, traditional linguistics is only concerned with the (dead) chunks of coral washed onto the beach.

6 For the significance of 'context' in Bakhtin's work, see Hirschkop 1989:14-7. Hirschkop (1989:16-7) defines 'context' as a 'series of largely invisible (pressure) forces and purposes, originating in the social location of the *speech act* and frequently conflicting with or contradicting one another'.

7 Giddens 1997:xxiii, 4, 375. In addition to the discursive consciousness, Giddens (1997:4-5, 7) distinguishes the subconscious as well as a practical consciousness, which consists of the practical know-how that enables people who act 'to go on' with their daily lives but which cannot be verbalized instantly.

8 'Dialogue' and 'dialogic', together with derivations like 'dialogizing' and 'dialogized', are key terms in Bakhtin's oeuvre (although he applies these terms in various meanings; see Morson and Emerson 1990:130-1). 'Dialogue' in this connection denotes 'communication between simultaneous differences' (Clark and Holquist 1984:9), a more extensive concept than the usual 'colloquy'. Rather than assuming the mutual incompatibility of opposing forces, in Bakhtin's view those forces conduct a continuous dialogue. Identity – of a person, a language or whichever cultural entity – is not approached in terms of 'the same as' but in those of 'simultaneous to'. That identity is not A *or* B, but A *and* B, in constant interaction (Clark and Holquist 1984:9-10).

9 Becker (1988:122) exemplifies five of these in the following dialogue:
1.A: 'What's the matter?'
B: 'Well, what you say about the apple is right, but I don't like your tone of voice.'
2.A: 'I'm just saying what the teacher said.'
B: 'Well, I don't see how it follows from what you said before.'
3.A: 'Let me diagram it on the blackboard.'
Becker distinguishes five types of relationship (thus, five types of context) in this dialogue – interpersonal (B's comment about the *tone* of the speaker), referential (the reference to what the speaker says), intertextual (the speaker's repetition of what the teacher said), intratextual (the reference to the lack of coherence in what the speaker says) and intermedial relationships (the proposal to draw a diagram).

logic aspects of the utterances may be distinguished (Bakhtin 1996a:279-80; Morson and Emerson 1990:131-9). One of these concerns the theme of the utterance. No theme is untouched by language and so the speaker (writer), in his utterance on a given subject, consciously or subconsciously processes prior utterances on the same subject,[10] recollecting his own or other people's utterances on or attitudes towards the theme as well as any texts he has read. Particularly in utterances occurring in non-literary prose (academic texts, policy documents), the processing of prior texts (in the shape of 'the consensus', for example, or of 'that which has already been established') takes place at the conscious level.[11] The utterance on a given theme thus originates at least in part from the dialogue between the speaker and prior utterances on that same theme.[12]

A second internal-dialogic property of utterances is that each utterance anticipates a response. Contrary to the implications of the well-known sender-message-recipient model, the speaker (writer) does not view the listener (reader) as passive, but anticipates the latter's understanding and response (associated inalienably therewith).[13] The speaker's (writer's) point of depar-

10 'On the various routes toward the object, in all its directions, the word encounters an alien word and cannot help encountering it in a living, tension-filled interaction. Only the mythical Adam, who approached a virginal and as yet verbally unqualified world with the first word, could really have escaped from start to finish this dialogic inter-orientation with the alien word that occurs in the object. Concrete historical human discourse does not have this privilege: it can deviate from such inter-orientation only on a conditional basis and only to a certain degree.' (Bakhtin 1996a:279.) Also see Bakhtin 1999a:93-4. The term 'prior texts' has been taken from Becker (1992:117-8, 1988:124-5).

11 Bakhtin 1996a:279. Poetry evades the natural orientation of linguistic utterances towards other utterances – the poet acts, so to speak, as the first person to approach the theme: 'In genres that are poetic in the narrow sense, the natural dialogization of the word is not put to artistic use, the word is sufficient unto itself and does not presume alien utterances beyond its own boundaries. Poetic style is by convention suspended from any mutual interaction with alien discourse, any allusion to alien discourse. [...] The language of the poet is *his* language, he is utterly immersed in it, inseparable from it, he makes use of each form, each word, each expression according to its unmediated power to assign meaning (as it were, "without quotation marks"), that is, as a pure and direct expression of his own intention. No matter what "agonies of the word" the poet endured in the process of creation, in the finished work language is an obedient organ, fully adequate to the author's intention.' (Bakhtin 1996a:285-6.)

12 Bakhtin 1996a:281; Morson and Emerson 1990:136-9. Compare with Bakhtin 1999a:69: 'Any utterance is a link in a very complexly organized chain of other utterances'.

13 'Understanding comes to fruition only in the response. Understanding and response are dialectically merged and mutually condition each other; one is impossible without the other.' (Bakhtin 1996a:282.) The response may take several shapes – it may be an immediate, verbal reaction, but it may also be expressed through an action (in the execution of an order, for example) or temporarily remain unspoken (such as in the case of lyrical genres) – described by Bakhtin as 'active responsive understanding with delayed action'. It is inevitable, though, for that which has been heard and actively understood, sooner or later to elicit a response in the shape of an utterance or behaviour on the part of the listener (Bakhtin 1999a:69).

ture is that his utterance will be entered into the conceptual system of the listener (reader), who is the conversational partner. Anticipating the conceptual horizon, the conversational partner's world, contributes substantially to the form of the utterance – the choice of words, the syntax, the intonation. This interaction also takes place in situations other than direct verbal dialogues and correspondences, in which the recipient is identical to the person whose response is anticipated. In situations where the person addressed is far less distinct – a subordinate, a stranger, a group of specialists in a given subject, like-minded people – this process is more complex and has an increased number of facets. In this manner, listeners and readers contribute to the form of utterances even before they are able to hear or read these.[14]

To conclude, some comment on the status of *text* in this context is warranted. Whereas spoken utterances leave no trace, utterances in writing do – they last as texts. Utterances in script, too, are performed by authors within a context of concrete, living dialogue occurring at a certain time and place, and are read by people within the framework of the dialogues of their own time and place. Text will always be an utterance in that the reader, at the end of the day, is bound to detect a concrete writer, a human voice.[15] In a particular situation and a new 'chain of utterances', the unique, strictly individual aspect that was the rationale for the written utterance and that was only valid under the specific circumstances prevalent at the time of writing, may be revealed.[16]

## *Meaning in context*

> Most legal scholars view words as objects, of a sort, that exist in an external world and are separate from the human mind. We use these words to build sentences and books, like we use stones to build walls and houses. The words possess a meaning, just like the objects possess a shape. A table that is round to one person cannot be square to another any more than a word can have different meanings to different people, without someone being in error. It is thought that the correct meaning of

[14] Bakhtin 1996a:280, 282, 1999a:69, 95-9; Morson and Emerson 1990:128-9. The attitude of the listener nevertheless is of crucial importance to the speaker – should the listener be asleep or otherwise 'absent-minded', the speaker would cease his utterance. One point on which Bakhtin criticized Roman Jacobson's communication model (sender-message-recipient) was that the attitude of the recipient played no part in it whatsoever (Morson and Emerson 1990:128). Most apt in this respect is Valentin Voloshinov's representation of the utterance as a bridge, dependent on both sides (Morson and Emerson 1990:129).

[15] Morson and Emerson 1990:427. Morson and Emerson (1990:164) mention the tendency to 'depersonalize' and 'disembody' authoritative texts, to counteract any notion that such texts are (just) someone's personal opinion.

[16] Bakhtin 1999a:105-7, 122. Stated differently: whereas reader and author form part of an unfinalizable world 'in which the activity of writing and reading is shaped by presentness', the textual world is a *represented* one (Morson and Emerson 1990:427-8).

> a word exists, like the truth exists. And that we should be capable of finding that correct meaning, if only we were more skilled. (Israël de Haan 1994:67 (originally: *Weekblad van het Recht* 10049, 1917).)

In the literature on and the government measures relevant to the Indonesian legal language, the 'meaning' aspect of language is the leitmotiv. The lack of clarity of legal texts and terminology is the main theme, both in the descriptions of the problems and in the solutions proposed. It is argued that the language of jurists must 'reflect the essence of the thinking' as adequately as possible, that too many synonyms (terms bearing the same meaning) and homonyms (terms bearing several meanings) are commonly applied and that legal texts are frequently open to more than one interpretation and are unintelligible to the layman.

The government has developed various initiatives to use the process of definition to arrive at a fixed meaning of legal terms, and to provide language studies for law students to improve their command of the language and achieve a clearer formulation (compare Chapter I). The core of these philosophies and activities is the attempt to do away with ambiguity. This attempt has its source in the implicit presumption that forms the foundation of all human communication, being that people are capable of understanding one another to the full.

Jurists' focus on the avoidance of ambiguity and on 'precise formulation' goes back a long way.[17] It agrees with the image of language as an instrument – the lawyer uses the language to 'put into words' and convey to another person a message or concept. Thus, like all tools and instruments, language, too, has to be precise and reflect a single meaning. The notion of verbal com-

[17] G. van den Bergh 1979:33-4, 38; compare Peters 1993:209, 211, 214. Also see Mellinkoff (1990:290; compare Chapter I): 'The standard answer to any criticism of the language of the law is that this language is *precise*. If the criticism is especially violent, the answer is modified only to the extent of saying that the language of the law is *more precise* than the ordinary speech, but customarily even that modest qualification is omitted. Say it is *cant, jargon, prolix, obsolete, stilted, wormlike, polysyllabic, repetitious, cacophonic, humorless*. Charge it with *verbosity* and *big words* and with being *needlessly involved*. [...] Call it what you will. *Precise* it is said to be, and that virtue is deemed sufficient, that the clincher in any argument.' J.M. van Dunné (1974) points out that the emphasis on unambiguous language usage in the Netherlands is primarily encountered in the so-called school of the 'fixed law finding' (*vaste rechtsvinding*). The supporters of this concept put legal certainty above fairness and justice and usually suppose that 'the law is *clear* and has but *a single correct application* and that it is precisely the judge's task to ensure that the law is indeed applied correctly' (Van Dunné 1974:9). Only when an article of a law is not altogether clear, interpretation (grammatical, systematic and/or historic) is called for, provided the scope of the law is adhered to. Equally, the Dutch legal principle of 'billijkheid' (fairness), that serves to harmonize, when necessary, the abstract rule of law with its concrete application, should be 'incorporated' into the very formulation of that rule as cogently as possible (Van Dunné 1974:11-2).

munication as a 'conveyance' is even older than the instrument metaphor and may be encountered in the widespread use of derivatives of the Latin verb *transferre* ('transfer, transpose', perfect participle *translatum*) in terms that relate to the act of translating. The image of translating, here, is that of transferring something (content, meaning, concept) from one language to another. The unspoken assumption expressed in these metaphors and in the literature and the measures taken with respect to the Indonesian legal language, is that the meaning of an utterance, in the sense of the aspect with which the speaker (writer) and listener (reader) are concerned, the 'message', 'essence of thinking', or that which unfolds within the human mind, exists separately to and distinguishable from the words of the concrete linguistic utterance.

As stated so floridly by Jacob Israël de Haan in the above quote, 'meaning' is thus seen as fixed, as the same for everyone, irrespective of the concrete context of the utterance.[18] In the Indonesian literature on legal language, too, sentences, phrases and words are consistently lifted out of their context of legal texts, to be cited as examples. Their meaning is to be found here and here alone and cannot, therefore, be anywhere else.[19] Should texts and words be found to possess several meanings, those texts must be modified and

18 See White 1990:233-4, Steiner 1975:276-8 and Hesselink 1992:74-5. This notion of meaning concords with the mathematics-physics tradition in that it focusses on the 'factual', on that which 'is' in absolute terms and is expressed in a neutral code, in the sense of one that is free from values. The concept is encountered in the doctrine of rational argumentation (having had enormous impact on jurisprudence, amongst other fields) and in various academic traditions, the core of which is a clear distinction between language and extralinguistic reality, along with a quest for 'facts'. H.M.J. Maier for one, in his PhD thesis (1985), deals extensively with the positivistic search for 'the truth behind the text' in the traditional philology on Malay literature. In the field of linguistics, the distinction between 'meaning' and 'interpretation' is drawn on principle. A sentence may be used and interpreted in several ways, but its meaning remains relatively constant in all cases. Context is altogether left out of the latter equation (Dik and Kooij 1979:239 and Uhlenbeck 1980:61). Moreover, in linguistics a distinction is sometimes made between *word* and *term* – words have meaning, terms denote concepts. Words are transformed into terms by means of definitions, thus 'robbing meaning of its agility', according to Uhlenbeck (1980:35, 33). Compare Voloshinov 1973:79-80.

19 W.J. Witteveen relates the gradual shift of *text* towards a central position within the law (replacing individual oratorical skill), over the centuries, to the tendency to come to view those texts as *inherently* authoritative. After all, the less visible the people behind and around a text, the easier it is to accept its normative nature. The idea that the meaning of a text is to be found primarily in the text *itself* corresponds to this train of thought. In the course of history, interpretation was often considered to be redundant, even objectionable – a view based on the assumption of it being possible to read texts *without* interpreting them. Issuing and distributing various explanations of authoritative texts and acknowledging that texts are open to interpretation was (and is) taken to undermine their autonomy and authority (Witteveen 1988a:151-2, 156-7, 173-4; compare Scholten 1931:2-3). Witteveen (1988a:174-5) draws attention to various rhetorical devices called into play to defend a particular interpretation, designating these the 'rhetoric of the correct response' such as 'the return to the text' – an expression that is frequently effective yet equally misleading. In this connection, compare Nasr Hamid Aboe Zaid (1996:73-4) about the role of the Koran within Islam.

words chosen that culminate in a text that is indeed open to a single explanation. Higher quality texts are obtained, for example, by improving lawyers' linguistic command; the more highly trained the builders, the greater the quality of the walls and houses they construct. With this in mind, definitions are used to attempt to pin down the meaning of words, thereby reshaping meaning into the fixed, ring-fenced form of a formulaic alternative (see, for example, Loth 1984:82).

It is undoubtedly true that improving jurists' command of the Indonesian language and adhering to the rules of grammar more consistently, along with a solid grounding in law, can enhance the uniformity and sometimes the quality, too, of legal texts. By the same token, standardization lists and dictionaries could heighten the degree of uniformity of the legal terminology, provided they are widely distributed and actually put to use. Nevertheless, the improvement can only be relative – one cannot hope for unambiguous texts, in the absolute sense, not even if all law students were to be extensively schooled in Indonesian, all lawyers were to compose in carefully formulated and grammatically perfect Indonesian and the standardization lists were far more comprehensive than those produced to date and used by all jurists.

Just as the instrument metaphor conceals important aspects of the phenomenon of verbal communication, so the notion of 'conveying a message by means of language' impedes a clear idea of the meaning of utterances in practice and of how that meaning is experienced by concrete speakers (writers) and listeners (readers). This notion results from a retrospective analysis of language usage and has become, as stated previously, one of many, deeply engrained metaphors used in connection with language. In daily life, however, the aspect of the 'meaning' of an utterance is not perceived as separate from the utterance itself and no 'message' to be 'put into words' presents itself to the speaker (writer). The meaning of an utterance is to be found in that which has brought the speaker (writer) in his concrete situation to make the utterance and forms part of the same practised, flowing movement with which the utterance was carried out. The speaker (writer) has at his disposal a well-nigh inexhaustible store of texts and fragments of texts he once read and phrases, expressions and words from his past, to be conjured up when speaking (writing) in new situations that demand more or less the same loading, intent, values or, in short, the same *meaning*. Contrary to what is implied by the message metaphor, the meaning of utterances cannot be separated from the concrete contexts in which they take place.

It is in those very contexts and in the specific speakers (writers) and listeners (readers) that constitute part of them that utterances have their source, their raison d'être. The actual meaning of an utterance cannot, therefore, be cast into a rephrasing, a proposition in dictionary-style meanings, but is to be found in the living impulse of which the utterance forms part. Trying to fathom the actual meaning of someone's words requires elaboration in terms of the unique context and the dialogues from which they have emanated.[20] At issue, here, is a unique complex of actual factors which has led the speaker (writer) to his impulse and has made him say what he says.[21] The meaning of an utterance thus is something extremely complicated that implies a whole range of answers or attunements.[22]

Thus, it is a fantasy to uphold an ideal of texts with a single meaning and

20 The exception is consulting a dictionary in order to 'discover' the meaning of a word or expression. Yet even in this instance, the dictionary meanings provided are mere abstractions and remain to be matched or fitted in with the text. The actual meaning of an utterance (*smysl*) therefore consists of answers to questions – only that which answers a question has meaning for the speaker (writer) or listener (reader). In this respect, Becker describes an interaction between the speaker and several environments or contexts (Becker 1988; compare with footnote 9). In doing so, he elaborates on John Dewey's thesis that 'meaning is to be observed in the relations of an organism with its particular environment' (Becker 1988:120-1). Morson (1986:6) defines meaning as a socially constituted 'field of answerability' (a 'field of all-that-can-be-answered'). The utterance must at all times be viewed in the light of the concrete context in which it arose: '[...] Bakhtin never chooses as examples of utterances those old linguistic chestnuts, "The cat is on the mat" or "The carpenter hit the nail with the hammer". Instead, he chooses utterances like "Well" or "Ah!" pronounced with a particular intonation that presumes, and partially creates, a context for the interaction of the speaker and the listener. Speech is *inter*locution. Understanding is active, is responsive, is a process. That process of understanding includes the listener's identification of the speaker's apparent and concealed motives and of the responses that the speaker invites and hopes to forestall. The interaction among speaker, listener, and context constitutes a "field of answerability", which *is* the meaning of the utterance.' Also see Bakhtin (1999a:83): 'When this individual sentence ["The sun has risen"] is analysed, it is usually perceived as a completed utterance in some extremely simplified situation: the sun really has risen and the speaker states: "The sun has risen". The speaker sees that the grass is green and announces: "The grass is green". Such senseless "communications" are often directly regarded as classic examples of the sentence. But in reality any communication like that, addressed to someone or evoking something, has a particular purpose, that is, it is a real link in the chain of speech communion in a particular sphere of human activity or everyday life.'

21 See Morson and Emerson 1990:126-7 and Bakhtin 1999b:105. Also see Bakhtin (1996a:340-1): 'In order to assess and divine the real meaning of others' words in everyday life, the following are surely of decisive significance: *who* precisely is speaking, and under *what* concrete circumstances? When we attempt to understand and make assessments in everyday life, we do not separate discourse from the personality speaking it (as we can in the ideological realm), because the personality is so materially present to us. And the entire situation is important: who is present during it, with what expression or mimicry is it uttered, with what shades of intonation?' James Boyd White (1990:34, 235 footnote 3) points out that well-known metaphors such as 'range of meaning' and 'semantic field' are deceptive in that they create the impression that meaning is two-dimensional, that it is possible for the meaning of an utterance to 'overlap' with the meaning of other utterances, that it can be demarcated and contained or, in other words, that it is *static*. These terms detract from the uniqueness of the meaning of an utterance, from its multidimensional nature, in just the same way as terms such as 'core meaning' and 'peripheral meaning' do.

22 Awareness of the multidimensional nature of communication usually only evolves when a hitch in the communication occurs (Becker 1988:121; also see footnote 9).

of complete understanding between people – the meaning of an utterance or text is context-linked and dependent upon the speakers (writers) and listeners (readers) involved and on the wider context.[23] And though the meanings of individual words may be abstracted, classified and housed in convenient dictionaries, such actions will never amount to anything more than abstracting actual reality. Moreover, in daily communication, dictionaries are only used in specific circumstances – when learning a new language, for example, or when having a vague notion of the meaning of a word but wanting to ascertain its applicability in a particular context. As a rule, the ingredients for new utterances stem from the lingual memory of the speaker (writer), arising from utterances that took place in concrete contexts in his past. Because of this, the meanings allocated to words and phrases in the daily practice of speakers (writers) and listeners (readers) are infinitely more varied, subtle and personal than dictionary meanings.

One could say that the meaning of an utterance derives a certain depth, or stratification, from the lingual memory of speakers (writers) and listeners (readers), which allows original utterances to be distinguished from expressions, clichés and proverbs. As no two people share exactly the same prior texts or the same linguistic or life experience, the complex of meanings attached to an utterance by an individual is unique.[24] Thus, people never attain full mutual understanding. In so far as they take part in the same communication streams

23 In terms of pure logic, too, text inevitably possesses more than one meaning. After all, language has a finite number of symbols, while required to serve an infinite number of settings (G. van den Bergh 1979:36 and Steiner 1975:375, 407).

24 White 1990:35, 43; compare Emerson 1986:24. Dwayne Booth (1986:153), applying Bakhtin's theories, somewhat refined 'his' list of previous texts, providing a fine illustration: '[E]ach of us has had different parents, read different books, met different people, conversed in different bars or dining rooms or truck stops. But what I [...] can utter will nevertheless always be some sort of complex amalgam of voices derived not only from my patria, [...] but more particularly, within any one society, from my economic class; my profession (we at the conference shared certain dialects, not to say jargons); my particular social circles (gourmet cooking clubs, chamber music societies, bowling leagues); my generation (*I* happen to know to be "cooking with gas" or to "consider joining the CCC until I find a job," yet most younger people today do not); my epoch (no one in the nineteenth century organized a conference anything like "The Politics of Interpretation", and if anybody from that time attended ours, much of what we said would have been unintelligible – not just because of lexical difficulties but because our language places quite different values on the very words we inherit from that time); my political party; the special institutions I have belonged to (my college, my trade school, my church [...] my neighborhood ethnic group); my family, with its private jokes and ethnic echoes; even my particular political "day" (the way I talked during Watergate is different from how I talk during Reagan's Revolution).' On the same subject, Steiner deploys the metaphor of a deeply-rooted plant or an iceberg, concealing underneath its surface 'a wealth of subconscious, deliberately concealed or declared associations' (Steiner 1975:172-3, compare 46, 292). Along with the increase in an individual's 'concentric spheres of association' and their gradual encompassing of community, province and country, he will begin to speak more 'at the surface' of himself (Steiner 1975:171-2). Compare with White 1990:254 and Israël de Haan 1994:67.

for some length of time, and have the same prior texts in common, the lion's share of new utterances will be self-evident, will not have to be stated explicitly. But someone learning a new language will not have recourse to this lingual, textual memory and therefore will be unable to make the distinction. In the case of the language student only, meaning – to begin with – is no more than what it says in the dictionary.[25]

The above also implies that language, to its speakers (writers) and listeners (readers), is not a valueless or neutral code. On the contrary, when they speak (write) or listen (read), they are involved in the utterance with their entire personas, their whole consciousness, including their ideas and values. One could say that those ideas and values are expressed in the *tone* of the utterance, that it is here that the author's stance is expressed in relation to the other utterances and circumstances leading him to make his.[26]

25 Becker 1992:117-8; compare Becker 1988:134-5. Becker (1992:119-20) relates passing on to his Malayan students the anecdote of Gregory Bateson about a computer asked to compute whether it could ever think like a human. Following some calculations, the computer printed its conclusion: 'That reminds me of a story'. The story prompted no response whatsoever among the Malayan students, the clue only being funny to initiates of that English sentence, to those having heard that sentence many times over. Lacking this imprint of the English language, the sentence is but one-dimensional and has no comedy value. Becker (1992:118) recounts his first stay in Malaysia: 'In Malay I had no memory to speak from. What prior texts Malay evoked for me were all English, except for a very few literary texts: the *Hikayat Hang Tuah*, the *Sejarah Melayu*, a few Malay poems by a friend, and a few Malay proverbs I had memorized once from a book. Essentially Malay was and remains one-dimensional to me.' See Steiner (1975:276-8) regarding the theoretical untenability of the distinction between 'translating word for word' and 'transferring meaning' (translating content). Here, too, the assumption contained in the first option is that a certain meaning, independent of context, is attached to the individual words. Translating, however, involves rendering explicit that which is implicit to the native speaker of the source-text language.

26 Bakhtin 1999c:164; compare Clark and Holquist (1984:10): 'Intonation is the sound that value makes'. Even in the absence of an author (for example, when a piece of writing has been produced by subsequent generations), the listener or reader will imagine one, will ascribe a voice to the utterance (Morson and Emerson 1990:133). The glossary in Bakhtin 1996 defines 'voice' as follows: 'This is the speaking personality, the speaking consciousness. A voice always has a will or desire behind it, its own timbre and overtones.' (Bakhtin 1996:434.) Also see Clark and Holquist (1984:10): 'The way values get shaped into expression, bringing differences into a tensile complex rather than into a static unity, is what Bakhtin understands as the activity of authoring. All of us who make utterances so understood, whether spoken or written, are thus authors. We operate out of a point of view and shape values into forms. How we do so is the means by which we articulate who we are amid the heteroglossia of possibilities open to us at any given moment. Bakhtin treats values not as an abstract axiology but as the practical work of building. By shaping answers in the constant activity of our dialogue with the world, we enact the architectonics of our own responsibility.' For an elaboration of the concept of 'value' in Bakhtin's work, see Hirschkop 1989:4.

## *Speech genres*

In his effort to expose certain misconceptions about language, Israël de Haan referred to the often applied image of 'building'. Like stones are used to build walls and houses, words and sentences are employed to construct texts (see p. 39-40). This image fits in neatly with the theme of traditional linguistics, being language structures, and with the systematic processes by which these structures are analysed in this discipline – texts are made up of sentences, that consist of words, that in turn consist of phonemes. The focus is both on the individual categories of units (phonemes, words, sentences, texts) and on the manner in which they jointly produce a greater entity (morphology, syntax). In the Indonesian literature on legal language and its ensuing initiatives, too, this systematic approach is the core feature – the focus is on building materials (words, sentences) and construction methods (grammar).

In this case, too, the reality is an entirely different kettle of fish than is proposed from an analytic-academic perspective. People writing a shopping list, a novel or a law are not conscious of the fact that they are constructing a text on the basis of words and sentences and that they are complying with the rules of grammar – they are writing a shopping list, a novel or a law. They do so along the lines of prior texts of the same category, guided by their mental picture of such texts or by samples in front of them on the table.[27] The writer (speaker) does not randomly select words and sentences he knows, but lets his utterance be guided by constants, in prior utterances, of a higher order than those words and sentences. He draws on that which Bakhtin calls 'genre' (*zhanr*), described in his work as a 'relatively stable [type] of [...] utterances' in a certain sphere of communication, a 'typical [form] of construction of the whole' and an 'horizon of expectations brought to bear on a certain class of text types'.[28]

27 See Bakhtin 1999a:87. The counterargument that systematically ordered texts such as grammar books and dictionaries do represent primary sources when acquiring, and producing text in, a foreign language, does not detract from this thesis. Anyone who has learnt a foreign language by means of such sources will, sooner or later, be told by a native speaker that 'that's not what we say (how we say it)'. The same applies to having a translation into a foreign language proofread by a native speaker – sentences that comply with the rules of grammar and with the dictionary will be found to be inconsistent with the conventions applicable to utterances in those contexts.

28 Bakhtin 1999a:60, 78, 1996:428, respectively. Compare with Becker (1988:125): 'A conversation today will draw upon prior conversations. A cowboy movie is about prior cowboy movies much more than it is about whatever may have happened in the American West in the second half of the 19th century. There are genres, everyday ones as well as literary ones – language games with history. Some of these "games" are quite intimate, like the repeated exchanges of a husband and wife, and some very public, like polite greetings or play-by-play reports of baseball games.' 'Genre', in this context, is a much more comprehensive concept than a literary genre. It is for this reason that English translations of Bakhtin's work sometimes use the term 'speech genre';

Speech genres come into existence through a grinding into the discourse of the function allocated to that discourse (business, technical, informal and the like) and of the specific circumstances under which it takes place. By this process, certain lexicological, semantic and syntactic aspects become intertwined with particular points of view, forms of thinking, nuances and accents.[29] Genres may be more prone to change than the forms and structures usually distinguished (lexicon, rules of grammar), but they are just as important to communication, if not more so. The genre to which an utterance belongs serves the listener (reader) as an initial guideline in interpreting the utterance, thus playing a pivotal role in the attainment of mutual understanding: 'After all, we respond to utterances, not to phonemes; fairy tales and novels, not syntactical or grammatical elements, are what affect us' (Morson and Emerson 1990:272). A certain type of context requires a certain type of utterance, with any sudden deviation from the expected being more likely to disrupt the communication than the deployment of a term or sentence structure that is uncommon within the context.[30] The genre the speaker (writer) has in

---

literary genres are but a category of the speech genre. Voloshinov also distinguishes a superior category of 'life genres' (*zhiznennye zhanry*), which is sometimes translated as 'behavioral genres' (Morson and Emerson 1990:291).

29 Bakhtin 1996a:288 9. Style, too, is an aspect of genre: 'In essence, language, or functional, styles are nothing other than generic styles for certain spheres of human activity and communication. Each sphere has and applies its own genres that correspond to its own specific conditions. There are also particular styles that correspond to these genres. A particular function (scientific, technical, commentarial, business, everyday) and the particular conditions of speech communication specific for each sphere give rise to particular genres, that is, certain relatively stable thematic, compositional, and stylistic types of utterances. Style is inseparably linked to particular thematic unities and – what is especially important – to particular compositional unities: to particular types of construction of the whole, types of its completion, and types of relations between the speaker and other participants in speech communication (listeners or readers, partners, the other's speech, and so forth). Style enters as one element into the generic unity of the utterance.' (Bakhtin 1999a:64.)

30 Should an adult, in conversation with another adult, for no obvious reason suddenly switch to a genre appropriate to conversing with children, the communication will be disrupted much more severely than the use of an incorrect sentence structure could bring about. This scenario was taken to an extreme in a famous Monty Python sketch in which a woman and her friend treat the former's adult son like a toddler. When the friend explodes, the son, in a business-like manner, dismisses the event as an everyday, trivial occurrence: (*Two ladies are sitting by the fire looking at a photo album.*) Mrs Nigger-Baiter: 'Oh, yes, he's such a clever little boy, just like his father.' Mrs Shazam: 'D'you think so, Mrs Nigger-Baiter?' Mrs Nigger-Baiter: 'Oh yes, spitting image.' (*The door opens. The son comes in.*) Son: 'Good afternoon, mother. Good afternoon, Mrs Nigger-Baiter.' Mrs Nigger-Baiter: 'Ooh, he's walking already!' Mrs Shazam: 'Yes, he's such a clever little boy, aren't you? Coochy coochy coo ...' Mrs Nigger-Baiter: 'Hello, coochy coo ...' Mrs Shazam: 'Hello, hello...' (*they chuck him under the chin*). Mrs Nigger-Baiter: 'Oochy coochy.' (*the son smiles a little tight smile*) 'Look at him laughing... ooh, he's a chirpy little fellow. Isn't he a chirpy little fellow ... eh? eh? Does he talk Does he talk, eh?' Son: 'Of course I talk, I'm Minister for Overseas Development.' Mrs Nigger-Baiter: 'Ooh, he's a clever little boy – he's a clever little boy. (*gets out a*

mind when he makes his utterance, thus guides him through the selection process inherent in the utterance, in the sense of his choice of the theme (the range of topics that may be discussed, that is), the words, sentence structures, style, intonation, attitude towards the partner in conversation or the reader (the audience), the manner of processing the prior utterances that engage the new one and so forth (Bakhtin 1999a:78, 80-1, 86). Some genres leave plenty of room for adaptation towards either the formal or the informal, according to the contingencies of the situation, whereas others (official genres, those with a high social status) are extremely limiting and stable.[31] In the *absence* of genres on which to base one's choices and attunements, these would perpetually have to be made afresh, making daily communication near impossible (Bakhtin 1999a:79; Morson and Emerson 1990:291).

*All* utterances belong to particular genres. It follows that their variety and heterogeneity are infinite – widely diverging literary genres, those active in daily life, such as greetings and words of leave (at times consisting of a single word) or inquiring after someone's health and the like, editorials and articles in newspapers (varying from one paper to the next), concise army orders, dialogues in all shapes and sizes between adults of different ages and children of different ages, legislation (both higher and lower), all manner of academic explanation et cetera et cetera.[32] Rather than describe the historical development of genres in terms of unfolding a beautifully conceived design, it would

---

*rattle*) Do you like your rattle? Do you like your rattle? Look at his little eyes following it ... look at his iggy piggy piggy little eyeballs eh ... oo ... he's got a tubby tumotum. Oh, he's got a tubby tum-tum.' Son: (*whilst Mrs Nigger-Baiter is talking*) 'Mother, could I have a quick cup of tea please. I have an important statement on Rhodesia to make in the Commons at six.' (*Sound of an explosion out of vision. Cut to reveal Mrs Nigger-Baiter's chair charred and smoking. Mrs Nigger-Baiter is no longer there. The upholstery is smouldering gently.*) Mrs Shazam: 'Oh, Mrs Nigger-Baiter's exploded.' Son: 'Good thing, too.' Mrs Shazam: 'She was my best friend.' Son: 'Oh, mother, don't be so sentimental. Things explode every day.' Mrs Shazam: 'Yes, I suppose so. Anyway, I didn't really like her that much.' (http://orangecow.org/pythonet/sketches/niggerbt.htm.)

31 By means of the mechanism Bakhtin terms 'reaccentuating' (*pereakcentuacija*), it is possible for genres to come into play in spheres of application other than the customary ones. A formal greeting, for instance, may be reaccentuated in an ironic, parodic way to become applicable to an informal setting (Bakhtin 1999a:79-80). Compare with Morson and Emerson 1990:293.

32 Bakhtin 1999a:60-1, 81-2. Bakhtin differentiates between primary (simple) and secundary (complex) genres. The primary ones encompass the numerous genres having arisen and arising from everyday spontaneous communication, from within the host of 'chains of utterances' that are repeated to a greater or lesser extent in recurrent situations in daily life. These genres are combined (absorbed or transformed, whichever the case may be) in various ways into secundary ones, such as those pertaining to art and science. For instance, a novel may include many a dialogue of the everyday kind; a deed may contain the statements of the parties appearing before the notary. Once a primary genre has been absorbed into a secundary one, the immediate relationship with the concrete practice is cut – henceforth taking place via the total of the secundary genre, that has its own form of relationship with reality (Bakhtin 1999a:62-3, Morson and Emerson 1990:294).

be more apt to compare it to a patchwork blanket that bears the marks of its own history. Precisely because genres never pre-eminently suit the use to which they are put, they are fairly easily adapted for future use.[33]

Equally, the fixed types of utterances are not valueless, any more than the utterances themselves are neutral or valueless – each genre implies certain values, as well as a certain perspective on (part of) the world (see Morson and Emerson 1990:291-2). 'Seeing/conceptualizing' and 'representing' are inextricably bound together in a single process – inherent in any genre is a certain horizon of what is seen and what is not. Viewed from this angle, genre may be taken to be a 'form-shaping ideology', a 'specific kind of creative activity embodying a specific sense of experience' (Morson and Emerson 1990:282-3).

A person's knowledge or command of language is described more accurately by the genres of which he disposes than by the rules of grammar and the vocabulary he knows. In the process of acquiring the native tongue, grammar and dictation only begin to figure once a child has started school. In the preceding years, in the phase in which the child learns to speak its language fluently, it does so on the basis of the dialogues in which it has incidentally participated and continues to participate, randomly taking part in the form of the genres to which those dialogues belong.[34] As the degree of differentiation in and complexity of the child's world increases, so does its number of genres.[35]

There is an important difference here between acquiring the mother tongue and learning a foreign language. The mother tongue, on the one hand, is not passed on to the child as a neatly packaged, ready-made system but rather as a string of concrete utterances and genres in a long chain of

33 One of the terms used in the literature is 'accretion', meaning something like 'growing together', 'attaching', 'appending' (Morson and Emerson 1990:292-3).

34 Morson and Emerson 1990:291. The role of dialogue in acquiring the native language is explicated in Dore 1995, amongst others. In *Seeing voices* (1991) Oliver Sacks elaborates on the developmental problems experienced by children who were born deaf. As a result of *missing out* on these dialogues, their *inner speech*, necessary for the generation of complex, abstract thought processes, fails to develop properly. This problem may largely be pre-empted by communicating with the child, from its earliest days, in sign language (Sacks 1991:66-75).

35 In some of the speech genres of young children, the mimicry or echo of those of adults may be detected, whereas they are absent in others. In the latter case, the repertoire of a Dutch girl aged four and a half may comprise the following genres: reporting on previous activities ('and then we played with plasticine and then I made a snake and then we played outside and then ...' et cetera); practising roles to be played ('I am Little Red Riding Hood and you are the Big Bad Wolf and I am going ...' et cetera); engaging in role play with others; playing alone while narrating; joining in with songs; reciting poems or songs learnt at school or elsewhere for adults (somewhat hurriedly, at times striking a shy-giggly tone); nagging for things only sparingly granted, such as sweets ('can I have a treat?').

random dialogues from the communication stream in which the child finds itself. A foreign language one decides to learn, on the other hand, *is* perceived as a 'package' by one's consciousness (fully-prepared thanks to the mother tongue) and, as a rule, is handed down in that shape – as a collection of words and rules.[36] Notwithstanding this perception, leaving the initial phase of learning words and grammar behind, the command of a foreign language, too, is best described in terms of having mastered a certain repertoire of genres. All said and done, a person's verbal communication skills cannot be measured by his knowledge of vocabulary and grammar but by his ability to manage in different situations and social circles or, in other words, by his command of a range of genres.[37]

In view of the above, genre ought to be an important theme in the investigation into the legal language of Indonesia. By examining the language usage wielded in teaching and practising law in terms of the genres that Indonesian law students and jurists have acquired over the course of time, a more realistic picture will be gained of the historical development of this language usage than can ever be the case when basing such an examination on the fallacy that Indonesian legal texts are perennially 'built up' from a zero starting point. Only when genre (and utterances rather than 'language structures') is allowed to set the scene can the historical nature of language become the focal point and the link between daily life and language be left intact.[38]

36 Voloshinov 1973:81. Valentin Voloshinov was one of Bakhtin's inner circle. Voloshinov 1973 is generally thought to be Bakhtin's.

37 'Many people who have an excellent command of a language often feel quite helpless in certain spheres of communication precisely because they do not have a practical command of the generic forms used in given spheres. Frequently a person who has an excellent command of speech in some areas of cultural communication, who is able to read a scholarly paper or engage in a scholarly discussion, who speaks very well on social questions, is silent or very awkward in social conversation. Here it is not a matter of an impoverished vocabulary or style, taken abstractly; this is entirely a matter of the inability to command a repertoire of genres of social conversation, the lack of a sufficient supply of those ideas about the whole of the utterance that help to cast one's speech quickly and naturally in certain compositional and stylistic forms, the inability to grasp a word promptly, to begin and end correctly (composition is very uncomplicated in these genres).' (Bakhtin 1999a:80.)

38 Morson and Emerson 1990:272. Bakhtin (1999a:65) refers to speech genres as the 'drive belts from the history of society to the history of language'. Compare Bakhtin (1999a:62): 'To ignore the nature of the utterance or to fail to consider the peculiarities of generic subcategories of speech in any area of linguistic study leads to perfunctoriness and excessive abstractness, distorts the historicity of the research, and weakens the link between language and life. After all, language enters life through concrete utterances (which manifest language) and life enters language through concrete utterances as well. The utterance is an exceptionally important node of problems.'

*Heteroglossia, social languages, language evolution*

> Language – like the concrete environment in which the consciousness of the verbal artist lives – is never unitary. It is unitary only as an abstract grammatical system of normative forms, taken in isolation from the concrete, ideological conceptualizations that fill it, and in isolation from the uninterrupted process of historical becoming that is a characteristic of all living language. Actual social life and historical becoming create within an abstractly unitary national language a multitude of concrete worlds, a multitude of bounded verbal-ideological and social belief systems; within these various systems (identical in the abstract) are elements of language filled with various semantic and axiological content and each with its own distinct sound. (Bakhtin 1996a:288.)

In the literature on Indonesia's legal language problem and the measures taken to try and overcome it, a significant role is played by the official standard for Indonesian, the body of grammar rules laid down on the instruction of the government, that is. The issues dealt with often concern lawyers' manner of expression in a certain context, to what extent it complied with the official standard, how a higher degree of compliance with that standard might be achieved and which new means of standardization (standardization lists, dictionaries and the like) ought to be produced for this purpose. This mindset, defined in terms of official standards, also pervades descriptions of the legal environment. Linguistically speaking, this environment is very orderly, having applied 'the Dutch language' (*bahasa Belanda*) as the norm in the Netherlands East Indies era and nowadays generally using 'Indonesian' (*bahasa Indonesia*).[39] Whether or not Indonesian jurists deviate in their use of language from the official standard does not detract from that transition – the legal language, too, is 'bahasa Indonesia'. 'English' (*bahasa Inggeris*) has also gained in importance, particularly since the second half of the 1960s, while adat law is expressed primarily in the various 'regional languages' (*bahasa daerah*). Moreover, this environment is characterized by strict boundaries – people either speak one language or they speak another, their utterances being classed accordingly. One could state that homogeneity is taken as the norm and heterogeneity as the deviant. Language use displaying 'mixed language' ('Indonesian' betraying a 'Dutch' influence, for example) is generally frowned upon (see Chapter I).

The above is not to say that the utterances designated as 'Indonesian' or 'Dutch' by the Indonesian literature on legal language cannot be arranged under those headings, nor that formulating a standard would not be helpful. The point here is that the act of labelling the use of language as 'Indonesian' or 'Dutch', as 'Indonesian legal language' or 'correct Indonesian', by its very

39 The descriptions by Mahadi and Sabaruddin Ahmad (1979:85), for example.

nature takes place in retrospect, carried out by people wanting to classify or assess utterances already made. In day-to-day speaking (listening) and writing (reading), however, such labels hardly figure. A speaker (writer) primarily aims to respond and be heard (read), whereas a listener (reader) primarily aims to understand. In the process, they routinely employ, and interpret within the framework of, prior utterances and speech genres that fit the situation. The prior utterances will, in one part, belong to the same (national or regional) language as the new utterance; yet in another they will be separate. The dialogic nature of utterances inherently allows utterances in other languages within the speaker's (writer's) or listener's (reader's) socio-ideological conceptual sphere to exert their influence (Bakhtin 1996a:275).

The traditional view of cumbersome language barriers to be overcome by speakers (writers) and listeners (readers) – a view evoked by linguistic terms such as 'bilinguality', 'code switching' and 'interference' – has now been disproved. Suzanne Romaine's work on bilinguality, for example, paints a picture of enormous diversity and liquidity, of a continuum of phenomena rather than accurately delineable categories, and of subtle 'transitions' rather than obtrusive barriers. In reality, being 'bilingual' generally is not experienced as fundamentally different from or more problematic than being 'monolingual'. Mixing national (regional) languages and switching from one to the other for 'true bilingual speakers' in principle takes place by the same process as a 'monolingual' speaker's change in style, genre or variety. *All* speakers, even those in communities passing off as monolingual, have at their disposal a certain repertoire of speech varieties (Romaine 1989:132, 282).

In essence, 'the language (languages) of speakers (writers) and listeners (readers)' in a communicative setting usually neither manifests itself nor is experienced as homogeneous, systematic or 'belonging to (or complying with the official rules for) national language X or Y'. Instead, the focus of the communication is on the concrete, unique situation of that very instant, and on the requirement for a reaction or an interpretation. 'A person's language' ('languages') in that scenario consists of a random amalgam of previous utterances and genres stemming from his or her past (to whichever national or regional languages those utterances and genres may belong), some of which are activated in the new situation. Notwithstanding the customary definitions and designations, 'language' in daily life is neither homogeneous nor systematic. Denominations such as 'Indonesian', 'Dutch', 'English', 'Javanese' or 'Indonesian legalese' are abstractions, ideals. They are socio-ideologically, culturally and power-politically charged concepts, as are 'language' and 'dialect'.[40] With hindsight it may be easy to draw dividing lines

40 According to Romaine (2000:2), the term 'dialect' is commonly used to designate any infe-

between utterances, in so far as their form is standard language;[41] within the actual communication, the boundaries are often far less distinct. For example, the geographical area in which 'English' or 'Flemish' is spoken, according to the official map, in reality turns out not to be an 'island' at all but to form part of a 'continuum in social and geographical space and time'.[42] Instead of everyday language use revealing linguistic unity, or a synchronic system, it evidences diversity and a continuous, historical process in real time of constantly changing forms.[43]

Bakhtin speaks of an incessant struggle in the human environment between centrifugal, 'unofficial' forces and centripetal, 'official' ones. The centrifugal forces are made up of man's actions in response to the random, ever new

---

rior version of a language. Max Weinreich's definition of a language as a 'dialect with an army and a navy' is well-known (Romaine 2000:13). Both 'regional' and 'social' dialects are distinguished – the former demarcated by geographical boundaries (rivers, mountains, large distance), the latter by social ones (between social classes). Social dialects make a point about who we are; regional dialects state where we are from (Romaine 2000:13). To differentiate between language and dialect, the terms 'autonomous' and 'heteronomous' are sometimes used. Thus, one could say that the Dutch dialects are dependent on or 'heteronomous' in relation to standard Dutch. What is meant by this, is that standard Dutch provides a sense of unity among the speakers of Dutch dialects, including those near the border with Germany, and serves them as a point of reference (Romaine 2000:14). In addition, 'registers' are distinguished, the characteristics of which are determined by the usage context, purpose, theme and content (the use of legal language, for example), rather than by their users (Romaine 2000:21). For more on languages, dialects, styles and registers, see Wardhaugh 1993:22-54.

41 That is, a language variety that has been 'deliberately codified so that it varies minimally in linguistic form but is maximally elaborated in function' (Romaine 2000:14, compare pp. 87-8). One of the examples of standardization supplied by Romaine relates to the many varieties of 'English': 'Standard languages do not arise via a "natural" course of linguistic evolution or suddenly spring into existence. They are created by conscious and deliberate planning, which may span centuries. [B]y the eighteenth century a single, unified standard for English had ceased to exist, as speakers of new varieties of English such as American English began to codify their own standards in their own dictionaries and grammars. That process continues today as new varieties of English such as Australian and even Indian English assert their autonomy.' (Romaine 2000:88, compare pp. 17-20.)

42 Romaine 2000:2. Not surprisingly, Romaine states that 'the very concept of discrete languages is probably a European cultural artefact fostered by processes such as literacy and standardization. Any attempt to count distinct languages will be an artefact of classificatory procedures rather than a reflection of communicative practices. Lexico-statistics will not yield any non-arbitrary technical definition of terms such as "language", "dialect", or "family".' (Romaine 2000:10, compare p. 88.)

43 Bakhtin 1996a:356-7. Steiner's words (1975:108), here, are very to the point: 'Time moves through every feature of language as a shaping force'. Also see Voloshinov (1973:66): '[A] *synchronic system, from the objective point of view, does not correspond to any real moment in the historical process of becoming*. And indeed, to the historian of language, with his diachronic point of view, a synchronic system is not a real entity; it merely serves as a conventional scale on which to register the deviations occurring at every real instant in time.' Compare Stewart 1986:44 and Morson 1986:7.

situations with which everyday life confronts him. These actions focus on the moment and thereby become unique, special, different from any other actions whatsoever. The centripetal forces, by contrast, focus on unification, uniformity and standardization.[44] In the sphere of verbal communication, too, such a force field is at work. One of the effects of the interplay between these opposing forces, partly externalizing towards infinite diversification, and partly internalizing towards uniformity, is that language has become and continues to be stratified, not only in the traditional linguistic sense (relating to formal characteristics such as phonetics) but, crucially, at the level of values and ideas termed the *metalinguistic* level[45] by Bakhtin: that which in the abstract is a unitary language, in reality consists of a multitude of 'concrete worlds', of ways in which to conceptualize and evaluate the world.[46] This natural, heterogeneous condition of language in daily practice, manifesting itself at the point of collision between the centrifugal and centripetal forces, may be referred to as 'heteroglossia' and the array of languages that occur at the metalinguistic level as 'languages of heteroglossia' or 'social languages'.[47]

44 See Steiner 1975:31. According to Bakhtin, it is the very ability to respond to the unforeseen in daily life that harbours the essence of human creativity – as something that is omnipresent, perpetual, immanent to constant, continuous processes. Long-term changes should not be seen as systematic developments but as disorganized, haphazard 'accretions' consisting of a plethora of minute changes (Morson and Emerson 1990:40). Bakhtin does not sketch an orderly and regular world but a chaotic, sloppy one that nevertheless is open to and has opportunity for freedom and creativity. One of the most important neologisms he applies in this respect is 'unfinalizability' (*nezavershennost*) – the last word in and about the world has not yet been and will never be spoken (Morson and Emerson 1990:36-7).

45 Bakhtin named his approach 'metalinguistics' (*metalingvistika*) because its objectives were wider, different from those of traditional linguistics. Whereas he emphasized the utterance, as a unique, unrepeatable manifestation, traditional linguistics confined itself to the 'repeatable' component, being the words and sentences. In Bakhtin's view, however, that component merely represents part of the utterance – words and sentences are made subservient to the unique intention of the particular speaker (writer) (Morson and Emerson 1990:125-6, 131; compare with the quote on p. 35 as well as footnote 5). Clark and Holquist (1984:10) employ the term 'translinguistics' because of the pejorative connotation of the prefix meta-.

46 See Morson and Emerson 1990:141. The specific formal-linguistic properties of heteroglot tongues may only be established in retrospect, as 'traces'.

47 Bakhtin 1996a:263; Morson and Emerson 1990:30; Clark and Holquist 1984:7. The glossary in Bakhtin 1996 provides the following elaboration on heteroglossia: 'The base condition governing the operation of meaning in any utterance. It is that which insures the primacy of context over text. [...] Heteroglossia is as close a conceptualization as is possible of that locus where centripetal and centrifugal forces collide; as such, it is that which systematic linguistics must always suppress.' (Bakhtin 1996:428.) The term 'social language' is circumscribed in Bakhtin 1996a as 'the concrete, living, integral mass [...] made up of all the markers that give language its social profile', a 'concrete socio-linguistic belief system that defines a distinct identity for itself within the boundaries of a language that is unitary only in the abstract' (Bakhtin 1996a:356). A comprehensive description of the process of defining a language norm in the Netherlands East Indies and Indonesia (namely 'high' or 'correct' Malay and *bahasa Indonesia*) is contained in Maier

During the genesis of social languages, the infinite intentional possibilities of language are 'realized in specific directions, filled with specific content, they are made concrete, particular, and are permeated with concrete value judgements' (Bakhtin 1996a:289). Throughout the process, numerous elements, such as shared experiences, assessments, notions and attitudes, knit together into ways of talking. It is not a systematic principle but a complex of coincidences, a daily process of adaptation and growth that determines the evolution of social languages.[48] The development of social languages is dependent on lasting or repetitive situations, allowing a norm or standard to arise amidst the natural, centrifugal tendencies of the language. The concept of 'speech community' may be applied here, defined by Romaine as 'a social group who claims a variety as theirs and maintains its distinctiveness from the variety spoken by its neighbors'.[49] The common denominator for the members of the group, rather than being an aspect of formal linguistics, may be found in the realm of metalinguistics: the members share a certain 'communicative competence', interactional behavioural forms, ways in which 'to language' in particular contexts. One does not need to participate to an equal extent in the same formal linguistic language variety to be able to join the community.[50] A person will normally belong to several speech communities at once and, depending on the situation, will identify with one community or another (Wardhaugh 1993:125-7).

The social circumstances and speech communities in which social lan-

---

1993 and 1997. For heteroglossia and the English language, see Den Hond 2002.

48 Bakhtin applies terms to this phenomenon that refer to the accretion of bones or blood vessels (Morson and Emerson 1990:141).

49 Romaine 2000:23. Romaine's approach fits in with the previous argument in the sense that, in her argument, the emphasis is on a wider horizon, one that encompasses interaction and communication, rather than on language in its narrow form. On speech communities and the problems encountered in attempting to define this concept, see Wardhaugh 1993:117-31. Also see Romaine 1982.

50 Romaine 2000:23, 25. Romaine here also refers to the concepts of 'Sprechbund' ('speech bond') and 'Sprachbund' ('language bond'), developed by the School of Prague; the former relates to 'shared ways of speaking which go beyond language boundaries', whereas the latter has to do with a kinship at the level of linguistic form. The example she provides (Romaine 2000:24) to illustrate the point is as follows: 'In some bilingual Gaelic/English communities along the east coast of Sutherland in Scotland, speakers who have only a receptive competence in Scottish Gaelic nevertheless are able to share in conversations and interactions with more fluent speakers. Even though they do not control the language well enough to use it, they understand what goes on and what behavior norms are appropriate. They have what we can call "communicative competence" even though their grammatical competence in Gaelic is weak. The community as a whole shares certain norms for interacting, whether in fluent Gaelic, non-fluent Gaelic, or English. Conversely, sharing a grammar does not necessarily entail that communication will be successful. Speakers who speak the same language do not always understand each other because they do not necessarily share the same conventions for interpreting each other's speech or use speech in the same way.'

guages are established are infinitely pluriform in nature and reach. Although genres impose a substantial degree of stratification, this is interlaced with other strata – for example those related to particular professions or to social classes of a certain generation (Bakhtin 1996a:288-9). Social languages may be long-lived or last just a single day. Thus, language stratification is a process in which social languages perpetually evolve or become extinct. Attempting to define these languages in formal linguistic terms will often prove impossible; they are 'potential dialects', only a few of which will actually develop into dialects (Bakhtin 1996a:356-7). The only link between these languages is that each provides a specific window on the world and has its own objects, meanings and values.

Moreover, social languages intersect in a great many ways, in turn causing new languages to evolve. In their daily lives, people participate in several social languages at once, being the languages of their social circles and speech communities – their partner, children of different ages, relatives, neighbours, acquaintances from school, colleagues, friends and so forth. The social language to be spoken varies along with the situation one finds oneself in. In the consciousness of a speaker (writer), however, the social languages do not exist in neat, separate compartments. On the contrary, the dialogic nature of natural language causes utterances in different social languages continuously to be related to one another (Morson and Emerson 1990:242-3). Therefore, daily heteroglossia is one incessantly dialogized, as in considering one's professional language by means of the language of a child, or of a religious conviction. Value systems and approaches to the world can thus be seen to interact all the time. One is conscious of the contradiction between the ideas and approaches implied by those languages, which calls for the latter to be put into perspective in the sense that their application in particular circumstances is no longer indisputable; one becomes conscious of *choosing* a language.[51]

[51] Bakhtin 1996a:295-6; compare Morson and Emerson 1990:143. To exemplify this, Bakhtin (1996a:296) describes a hypothetical peasant who lives in total isolation and does not write or think. Even he participates in several languages (communication with his family, saying his prayers, formal communication with local authorities and the like), but his consciousness fails to connect those languages to one another: '[T]hese languages were not dialogically coordinated in the linguistic consciousness of the peasant; he passed from one to the other without thinking, automatically: each was indisputably in its own place, and the place of each was indisputable. [...] As soon as a critical interanimation of languages began to occur in the consciousness of our peasant, as soon as it became clear that these were not only various different languages but even internally variegated languages, that the ideological systems and approaches to the world that were indissolubly connected with these languages contradicted each other and in no way could live in peace and quiet with one another – then the inviolability and predetermined quality of these languages came to an end, and the necessity of actively choosing one's orientation among them began.'

Speakers of a social language experience that tongue in an intrinsically different way from non-speakers. For speakers, it is 'directly intentional', which is to say that they are able to denote and express directly and fully in that language. Because they are part of the same communication stream and share the same conceptual horizons, or, to use a Beckerian term, because they already are fully 'tuned in', the meaning of the utterances in their social language is largely self-evident; to them, 'a nod's as good as a wink'. Outsiders, on the other hand, may treat the language as an object, as 'local colour', turning the intentions evoked by those languages, once wrested from living discourse, into 'objects', limited in their meaning and expression (Bakhtin 1996a:289). In addition to formal differences being apparent between the language use of speakers and non-speakers, in the domain of word choice and syntax, the invisible difference, in 'lingual memory', also plays a role here.

In view of the above, it should be abundantly clear that language has an innate tendency to change. After all, being generated in response to the ever-changing contexts of concrete reality, all utterances carry within them a new, unrepeatable aspect. The speaker is motivated by his desire to express his point of view within the new situation, so as to shape his values.[52] The centripetal forces exerting themselves by way of the lingual standards applicable in this social circle or that, are incapable of fully nullifying the push for innovation. Changes in the 'formal sediments' of lingual communication may be traced back to changing contexts, both due to the 'natural circumstances' with which we are presented (advancing technology, global politics, environmental issues) and to the interplay of forces between social groupings and their languages within society as a whole. Put under pressure by the forces springing from those contexts, speakers modify their language customs.[53]

Such modifications will initially appear in the vocabulary but when they develop into long-term, widespread changes, they can gradually 'crystallize' into new styles and, in the long run, even into new grammatical standards.[54] Language change in this respect occurs along a continuum that 'extends from the most idiosyncratic ways of speaking to the most indisputable standards of grammar', in a process of 'grammaticization' or, by contrast, 'degrammaticization' (Morson and Emerson 1990:162). The picture created by language

52 Heteroglossia implies a conflict of values that, in the long run, imprints on the language with formal traces, thus being the driving force behind language change (Morson 1986:7).

53 'Content as *new*; form as stereotyped, congealed, old (familiar) content. Form serves as a necessary bridge to new, still unknown content.' (Bakhtin 1999c:165.)

54 Morson and Emerson 1990:162; Voloshinov 1973:125. The difference between style and grammar is a question of degree, not of nature. No clear boundary can be drawn: 'This borderline is fluid because of the very mode of existence of language, in which, simultaneously, some forms are undergoing grammaticization while others are undergoing degrammaticization' (Voloshinov 1973:126).

change, far from being regular or determined by some systematic principle, is one of random, coincidental accretions: 'Each language reflects in its particular unsystematic clustering and clumping the contingent historical and social forces that have made it' (Morson and Emerson 1990:141).

### *Law's language game*

> The law works by the translation of authoritative texts into the present moment, a kind of pushing forward of what was written in one context into another, where it has a necessarily somewhat different meaning. (White 1990:246.)

Since the 1970s in particular, numerous concrete examples have been produced to illustrate the problems with legal language usage in Indonesia. Each example consists of a word or a fragment of a text, while the contexts from which the examples are derived (the bigger text, the circumstances of its generation and the like) are not taken into consideration. The drawback of this approach is that the living, lingual world that has issued the texts is largely omitted from the overall picture. As a consequence, so are the factors that determine the present and future usage of juridical language. Why do Indonesian jurists speak and write as they do, what is it that drives them, guides them to do so? Seen from the perspective described in the sections above, to date the Indonesian literature on legal language has been preoccupied almost exclusively with the formal-linguistic aspect, with the 'dead traces' of the verbal communication amongst Indonesian lawyers.

Nevertheless, the texts and words cited, too, have their origins in utterances, in acts of lingual orientation (*languaging*) by concrete people towards the concrete contexts of a living and changeable world. One may then ask, these texts, of which social languages and genres are they 'traces'? In which circumstances were they (or are similar texts) written down, and by whom? Which speech communities were (and are) involved? Which were (are) the unifying factors in those speech communities and how did they come into existence? How did the speech communities, languages and genres develop over time? Chapters III and IV present an outline of the world of Indonesian jurists and their languages since the beginning of the twentieth century, along the lines of these questions, with the intention of bringing to light the nature and causes of the problems encountered in the legal language. In the remaining sections of this chapter, the above questions will guide a description of the lingual world of jurists elsewhere, namely in countries where over the previous century the legal language has *not* been a theme long mulled over in legal circles and where *no* special measures have been taken in that area. The standard thus formulated will be applied, in the next two chapters, in order to scrutinize the situation in Indonesia.

An investigation into the languages and texts of the legal world should be preceded by establishing the features of that world. What is it that jurists do; how to define 'doing law'? In the quote at the beginning of this section, James Boyd White mentions the 'translation' of 'authoritative' texts as the main feature. From this perspective, doing law, rather than being an activity in which language performs the function of an instrument, is a lingual activity, a way of communicating, speaking and writing. To apply Gierke's famous tenet, language is not the cloak of the law but its very body (see Chapter I). Indeed, jurists engage in reading texts and listening to others – whether it concerns a judge preparing and pronouncing a judgement based on the evidence presented during the proceedings and pleadings as well as other documents and the case law, a solicitor making a statement based on consultations with his client, the applicable law and judicial precedents, a notary drawing up and executing a deed on the basis of the legislation in force and a consultation with the parties, a corporate lawyer drafting a contract, or legislation specialists drafting an order in council based on research and previous legislation. Then, according to their findings, they produce new, mostly written texts.[55]

[55] Incidentally, White's description refers exclusively to the legal world itself, to the jurists doing law rather than to the place or function of the law in society or in the state. Robert Cover (1986:1601), on the other hand, points out that legal interpretation in actual fact takes place amidst 'pain and death'. (Thanks to Brian Tamanaha for acquainting me with this article.) Events such as erecting a fence, theft, murder or a traffic accident may give rise to legal action. In the process of doing so, these actions involving force or physical violence are translated into legal texts, to justify, to repudiate or to convict. In turn, the texts into which law being or having been done culminates, justify the (organized) application of renewed violence – perhaps in the shape of removing the fence, enforcing payment or taking into custody. The interpretation and experience of the law in action varies enormously between those who are subjected to the violence and those meting it out (Cover 1986:1602 footnote 2, 1607-9, 1629). Most apt is Cover's description (1986:1607-8) of the 'civil façade' of criminal law: 'The act of sentencing a convicted defendant is among the most routine of acts performed by judges. Yet it is immensely revealing of the way in which interpretation is distinctively shaped by violence. First, imagine the event from the perspective of the defendant. The defendant's world is threatened. But he sits, usually quietly, as if engaged in a civil discourse. If convicted, the defendant customarily walks – escorted – to prolonged confinement, usually without significant disturbance to the civil appearance of the event. It is, of course, grotesque to assume that the civil façade is "voluntary" except in the sense that it represents the defendant's autonomous recognition of the overwhelming array of violence ranged against him, and of the hopelessness of resistance or outcry. [...] I think it is unquestionably the case in the United States that most prisoners walk into prison because they know they will be dragged or beaten into prison if they do not walk. They do not organize force against being dragged because they know that if they wage this kind of battle they will lose – very possibly lose their lives. [W]e [do not] talk our prisoners into jail. The "interpretations" or "conversations" that are the preconditions for violent incarceration are themselves implements of violence. To obscure this fact is precisely analogous to ignoring the background screams or visible instruments of torture in an inquisitor's interrogation, the experience of the prisoner is, from the outset, an experience of being violently dominated, and it is colored from the beginning by the fear of being violently treated.' See Gaakeer 1998:58-60.

That which unites jurists in their widely diverging roles is their common participation – or at the very least their specialist expertise – in what could be termed 'law's language game'.[56] By employing a communal language that could be called the 'basic legal language', jurists are able to communicate the ground rules of the game and the props required to play it. Without exception, they acquired their understanding of the rules and the attributes of the game (comprising in particular a sizeable body of texts), when reading law. By virtue of their study, they avail of a certain 'stock of knowledge' that may be designated the *legal meaning system*, to quote Brian Tamanaha.[57]

For example, during their training, all Dutch jurists learn how the rule of law and the three powers (the legislative, the executive and the judiciary) function, broadly speaking; they are taught the most important sources of law and its various branches (constitutional, administrative, criminal, civil and commercial law) and gain a degree of insight into the workings of legal procedure.[58] The body of knowledge commonly possessed makes jurists the specialist players of the law game. It is because of this shared knowledge that the group of jurists within a given legal tradition (the Dutch tradition, for instance, or the American) may be called an *intersubjective legal community* (Tamanaha 1993:111-3). This community can be subdivided into various subcommunities that may or may not overlap, depending on further professional specialization.

The board on which lawyers' specialized knowledge best comes into its own is that of the so-called *state legal system*, a highly organized aggregate of the acts of legal actors (Tamanaha 1993:113-5). Some legal actors may not belong to the intersubjective legal community (some players are less specialized than others), whereas others that do may not form part of the state legal system (some specialists do not participate in the game) – policemen and bailiffs are part of the state legal system but do not share in the intersubjective meaning system

56 I have derived the term 'language game' (Dutch 'taalspel') from Witteveen 1988a:156.

57 Tamanaha 1993:111. In keeping with Roy D'Andrade's differentiation in cultural meaning systems, Tamanaha (1993:112) lists four functions of meaning within the intersubjective legal community: meanings can depict the world (the representative function, in this case knowledge of the law); they can create entities (the constructive function, in this case legal institutions such as property, legal entities, marriage, courts of law and legal reality in general); they can steer towards certain behaviours (the directive function, here, for example, the standard for a judge's conduct) and, finally, they can appeal to emotions (the evocative function, in this case the feelings evoked by actors on the legal stage in the course of their work).

58 Tamanaha (1993:112) describes the U.S. legal meaning system, the lowest common denominator of knowledge among American lawyers, as 'a core set of linking aspects of the overall legal meaning system, primarily that inculcated in the course of a law school education. For example, at a minimum, all lawyers in the U.S. legal tradition share the fundamental story of the rule of law, along with basic notions about legal institutions, and a core base of knowledge about substantive law and procedural law, and they know the legal language.'

(they are not lawyers), whereas the opposite is true for law professors (except when they also act in another capacity, such as that of a judge or solicitor). The state legal system is capable of continuation should the intersubjective legal community cease to exist (the game can be played without specialists). But should the reverse happen, should the state legal system collapse, that is, that community would simply vanish: not only does the monopoly on the specialized knowledge of the legal system endow the community with its very identity and position of power, it is the a priori *source* of its existence per se. Should the board cease to exist, so would the subject of communal knowledge, as well as the arena in which this category of players is able to act out its leading role. On the other hand, the continued existence of the state legal system safeguards the monopoly of the intersubjective legal community, by virtue of the trend towards ever greater specialization, and the important posts within that system will, by and large, be held by members of the community (Tamanaha 1993:114-5).

Acceding to the state legal system takes place via a route other than joining the intersubjective legal community. A position in the state legal system is allocated – one is appointed judge or bailiff – whereas admission into the community of jurists and more specialized subcommunities involves a much more extensive path of preparation:

> The very ability to formulate a decision in terms that would be recognizably legal depends on one's having internalized the norms, categorical distinctions, and evidentiary criteria that make up one's understanding of what law is. That understanding is developed in the course of an educational experience whose materials are the unfolding succession of case holdings, dissents, legislative actions, etc., that are the stuff of law school instruction and of the later instruction one receives in a clerkship or as a junior associate.[59]

[59] Fish 1987:401, 405-6 (reference to this quote is made in Tamanaha 1993:132-3). Also see Giddens' remarks (1997:330-1) on a dialogue between a judge, a solicitor and a prosecutor about an accused who has pleaded guilty to the charge of theft:
'P(ublic) D(efender): Your honour, we request immediate sentencing and waive the probation report.
Judge: What's his record?
PD: He has a prior drunk and a GTA [grand theft, auto]. Nothing serious. This is just a shoplifting case. He did enter the K-Mart with intent to steal. But really all we have here is a petty theft.
Judge: What do the people have?
D(istrict) A(ttorney): Nothing either way.
Judge: Any objections to immediate sentencing?
DA: No.
Judge: How long has he been in?
PD: Eighty-three days.
Judge: I make this a misdemeanor by PC article 17 and sentence you to ninety days in County Jail, with credit for time served.
[...] Each turn in the talk exchanged between participants is grasped as meaningful by them (and by the reader) only by the tacit invocation of institutional features of the system of criminal

The jurist-to-be must be initiated into all aspects of the legal tradition (Tamanaha 1993:122). First, this requires a course in law to be completed. In addition to acquiring a certain body of knowledge (theories, legal principles, legislation), the law student must also master the skills of learning to think, speak and write like a lawyer (Tamanaha 1993:113; compare Hesselink 1992:75). These skills can only be gained from special study components such as moot courts and work placements as well as in practice. At issue are a fundamental attitude and routines one is only able to internalize through constant repetition of the same action, as lucidly expressed in the above quote from Stanley Fish.[60]

Just as moves are made on the game board, so texts (written, as a rule) are produced within the extended context of the state legal system. In the law game, such texts are the subject of *legal acts*, being the acts through which the respective jurist intends to bring about *legal effects*.[61] These are consequences in the sense of the generation or the voiding of rights and/or obligations that may be linked to those acts by means of the (abstract) rules of the law in force ('positive' law).[62] By virtue of these legal acts, the texts acquire the force of law, they become binding, in other words. Pronouncing judgement, presenting statements of claim and counterclaim, executing notarial deeds, concluding contracts and submitting draft orders in council – all are legal

justice. These are drawn upon by each speaker, who (rightly) assumes them to be mutual knowledge held also by the others. Note that the content of such mutual knowledge presumes vastly more than just awareness of the tactics of "proper procedure" in such cases, although that is also involved. Each participant knows a vast amount about what a "legal system" is, about normative procedures of law, about what prisoners, advocates, judges do, etc. In order to "bring off" the interaction, the participants make use of their knowledge of the institutional order in which they are involved in such a way as to render their interchange "meaningful".'

60 Pim de Vos (1997:117) points out that in the Netherlands, during the first three years as a novice solicitor, each note is checked by the patron. Equally, Indonesian judges at courts of the first instance would have their judgements returned by their colleagues of a higher instance, marked with numerous crossings-out and ample commentary (Pompe 1996:223-4). It is precisely to train students in these kinds of skills that components such as 'moot court', 'legal clinic' and the like are incorporated into the curriculum. The report by the committee chaired by J.H. Carpentier Alting, too, which argued in favour of establishing a 'rechtshogeschool' (law college) in the Netherlands East Indies (see Chapter III), pointed out the importance of debating circles, practical exercises in the shape of dissertations and practice in defending arguments (*Verslag commissie hervorming Rechtsschool* 1920:50).

61 Legal acts do not, per definition, presuppose written texts – most agreements legitimately come about, in daily life, without a single word being put on paper. It is typical of jurists, however, that they nearly always commit their moves in the law game to paper.

62 Franken 1985:192. Art. 3:33 of the Burgerlijk Wetboek (BW, Civil Code) reads: 'A legal act (Dutch 'rechtshandeling') requires a will aimed at legal effect, a will that has revealed itself in a statement'. Besides legal acts, there are material ones, the difference being that the latter provoke a legal effect irrespective of any intention to do so. Examples of material acts are committing a so-called unlawful deed (art. 6:162 BW) and writing an academic treatise (art. 1 Auteurswet (Copyright Act) 1912).

acts endowing the corresponding texts with the force of law. Because of this, the legal situation outlined or implied in those texts sets in and they can thus be defined as *texts intended to have legal effect.* They are islands in an ocean of oral and written utterances that are devoid of such intention – comments and scribbles in the corridors, during meetings or even the deliberations 'in chambers', the meetings between solicitors and their clients and so forth. Utterances such as these carry far less weight to both those making them and those coming into contact with them than do texts in the category mentioned above – the former do not qualify as 'moves' in the law game, are not considered liable to acquire the force of law.

A feature of texts intended to have legal effect, is that they explicitly or implicitly refer to other texts that, in the law game, are accepted as *authoritative.* The legal effect intended in the new texts is only able to come into its own because of the explicit or implicit activation of the authoritative texts and the rules in force embedded therein.[63] Thus a judge, in formulating his judgement, will implicitly build on the applicable laws, on any prior judgements pertaining to similar cases and on legal handbooks; thus a notarial deed must comply in both form and content with the applicable legal requirements[64] and when formulating statements of claim and counterclaim, contracts and orders in council, too, such texts will be drawn on whenever necessary. The authority only adheres to the text of the law (or judgement) itself, not to any

63 In this regard, Broekman (1979:95) mentions the *textuality* of the law: 'One feature of each form of oral law, each manifestation of non-formal, topical-rhetorical law, in our continental system of legislation, is that it *must* possess a core of formal, written law by way of reference. There is no such thing as positive law without a dossier, without records, without legal clauses or, in short, without a textual deposit.' (Compare White 1985:240.) Witteveen's (1988a:156) comment about authoritative texts is: 'The text creates the normative model for ordering social relationships. The legal text uses normative language to describe possible conditions in the world and legitimizes certain kinds of behaviour by participants in social situations. In law's language game, the user activates textually embedded legal constructions, to facilitate doing law.' There was a time when text did not occupy this central position within the law – in the era of classical rhetoric, the rules established by legislative councils did not automatically become legally binding. In specific circumstances, the public could judge unwritten rules (common law) to take precedent (Witteveen 1988a:151). Witteveen (1988a:151-3) describes the developments from those days up until the positivism of the nineteenth century, in which epoch text attained the most central position in the legal discourse ever and was regarded as playing a fully autonomous role.

64 The form of notarial deeds in particular is subject to various stringent legal requirements. Article 26 clause 1 of the Reglement op het notaris-ambt (*Stb.* 1860, no. 3) provides an excellent example. In translation: 'Notarial deeds must be written legibly and with uninterrupted cohesion and must not contain abbreviations, blank sections or intervals, unless pre-printed forms exist for some deeds, as issued by any authority; prior to signatures being put to the deed, any boxes of necessity left blank in its body must be rendered useless for further completion by means of one or more clearly visible marks in ink; all numbers that establish the quantity or extent of the objects listed in the deeds, as well as any dates, must be expressed in letters but may be repeated in or preceded by numbers'.

translation or interpretation, unless the latter is legally authoritative and has been laid down in the form of legal precedent or in authoritative literature, in other words, unless the interpretation has become *doctrine*.[65] The texts at issue here are counted amongst what are termed 'formal legal sources', the highest ranking of which are acts of Parliament, the body of court decisions and treaties.[66] Orders in council, new court decisions and contracts, in turn, will become sources of law, although the latter two will usually apply only to the parties concerned and all three types of text derive their authority from a superior source of law. Of the highest of these sources, law[67] and treaty occupy a special position in that these text categories do not require validation against a higher ranking text to be authoritative – their authority is a matter of a priori acknowledgement.[68]

Ultimately, the (continued) existence of a system of law depends on such (continued) a priori acknowledgement of the authority of particular texts or, in a wider perspective, of the social order implicit in that acknowledgement. This applies not only to the legal actors but also to the people and institutions on the outside (civilians, the legislature and the executive). In this regard, Giddens mentions the acceptance of the *facticity* of the institutional order of the law, in the sense of accepting as 'real' the order of the relationships in which the interaction between jurists takes place and finds expression.[69] To embroider on the game metaphor – not only must the players be prepared to play the game by the rules, non-players must refrain from interfering in it while simultaneously accepting its implications and results. The community of jurists, in this framework, may be dubbed an *imagined community*, after Benedict Anderson (1985:15-6), or a *discourse community*, after White:

> [The law] is the constitution of a world by the distribution of authority within it; it establishes the terms on which its actors may talk in conflict or cooperation among themselves. The law establishes roles and relations and voices, positions

65 It is interesting to note, here, that in cases in legal history where a 'translation' was adopted, in the *formal-legal* sense, the words of the translation prompted judges to embark upon a whole new train of interpretation and decision-making. See footnote 78.

66 Franken 1985:99-101. The fourth formal source of law, custom, is *a*textual. Dutch law, in certain cases, refers explicitly to custom as a source of law (art. 6:248 clause 1 BW (contract law), for instance), but does not do so in others (Franken 1985:106-9).

67 Legislation comprises a profusion of text categories, ranging from by-law to statutory law (called *wetten* in Dutch, being the product of central government and the Staten-Generaal, the Dutch Parliament).

68 To quote Witteveen (1988b:4), the legislator is 'the only entity that may authoritatively determine the rights and obligations of those who are subject to its authority'. For more about authoritative texts in law and in jurisprudence, see Hesselink 1992:71-87.

69 Giddens 1997:331. Because of both the implicit pressure to acknowledge the rule of law and the incessant exercises intended to cause thinking and writing like a lawyer to become second nature, one could speak of 'being indoctrinated' into a jurist (Tamanaha 1993:113, 180, 182).

> from which and audiences to which one may speak, and it gives us as speakers the materials and methods of a discourse. It is a way of creating a rhetorical community over time. It is this discourse, working in the social context of its own creation, this language in the fullest sense of the term, that *is* the law. It makes us members of a common world.[70]

Just as the world of the game is evoked through rules and players, so jurists, through their texts and (largely) lingual acts, create the world in which they work. It is law's language game that spawns the legal community and maintains its cohesion, not so much because of the geographical places where the game is played but because of the 'social location' which it gives birth to.[71]

### *Languages and genres of the legal world*

The range of examples provided in the previous section amply demonstrates that the legal world knows a great many social situations and, accordingly, a host of (social) languages. A judge's lingual repertoire differs from that of a solicitor, whose repertoire, in turn, differs from that of a notary and that of a company lawyer. Many a social language is generated when jurists and other players in their segment of the law game work in a single location. As is the case absolutely everywhere, there is an inexhaustible diversity in languages. No two people speak in the same way, however equal the paths in life, education and career they have trodden. And in the workplace, one continually comes into contact with a variety of languages, which, over time, will be reflected in one's own repertoire and genres. The meetings, acts and routines of daily legal life – meetings, hearings, deliberations in chambers, all manner of conversations amongst each other or with outsiders, whether in a formal or an informal setting, about all kinds of topics (business, private), luncheons, drinks, taking notes and writing memos, in rough or drafts – consistently engender new languages and genres, while others simply vanish. The languages spoken in one court (or firm of solicitors or legal department and so forth) are not the same as those spoken in another.

The legal world thus encompasses a colourful array of speech communi-

70 White 1984:266. The representation of the law as a discourse community or a culture of argument is a leitmotiv in White's oeuvre – see White 1990:16, 27-8, 79-80 and 1985:35: 'In this way we might come to see the law less as a bureaucracy or a set of rules than as a community of speakers of a certain kind; as a culture of argument, perpetually remade by its participants'. Compare with Tamanaha (1993:40): 'In effect, for legal actors these prescribed ceremonial forms set up by the interactive rules carve out a separate realm of discourse and action and identify that realm as law'. Also see Tamanaha (1993:178-82) on the autonomous status of the law.

71 Hirschkop 1989:17. Hirschkop quotes Francis Mulhern's comment that communities, rather than existing in particular places, consist of practices of collective identification.

ties, each characterized by typical language usage. Yet the legal community as a whole may also be called a speech community. Although the majority of jurists do not have a common physical location where they carry out their work, within society they are collectively united through the law game (their *social* location) and the training dedicated to their participation along with the corresponding language and texts. They are also in contact with one another through all kinds of channels such as professional organizations, conferences, internet, courses, law magazines and other relevant literature.

On the basis of the above section, the rich variety of utterances (texts) in the legal world may be divided into several categories. First, a distinction may be drawn between utterances pertaining to the state legal system (on and around the 'game board') and those falling beyond its scope – texts related to the teaching of law and to research (books, syllabi, lectures, dissertations), as well as the general press (articles in newspapers and the like). In the Indonesian literature on legal language, examples are cited from texts from both within the law game (legislation, court decisions, notarial deeds) and from outside it (legal handbooks, dissertations) (see Chapter I)).

Secondly, the category of texts belonging to the state legal system can be divided into texts intended to have legal effect and those in which such an objective is absent, the latter being in the majority. The texts in the first subcategory represent the core of 'doing law', the formal moves in the law game. This category could be referred to as comprising 'legal texts in the narrower sense'. The utterances in these two subcategories originate in different languages (forms of *languaging*), that nevertheless exert a mutual influence. The utterance that is statute thus embroiders on a long chain of utterances (previous versions, drafts, recommendations et cetera) which qualified only partly as formal moves in the law game (that is to say, had legal effect), which, in turn, embroidered partly on texts that qualified wholly as such (earlier statutes, for instance). More generally speaking, the dialogic nature of language occasions even utterances that belong to different social languages to be oriented towards each other as a matter of course.

A special feature of texts intended to have legal effect is their obvious moulding into genres. Whether one scrutinizes laws, court decisions (both the verbally delivered version and its written counterpart), deeds or the various texts generated in the course of proceedings, all are characterized by a fixed format and standard formulae, phrases and terms. Writing a new law automatically entails a certain lay-out (considerations, articles, promulgation form), a certain style of formulating (striking the right 'tone' – general, abstract, neutral) and certain phrases and expressions (see G. van den Bergh 1979:14-5). Pinpointing the precise 'legal character' of legal language (certain words or expressions) is an impossibility – it lurks in its entirety. It is the 'typical construction of the whole' that invokes recognition of 'typical legalese'. In comparison with other utterances, legal texts in the narrow sense stand out because of the relative constancy of their fixed formats and their fairly conservative, at times archaic nature.

This particular feature of legal texts (in the narrow sense) seems to have its origins in the law's foundation in popular law, the oral tradition. The quote below from Mellinkoff about British law exemplifies this:

> There was small place in early Anglo-Saxon England for a law of contract; the open sale before a witness, the pledge of faith with oath and surety, the Biblical handshake – these generally sufficed. Action more than words. And the words spoken important more for their immediate effect than for promise. The solemn words of oath-taking created an immediate relationship, and put in pawn a part of a man's personality. Particular words – not words of inherent precise meaning, but magical words that could stir a God or wreck a soul.[72]

The word formed part of a ritual, a quintessential requirement of which was exact replication. At issue were formulae and incantations that could not be put down on paper and therefore had to be committed to memory.[73]

This aspect of doing law reverberates to date in the highly 'formulaic' nature of texts and in the strong urge to duplicate the manner of formulating.[74] The necessity to apply fixed wording may have diminished as the role of written text increased; however, the nature of written text must also be clear, perhaps precisely because of being written. The authority of a law rests in the very nature of the text, in the fact that it is a *law*. Now the meaning of verbal utterances, performed in a context of concrete, ritual acts by concrete people, is 'secured', as it were, in the sense that all those directly involved, by virtue of their presence, understand the meaning of the utterance and of the acts.

A written legal text, by contrast, is also, maybe exclusively even, intended to exert its influence amongst people who were *absent* during its generation.[75]

72 Mellinkoff 1990:41. Mellinkoff's statement beautifully testifies to language as a behaviour, to *languaging* – it is the actions rather than the words that count and in so far as words were used at all, they formed part of the enactment of ritual. For the Dutch legal language of the fourteenth and fifteenth centuries, see Drucker 1916, I:3-16.

73 Mellinkoff 1990:41-2, also see pp. 114-6, 298-301. This also explains the frequent use of particular sets of words (preferably alliterating), that gave the law 'rhythm' (Mellinkoff 1990:42-5). Also see Van Dunné 1988a:8-9, 11-2, 29.

74 This feature of doing law also is evident in the substantial body of regulations governing the law of procedure and in the constant use made of sample forms, model contracts, model books and such like (compare Tamanaha 1993:128 footnote 43).

75 On this topic Witteveen speaks of a 'duplication of the rhetorical situation': contrary to situations of verbal communication, the production of the text and its observance take place in different situations. During the phase of the production of the text, the reader is merely present in the capacity of a 'model reader', whereas during the phase of the text being read or interpreted, the

Its nature ('act of Parliament', 'deed', for example) is therefore often stated explicitly at the top of the text. Moreover, legal provisions prescribe the sections (regarding content) and fixed components (such as the preliminary wording) certain texts are required to contain, or impose the circumstances under which the text is to be generated (this can also be reflected in the text – consider, for instance, the prescribed presence of one or more witnesses to the execution of certain notarial deeds).[76] One could put that adhering to fixed forms contributes to a law's status as a law, to a notarial deed's status as a notarial deed and to the text in question being taken as legal and binding – not a text by just any random individual, but one produced anonymously, objectively.[77]

The above is not to say that the languages of the law game (legal texts in the narrow sense, intended to have legal effect, that is) are immutable. On the contrary, the tendency to change that is inherent in all natural language also exerts itself within the legal language. Here, too, changes initially crop up in the words and terms used, to be followed much later, in the very long term, by modification of the most constant, most deeply ingrained aspect of language, being its grammar. Long-term changes in the grammar of the languages of legislation used by jurists, over time, will unavoidably steal into the law and other legal texts.

The processes of change taking place within the various legal languages, in both the narrower and the wider sense, are partially determined by the role

---

author is merely present in the capacity of an 'implied author'; reader and author, respectively, fulfil roles here as textual strategies. The text functions as the intermediary between the phases of production and interpretation (Witteveen 1988a:173, 252, compare p. 150).

76 See footnote 64. By way of the legal provisions concerning the format of Dutch court decisions, Hofhuis (1988:53) lists only art. 121 of the Constitution (court decisions must state the grounds on which they were reached) and art. 59 Reglement op de burgerlijke rechtsvordering (hereafter Rv, Regulations for civil proceedings) (concerning the distinction between the grounds relating to the facts and to the law; the latter point is evident in court decisions, in their consideration of the facts prior to setting out the legal deliberations).

77 Tamanaha's (1993:39) term for the language genres of the law is 'stylized modes of discourse', which is to say 'the peculiar set of prescribed ways in which legal discourse occurs', 'rules of conduct or form which legal actors use to identify a given item as having legal status or a given set of actions as those of a legal institution'. Different prescriptions for form apply to different types of text: 'To be recognized as valid, bills must be written in a certain form with certain preliminary language. Complaints filed in court must be written in certain ways, as must Answers to these Complaints – the very existence of such entities as Complaints and Answers are determined by these rules.' (Tamanaha 1993:39-40.) Moreover, prescribed forms are also in force with respect to the current oral discourse: 'Legislators follow rules of order which dictate who can speak, when, and what significance is attached to what is said, how long a person can speak, what can be voted on, when a vote can be taken, and the significance of the vote. Legal actors in court proceedings follow a prescribed order and mode of speaking, with limits on who can speak, in what order, and even what can be said, with consequences attached to violations of the prescribed rules.' (Tamanaha 1993:40.)

of legally authoritative texts. Legislation in particular is of major influence. New words, terms, definitions and expressions in legislation, relating to new sociological or technological phenomena in society, find their way into the language usage of judges, authors, lecturers and students. They represent the main leads towards shaping the new theory on the area of law at issue. In court decisions and in the literature on the law, the legal terms and definitions can be elaborated upon, for example in court, when the parties to a case question the meaning of a word in a newly arisen context.[78] Inasmuch as the interpretations by judges and respected legal authors will be accepted by the wider legal audience, they will in turn be incorporated into new literature and court decisions and will contribute to the generation of new legislation.[79] Incidentally, the self-perpetuating impact of legal usage holds true for terms, expressions and definitions, not for grammar – lawyers do not speak in the way the law is formulated. Sometimes the legislator pays special attention to the wording of the law – for example, those who drafted the Dutch Nieuw Burgerlijk Wetboek (New Civil Code) deliberately aimed to create a modern code in *plain* language and, in doing so, tied in with a highly topical legal theme.[80]

78 A well-known example from Dutch law is the term 'onrechtmatig' (unlawful) as contained in art. 1401 of the Burgerlijk Wetboek of 1838, now rescinded, that reads as follows: 'Every unlawful act [Dutch 'onrechtmatige daad'] that causes detriment to another compels the party to blame for the detriment to compensate the losses suffered'. In the corresponding art. 1382 of the French *Code civile*, on which the Dutch Code was largely based, no term to signify something like 'unlawful' occurred, however (this text only contained 'tout fait quelconque ...'/every act that ...). In the course of time, in concrete disputes in which the question arose as to the 'unlawfulness' of a particular act (or a particular failure), Dutch judges have pronounced many a decision to attempt and interpret the concept of 'unlawfulness' more closely. The most famous ruling was given by the Hoge Raad (Supreme Court of the Netherlands) in the case of Lindenbaum vs Cohen, in which an act (or failure) was considered to be 'unlawful' when: (1) another person's rights are infringed upon; (2) the act is in conflict with the legal obligations of the person committing the act; (3) the act offends public decency; or (4) the act is contrary to the care befitting in social relationships in respect of another person or property (Hijma and Olthof 1988:265). The text cited from the ruling itself was based on that from an earlier draft act to amend art. 1401 (Schut 1985:49).

79 In the new article pertaining to the *onrechtmatige daad*, art. 6:162 BW, the ruling in the Lindenbaum vs Cohen case (see previous note) can be retraced. Here, an unlawful deed is defined as (1) 'an infringement of a right'; (2) 'an act or failure in conflict with a legal obligation'; or (3) 'an act or failure contrary to that which, according to unwritten law, is befitting in social relationships' (barring grounds to justify the act or failure). Parts (1) and (2) of the ruling are to be found in (1) and (2) of art. 6:162 BW, whereas (3) and (4) of that ruling have been contracted into (3) of the article (Hijma and Olthof 1988:265; compare with Schut 1985:46). In addition to 'unlawfulness', the terms 'act' ('daad'), 'detriment' ('schade') and 'blame' ('schuld') had also been interpreted authoritatively in a large number of sentences and rulings, some of which were incorporated into the Nieuw Burgerlijk Wetboek (New Civil Code) (see Hijma and Olthof 1988:264-6, for example).

80 For a critical commentary on the wording of the Nieuw Burgerlijk Wetboek, see Van Dunné

In the legal languages used outside of the scope of the state legal system, for example in the literature on the subject, lectures and working groups, syllabi and study books, articles and columns in newspapers and magazines, much less of an urge to preserve is present. In producing the latter texts, too, prior texts and the fixed forms of the genre in question are consciously or subconsciously drawn on. Yet the function of these texts, as well as the manner in which they are treated, is much less stringently prescribed than is the case with legal texts in the narrow sense. Besides, texts in the latter category do not need to refer to literature on legal topics or to articles from magazines for those texts to qualify as valid 'moves' in the law game. Nevertheless, the legal languages used in the spheres of teaching, research and public opinion have an enormous impact on the languages of the law game. Jurists are trained in these spheres, legal theory is developed there and the sociopolitical debate about the law finds expression there.[81]

Regarding the development of the languages and texts of legal scholars, lecturers, students and columnists, but also those of judges, Bakhtin draws a most instructive distinction between others' words that are 'authoritative' and those that are 'internally persuasive' (if not both at the same time).[82] After all,

---

1988b. Hofhuis (1988:52) points out that the formulation of rulings by the Hoge Raad sometimes reappears in decisions by lower ranking judges. In the Netherlands an important modification of the genre made up of court decisions is the gradual replacement of the style 'having considered' with the use of direct speech in the sense of a narrative (Hofhuis 1988:53-4; compare M. Reinsma and R. Reinsma 1976).

81 Witteveen (1988a:156) calls the sociopolitical debate about the law 'the discourse in which the business of the law is given shape'. Also see Witteveen 1988a:220.

82 To clarify the distinction between 'authoritative discourse' (*avtoritetnoe slovo*) and 'internally persuasive discourse' (*vnutrenne-ubeditel'noe slovo*) Bakhtin (1996a:341-2) refers to the two basic methods taught in school for learning and reproducing texts – 'learning by heart' (compare to authoritative discourse) and 'recounting in your own words' (compare with internally persuasive discourse). Utterances can be both authoritative and internally persuasive, but are usually either one or the other. Authoritative texts fulfil a role in all social groups, irrespective of their nature or size: 'In each epoch, in each social circle, in each small world of family, friends, acquaintances, and comrades in which a human being grows and lives, there are always authoritative utterances that set the tone – artistic, scientific, and journalistic works on which one relies, to which one refers, which are cited, imitated, and followed. In each epoch, in all areas of life and activity, there are particular traditions that are expressed and retained in verbal vestments: in written works, in utterances, in sayings, and so forth. There are always some verbally expressed leading ideas of the "masters of thought" of a given epoch, some basic tasks, slogans, and so forth.' (Bakhtin 1999a:88-9; also see Morson and Emerson 1990:219.)

The authority embodied can be authority per se but could also be the authority of a tradition, a dictum or an official line (Bakhtin 1996a:244). This type of discourse characteristically is felt to be 'organically connected to a past that is felt to be hierarchically higher': 'It is, so to speak, the word of the fathers. Its authority was already *acknowledged* in the past. It is a *prior* discourse. It is therefore not a question of choosing it from among other possible discourses that are its equal. It is given (it sounds) in lofty spheres, not those of familiar contact. Its language is a special (as it were, hieratic) language. It can be profaned. It is akin to taboo, i.e., a name that must not be

the scholarly debate, the literature on law, dissertations by law students and articles on legal matters in newspapers, they all draw on personal opinions and texts that are authoritative in the legal sense, but also on the languages of and texts by other people that, to the authors, are 'authoritative' (the words of some respected lecturers, for example, or of an authoritarian leader figure, religious doctrines, Bible texts, acknowledged scientific facts, proverbs, slogans) or 'internally persuasive' (words spoken by inspiring masters, senior colleagues, certain friends, authors) in another sense.

Legal texts in the narrow sense, too, are subject to the influences of other people's texts, whether authoritative or internally persuasive. In the case of a new law, these may comprise the (reasoned) observation that the earlier law (assuming there is one) 'no longer stands the test of time', descriptions of the actual situation to be realized by means of the new law (in the shape of a preceding 'translation' of the future law text into 'facts'), the earlier law itself, possibly other laws to which the act-to-be may refer, academic literature on topics to be dealt with in the new act, the personal opinions and preferences of the specialists involved in drafting the act, the various texts produced during the parliamentary development of the act and court decisions regarding the matters to be settled by the law, as well as any considerations in respect of

---

taken in vain.' (Bakhtin 1996a:342.) As the authority of a discourse increases, so a clearer boundary is required to separate it from the surrounding discourse and so less dialogizing is admitted; the reciting (and interpretation) of holy texts in 'strict' Christian and Islamic circles compared to their application in more liberal circles exemplifies this point. The issue in this discourse is blind obedience (or wholehearted rejection), rather than internalization and assimilation: 'Therefore authoritative discourse permits no play with the context framing it, no play with its borders, no gradual and flexible transitions, no spontaneously creative stylizing variants on it. It enters our verbal consciousness as a compact and indivisible mass; one must either totally affirm it, or totally reject it.' (Bakhtin 1996a:343.) Internally persuasive discourse, on the other hand, activates the consciousness of the individual, precisely to stimulate 'independent ideological life' (Bakhtin 1996a:345). It is processed in the conscious mind by means of assimilation and is therefore closely interwoven with 'one's own discourse' (Bakhtin 1996a:345), the result being that 'in the everyday rounds of our consciousness, the internally persuasive word is half-ours and half-someone else's. Its creativity and productiveness consist precisely in the fact that such a word awakens new and independent words, that it organizes masses of our words from within, and does not remain in an isolated and static condition. It is not so much interpreted by us as it is further, that is, freely, developed, applied to new material, new conditions; it enters into interanimating relationships with new contexts. More than that, it enters into an intense interaction, a *struggle* with other internally persuasive discourses. Our ideological development is just such an intense struggle within us for hegemony among various available verbal and ideological points of view, approaches, directions and values. The semantic structure of an internally persuasive discourse is *not finite*, it is *open*; in each of the new contexts that dialogize it, this discourse is able to reveal ever newer *ways to mean*.' (Bakhtin 1996a:346.) According to Bakhtin (1996a:348) a person's history of gaining ideological awareness is characterized by an incessant struggle and dialogic relationship between the authoritative and internally persuasive discourses.

the wording to be used.[83] Words, expressions and phrases used in those texts will be transferred to the new act – consciously or subconsciously adopted, or rephrased. The publication of new texts and their processing in the consciousness of researchers, lecturers and future lawyers, provoke change and innovation in the legal discourse, both outside of the actual game and within it.[84]

It has already been pointed out that speakers of a social language experience this in a way that is fundamentally different from non-speakers. The languages of the legal domain are notorious, in this respect – complaints about the unintelligibility of legal language usage are as old as the law itself (see Chapter I). Leaving aside the frustration caused by the gobbledegook quality of the legal languages precisely because the languages of a public domain like the law attract a relatively large amount of attention from laymen, the reason for the complaints may lie in the fact that a huge and highly specialized body of knowledge is necessary to produce legal texts in the narrow sense.

When jurists set to work, to quote Tamanaha (1993:115-30), they automatically switch to the *internal legal attitude* and the corresponding cognitive style. In doing so, the basic legal language and the legal meaning system are activated, as are the social languages, genres and prior texts belonging to the particular profession, that were acquired and studied during their training and further professional specialization. A sheer network of definitions is mobilized – cognizance of a single legal term commonly demands that of various others because the majority of terms can only be defined by using others.[85] Moreover, new attitudes and interpretations in recent court decisions and literature come under the texts one is supposed to be able to draw on. Certain methods of reasoning, techniques (how to read a case, for instance) and relevant arguments are also activated. All lawyers affiliated with, say, a

83 To formulate a judgement, a judge may draw on the claim or charge, couched in the summons, legal provisions prescribing the format of judgements, any legislation in need of an interpretation in the case at hand, prior court decisions in similar cases, especially those by a higher ranking court of justice, the factual situation the judge envisages bringing about, the opinions of prominent academic experts on the subject and the texts generated in the course of the hearing, such as statements by the defendant and witnesses.

84 Traces of very old texts that are both authoritative and internally persuasive are to be found in the 1838 Burgerlijk Wetboek. Wiarda (1988:20-4) discusses these in the following order: texts from the Five Books of Moses (Wiarda points out that the authors of the Burgerlijk Wetboek were familiar with this work in the shape of the 1637 'Statenvertaling' – the Authorized Dutch Version of the Bible) on issues such as the male as the head of the marital union or impediments to marriage; texts from the New Testament; texts by Cicero, Celsus and particularly Gaius, whose writing has left its mark on the lay-out and terminology (translated literally, in places) of the Burgerlijk Wetboek; the text pertaining to the 1579 Union of Utrecht; the *Massachusetts Body of Liberties* dating back to 1641; Hugo de Groot's oeuvre, his Dutch neologisms included; the *Déclaration des Droits de l'Homme et du Citoyen* of 24-6-1793 and the *Code civile*, which came into force in the Netherlands in 1810.

85 G.R. de Groot (1988:94) speaks of legal terminology as being strongly *system-linked*.

particular court of justice or firm of solicitors are linked by such a substantial body of knowledge and skills. Even though this may not actually be called upon in every situation and every language in the workplace, one is assumed to be able to activate it whenever necessary.

It follows that understanding a lawyer's argument is beyond most not legally trained readers (listeners). Switched to internal legal attitude, a lawyer has accessed his own reality and will work under a different horizon, as it were, from which non-lawyers are barred (Tamanaha 1993:87, 128). That which applies to language in general, is true here, too – lawyers do not construct their texts word by word, cementing the structure with grammar, but skilfully draw on their lingual memory, on their recollection of prior texts in the same category as the text in the making. In doing so, the divide with the outside world is all the more distinct because the professional attitude maintains a forceful grip indeed on the lawyer – the routines of thinking and speaking like a lawyer are the product of many years' education and training.

### *Summary*

Towards the close of Chapter I attention was drawn to the metaphor of language as an instrument that serves the lawyer in his practice of the law. Although this notion of language is rarely stated explicitly, it permeates the literature on the Indonesian legal language and the range of government measures taken to date. This perspective tears language out of its context and separates it from 'language user' (speaker/writer, jurist) and theme (law). The objection to this abstract approach to language is that it fails to take on board the concrete causes of the complaints about the legal language. Also, the instrument metaphor obscures important aspects of the phenomenon of language in practice.

To create a different image of language, numerous other approaches are conceivable. The point of departure of this chapter was the basic question as to what exactly takes place when people communicate by means of language. The approach chosen to deal with that question is one of a sociolinguistic colouring. The work of Mikhail Bakhtin, in particular, has been applied to attempt to rid language of several widely held misconceptions. On the basis of the general theory on language set out in the opening sections of this chapter, the language usage in legal circles was subsequently examined.

The first section picked up on one of the many illuminating insights into the workings of language that Bakhtin provides – an utterance is not pieced together consciously but in a practised manner, it 'accompanies' the 'living impulse' of the speaker or writer intending to respond to a particular concrete situation. This notion beautifully expresses that the context of an utterance is of the utmost importance to gaining an understanding of the functioning of language in daily practice – *languaging* is attuning oneself to a perpetually changing context (Alton Becker). That context is multifaceted – the utterance is a response not only to any prior utterance by a partner in conversation but also to the opinions or prior utterances of the speaker himself or of other people on the same subject, to the anticipated counterresponse by the partner in conversation, and so forth.

In turn, the contextual approach evokes a different idea of the theme of this chapter's second section, which is meaning. The Indonesian literature on legal language and the measures taken in dealing with that subject largely treat this aspect of language in terms of aiming for unambiguous texts and of producing dictionaries to establish the meaning of legal terms. That the result of the measures taken can only ever be relative cannot but be concluded as soon as one acknowledges that the complete absence of ambiguity is an unattainable ideal – in the concrete practice of speaking and writing, meaning has little to do with dictionaries and everything with the concrete reasons prompting a person to say what he says. Asking what an utterance means is asking for its raison d'être, for its rationale, and these, too, are to be found in the complex context in which the utterance originated. Aiming to achieve neutral, valueless language usage will also be in vain – whether they like it or not, people engage in their speaking and writing heart and soul, opinions, values and all. Whereas the instrumental perspective segregated the language, as it were, from both the speaker and the theme, the viewpoint described here concentrates on the inseparable cohesion of these three aspects.

The third section explored the question as to how people construct their utterances. They do not do so from individual words and sentences, but are led by their concept of the kind of utterance they envisage – a person writing a shopping list will, from the outset, tune in to writing a shopping list; a person formulating a court decision tunes in to formulating a court decision, and so forth. In other words, one is guided by a corresponding *genre*, the 'typical form of construction of the whole'. Genres imply a certain scope of expectations with regard to the themes, the words, sentence constructions, style, intonation and points of view to be communicated. Approaching the Indonesian legal language issue by means of genres would yield far better insight into the processes of development of certain texts and into any choices (to be) made when generating them than working on the false assumption that those texts were (are) perennially constructed out of a void.

The fourth section argued that the Indonesian literature on legal language sketches but a primitive 'lingual map' of Indonesian law. The differentiation is limited to the languages of the various legal genres (legislation, court decisions, notarial deeds, legal literature) and to a handful of national and regional languages, the latter in view of adat law. The approach in official terms, such as 'Indonesian' (*bahasa Indonesia*) and 'Dutch' (*bahasa Belanda*), ignores the endless variety in people's actual language usage – no two people speak in the same way. Any official classification into unitary languages masks an infinitely varied and continuously changing world of 'social languages', formed around shared experiences, values and beliefs within social situations, where styles, dialects and even (national and regional) languages blend together fluently and mostly without being noticed, which is highly manifest in a multilingual society such as the Indonesian.

In a reality like this, speakers and writers rarely think in terms of 'Language X' (in the case of monolingual people: '*Style* X') or 'Language Y' ('*Style* Y') or of switching between those languages (styles). Instead they are motivated by the routines discussed above – they dispose of an extremely personal repertoire of languages (styles) and prior texts on which they can draw effortlessly and stylishly as the situation demands. At times the official standard is operative ('what is allowed, what is not? what belongs to language X, what to Y?'), more commonly, it is not. There is a clear divide between the speakers of a social language and outsiders. The latter neither possess the degree of 'being tuned in' of the speakers, nor have they the prior texts in common, as a result of which they miss many meaningful aspects of what they are told.

The fifth section made the transition to the world of the law. The instrument metaphor denies language the lofty position in the law to which it is entitled – doing law *is* languaging. Jurists produce texts, they 'translate' authoritative texts with a concrete situation in the present in mind (James Boyd White). Though jurists play different roles in law's language game, they all share in what may be termed the 'basic legal language' – they are able to communicate with one another, as an intersubjective community, about the basic rules of the game and the corresponding attributes, such as a substantial body of texts. They owe this legal meaning system (Brian Tamanaha) to their education in law. On the one hand, not all jurists play on the game board or state legal system – some write books or give lectures. On the other, some people who do participate in the law game are not jurists – policemen, for example, play a major role, too. But because the members of the intersubjective legal community possess specialized knowledge, they are the leaders of the law game. To be admitted into that community, one must graduate from law school and learn to 'think and speak like a lawyer'. In addition to learning texts, one must therefore also internalize certain languages and genres.

The texts produced by jurists, the 'moves' on the board of the law game, constitute part of legal acts, that is to say, of acts with which the player intends to bring about legal effect. The legal acts endow the texts with the force of law. A prerequisite for this acquisition, however, is for the text to refer to authoritative texts, of which statutes are first and foremost. The authority of a statute itself is not derived from a higher ranking source but is acknowledged a priori. It is on this a priori acceptance of certain kinds of text that the law is based – the world of the law is erected out of texts, is an imagined community (Benedict Anderson) or a discourse community (White).

The sixth section examined the languages and texts of the legal world. A colourful array exists of social situations and speech communities and, thus, of social languages. The intersubjective community of jurists also is a speech community – the jurists share a *social* location (Ken Hirschkop), a common basic legal language with inherent knowledge and skills that relate to the state legal system, and keep in touch with each other through various, mostly national, channels and institutions. A distinction can be drawn between the texts on the board of the law game (texts within the scope of the state legal system) and those outside of the game (teaching, research, public opinion). The former text category can then be subdivided into the formal 'moves' in the game (legal texts in the narrow sense) and other kinds of text (with which no legal effect is intended). The Indonesian literature on legal language provides examples from different categories of text. Genres play a comparatively large part in legal texts in the narrow sense – the language of laws, sentences and deeds of old is conservative to the point of being archaic, the origins of which lie in popular law, the oral culture that, to a considerable degree, has engendered the law. Another reason for adhering to fixed formats is that these establish the nature of the text – texts such as acts of Parliament and deeds carry authority and must therefore make their status abundantly obvious.

Notwithstanding the conservative wording and the fixed formats, even the language in this category of legal texts is subject to the changes that affect all language. Examining the changes that course through the different categories of languages and texts in the legal world, the main influence on terms, expressions and definitions probably comes from legislation – the items changed will steal their way into court decisions, literature and dissertations. Their interpretations in court decisions and literature on the subject may, in turn, become authoritative, take on the status of doctrine. The opposite is also true – the languages used in teaching, research and public opinion pieces (articles on the law in newspapers and magazines) affect the texts inside of the scope of the game. After all, those languages are used to train jurists, to formulate doctrine and to conduct the sociopolitical debate. To put into perspective the effect of 'texts by others' on the intellectual development of Indonesian lawyers, by way of example, and accordingly the innovation of legal discourse and doing law, too, the distinction between 'authoritative texts' and 'internally persuasive texts' (Bakhtin) may be applied.

The divide between the speakers and the non-speakers of social languages is intensified in the area of law – the 'internal legal attitude' (Tamanaha) with which jurists produce their texts requires a substantial repertoire of knowledge and skills. The deeply entrenched routines of 'thinking and writing like a lawyer' represent an additional obstacle to bridging the gap.

The description given in this chapter is based on literature that primarily refers to the conditions in the United States and in the Netherlands, both countries in which 'legal language' has not been a major theme for jurists, at least not in the previous century. In chapters III and IV we will return to Indonesia, the legal language usage of which, as well as the development of that usage over time, will be examined from the new perspective sketched. Thus it is intended to arrive at a more realistic understanding of Indonesian lawyers' speaking and writing and of the way in which they 'experience' language – and correspondingly to gain a better idea of the cause of and the background to the dissatisfaction with the legal language.

**CHAPTER III**

# Dutch as the legal language

## *An education for native[1] jurists*

The year 1909 saw the Opleidingsschool voor Inlandsche Rechtskundigen (OSVIR or OVIR, School for the Training of Native Jurists) – popularly called the Rechtsschool (Law School) – open its doors at no. 10 Koningsplein Zuid in Batavia,[2] and may thus be taken as the starting point of the teaching of law

1 The Dutch term 'inlander' (adjective 'inlands(ch)), translated as 'native', now has pejorative connotations. It was perfectly ordinary in colonial times, not only in everyday life but also in the official sense, to designate the native, indigenous population of the Netherlands East Indies. The term was applied in legislation to draw a distinction with 'uitlander' (stranger) or 'buitenlander' (foreigner), but in a legal context was also used in relation to the Netherlands, namely to designate the Dutch (Kollewijn 1955:5). The term 'Inlander' appears in art. 6 Algemeene Bepalingen van Wetgeving voor Nederlandsch-Indië (AB, General Regulations concerning Legislation for the Netherlands East Indies, promulgated in *Stb.* 1847, no. 23 in conjunction with no. 57), for instance, in which the inhabitants of the Netherlands East Indies were divided into Europeans and those equated with them and 'Inlanders' and those equated with them. In *Stb.* 1855, no. 79, those equated with the Natives are specified separately as 'Vreemde Oosterlingen' (Foreign Orientals); according to art. 8 AB, they ranked among them 'Arabs, Moors, Chinese, and all others who are Muslims or Pagans'. This distinction is also encountered in art. 75 and 109 of the Regeeringsreglement (Government Regulations, *Stb.* 1855, no. 2), the organic law for the Netherlands East Indies, as well as in its successor, the Indische Staatsregeling (Indies State Regulations, *Stb.* 1925, nos. 415, 416 and 447). The rules in respect of the legislation to be applied and the courts appointed to determine their cases differed for the various population classes (Dekker and Van Katwijk 1993a:13). For authenticity's sake, the terms 'native'/'Inlander'/'inlands' will be used in their historical meanings.

2 The foundation of the school took place by Governor General's Decree (*Besluit*) no. 2 dated 25-10-1908 (*Stb.* no. 621), its abolition by *Stb.* no. 24 dated 23-5-1922. The statutes were laid down in Governor General's Decree no. 14 dated 29-1-1909 (*Stb.* no. 93). The school initially admitted Natives of Java and Madura only, but amendments of the statutes in 1915 and 1922 also enabled Natives from the Buitengewesten (Outer Territories) and non-Natives to attend (see *Stb.* 1915, no. 364 and Governor General's Decree no. 24 dated 23-5-1922, respectively). Furthermore, from the latter amendment until the closure of the school in 1928, the course was to be called officially the 'Rechtsschool' (*Gedenkboek Rechtsschool* 1929:86). The school and its living quarters partially moved, in 1920, to a newly constructed site in Pegangsaän, Weltevreden, officially opened on the 25th of September of that year by the then Director of Justice, H.J. Schreuer. The previous location at no. 10, Koningsplein Zuid was maintained for some time to teach and house the pupils

Fig. 2. Pati *landraad*, 1867 (KITLV collection no. 3516)

in what is now Indonesia. The recommendation to found the school had been put forward by an advisory committee chaired by the influential Adviseur voor Inlandsche en Arabische Zaken (Advisor for Native and Arabic Affairs), C. Snouck Hurgronje, with as his fellow committee members the Prosecutor General of the Hooggerechtshof (Supreme Court), B.H.P. van der Zwaan, and the Secretary of the Departement van Onderwijs en Eeredienst (Department of Education and Worship), M.S. Koster, a former teacher at the Opleidingsschool voor Inlandsche Ambtenaren (OSVIA, School for the Training of Native Civil Servants) (Achmad Djajadiningrat 1936:222; compare Van Helsdingen 1929a:12). The objective of the recommendation was to get legally trained personnel up to speed to fill important posts at the *landraad*,[3] the main court

of the preparatory programme; it was vacated altogether during the academic year of 1923-24 (*Gedenkboek Rechtsschool* 1929:86).

3 A *landraad* was the ordinary court for the native population (see footnote 1) and had its seat

to hear the cases of Natives. An *inlands rechtskundige* (native jurist) – the title obtained upon graduation – would be able to assist the European chairman of a *landraad,* commonly snowed under, in the role of *griffier* (registrar, clerk of the court) or member and might, in the long run, even come to replace him.[4]

The rationale for establishing the Rechtsschool was that the training of native judicial officers would have several advantages over the recruitment of more Europeans to fill judicial posts. First, the shortage of legally trained personnel could be more easily replenished from the ranks of the Natives than from those of the Europeans.[5] Secondly, the administration of justice in respect of Natives could be entrusted to people who '*better* than the Dutch are acquainted with the native tongue, social mores and customs, as well as the

---

in the capital of each regency (art. 89 and 94 Reglement op de regterlijke organisatie en het beleid der justitie in Nederlandsch-Indië, hereafter RO, Regulations for the organization of the judiciary and the policy for the administration of the Netherlands East Indies). A *landraad* consisted of a civil servant versed in the law, who acted as the chairman (some were assisted by a legally trained deputy chairman), the regent (if there was one) and several 'distinguished Native Chiefs' as the members, aided by a *griffier* (registrar) (art. 92 clause 1, 2 RO). The *landraad* was the proper authority to hear and try all civil and criminal matters involving Natives and Foreign Orientals as defendants, provided no other court had prior jurisdiction (art. 94-95 RO, see Dekker and Van Katwijk 1993a:27). *Rechtskundigen* were to be appointed as *ambtenaar ter beschikking* or *a.t.b.* (official seconded) to the *landraad,* following which appointment they could, in principle, progress to the successive positions of prosecutor, salaried member, deputy chairman and chairman of the *landraad.* From 1914 onwards, they could actually be appointed to these positions in the *landraden* of Java and Madura. The remuneration for the respective posts was fixed at Dfl 75, Dfl 100, Dfl 200, Dfl 300 and Dfl 400 per calendar month (Governor General's Decree no. 18 dated 23-6-1911 (*Stb.* no. 381) and *Stb.* 1914, no. 277 in conjunction with 1915, no. 369). Some time later, it became possible for a native *rechtskundige* to be appointed as official seconded to the presidents of the Hooggerechtshof, the *raden van justitie,* the Prosecutor General and the prosecutors at the *raden van justitie* (see André de la Porte 1933:117, for example). Compare Fasseur 1993:239-41, 245-6.

4 The increase in the number of cases dealt with by the *landraad* had been caused in part by the abolition of the *rechtbank van ommegang* (circuit court) in 1901 (*Stb.* no. 13). Since 1879 (*Stb.* no. 106), the duties of the chairmen and the prosecutors at the latter courts had already been transferred gradually to the chairmen and the prosecutors at the *landraden* (see *Rechtswezen* 1919:568-9).

5 Since the 1870s in particular the demand for legally trained civil servants had been rising steadily, due to a measure taken in 1869 (*Stb.* no. 47), whereby the chairmanship of the courts for the Natives and the extraordinary jurisdiction of the *residentiegerechten* (residency courts) was to be transferred gradually from the civil servants of the Binnenlandsch Bestuur (Administration of the Interior) to chairmen trained in the law (also see *Stb.* 1873, no. 157). The *landraad* courts of Java and Madura were the first to have such chairmen appointed, followed by the courts for Natives in the Outer Territories. The new *landraad* chairmen at Java and Madura doubled as *residentierechter* (judge of the residency court) (André de la Porte 1933:123). The final measure taken in this respect was to establish the so-called *landgerecht* (petty crimes court), charged with the administration of justice in cases of petty crime involving all classes of the population. Thus, the resident was relieved of the duties known as *politierechtspraak* (police court) over the Natives (*Stb.* 1914, no. 317, taken effect on 1-11-1917).

thought processes and attitudes of the native litigants and defendants'.[6]

In a letter dated 5 July 1904 Snouck Hurgronje had already brought to the attention of the Governor General the 'lack of mental contact between judges and those seeking justice' and to 'the inefficacy, indeed the unreliability of the European administration of justice with respect to the Natives' – most European judges were so ignorant of the native languages and native society that much of what was actually at issue in a given case escaped their notice. He quoted a number of judicial officers who had told him that they 'considered themselves fortunate to be relieved of their involvement in the administration of justice over Natives, as during the execution of their duties, the conviction had not infrequently thrust itself upon them that their court decisions, though taken to the best of their ability and in keeping with the law, lacked a solid foundation' (Gobée and Adriaanse 1957:496-7). This enabled others, who did speak the languages of the accused or the parties, such as the *jaksa* (otherwise known as *inlands officier van justitie*, native prosecutor) and the clerks, to exert undue influence on both those seeking justice and the process of the law (see pp. 100-21).[7] Training and appointing indigenous judicial officers would be most beneficial to the government's administration of justice with respect to the Natives, Snouck's letter concluded.[8]

The third advantage envisaged was that the decision to educate Natives to fill these prestigious posts might yield some positive political effects.[9] Finally, compared with recruiting more European judicial officers, this solu-

6 Explanatory memorandum accompanying the draft act, cited in Van Helsdingen 1929a:10.

7 Gobée and Adriaanse 1957:497. Complaints about the role of the *jaksa* and other native civil servants involved in proceedings were nothing new (see, for example, the missive written on 12-4-1849 by G.L. Baud, the then Minister for the Colonies, to Scholten of Oud-Haarlem (cited in Immink 1882:199), correspondence of 14-4-1864 by the Attorney General W. Rappard to the Governor General (cited in Immink 1882:237), Piepers 1884:106 and Mounier 1900:149). In a 1907 article in the *Indische Gids*, J.W.T. Cohen Stuart, former Director of the Department of Justice, warned against the danger of public safety becoming compromised as a result – judges simply were unable to establish the facts or to distinguish these from fiction, thus being fairly easily inclined to decide on 'kurang terang' ('insufficiently clear', not proven, that is, meaning acquittal) (Cohen Stuart 1907:1330-2). See the description in Augusta de Wit's *De godin die wacht* (1916): 'The interrogation began. The President [of the *landraad*], who did not understand Sundanese, put his questions to the *jaksa* in Malay; and the *jaksa* conveyed them in Sundanese to the accused and the witnesses who did not understand Malay. The case thus proceeded, slowly, like pouring from a corked bottle; drop by drop the words came out, and were poured then into this cup, then into that, and were carried hither and thither, were spilt and filled up again.' (De Wit 1916:54.)

8 It was also argued that, as a matter of principle, it would only be proper and fitting for justice to be done 'kind by kind'. This line of reasoning had been put forward by Cohen Stuart, too, in the article mentioned above; in his opinion, the 'administration of justice by Europeans over Natives [...] could *never* be right', as 'Natives [could only be] understood fully by Natives [...]' (Cohen Stuart 1907:1329, 1334).

9 Explanatory memorandum accompanying the draft act (cited in Van Helsdingen 1929a:10).

tion would render substantial savings for the colonial government – because the Rechtsschool diploma was inferior to a university degree in law obtained in the Netherlands (nor did it grant the use of the title of *meester in de rechten* (master of laws, abbreviated title 'Mr.', LL.M)), the salary of a native *rechtskundige* could be kept well below that of a European in the same post.[10]

The decision to found the Rechtsschool fitted in neatly with the Ethical policy practised at the start of the twentieth century. This was neither the first course provided by the colonial government for the youngsters of the indigenous upper crust, nor the first to teach law.[11] Moreover, the colonial government already had native judges in its ranks.[12] But Natives dispens-

10 Explanatory memorandum accompanying the draft act (cited in Van Helsdingen 1929a:10), see the comments by the advisory committee mentioned, as discussed in Neytzell de Wilde 1929:28.

11 In 1893, by way of experiment, the Magelang school known as the Hoofdenschool (Chiefs' School, school for the native elite) had added the subjects 'principles of law' and 'constitutional and administrative law of the Netherlands East Indies' to its syllabus (in addition to other subjects, such as surveying) (*Bijblad* (hereafter *Bb.*, Supplementary Gazette) no. 4914; *Algemeen verslag inlandsch onderwijs* 1901; Driessen 1897:254-5, 259-62). The aim was to remodel the existing, general education into a vocational one, not in the least to better prepare the future *jaksa* and members of the courts for Natives for their duties. The proposal to establish a school specifically for *jaksa*, originally put forward in 1865 by J.A. van der Chijs, by 1890 had firmly run aground (Driessen 1897:254-9). When the trial in Magelang turned out well, this Hoofdenschool and those in Bandung and Probolinggo were restructured, in 1900, into 'Opleidingsschool voor Inlandsche Ambtenaren' (OSVIA). In 1910 such schools were also founded in Serang, Madioen, Blitar and Makassar (*Stb.* 1910, nos. 458 and 460). The last two of the five-year OSVIA curriculum included law as a compulsory subject (*Bb.* no. 5516 sub B art. 5). The later educational programmes for native civil servants, the Bestuursschool (School for Administrators), Middelbare Opleidingsschool voor Inlandsche Ambtenaren (MOSVIA, Middle School for the Training of Native Civil Servants) and the Bestuursacademie (Civil Administration Academy), founded in 1914, 1927 and 1938 respectively, would also provide courses in law.

12 The Netherlands East Indies had two separate justice systems, one governmental and the other for *inheemse rechtspraak* (indigenous administration of justice). The former, to which all population groups were subject, was operated in the name of the crown; it was divided into a European and a Native branch, the *inlandse rechtspraak*. The indigenous system applied exclusively to the indigenous population. Most of the indigenous administration of justice took place in the autonomous regions and was entrusted to the rulers or the judges appointed by them (Dekker and Van Katwijk 1993a:18-9). In addition to this indigenous justice, native judges presided over two institutions that came under the auspices of government justice, being the *districtsgerecht* (district court) and the *regentschapsgerecht* (regency court). The district head and the *regent* (or *patih*), respectively, functioned as sole judges, assisted by native counsellors, a *penghulu* (state-paid religious official) (in the case of the regency court) and a *jaksa*. Their jurisdiction was confined to small claims and petty crimes committed by Natives only. Court decisions taken in civil cases heard by the district court could be appealed at the regency court while review of the regent's decisions would be undertaken by the *landraad* (Dekker and Van Katwijk 1993a:28-9). This kind of administration of justice, carried out by these institutions, clearly was of a different nature than that practised by the *landraad* and the European courts, as is evident from the fact that the cases were heard without any involvement of jurists while the procedural rules were

Fig. 3. Hoesein Djajadiningrat, Leiden, ca 1900 (see footnote 13)
(KITLV collection no. 6353)

ing justice *on an equal footing with the European landraad chairmen* (university-trained advocates, on Java and Madura at least), on occasion having jurisdiction over Europeans! To many a contemporary, it was simply unthinkable.[13] At the dawn of the twentieth century the intersubjective legal community in the Netherlands East Indies, united in and around the colonial legal system (see Chapter II), was an exclusively Dutch affair. The draft act in respect of the Rechtsschool was opposed by some of the highest authorities, W.A.P.F.L. Winckel, the former president of the Hooggerechtshof, I.A. Nederburgh, justice on that same body and W.F. Haase, lecturer in jurisprudence at the Probolinggo OSVIA and member of the *raad van justitie* (council of justice) at Semarang among them.[14]

An article by Haase in *De Locomotief* of 23 October 1907, entitled 'Inlandsche landraadsvoorzitters; Non tali auxilio' (Native *landraad* chairmen; Non tali auxilio), seems particularly to have impressed the Dutch Eerste Kamer (Upper House) (*De wording der Rechtsschool* 1929:44; Van Helsdingen 1929a:9-11). The

---

extremely minimal – the original version of the Inlandsch Reglement (IR, Native Code) contained sixteen stipulations for procedure at a district court (art. 93-108) and fourteen for that at a regency court (art. 109-122), compared with 242 clauses regarding procedure at the *landraad* (inclusive of the rules for appealing and *cassatie* (cassation) (art. 123-237, 241-367)).

13 The draft act in respect of the Rechtsschool was preceded, in 1905, by a Governor General's Decree stating that 'no Native who meets the requirements imposed by law on any judicial office shall be excluded from that office because of being a Native' (*Bb.* no. 6395). The Decree had been occasioned by a petition submitted to the government by the Regent of Serang, R.T. (Raden Tumenggung) Achmad Djajadiningrat, in 1903. In his letter he enquired on behalf of his brother Hoesein, who intended to embark on a course in law, whether Natives would be admitted to the judiciary were they to satisfy the requirements of competence imposed on such admission. Up until that time, no Native had been accepted into the judiciary or the administration of the Interior and any Native making his way up the colonial civil service ladder at all could count on severe opposition from amongst those ranks (see Achmad Djajadiningrat 1936:222-3 and Fasseur 1993:290-1). From 1890 onwards, Snouck Hurgronje himself laboured wholeheartedly for the education of Achmad Djajadiningrat and his siblings (Achmad Djajadiningrat 1936:62; compare Gobée and Adriaanse 1957:496).

Regarding the jurisdiction over Europeans – any civil dispute which involved a Native being summonsed had to be heard by the *landraad*, even if the plaintiff was a European (art. 94 IR). In a few rare circumstances it was also possible for a European to be summonsed to appear before the *landraad* (André de la Porte 1933:79). The then Minister for the Colonies, D. Fock, in his Memorandum of Reply to a question from parliament, addressed to the States General (dated 18-10-1907), commented that entrusting native judges with jurisdiction over Europeans was not envisaged for the time being. Whether or not this might arise at any time in the future, he felt he could not fathom (*De wording der Rechtsschool* 1929:39). From 1901 (*Stb.* no. 15 in conjunction with no. 273), the chairman of the *landraad* doubled as residency judge, in which capacity he was authorized to take cognizance of small claims between Europeans (art. 116c, f RO) and also, up until the introduction of the *landgerecht* in 1914 (*Stb.* no. 17), to try petty crimes committed by Europeans (Dekker and Van Katwijk 1993a:26; compare Van Helsdingen 1929a:19).

14 *De wording der Rechtsschool* 1929:44; compare Lev 1976:145-6. On the OSVIA, see footnote 11.

crux of Haase's article was the hypothesis that Natives were lacking in integrity, an indispensable trait for any post in the judiciary. According to the author, a native judge would as yet lack 'the self-reliance, the independence and the moral courage to stand firm in his convictions'.[15] However eminently educated, it would be a fallacy to think that such a judge or his decisions would be able to wield any authority whatsoever in the current social conditions. Their modest salary, a factor not to be underestimated in a country where *rang* (position) and *wang* (money) were 'virtually synonymous', would cause native and European civil servants alike to treat them with the same condescension they meted out to graduates of the Dokter Djawa-school (school for 'Javanese doctors') and of the School tot Opleiding van Inlandsche Artsen (STOVIA, School for the Education of Native Doctors) – 'half-baked jurists', 'mèster-bamboe' or 'presidèn-bamboe'.[16] It was therefore in everyone's best interest, according to Haase, not to upset the status quo. Whatever faults the European judges might have, they most certainly could not be found wanting in integrity (Haase 1907).

Haase's argument is strongly coloured by the racial prejudice of his colonial times. Nonetheless, he had a point in that the new course represented a move into uncharted territory, in several respects. As mentioned, the intersubjective legal community in the Netherlands East Indies had, up until that time, been an exclusively Dutch/European domain. Native *rechtskundigen* in general, but future deputy chairmen or chairmen in particular, would enter a world in which Dutch was spoken, in which all legislation, literature and court decisions (published and discussed in the law journals *Recht in Nederlandsch-Indië* and *Indisch Weekblad van het Recht* – see Dekker and Van Katwijk 1992:1-12) were written in Dutch and in which the court decisions they themselves had fashioned in the Dutch language[17] would be exposed to review, on appeal,

15 Van Helsdingen 1929a:10. Compare with Cohen Stuart (1907:1326) on native civil servants employed in the prosecution service: 'They possess in common with all other Natives this weak side in particular – a lack of independence and little moral fortitude. They display a strong tendency to yield their insights and attitudes to those of their superiors, as well as being extremely susceptible to temptation. They have no resistance to the influence of kin, friends, superiors and succumb especially easily to gifts on offer.'

16 Old spelling. Haase 1907. The term 'pokrol bambu' ('pokrol' is a corruption of 'procureur' (procurator)) continues to be applied to 'would-be' or amateur advocates.

17 In accordance with the Inlandsch Reglement (*Stb.* 1847, nos. 23 and 63 in conjunction with *Stb.* 1848, no. 16 and *Stb.* 1849, nos. 60 and 63), the *dispositief* (the actual pronouncement) of court decisions in criminal cases also had to be recorded in the *landtaal* (local language) (art. 313 clause 1, as amended by *Stb.* 1873, no. 113). A.J. Immink, an authority on the law of the Netherlands East Indies, proposed that 'landtaal' ought to be taken to be the (mother) tongue of the region in which the court operated (as opposed to Malay). The prescription probably arose to enable the indigenous members of the court to verify the judgement's conformity with the decision reached prior to putting their signatures to it (Immink 1889:425). The defendant, incidentally, was entitled

by a Dutch judge (of a *raad van justitie*). To what extent the new course could prepare Natives for their intended role and to what extent native *rechtskundigen* would be capable of fulfilling that role in the compartmentalized colonial society could not be predicted with any great accuracy. Moreover, it was not clear whether the relatively short course (the law programme had a three year curriculum) could deliver graduates who would turn out to be the equals of European, university-trained law officials.[18]

Then there was the issue of professional integrity – it was clear from the start that the steadfastness of the future *rechtskundigen* would be sorely tried in their place of work. Natives with powers formerly reserved for European civil servants were bound to meet with resistance – from both other native civil servants and their European counterparts. Also, decisions taken by the *landraad* were not just any official decisions – they were invested with a particular type of authority, in the sense that (once they had become irrevocable) they were inviolable and applicable to all. And they were a source of new law! (See Chapter II.)

The objections raised failed to deter the newly installed Minister for the Colonies A.W.F. Idenburg, however. In a speech that convinced the members of the Upper House, too, he made it plain that the arguments in favour, as provided by Snouck Hurgronje, the former Director of the Justice Department J.W.T. Cohen Stuart and others, outweighed those against. The critics of the draft may have had ample authority to voice their concerns, but no one was more expert than Snouck on 'the character of the Native' – so was it not highly significant that Snouck of all people should be in favour of the plan? Integrity, according to Snouck, was nothing to do with the national character;[19] rather, it was partly a question of upbringing and education and partly one determined

to request a translation of the judgement (both in the first instance and of any retrial), free of charge, into his 'local language', in case he belonged to the indigenous population and had no understanding of Malay (clause 2). It follows that defendants classed as 'Foreign Orientals', were only able to request a transcript in Malay. According to A. van den Bergh (1900:467), who boasted 17 years' experience at 15 different *landraad* courts, the majority of chairmen were not well-placed to verify the translations in the 'local language'. To the chairman, and often also to the registrar, it would therefore '[be] a hazardous undertaking to sign those translations'.

18 In the Tweede Kamer (Lower House) the question was raised as to whether the plan did not represent a step backwards on the path embarked on in 1869, when it had been decided that European colonial administrative officers would gradually be relieved from their judicial duties (*Stb.* 1869, no. 47), with the vacancies to be filled by academically trained judicial officers (*De wording der Rechtsschool* 1929:37).

19 In his letter of 5-7-1904 Snouck Hurgronje had already drawn attention to the corruption in European administrative circles in the East Indies throughout the previous centuries (Gobée and Adriaanse 1957:494-6). The improvement in this situation over the last few decades (though not yet equal to that in Europe), 'surely no-one [would] ascribe in earnest to any improvement in the European race in general nor even, in the first instance, to a rise in the quality of its representatives in these regions' (Gobée and Adriaanse 1957:495).

by factors relating to one acquitting oneself of one's official duties (Cohen Stuart 1907:1326). Future judicial officers would therefore need to be brought up and educated in a thorough, European fashion (Gobée and Adriaanse 1957:498-9, 501; Cohen Stuart 1907:1326-9). And during his training, the future judge would 'undoubtedly [be] more imbued than others with respect for and insight into the requirements of the law' (Gobée and Adriaanse 1957:495).

The conditions under which the work was to be done, were considerably more favourable to the performance of the job than those under which native administrative officers operated.[20] The positive experiences gained with Natives qualified as 'Surinam jurists' (those engaging in law by virtue of a practitioner's examination) as well as with indigenous judges in British India (whose court decisions were not in any way inferior to those taken by their British colleagues) served to underline that the government truly was not going too far.[21] What it ultimately came down to, according to the Minister, was a question of faith.[22] The conservative-minded would simply

20 All said and done, native judicial officers were thought to be more resistant to being 'forced back' into traditional cultural patterns than native administrative officers, both as a result of the greater duration of their course and by virtue of 'the nature of their studies equipping them with insights into the significance of family, society and state that differ dramatically from those they would most probably have acquired in their fatherland' (Gobée and Adriaanse 1957:499-500). In the daily practice of the job, unlike administrative officers, *rechtskundigen* would not come into close contact with the population on a regular basis and would therefore less frequently be exposed to bribery. The higher remuneration, too, was a favourable factor. Furthermore, a more stringent measure of integrity was applied to members of the judiciary than to other civil servants, both internally and externally (Gobée and Adriaanse 1957:495-6, 499-501). Finally, European judicial officers might be able to play a positive role by providing their native colleagues with moral support – something higher-ranking native administrative officers often had to do without (see footnote 13) – for example by communicating with them in the Dutch language. This was highlighted because it was claimed that European administrative officers would often not permit native officials to address them in Dutch (Gobée and Adriaanse 1957:499-500). (The European administrative officer G.L. Gonggrijp repeatedly refuted this accusation in his letters to the editor of the *Bataviaasch Handelsblad*, written from 1911 until 1914 under the pseudonym of 'Opheffer' (Elevator) – see Gonggrijp 1944:106-10, 121-3.) It is interesting to note, here, the experiences recorded at a later date by the retired *wedana* (district head) Soerianata. Having summed up his successive positions (*jurutulis controleur* (controller's scribe), *jurutulis assistent-resident* (assistant resident's scribe), *mantri kabupaten* (regent's clerk), *jaksa*, assistant *wedana* and *wedana*), he comments that his superiors in the colonial administrative civil service would not permit him to speak Dutch. He continues: 'Only once I [had] reached the position of *jaksa*, some 10 to 12 years later, I could freely speak Dutch with the chairman of the *landraad*, though in the meantime [since sitting the examination at the Hoofdenschool in 1896] I had forgotten most of it, so that I could not express myself adequately' (Deenik, Zandvoort and Sadikin 1929:96).

21 *De wording der Rechtsschool* 1929:50-1. The Minister was inspired by the words of Sir John Strachey in his *India; Its administration and progress* (originally published in 1888) (*De wording der Rechtsschool* 1929:51; compare Cohen Stuart 1907:1326-9).

22 A reference to a letter written in response to Haase's article, signed 'A Javanese', published in *De Locomotief* of 26-10-1907 (compare *De wording der Rechtsschool* 1929:49).

Fig. 4. Opening ceremony of the Rechtsschool (KITLV collection no. 6571)

have to grow accustomed 'to the thought that, as the spiritual forces present in the Native would develop and the emancipation of the population would progress, native civil servants, too, might issue decisions to which European civil servants, yes! even European administrative officers, would have to submit' (*De wording der Rechtsschool* 1929:49).

## *'The Sun of Justice casts its rays upon us'*[23]

Thus, a college came into being that, without a shadow of a doubt, was the most exclusive, the most elite educational establishment for Natives at the turn of the twentieth century. The curriculum consisted of a preparatory programme and a law programme, each lasting three years (Rechtsschool Statutes art. 3 clause 1). Stringent criteria concerning the proficiency in Dutch were to ensure that only youngsters from the native upper crust, where Dutch was spoken, could be admitted.[24] In addition, the students-to-be would need to be

23 Motto, displayed on the inside page of the *Gedenkboek Rechtsschool* 1929. The motto was manifest in the emblem of a golden sun that decorated the Rechtsschool student's cap.

24 The college initially admitted students from Java and Madura only, as it was intended to employ the *rechtskundigen* predominantly in their area of origin; a mere handful of places in the

Fig. 5. OSVIA students, Bandung, 1903 (KITLV collection no. 5180)

highly motivated and supported by their parents, because the course did not come cheap – depending on the means of the parents, the fees for boarders were five to twelve times higher than for an OSVIA student, whereas day students with lodgings elsewhere paid one and a half to four times more (excluding subsistence, of course).[25] The number of places for Rechtsschool students

Outer Territories employed legally-trained personnel in the courts for Natives at the time the Rechtsschool was founded. From 1915, however, the college also admitted students from the Outer Territories and increased its number of student places. Applicants to the college's preparatory programme had to have completed the Europese Lagere School (ELS, European Primary School) or demonstrate an equivalent level of cognitive development, especially in Dutch (Rechtsschool Statutes art. 10 clause 3). For future OSVIA students it sufficed either to have passed the state native 'first class' school with Dutch as an exam subject or to have completed the fifth grade of the ELS with good results (or to have attained an equivalent level of cognitive development, especially in Dutch) (OSVIA Statutes art. 8 clause 3). Students could be admitted to the Rechtsschool's law programme once they had either completed the preparatory programme or had taken an entrance exam in which they had demonstrated 'having acquired at least an equivalent body of knowledge and reached at least the same level of mental development' and had been judged suitable following an assessment of their 'ethical progress' (Rechtsschool Statutes art. 10 clause 4).

25 Compare articles 9 of the Rechtsschool Statutes (Governor General's Decree dated 29-1-1909

was considerably lower than the capacity of the OSVIAs – the Rechtsschool could accommodate a total of 72 students (in both programmes, that is), while the three OSVIAs at Magelang, Bandung and Probolinggo together had 420 places available, the latter figure rising further with the establishment, in 1910, of three new OSVIAs at Serang, Madiun and Blitar.[26]

The tutoring of students was not confined to lessons – the staff were instructed to 'nurture and develop morals and virtues' in their extracurricular contact with the students, too.[27] These were required either to board at the school's living quarters (where each had a room to himself, in contrast to boarding Osvians) or to lodge with a European family approved by the Supervisory Committee.[28] The boarding part of the course was not to become 'a simple matter of sharing digs' but had to amount to 'an institution for joint upbringing'.[29]

---

no. 14, *Stb.* no. 93) and 7 of the OSVIA Statutes (included in part B of the Governor General's Decree dated 5-10-1908 no. 1, *Stb.* no. 593). The conditions for exemption from the tuition fees, in case of limited means, were also much less harsh for the OSVIA than for the Rechtsschool. OSVIA students from families with an income of less than Dfl 150 p.c.m. could attend free of charge, provided they showed 'good aptitude' (OSVIA Statutes art. 7 clause 4). Free tuition at the Rechtsschool, however, initially was only granted to those students who displayed 'exceptional aptitude and outstanding character', as assessed by the Supervisory Committee (Rechtsschool Statutes art. 9 clause 4), though this particular rule was relaxed over time (*Stb.* 1913, no. 379; compare Neytzell de Wilde 1913:98). A second difference was that siblings at the OSVIA qualified for a fee reduction (art. 7 clause 1), an arrangement which was absent from the Rechtsschool Statutes. (This meant that, with two sons attending the OSVIA and an income of Dfl 300 per month, school fees of Dfl 6.50 per month were due, whereas the same two sons boarding at the Rechtsschool would, in principle, cost Dfl 70 per month.) It should be noted, though, that the OSVIA had a seven-year curriculum, one year more than the Rechtsschool. And it was possible, at both the OSVIA and the Rechtsschool, for the normal rates to be disregarded 'due to exceptional circumstances' (compare articles 9 clause 3 of the Rechtsschool Statutes and 7 clause 5 of those of the OSVIA).

26 Compare articles 3 clause 2 of the Rechtsschool Statutes and 3 clause 1 of those of the OSVIA; also see footnote 11.

27 Rechtsschool Statutes art. 7. According to a circular from the Supervisory Committee dated 31-3-1909, the Rechtsschool would 'provide an education ensuring that the general knowledge necessary and the understanding of the law required are achieved, while the organization of the course, extending to the living quarters for the boarders, is of such a nature that integrity, independence and impartiality in respect of all will be promoted amongst and instilled into the students with good result' (circular Supervisory Committee, cited in Neytzell de Wilde 1929:28-9).

28 Rechtsschool Statutes art. 8 clause 1 and Lev 1976:151. Boarding was not mandatory for Osvians, though accommodation could be made available to students whose parents resided elsewhere (OSVIA Statutes art. 3 clause 3). In 1922 it became possible for graduates of the five-year Hoogere Burger School (HBS, Higher Civilian School) or of an equivalent course to enroll in the Rechtsschool's evening programme, lasting two years, and to sit the external candidates' final examination. Kan Teng Tjoan had already done so in 1920 (*Gedenkboek Rechtsschool* 1929:86, 92).

29 Gobée and Adriaanse 1957:510; compare *De wording der Rechtsschool* 1929:41. The idea was to pre-empt situations such as had occurred at the Instituut voor de Javaansche Taal (Institute for the Javanese Language) at Surakarta (1832-43, for more information, see Fasseur 1993:60-9) and the STOVIA. At the latter establishment insufficient supervision had given the students free rein

Fig. 6. A room in the living quarters of the Rechtsschool
(*Gedenkboek Rechtsschool* 1929: opposite p. 50)

A resident teacher was in charge of the daily supervision of the living quarters; the housekeeping was carried out by a European woman.[30] The below fragment of Daniel Lev's interview with M. Besar Martokoesoemo, LL.M, who took the exams in 1915 and would later become the first Indonesian advocate, paints a picture of daily life at the school:

> The schedule was very strict. They awoke early to bathe, eat, and off to lectures. Then back to the dormitory for study in the early afternoon, food, a nap, a walk in the Koningsplein, back to study. He laughed as he recounted how they were taught to eat with Dutch manners, taught to dance. (Lev 1976:151.)

The Rechtsschool not only educated its students but raised them with the manners and the etiquette of the Dutch in the Netherlands East Indies. The Supervisory Committee actively encouraged teachers to invite their pupils to

to spend their leisure time mostly in the *kampong*, in the company of dubious characters, with a detrimental effect on the 'development of their character and moral uprightness' that could only be guessed at (Cohen Stuart 1907:1338). Compare Besar Martokoesoemo in Lev 1976:151.

30 Lev 1976:151; Rechtsschool Statutes art. 2 clause 4; *Gedenkboek Rechtsschool* 1929:91, 98. By way of comparison: at the STOVIA two retired soldiers supervised the living quarters, which accommodated approximately 150 males aged between twelve and thirty (Cohen Stuart 1907:1337-8).

high tea or to take turns in having them over for supper, 'so that they may thus become exposed to Western family life' (Van Helsdingen 1929b:71; compare Neytzell de Wilde 1913:99). The future *rechtskundige* had to be eased away as much as possible from his indigenous background.[31] The preparatory programme, introduced at the suggestion of the Snouck Hurgronje Committee, was intended not only to lay the foundation for a successful negotiation of the law programme (in those days, very few native youngsters were admitted to the Hoogere Burger School (HBS, Higher Civilian School, the only institute for secondary education in the Indies),[32] but also to have expert staff begin to guide the pupils while still impressionable, in their teens, and to keep them away from the 'Native methods of education of the old guard' (Gobée and Adriaanse 1957:510).

The 'European upbringing' is reflected in the extracurricular activities recorded in the *Gedenkboek Rechtsschool* (Rechtsschool Memorial Book). The students engaged in debate ('so many heads, so many points of view') in the 'Rederijkerskamer' (Chamber of Rhetoric) on the topics of Bandung as the seat of the Rechtshoogeschool, on whether a man could love two or more women at the same time, on the relationship between the church and the state and on whether 'it was permitted for Indonesian girls to dance in a European manner' (*Gedenkboek Rechtsschool* 1929:61-2, 68). They enjoyed a 'swinging party' at 'De Gezelligheid',[33] the oldest school society, played a round at the chess club, played football or tennis or exercised on the parallel bars or the rings at the gym club 'Barbaar' (Barbarian) (Hadi 1929; Boeto 1929). They contributed

31 Both the Supervisory Committee of the Rechtsschool and the colonial government had misgivings about 'Islam', from a twofold perspective – on the one hand, the objective of inviting students into the homes of teachers was to imprint upon them a picture of Western, *monogamous* family life – here, students would be able to experience 'the exalted position that was generally assumed by the European woman, which would be a shining example in their mind's eye and might arouse in them the desire in the future also to shape such an environment for themselves, over which just a single woman, instead of several, whether concomitantly or successively, would hold gentle sway' (Van Helsdingen 1929b:71). On the other hand, they were apprehensive about causing affront to (Muslim) students and their parents should Western family life be too overtly Christian, for example by saying grace or reading Holy Scripture at the dinner table. For this reason, Van Helsdingen, apparently known as a devout Christian, was allowed to hold tea parties but not to invite students to his table. He had been requested, initially, to have students over for dinner and dispense with Christian custom but Van Helsdingen refused these terms and eventually did invite the students on passing the course (Van Helsdingen 1929b:71-3). Van Helsdingen (1929b:75) speaks of a '*phobic* anxiety over Islam'.

32 The syllabus comprised Dutch, French, general history, mathematics and natural sciences (Rechtsschool Statutes art. 4 clause 1).

33 Roughly translated, something like 'cosy corner'. 'Gezelligheid' denotes an atmosphere of warmth, comfort, good company and a good time. The notion is held to be typically Dutch and does not translate. It is telling that the first student society formed within the Rechtsschool was given this particular name.

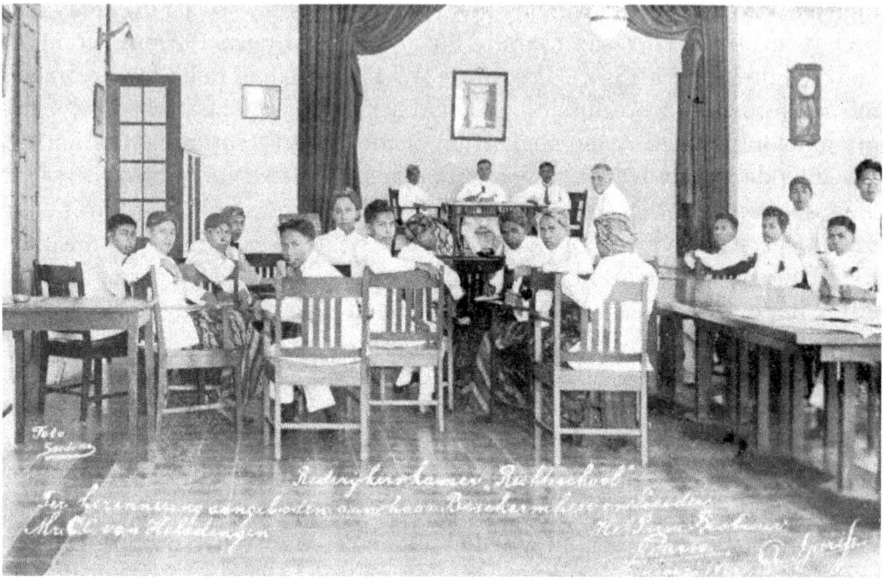

Fig. 7. Gathering of the 'Rederijkerskamer', the debating club (*Gedenkboek Rechtsschool* 1929: opposite p. 62)

Fig. 8. The Rechtsschool football team (source: *Gedenkboek Rechtsschool* 1929: opposite p. 68)

to the school paper, the *Rariteiten-winkel* (Curio Shop). The Javanese students (outnumbering all others), in particular, could while away their Sundays at 'Paromosastro' (possibly named after a treatise on traditional Javanese poetry and music conventions), a society started by students of Javanese that provided courses on that day in Javanese, its literature and song, or at the music society, specializing in Javanese music, song and dance. Thus, the annual gala nights saw 'the performance of European music and theatre as well as episodes from the wayang tales (shadow plays)' (*Gedenkboek Rechtsschool* 1929:68, 83-4).

As mentioned above, the future *rechtskundigen* were being prepared for positions in a world in which Dutch was the principal language – the language spoken among the members of the intersubjective legal community; the language in which legislation and court decisions were drafted; the language, too, of literature expounding on legal theory, discussing branches of law and analysing legislation. Future judicial officers were required to have a thorough command of those Dutch-language theories and sources of law.[34] They were instructed in these subjects in Dutch, the official language of education.[35]

34 The emphasis on professional expertise distinguished the Rechtsschool from the OSVIA. Like the STOVIA, though unlike the OSVIA, that offered a broader spectrum of general studies, the objective of the Rechtsschool was to teach vocational skills. This is evident from, for instance, the exam rules stipulated in the Rechtsschool Statutes. The OSVIA Statutes mention 'public examinations' by way of concluding either the lower or the upper programme, without elaborating further, to which is added that, in determining the results, 'the progress demonstrated in the course of the entire school year [will especially be] taken into account' (OSVIA Statutes art. 10 clause 4). The Rechtsschool Statutes, on the other hand, mention a final examination in all the subjects of the law programme barring Dutch (Rechtsschool Statutes art. 14 clause 3).
Considering the careers open to the graduates from these two types of schools, the difference is obvious. OSVIA school leavers would become employed in the hierarchical structure of the administration machine for Natives and be required to carry out widely divergent tasks. In doing so, the smooth functioning of the machinery would benefit more from qualities such as the ability to improvize and flexibility, in respect of superiors, for example, than from an excellent command of specialized subjects such as law. Administrative officers benefitted particularly from a broad understanding of various subjects and the OSVIA curriculum therefore offered a broad spectrum – the geography and history of the Netherlands East Indies, natural science, arithmetic, algebra, geometry, land survey, freehand drawing, (principles of) law, constitutional and administrative law of the Netherlands East Indies, state economics, plotting and levelling and, finally, line drawing and cartography (OSVIA Statutes art. 5 clause 1).
By contrast, thorough specialist knowledge of the law was essential to *rechtskundigen* – they would, after all, be entrusted with a highly specialized office and were required to operate in a 'closely defined sphere of work' (Gobée and Adriaanse 1957:501). Apart from Malay, the Rechtsschool curriculum comprised the subjects of introduction to law, political science of the Netherlands, constitutional law of the Netherlands East Indies, substantive criminal law of the Netherlands East Indies, the Burgerlijk Wetboek (Civil Code), sections of the Wetboek van Koophandel (Commercial Code), folk law (particularly family and succession law, property law and contract law) and the Inlandsch Reglement (Rechtsschool Statutes art. 4 clause 1).

35 The Rechtsschool Statutes did not dictate an official school language, as opposed to those of the OSVIA. The latter stipulated that Dutch be used except when teaching Malay or the regional

Fig. 9. Bird's-eye view of the Rechtsschool at Pegangsaän, Batavia (in front, the recreation hall; at the back, the school building; to the left and right, the living quarters) (*Gedenkboek Rechtsschool* 1929: opposite p. 38)

In other words, Dutch was the language 'in which they became jurists', in which both the concept and the reality of law took shape in their consciouSness. Indigenous languages hardly figured at all at the Rechtsschool, not even formally, as curriculum subjects.[36] Contrary to OSVIA or STOVIA graduates,

languages (OSVIA Statutes art. 5 clauses 1, 3; compare footnote 36). Such a stipulation presumably was absent from the Rechtsschool Statutes because it was inconceivable for any language *other than Dutch* to be used.

36 Six years of Dutch language and literature and three years of French (throughout the preparatory programme) were in stark contrast to a single year's instruction in Malay, in the final year (Rechtsschool Statutes art. 4 clause 1). The teachers, successively, were G.V. Lettinga, W.B. Regenhardt and F.K. Meeter, all of whom came from the armed forces (lieutenant first class, captain and infantry captain retired, respectively; *Gedenkboek Rechtsschool* 1929:90). There was no final exam in the subject of Dutch, incidentally (attention was paid to 'the skilled expression of concepts in that language'; Rechtsschool Statutes art. 14 clause 3), though there was one in Malay! French had been incorporated into the syllabus by virtue of the 'edification' supposedly inherent in learning a foreign language besides Dutch, as well as of the kinship between Dutch and French law (Gobée and Adriaanse 1957:511). Dutch was a mandatory subject at the OSVIA for the first

for example, *rechtskundigen* would remain professionally bound up with the Dutch language – doctors could use the Malay translations of their textbooks without any impact on the quality of their work, but *rechtskundigen* were tied to the original version of laws and court decisions, in Dutch (see Chapter II). Making intensive use of and producing texts in Dutch would play a pivotal role in the positions they would hold, whether as a registrar or as a chairman of a *landraad*.

While progressing through the course, the lingual repertoire of the students was subject to constant change. Daily life, involving a fixed schedule at fixed places, along with the intensity of the contact between students and teachers, is bound to have encouraged the development of numerous conventions and, correspondingly, social languages and genres (Giddens 1997:70-1; compare Chapter II). There were the languages and genres of the classroom, of the lessons in Dutch or Malay, on the Inlandsch Reglement (Native Code) or the Wetboek van Koophandel (Commercial Code). Languages spoken at mealtimes, during the dash to the classroom or the stroll to the tennis court, the debates at the Chamber of Rhetoric or the do's at 'De Gezelligheid'. Then there were the languages of the corridors of the living quarters and those spoken in each other's rooms or while taking a walk through the town. Dutch will have been spoken, in the main – a form of Dutch that, as a rule, must have complied neatly with the standard applied at school, as the lessons taught in Dutch, the

---

five years, the subject only being taught in the last two 'where necessary' (OSVIA Statutes art. 5 clause 1). Malay and the regional language in question, which meant Sundanese (for Bandung), Javanese (for Magelang) or Javanese together with Madurese (for Probolinggo), were compulsory throughout the seven years of the programme.

The experts involved in founding the Rechtsschool had been at variance on the subject of language instruction. Cohen Stuart had argued in favour of a thorough command of Javanese, Sundanese or Madurese rather than of Malay, which, all said and done, was not the mother tongue of the majority of students. The command of their native language developed at home did not suffice – surely Dutch children were taught Dutch at school? Partly on the basis of the experiences gained in British India, he noted, additionally, that what was expected from the future *rechtskundigen* extended well beyond merely speaking, understanding and writing said languages – they would also be called upon to *translate* rapidly from those languages into Dutch and vice versa so as 'to be able to convey accurately in their mother tongue the provisions of our Dutch statutes and to translate the evidence given by witnesses off the cuff from one language into another' (Cohen Stuart 1907:1345). Snouck Hurgronje, on the other hand, was of the opinion that the students, who would already be native speakers of one native language, would have little difficulty in acquiring the others (Gobée and Adriaanse 1957:497). This opinion was strengthened by his lack of faith in the usefulness, if any, of the translations mentioned by Cohen Stuart, even when the translator proved to be well-trained – as early as 1902, he had written to the Director of Justice, stating that a translation of a regulation into Malay could not 'ever amount to much more than a botch-up' even when carried out by the most skilled of translators (letter dated 29-12-1902, cited in Gobée and Adriaanse 1957:1791, and letter dated 26-5-1896, cited in Gobée and Adriaanse 1957:1785). As far as he was concerned, it was the teaching of law that mattered. See Neytzell de Wilde 1913:100-1.

lessons in Dutch and the fairly close involvement of the staff in the education as well as the upbringing of the future *rechtskundigen* will have had a strong centripetal effect.[37] It was the language of public events but undoubtedly also that of informal meetings and gatherings, of the students spending time together.[38] Dutch not only was a language in which the students were already fairly proficient upon their arrival at the school, it was also the language of the new life upon which all students embarked when admitted to the school.

Of enormous importance, here, is the potent esprit de corps that is bound to have united the Rechtsschool students (and the *rechtskundigen* they became) from the very beginning. They were conscious of being viewed and treated as the 'cream of the crop' of indigenous youngsters.[39] The 'pilgrimage' undertaken by most of the students to the powerhouse of the Netherlands East Indies, Batavia, and their communal lives once there, away from home and hearth, must also have contributed to the team spirit (Anderson 1985:127). Yet the feeling of membership of an exclusive group may, above all, have been inspired by the very nature of the education they were receiving. Their initiation into the law and its foundations, the course itself, that valued highly the nurture of an independent, critical mind – these will have opened up a new perspective on the world at large that differed in important respects from the way in which most students must have perceived colonial reality before embarking on the course.[40]

The classes, the legal literature and the conversations with teachers also had a profound personal effect on the students. Being internally persuasive texts, particular sections are bound to have permeated the process of growing awareness they underwent and to have been absorbed into their verbal-ideological horizon (compare Chapter II). Here was a new language, one that

[37] See Chapter II. Conversely, the languages and genres of the legal literature, of the sources of law and of the teachers are likely to have found their way into the utterances of the students (and of the *rechtskundigen* they later became) related to their studies (and profession, respectively).

[38] Javanese may have been spoken occasionally in small groups of students of Javanese origin (the majority by far) when discussing the subjects to which that language pertained, such as family, home, childhood and the like. Malay will have been used mostly outside of the school. The influences of discourse other than that in the Dutch language will have diminished in direct proportion to the degree to which students became 'eased away' from the home culture.

[39] In the interview with Lev cited above, Besar Martokoesoemo described the difference with the STOVIA students: 'He mentioned the differences between the Rechtsschool and the medical school for Indonesian students. Rechtsschool students got twenty-five guilders a month, private rooms in the dormitory, good food, and a good introduction to Dutch culture. Medical students got fifteen guilders a month, slept many to the room, dressed sloppily, and got poor food and care.' (Lev 1976:151.)

[40] Van Helsdingen 1929c:63. Compare Lev (1972:256-7), who points out that the national Indonesian legal community developed by and large in the big towns. Rather than the *droit coûtumier* (customary law), the unifying factor was the *droit écrit* (written law).

Fig. 10. The last cohort of Rechtsschool graduates (in the middle, Moehamad Hamid, the first *rechtskundige* without a university degree to make chairman of a *landraad* – see footnote 44) (*Gedenkboek Rechtsschool* 1929: opposite table of contents)

spoke of the equality of all citizens before an impartial judge, one that was translatable into the languages of 'all civilized peoples', also one (capable of being) used to generate power. This language was Dutch. Speaking it therefore cannot but have been an important team characteristic of the students and alumni of the Rechtsschool.[41]

The school trained a total of 211 students to become *rechtskundigen*.[42] In

41 See Anderson (1985:127): 'Much the most important thing about language is its capacity for generating imagined communities, building in effect *particular solidarities*'.

42 Representing approximately one third of all admissions in the history of the school (Lev 1976:146). The number of *rechtskundigen* is derived from the chronicle of the years 1909-26 included in the memorial book, plus the number of school leavers in the years 1927 and 1928 as listed (*Gedenkboek Rechtsschool* 1929:85-7, 93-7). There is a discrepancy between the list of school leavers in 1922 and 1923 and the chronicle, of one and two students in the respective years. Of the 211 *rechtskundigen*, 192 were full-time students who completed the entire programme and nineteen were external candidates. Judging by the names, some twenty non-native students took the course, comprising twelve foreign orientals (the names are Chinese) and about nine Europeans, most of them as external candidates (*Gedenkboek Rechtsschool* 1929:92-7). The lists of full-time

1929, the year in which the memorial book was brought out, at least 130 of them were employed by judicial bodies.[43] Others, the previously quoted Besar Martokoesoemo amongst them, had been in the employ of a court but had resigned. Some had gone on to achieve a master of laws at Leiden University or the Batavia Rechtshoogeschool and had thereafter found employment outside of the judiciary (Lev 1976:153-4). Within the judiciary, *rechtskundigen* not only worked at the *landraden* (from 1925, holding the office of chairmen, too), but also at the *landgerechten* (petty crimes courts) as *fiscaal-griffiers* (secretary to the court) or as judges, if boasting the master's title; at the *raden van justitie* (councils of justice), either as *ambtenaren ter beschikking* (official seconded) or as members; at the Hooggerechtshof, the prosecution service and the Prosecutor General's Office.[44]

## *The* landraad *in 1910*

Having completed the Rechtsschool, the *rechtskundige* would embark on the next phase of his education, at some *landraad* on Java, Madura or the Outer Territories.[45] He had become versed in the theory of the law but lacked insight

students and external candidates contain a single name only that is definitely female – Miss F. Opperman (external candidate, final exam 1924; *Gedenkboek Rechtsschool* 1929:92).

43 This figure only relates to the 192 full-time students. The positions held by the external candidate alumni are not given in the memorial book. At the time the book came out, four *rechtskundigen* were deceased, their last positions also having been at a court of law (*Gedenkboek Rechtsschool* 1929:93-4). In the years of 1928-29 one hundred *rechtskundigen* were employed at the various *landraden* – 41 as chairman, associate chairman or deputy chairman, 24 as member and 35 as official seconded. At the *landgerecht* 23 school leavers had found employment, three of whom as *landrechter* (petty crimes court judge) and nineteen as *fiscaal-griffier*. Ten *rechtskundigen* had been appointed to the *raden van justitie*, of whom one as a member (the future president of the Indonesian Supreme Court, Koesoemah Atmadja, who passed his exams in 1919) and nine as official seconded, with an eleventh alumnus also employed by a *raad van justitie* though seconded to the prosecution department. Including the members of the various *landraden*, in 1928-29, no less than 69 Rechtsschool alumni, more than a third of the total, held a judgeship.

44 Van Helsdingen 1929a:13; also see footnote 3. The first *rechtskundige* without a university degree to make chairman of a *landraad* was Moehamad (Mohamad) Hamid (see Fig. 10). On 16-1-1925 he was appointed chairman of the *landraad* at Kraksaän on East Java. Prior to taking up this post, he had held the office of deputy chairman of a *landraad* (another first), the Batavia and Tangerang one, since 23-6-1920. Hamid, who died in 1958, was to be paid tribute to, in *Hukum*, in that same year as the first *rechtskundige* to have served as a *landraad* judge. Gondokoesoemo, who achieved the master of laws at Leiden University after completing the Rechtsschool, and who, in 1922, became the first *rechtskundige* with a doctorate, was appointed chairman of the *landraad* at Pacitan on East Java in 1925 (*Regeeringsalmanak* 1924, II and 1926, II). By virtue of their chairmanships, Hamid and Gondokoesoemo also held the office of residency judge for their respective areas of jurisdiction (see footnote 13).

45 In 1928 *rechtskundigen* were not only employed at Java and Madura, but also at Sumatra

into its practice in court, into the functioning of the various procedures and into the application of documents. Modules such as 'moot court' and 'legal clinic' had not formed part of the programme of study so 'thinking and writing like a lawyer' and 'the tricks of the trade' could only be learnt through hands-on experience in the daily practice of the law.[46] As a rule, the 'newly outed' judicial officer, seconded to the president of the *landraad*, was put to work in the *griffie* (court registry), often in the role of *(buitengewoon) substituut-griffier* (deputy registrar (extraordinary)).[47] He would normally be appointed *fiscaal-griffier* at a *landgerecht* at some later date and would subsequently fulfil the roles of member, deputy chairman and chairman of a *landraad*.[48]

The employment of native *rechtskundigen* is bound to have had a significant impact on the status quo of the *landraad*. Articles written by civil servants engaged in the administration of the interior and in the judiciary, in Netherlands East Indies periodicals such as the *Tijdschrift voor Binnenlandsch Bestuur* (Journal of Administration of the Interior) and the *Indisch Tijdschrift van het Recht* (Indies Law Journal) as well as presentations held at the Indisch Genootschap (Indies Society) in The Hague, afford a glimpse into the prevalent hierarchy before that time.[49] Countless articles deal with the roles performed

---

(Padang, Palembang, Pangkalpinang, Pematang Siantar, Sawahlunto, Tanjung Balei and Tebing Tinggi), Borneo (Banjarmasin and Kandangan), Celebes (Makassar, Bantaeng) and the Moluccas (Ternate) (*Gedenkboek Rechtsschool* 1929:93-7).

46 See Chapter II and W.F. Wertheim, who describes having to familiarize himself with the 'official style of writing letters' in his first period of office at the Justice Department (Wertheim and Wertheim-Gijse Weenink 1991:125).

47 This is how the *rechtskundige* mentioned as the first of the school leavers, Soedirman (1912), began his career in the judiciary, in 1913 – as a *buitengewoon substituut-griffier* at the *landraad* of Banyumas and Cilacap (*Regeeringsalmanak* 1914, II:76). Native *rechtskundigen* were not alone in obtaining their first post at a registry – European judicial officers, too, set their first steps on the legal ladder there. The *Regeeringsalmanak* records J. Vriesendorp as Soedirman's colleague, for example. Europeans were more commonly employed by a *raad van justitie* or at the Hooggerechtshof, however, though the *landraad* was a possible domain for them, too (compare Boekhoudt 1916:327, Jonkman 1971:50 and Van Wageningen 1920:263).

48 In addition to the *Regeeringsalmanak*, the book *Orang Indonesia jang terkemoeka di Djawa*, published in 1944 by the Japanese military authorities (Gunseikanbu) and reissued in 1973, is a rich and easy-reference source. This first Indonesian 'Who is who?' lists all Indonesians having enjoyed higher education and/or a special position in society, along with their date and place of birth and successive places of employment. These people's names are ordered according to their sphere of work at the time of recording the data (for more on this publication, see Anderson 1961:20-1). For this work, the 1973 reprint has been used.

49 In 1915 the *Indisch Tijdschrift van het Recht* became the publication of the Nederlandsch-Indische Juristen Vereeniging (Netherlands East Indies Jurists' Society). It had previously been published under the title of *Recht in Nederlandsch-Indië* and incorporated the existing *Indisch Weekblad van het Recht* (Dekker and Van Katwijk 1992:9). The legal journals published in the Netherlands East Indies and in Indonesia from 1849 to 1958 are listed in Dekker and Van Katwijk 1992:1-12.

Fig. 11. Indramayu landraad, 1901-02 (behind the table, *landraad* president J.M.Ch.E. le Rütte (presumably); in front of the table, the accused (in the middle) and two witnesses; on the right of the table registrar J.M. de Wendt (5th from the right), *jaksa* Raden Soedjalma (4th from the right) and the *penghulu* (chief administrator of the mosque); behind the registrar the bailiff, Wangsa Wardaja; to the left of the table, two *landraad* members) (KITLV collection no. 19590)

by the chairman of the *landraad*, its members, the registrar and the *jaksa*, both in their individual capacities and in relation to one another. In the period that saw the first appointments of *rechtskundigen* to the *landraad*, the chairman in many respects held a unique position. With the possible exception of a deputy chairman or chairman extraordinary, he was the only *totok* (full-blooded Dutchman) and the only officer of the court qualified in law. The functionaries of the registry office, including the registrar himself, usually were of Indo-European origin[50] whereas, by legal provision, both the *jaksa* and the members

50 See part II of the successive *regeeringsalmanakken* and also Boekhoudt 1916:335, Mounier 1900:150, Idema 1938:172 and Wirjono Prodjodikoro 1974:14. Apart from Soedirman and Vriesendorp (see footnote 47), the following persons are mentioned as *substituut-griffier* at Cilacap: H.A. Meijer, R. Scheerder and P.J.H. Lapré.

of the *landraad* were recruited from amongst the indigenous population.[51] As was the case in all of society, lower ranking staff (such as scribes) normally also came from amongst the Natives.

By comparison with the staff, whose entire lives and careers might centre on the *landraad,* the chairman was a mere passer-by. He would stay for a few years and upon stepping down would be replaced by a new chairman, another passer-by. The job afforded no opportunity to grow roots, to familiarize oneself or get to grips with the lives and concerns of the *blijvers* (settlers). Over and above the limitations imposed by both the period of time spent there and the gap between the colonial castes, his socialization was hampered by the language difference. In court, most *landraad* chairmen employed a form of Malay.[52] Even if they could speak the 'local language' (Javanese, for example), studied during their training in Delft or Leiden and put to use in successive postings on Central or East Java, this would have made little difference to their relationships with other civil servants at the *landraad.* Defining command of language in terms of having at one's disposal a certain repertoire of social languages and speech genres (see Chapter II), and taking into account the colonial set-up, one realizes that communication must, by and large, have been limited to those business relations that were strictly necessary.

The chairman of a *landraad,* one could therefore state, operated amidst a network of social relations, hierarchies and loyalties that largely escaped his powers of observation. As with many other aspects of colonial life, two separate though occasionally intertwined worlds existed alongside one another. The activities of the *blijvers,* not a jurist among them, were governed primarily by considerations and interests other than the legal-official pragmatism that dictated the chairman's professional conduct. Moreover, the defendants and the parties in civil proceedings also belonged to this alien, non-Dutch speaking world, a circumstance that substantially hampered the reliability of the judicial process.

The relationship between the chairman and the registrar is examined in several articles. In terms of his education, the former far outshone the latter, the master of laws prerequisite upon the chairmanship making the *kleinambtenaarsexamen* (petty official's certificate) required for the job of registrar pale into insignificance.[53] Conversely, the registrar usually was the *landraad*'s

[51] For more on the *jaksa,* see art. 62, 92 clause 6 RO and art. 55-64 IR; for more on the *landraad* members, see art. 92 clause 1 and 6 RO.

[52] See footnote 7, Immink 1889:362, Mounier 1900:154-5, A. van den Bergh 1902:238-9, Cohen Stuart 1907:1330-1, Lev 1976:159.

[53] Idema 1938:171. From 1869 onwards, the administrative officers who, by virtue of their office, carried out the task of chairman of a *landraad,* were replaced by jurists (*Stb.* 1869, no. 47 for Java and Madura; in the Outer Territories, the substitution took place on the basis of a string of provisions enacted between 1874-1908. See Dekker and Van Katwijk 1993a:49).

Fig. 12. Madiun *landraad,* ca 1920 (KITLV collection no. 2640)

most thoroughly experienced civil servant. Reaching his position commonly involved a lengthy career with that same *landraad*. Year upon year of routinely fulfilling his duties (such as updating the court records, overseeing the despatch and receipt of documents, recording the proceedings and reimbursing the witnesses – see Boekhoudt 1916:337 and Winckel 1920:171-6), coupled with his excellent command of the local languages, made the registrar the pivot around which the *landraad* revolved. He knew the procedures of the Inlandsch Reglement inside out, as well as all the time limits, formalities and tariffs applicable to the day-to-day running of the court.[54] By contrast, the president of a *landraad* never remained in the same post for more than a few years before being transferred to his next position. And when green, his expertise in the actual practice of the Inlandsch Reglement, which had not been an examination subject, was also inferior to that of the registrar (Van Wageningen 1920:264).

[54] Idema 1938:172; compare Van Wageningen 1920:264-6. Some registrars and other registry officials cashed in on their informal position of power by charging considerable sums of money for drawing up certain documents (Rutgers 1911:135, 145).

However experienced a registrar became in the affairs of the *landraad*, he was still not a jurist.[55] This is abundantly clear from the problems encountered in writing the reports of the court sessions, for which the registrar was responsible (art. 190-1, 314 IR). In the case of criminal proceedings, the official report and the decision in the case had to be sent off 'for examination' to the *raad van justitie* (art. 301t Reglement op de strafvordering (hereafter Sv, Regulations for criminal proceedings), 427 IR; compare Rutgers 1911:461). Writing the report in the Dutch language or rather, in a manner of Dutch acceptable to the legally trained chairman, presented many a registrar with considerable difficulty. As a result, with the increasing workload of the *landraad*, sizeable backlogs in the despatches to the *raad van justitie* ensued.[56] From the dawn of the twentieth century, therefore, it became customary for the chairman to dictate the report and the decision, either to the registrar himself or to one of his registry colleagues.[57] But the dictation, if carried out in the course of the hearing, continuously interrupted the proceedings in question.[58] Dictating did not intrinsically

55 The registrar may not have been trained in the law, he nevertheless had an understanding of criminal procedure. Mounier (1900:150) mentions incidences of a registrar submitting a report of a criminal offence substantiated by two identical witness statements. In reality, the two witnesses may have had a completely different version of events but, it was argued, an accused could only be found guilty on the basis of two corresponding statements.

56 Pilon (1920:30-1) lists the circulars on this topic sent by the Hooggerechtshof to the chairmen of the *landraad* in the period 1884-1916. Younger chairmen in particular experienced these circulars, from both the Hooggerechtshof and the *raden van justitie*, as extremely stressful (Van Wageningen 1916:317-8; compare Idema 1938:184-5).

57 The solution of dictating the reports had been suggested in a Hooggerechtshof circular of 1907 (Pilon 1920:30-1). Justice W. Boekhoudt, retiring from the Hooggerechtshof, provided the following description: '[I]n the afternoon of the court day, the reports of the hearings as well as the decisions [were] dictated, so that on the very same day everything was ready, in draft form, to be copied in neat over the next two days by the same functionary of the registry, if necessary assisted by lower ranking staff' (Boekhoudt 1916:336; also see Pilon 1920:30-2). Boekhoudt's 'same day' organized method cannot have been the norm, as is apparent from the persistent backlogs. Apart from dictation being necessary because the registrar was insufficiently proficient in Dutch, it may also have been the case that the inexperienced *Dutch substituut-griffier* (customarily a student judicial officer on work placement) failed to understand a word of the local language and/or Malay spoken during the trial (Rutgers 1911:141).

58 See Rutgers (1911:141-2): 'In my opinion, this dictation business is wrong entirely, as it continually interrupts the proceedings which thereby lose their flow; furthermore, the hearing becomes terribly long-winded, especially for the Native members who are half asleep by the time a witness statement has been dictated and with each new witness appearing before the court, they have all but forgotten the previous one's story. When putting questions to the witnesses, the President is all the while considering how to dictate the question and the answer he receives, resulting in more care being taken over the beautiful report than over the examination itself. If the President has no command of the local language, a witness statement may have to be repeated twice over – first the witness tells his story in the local language, then the *jaksa* puts it to the court in Malay, then the President puts it into Dutch in his dictation; for the members, especially, this seems to me to be intolerable.' Rutgers advised the president to note down the

solve the problem either, merely shifting the burden from the registrar to the chairman of the *landraad*. Lack of time available for dictation meant that some reports were left for months on end. A perpetual conflict of interests thus arose between the chairman, keen to hear new cases in order to comply with the time limits set for pre-trial detention and other such considerations, and the registrar, bound by the time limits set for despatching the records for examination and thus keen to hear fewer cases (Pilon 1920:32-7).

The role of the *jaksa*, too, has been widely discussed by administrative and judicial officers.[59] Although the *jaksa* or *hoofddjaksa* (head *jaksa*)[60] was referred to as the 'native prosecutor' and his office as the *openbaar ministerie* (prosecution service), his official responsibilities showed little resemblance to those of the prosecutors at the European courts and their prosecution service. Whether a *landraad* heard criminal cases or civil ones, the session was only valid provided the *jaksa* was present (art. 92 clause 6 RO). In civil cases, the *landraad* had to hear the counsel of the *jaksa* before deciding upon the matter (art. 164 clause 1 IR; compare Rutgers 1911:191-292). Contrary to the officers of the European prosecution service, however, the *jaksa* played no role in either of the processes of bringing cases to trial or executing a sentence; and he was answerable to the *resident* and the chairman of the *landraad* for the detection of crime and the investigation at trial, respectively.[61] The remit of the *jaksa* encompassed detecting offences punishable by law, questioning the suspect and, during the trial, also the witnesses, advising on the matter during the deliberation and applying for a retrial (*revisie*) in the case of sentenced criminal offences (*misdrijven*) and for appeal review (*hoger beroep*) in the case of summary ones (*overtredingen*) (art. 58-60, 63, 263, 317b, 346 IR; art. 283 Sv).

Initially, according to the original text of the Inlandsch Reglement (*Staatsblad* (hereafter *Stb.*, State Gazette) 1848, no. 16), the authority of the *jaksa* had been considerably greater. He had played an important role in the pre-trial investigation, the phase in which the nature and scope of the proceedings would be determined and evidence would be gathered.[62] In practice, though, the

main points only, so as to enable him to check the report later on. In his view, this would more than compensate for 'any mistakes in language and style creeping into the non-dictated court reports' (Rutgers 1911:142).

59 For extensive information on the *landraad* in practice, see Wormser 1946.

60 The Inlandsch Reglement draws a distinction between the titles of *hoofddjaksa* and *djaksa* (in Dutch spelling), the former applying to those holding the position in a residency capital, the latter to those doing so anywhere else (art. 55-57 IR). See Rutgers 1911:33 and Idema 1938:76-7, 79.

61 Idema 1938:68-70, 83-4; compare Jonkers 1940:28-31. For more on the development of the office of the *jaksa* over the years, see Jonkers 1940:66-87 and Driessen 1897:33-6, 164-262.

62 One of the tasks of the *jaksa* was to draw up the *akte van beschuldiging* (the indictment), the instrument that determined the legal scope of the procedure (art. 246 in conjunction with 273 IR; also see Idema 1938:71).

*jaksa* frequently acted in such flagrant breach of the legal provisions that, as the *landraad* gained a more legal footing (for example by having the office of chairman held by a lawyer) in the second half of the nineteenth century, his authority was gradually reduced (Idema 1938:71-3, 75). Furthermore, with a particular view to training the *jaksa*, the subjects 'Principles of Law' and 'Constitutional and Administrative Law of the Netherlands East Indies' were introduced into the curriculum of the *Hoofdenschool* (Chiefs' school, school for the native elite) or OSVIA, as it came to be called.[63]

In a formal legal sense, the scope of the authority of a *jaksa* was limited during trial, too. In civil cases, he was required just once to provide counsel and in criminal ones, he was allowed to read the translated *akte van verwijzing* (comparable to a summons) and to question the accused and the witnesses 'to establish the truth' (art. 245, 263 IR). Nevertheless, it was the *jaksa* rather than the chairman who often played the lead role in the court room (Rutgers 1911:139; compare Idema 1938:80-1), a role reversal that sprang from the requirement for an interpreter laid down in the Inlandsch Reglement, should the accused or a witness have insufficient command of the language in which the judicial investigation was conducted (art. 275 clause 1 IR). Though officially contrary to the regulations, it had become common practice to call upon the *jaksa*, semi-officially, to interpret.[64] The most customary communication method was for the chairman to put the questions to the *jaksa* in Malay and for the *jaksa* to pass these on, translated into the local language, to the accused or witnesses and vice versa.[65] In reality, however, the chairman often had no notion of what passed between the *jaksa* and the interviewees, to the extent that

63 See footnote 11 and Driessen 1897:259-62. According to Cohen Stuart (1907:1325), 'the Native civil servants from the OSVIAs, in particular, [are proving] their worth to the Prosecution Service. In performing their tasks, they show evidence of great astuteness and a flair for dealing with legal issues, although by the very nature of an OSVIA, aimed at training administrative officers rather than law graduates, they possess but a scant notion of the law.' Compare A. van den Bergh 1900:470.

64 Immink 1889:362-3; compare Rutgers 1911:138-40, 397 and Winckel 1920:44. This custom was contrary to the legal provisions because those barred from giving evidence (the *jaksa* amongst them) were also disqualified from interpreting (art. 275 clause 2 IR; see Immink 1889:363). Also see Fasseur 1993:242.

65 Or in Cohen Stuart's critical phrasing (1907:1330-1): 'The performance of a court session in the Indies therefore comes down to: a judge posing questions in Malay, in which language he cannot but inadequately formulate his thoughts; a civil servant of the Prosecution Service who has an inadequate understanding of Malay, frequently fails to grasp the tenor of the question posed and therefore cannot but relay it inadequately to the accused or the witnesses; an accused or witness who often fails to understand the question properly; a civil servant of the P.S. who transmits the answer to his best ability, though frequently containing some small, apparently insignificant twisting of the words, in inadequate Malay, which the judge often fails to understand properly'. See footnote 7. The 'translation chain' of Dutch into Malay into Javanese and vice versa also occurred – see Sibenius Trip 1905:10, for example.

Fig. 13. Binjai *landraad,* ca 1930-33 (KITLV collection no. 51732)

Fig. 14. Purbolinggo *landraad,* 1937 (KITLV collection no. 30628)

D. Mounier, in his presentation to the Indisch Genootschap in 1900, lamented that 'the *jaksa*, after all, [is] well-nigh the only person who has conduct of the case with the accused and, [in civil cases], frequently also with the plaintiffs and the defendants'.[66] Both Immink's report that 'judicial investigations [...] usually [are] held in the Malay language' and Rutgers's statement that 'the trial is conducted [...] in the native language', are true – the former from the point of view of the *landraad* president; the latter from that of the interviewees (see Immink 1889:362 and Rutgers 1911:138).

Rutgers (1911:138-9) paints an interesting picture of the complexity of communication during trial and of the considerations involved in the chairman's choice of language:

> Java and Madura know many *landraad* chairmen who are fairly proficient in the native language, or have an adequate understanding, at least. They do not require every word spoken during the hearing to be translated. The Chairman's own communication with the Natives is problematic, however. Even should he know the language well, a nervous witness will *never* understand a European, though he might utter exactly the same words as the *jaksa*. Most Presidents therefore delegate the communication with the accused to the *jaksa* in that they supply the latter with the questions to be put; the answers do not require translation if the President understands them. In the opposite scenario, whereby the President does not understand the language spoken by the Natives, the *jaksa* is also called upon to translate their responses. For the sake of convenience, so as to maintain the thread of the proceedings, he will put a number of questions in a row and will translate these along with the answers supplied in one continuous batch. During the question and answer session, therefore, the President remains idle. Only once the *jaksa* has completed a series of questions and is translating back will the President become aware of the nature and content of the questions the *jaksa* has asked. Frequently, these are questions deemed rather incorrect by the President which he would never, in that manner, that is, have put himself. It goes without saying that, in the process, the President's control over the case is doomed to failure.

The world in which the *jaksa* lived and worked was not the same one the chairman inhabited. In his last two years at the OSVIA, the *jaksa* might have

[66] Mounier 1900:149. Compare with Cohen Stuart (1907:1330): 'Many judicial officers in the Indies claim to have a sufficient command of the local language to be able to "follow" the interpreting and to ascertain whether questions and answers are relayed properly. It is hard to believe this, however. One who has no *full* command of a language, has no facility for judging the accuracy of interpreting.' Boekhoudt (1916:334) reports that, for this very reason, he never relied on the *jaksa* alone to carry out the interpreting but also involved the members and the *penghulu* (in so far as these had demonstrated their suitability) – both of which solutions nevertheless were also contrary to the IR (see footnote 64). J. Sibenius Trip, the chairman of a circuit court, therefore appointed a clerk to function as the interpreter, which arrangement was in keeping with the regulations (Sibenius Trip 1905:10).

received instruction in the two legal subjects mentioned and perhaps he sometimes consulted Haase and Boekhoudt's well-known Dutch-Malay handbook on preliminary criminal investigations.[67] But he was not a jurist, any more than the registrar; like the latter, he was neither familiar with the legal meaning system nor did he speak the basic legal language (see Chapter II). A *jaksa* often came from a job as administrative officer (an assistant *wedono* (district head), for example), which remained an attractive proposition, particularly in view of the higher remuneration and the greater degree of freedom (Rutgers 1911:33; compare Driessen 1897:259 and Idema 1938:82). A few years of *jaksa*-hood combined well with a civil service career. By contrast with European prosecutors, the *jaksa* enjoyed no independence from the administrative power whatsoever – *hoofddjaksa* were answerable directly to the *resident* and to the *assistent-resident* for the police (where appointed); *jaksa* were answerable to the *resident* (or, in residency departments, to the *assistent-resident*) and the regents (art. 56-57 IR). Translating the chairman's questions and the defendant's answers confirmed his position as a cog in the civil service apparatus. Moreover, the 'impartiality' of the *jaksa* during the trial was hardly helped by his having played a central role in the pre-trial investigation that had resulted in the accused having to stand trial (see Cohen Stuart 1907:1330). Did it not behove, then, to finish what he had started?

The multitude of complaints about the performance of the *jaksa* testifies to a set of priorities, loyalties and attitudes towards the administration of justice that were entirely his own; there were complaints about *jaksa* who arranged for different witnesses to provide coinciding statements;[68] about a *jaksa* who replaced a lost piece of evidence himself (Idema 1838:75); about both trick questions (Rutgers 1911:139; Sibenius Trip 1905:10; Idema 1938:198) and lead-

67 The *Handleiding ten gebruike bij het voorloopig onderzoek in strafzaken/Boekoe Penoentoen akan dipakai oléh prijaji2 dalam pemeriksaan 'voorloopig onderzoek'* (Handbook to be used in the preliminary investigation of crimes) by W.F. Haase and W. Boekhoudt was issued three times between 1904-08. (These data are derived from the third edition, which was published privately, available from G. Kolff & Co. at Batavia.) The sixth edition was brought out in 1928.

68 Mounier 1900:149. Sibenius Trip (1905:11) relates the following about his arrival in Kediri on the eve of a trial: 'I arrived at Kediri the night before, around eleven o'clock, and found the *hoofddjaksa* waiting for me in my lodgings. I asked him whether the witnesses had all arrived, to which he replied in the affirmative. But, he said, you cannot hold court tomorrow and to my inquiry: whyever not? he answered "seksi-seksi belom di tjotjokken" ('the testimony of the witnesses has not yet been synchronized). As I did not understand this particular expression, the clerk explained to me: because the witnesses haven't been tested on their lessons yet, wherefore the *hoofddjaksa* does not know whether the witnesses remember what was written down as their statements during the preliminary investigation. I then instructed the *hoofddjaksa* to refrain from this "tjotjokken" ('synchronizing') both on this occasion and on any future ones. When I arrived in the Kaboepaten the next morning, I encountered a most bleary-eyed *hoofddjaksa*. It would seem that he had been "tjotjokken" all night long.'

ing questions[69] being put to the accused; about arranging witness statements as well as a confession concerning a crime that had not taken place[70] and so forth. It comes as no surprise, therefore, that the Dutch civil servants engaged in the administration of justice generally entertained a great deal of scepticism towards the *jaksa*.[71] The chairman of the *landraad*, incapable of obtaining an accurate picture himself of the true events surrounding the charges before him, in many cases had no option but to pronounce a discharge from further prosecution or a full acquittal – commonly called 'kurang terang' (insufficiently clear).[72]

In addition to the chairman, the registrar and the *jaksa*, a minimum of two people were required to attend the *landraad* sessions in the capacity of member.[73] According to the 1847 Reglement op de regterlijke organisatie en het beleid der justitie in Nederlandsch-Indië (RO, Regulations for the organization of the judiciary and the policy for the administration of the Netherlands East Indies), the members should consist of the regent, if appointed, and several 'distinguished Native Chiefs', to be installed by or on behalf of the Governor General.[74] Later on it was decided that these 'distinguished chiefs' ought to be

69 Idema (1938:198) lists the successive (open) questions that were supposed to be – and were, commonly – put to the accused with a view to determining his identity: '[Art.] 255 [IR, originally art. 244] follows: the identity questions: name "djenengmoe sapa"? place of birth: "lahir endih"? profession: "pegawean apa"? [...] In practice, the course of events can be very different, typically when the *Jaksa* gets straight to the point: "Aren't you Wagimin, born at such and so a place, a *tani* [farmer] by trade?" Answer: "Noen inggih doro" [Yes, sir], accompanied by a sembah [bow].'

70 Mounier (1900:149) recollects several murder trials 'in which the examination of the case had been concluded, the evidence provided by witnesses being in agreement, a so-called confession having been made and the *jaksa* having demanded that the accused be sentenced to death, when the entire show came to an end at exactly the right moment with the ushering in of the murder victim on whose behalf the procedure seemed to have been staged'.

71 For example, J. van der Vinne, Director of the Means and Domains of the Colony, and C.J. Scholten van Oud Haarlem, president of both the Hooggerechtshoven of the Netherlands East Indies, mention the enormous power and influence of the native prosecutors, who were said to surpass by far their fellow countrymen in 'knowledge, skill and cunning' (memoranda of 1-4-1845 and 30-4-1845, respectively, cited in Immink 1882:132-3). There were some highly memorable cases, both positive and negative. The former category included R.M.T.P. Adiningrat, who had been a *jaksa* of such distinction that in 1875 he was called upon to instruct future *jaksa* (Idema 1938:78). Nitisastro took the biscuit in terms of notoriety – *hoofddjaksa* at Probolinggo and held in high esteem by the European governors, he turned out to have been the longtime leader of 'a dangerous gang of robbers and murderers' (Immink 1882:133-4). Dirk van Hogendorp (1799:21), writing much earlier, also expressed his displeasure with the conduct of some native civil servants at the courts.

72 See footnote 7 and Cohen Stuart 1907:1331, Van Dissel 1913:55, Van der Linden 1911:24, 26-7 and Idema 1938:193-4. According to Boekhoudt (1916:350), the sentences of the *landraad* were commonly reported in the press as 'korang-terang [old spelling] Landraden'.

73 Art. 92 clause 6 RO. For more on the members, see Winckel 1920:160-3 and André de la Porte 1933:116-7.

74 Art. 92 clause 1 RO. It was determined at a later date that the regent, who by law was a

selected from amongst the *patih* (high-ranking official below regent), heads of district and subdistrict, *onder-collecteurs* (deputy collectors), *mantri kabupaten* (regent's clerks) and *mantri polisi* (police clerks) operating in the territory over which the *landraad* had jurisdiction (*Stb.* 1913, no. 678). In addition to these 'State Gazette members' (Dutch 'Staatsblad-leden'), retired native chiefs could also be appointed (*Bb.* no. 2429; compare Winckel 1920:161-2). Moreover, from 1914 it became possible to appoint salaried native *rechtskundigen;* with the exception of the *landraad* of Batavia, Semarang and Surabaya, all others merely contributed towards their members' expenses (Winckel 1920:162). From a formal-legal point of view, the members of the court fulfilled an important role – the *landraad,* in actual fact, was a judicial tribunal and its decisions were required to have been arrived at through a poll of the chairman and the members (art. 40 in conjunction with art. 39 clause 1, 3 RO).

Justice W. Boekhoudt, retiring from the Hooggerechtshof and addressing his former, more junior colleagues in his leaving speech, was full of praise for the native members of the *landraad,* from whom he claimed to have learnt much and whose presence, in his opinion, had considerably enhanced the value of the decisions taken during his chairmanship.[75] But, according to Boekhoudt (1916:334), a certain amount of effort on the part of the *landraad* chairman himself was required to achieve this – during the investigation, he would have to engage 'in a continuously lively exchange of thought' with the members and to show his unequivocal appreciation of their advice and cooperation. Hardly anything resembling such an interaction between chairman and members existed at many *landraden,* though. The members, unsalaried, mostly lacked even rudimentary knowledge of the law, to say nothing of their interest in it, and usually met with the chairman's dismissive attitude. As a rule, they were 'the most passive judges' ever, in that they kept quiet throughout the trial and blindly followed the chairman's lead during the ballot – *seemingly* in any event.[76] Yet the members would leave no stone unturned to procure a given decision in cases in which they had an interest, for example because they had been involved in the pre-trial investigation in the capacity of administrative officer – pressure would be exerted on the witnesses and

member of the *landraad,* was obliged to attend a minimum of two sessions per month (*Bb.* no. 4037). Winckel (1920:160) ascribes this measure to the persistent absence of some regents during court sessions once the chairmanship had passed from administrative officers to jurists.

75 Boekhoudt 1916:334. Sibenius Trip (1905:10-1), too, sketches a reasonably positive picture of his working relationship with the members (the circuit court, in this case).

76 Boekhoudt 1916:333; compare Soesanto Tirtoprodjo 1932:499. Regarding the qualification of 'seemingly': Sibenius Trip (1905:10) cites an example of such a 'Bagimana toewan poenja soeka' (As your Lordship prefers), which turned out, upon closer examination, to harbour the opposite meaning (being: we, the members, are of a *different* opinion). He also mentions another judge who took this members' pronouncement at face value (see Idema 1938:194).

during the ballot, they would vote for the desired verdict, whether or not this infringed upon the prescribed impartiality and whether or not there was any evidence to this effect.[77] And should a member with an interest in the case additionally have a subordinate with a seat on the *landraad*, a decision might ensue from the vote that had been brought about in direct contravention to the procedural rules.

Many a chairman of a *landraad* thus shunned entering into open consultation and discussion with the members, particularly in criminal trials. Though strictly speaking contrary to the law, he would attempt instead to persuade them with an elaborate plea to vote this way or that (Mounier 1900:146; A. van den Bergh 1900:466; Boekhoudt 1916:334). It was sometimes said, for this reason, that the *landraad* did not actually constitute a court (a tribunal, that is) but had a sole judge (Mounier 1900:146, 148; Idema 1938:176; Wormser 1946:5). Other chairmen, however, considering themselves bound by the law through thick and thin, did conclude the session with a vote and subsequently found themselves saddled with a decision they knew to have been effected unlawfully.[78]

The picture evoked by these descriptions is reminiscent of the section before, on the *jaksa*. It is a picture of commonly divergent, at times conflicting agendas, one of entirely different priorities and interests.[79] There was a difference in lingual background, the sum of which is always greater than the total of the vocabularies and grammars – at issue were different life stories, authoritative and internally persuasive texts, value systems, ways of interacting and so forth (see Chapter II). This is beautifully exemplified in the following description, depicting the behaviour of the native members of the *landraad* on the one hand, and the comment of the European jurist on the other. In the case described, a regent acts as *zaakwaarnemer* (representative, see below) for one of the parties in a legal action brought before a *landraad* of which his subordinates formed part:

77 A. van den Bergh 1900:465-6; compare Mounier 1900:147-8, Nemoo 1900 and Idema 1938:175-6.

78 A. van den Bergh (1900:467) argues in favour of this course of action. In his opinion, drawing up 'a decision [...] contrary to one's own opinion [...] can be a good exercise [for the chairman] in impartial judgement and self-denial', even though it may be 'abnormal and sometimes amazingly difficult'. Also see Mounier (1900:146), who considers the method commonly employed by many *landraad* chairmen, described above, 'a violation of a truly free and independent consultation', notwithstanding the non-lawful actions of many *landraad* members.

79 Witnesses, too, could have a secret agenda – such as an axe to grind with the accused. Sibenius Trip (1905:10) has one such witness say: 'Sir is right, neither of us knows anything about the case, but this man (pointing at the accused) [...] bothered us so badly that we agreed to *bantu* [help] the *negeri* [authorities]'. Further instances of false evidence provided by witnesses are given in the same article.

> Every time the regent stood up to speak on behalf of his client, the members of the *landraad* would slide their chairs back and sit on the floor until the regent had finished. Thus, the same image was created as one I can show you on a photograph of the president and the registrar, namely a head emerging only just above the edge of the table, to the wholehearted indignation of the other party. (Mounier 1900:148.)

The members lacked awareness of the principles and sources of law, of the texts that determined the chairman's thoughts and actions. The gap in their knowledge was impossible to bridge – because of the limited time span of their involvement in the *landraad* process (hearings only[80]), the near absence of legal literature in Malay (not to mention in any of the regional languages) and, above all, their disadvantage compared with the chairman's education and experience. Also taking into consideration the difference between being brought up in the Netherlands East Indies or being brought up in the Netherlands, one may safely assume that the divide separating the chairman from the members (as well as the *jaksa*) was probably greater, normally, than that between a judge and those before him in the Netherlands.

To finish, the subjects of legal proceedings ought to be mentioned, be they a party in a civil case or a defendant in a criminal one. When drawing up the Inlandsch Reglement, that governed the procedure at the *landraad*, the legislator intended as low a threshold as possible for Natives seeking access to justice. The usual lack of a grounding in law on the part of the residents and assistant residents who initially wielded the gavel was also borne in mind (see footnote 18; compare Rutgers 1911:2). Compared to the procedural law applicable to European courts, laid down in the regulations for (civil) legal actions and prosecutions, the provisions of the Inlandsch Reglement seem most concise and uncomplicated.[81] The idea behind the code was that the cases of Natives were comparatively straightforward and that the Native seeking justice ought to be able to access the courts through simple procedures without

80 Moreover, the composition of the *landraad* was subject to frequent change because of the official commitments the members (if still in active service) might have elsewhere (Mounier 1900:144; compare Idema 1938:175).

81 'Straightforward' or 'uncomplicated' was one side of the coin, the other side being 'fewer fail-safes'. See Lev 1985:161, for example. As regards its size, the Reglement op de rechtsvordering (abbreviated to Rv; in full: Reglement op de burgerlijke rechtsvordering voor de raden van justitie en het Hooggerechtshof van Nederlandsch-Indië, alsmede voor de residentiegerechten op Java en Madura (Regulations for civil proceedings pertaining to the *raden van justitie* and the Hooggerechtshof of the Netherlands East Indies, as well as for the residency courts at Java and Madura)), promulgated in *Stb.* 1847, no. 52, contained 1,937 articles and the Reglement op de strafvordering voor de raden van justitie op Java en het Hooggerechtshof van Nederlandsch-Indië (abbreviated to Sv, Regulations for criminal proceedings pertaining to the *raden van justitie* on Java and the Hooggerechtshof of the Netherlands East Indies), promulgated in *Stb.* 1847, no. 40, contained 424, a total of 2,361 articles. The 1847 Inlandsch Reglement, on the other hand, contained a mere 394.

recourse to (expensive and scarce) legal aid. The small number of advocates operating in the Netherlands East Indies (several hundreds, serving a population of tens of millions) was a contributory factor to the initiative. Thus, it fell to the chairman of the *landraad*, in particular, to ensure, on countless occasions in the course of the legal procedure, that the interests of the litigants were duly served (Rutgers 1911:256; compare Winckel 1920:183-4).

The procedure to be followed to bring a civil case before the court provides an excellent example of the points of departure mentioned. To commence proceedings at a *landraad*, the plaintiff was merely called upon to submit a petition to the chairman (in practice, this occurred by post) that detailed his demand (art. 126 clause 1 IR; compare Rutgers 1911:258). The only requirement imposed on the format of the petition was that it had been duly signed by the plaintiff; no demands whatsoever were placed on its contents. In case the plaintiff was illiterate, to the extent even of not being able to sign his name, he could communicate his demand verbally to the chairman of the *landraad*. Many *landraden* provided a weekly clinic for oral petitions.[82]

Despite the relative simplicity of the rules, the divide between the world inhabited by most native litigants and that of *landraad* procedure was huge, perhaps most clearly exemplified by the enormous popularity of the *zaakwaarnemer* or 'pokrol bambu' (see footnote 16). Notwithstanding the principle of enabling Natives to find their way around a *landraad* without the help of a third party, the parties were allowed to be assisted or represented by an 'authorized person' (as were defendants charged with an *overtreding* or summary offence).[83] In (serious) crime cases (*misdrijven*), the accused could be assisted by 'counsel' (*raadsman*) during the trial, to be selected from amongst

82 The chairman was required to hear the plaintiff (or his legal representative – see below) *himself*, though he could entrust another *landraad* employee with taking minutes (art. 127 IR; compare Rutgers 1911:259 and Boekhoudt 1916:345). Immink (1889:43) provides a different interpretation of art. 127. According to Rutgers (1911:258), Natives were 'very frequently' able to write their names only. The judge's assistance to the illiterate plaintiff was in exception to the main clause of art. 37 clause 1 RO, which determined that 'no judge [...], in a dispute that [had been] brought before him [...], or of which he could reasonably assume that it [might] be brought before him, either directly or indirectly, shall provide advice or offer help to the parties or their legal representatives' (see Immink 1889:43 and Rutgers 1911:259). Defendants were at a disadvantage in this respect, because the Inlandsch Reglement does not stipulate that a response to a claim could be oral. In practice, the majority of the *landraad* admitted responses in writing (signed by the defendant, that is) only (Rutgers 1911:261).

83 See art. 130 and 340 IR; compare with Immink 1889:41-4, 530-1 and Rutgers 1911:262, 435-6. For more on the 'authorized person', see Lev 1973a, pp. 8-9 in particular. Incidentally, the *landraad* did have the authority to order parties represented during a hearing to appear in person – art. 130 clause 3 IR. In procedures before the *raad van justitie* or the Hooggerechtshof professional representation was mandatory – see art. 106 Rv. According to Rutgers (1911:256), the fact that one of the parties (a European) was capable of employing an advocate whereas the other (a Native) was not, compelled the judge to act in more than a passive capacity.

the advocates registered with the *raad van justitie*.[84] The help of a third party was indeed relied upon, in most cases.

In addition to the majority of Natives by far being unable to compose a petition,[85] they also could not manage without the expertise of someone who more or less knew his way around the *landraad*. The government did not provide for this demand; European advocates were out of bounds, in terms of both cost and social status – the advocates were Europeans who operated in an urban environment, belonged to high society and only spoke Dutch and Malay.[86] For this reason, litigants procured the services of people who were not trained in the law but who were said (or who spread the word by way of PR) to be experienced in bringing and conducting cases before the *landraad*. These 'amateur jurists' or 'pokrol bambu' fulfilled the function of interpreter, mediating between the language of the *wong cilik* (little man), on the one hand, and the colonial law, on the other. As described in great detail by Lev (1973a:4-13), they could come from all manner of backgrounds, but had in common their ability to read and write, some experience in *landraad* procedure and, as a rule, their origin in the lower social classes.

The number of *zaakwaarnemers* or amateur jurists grew steadily from the 1850s onwards and in 1927 the Zaakwaarnemersbond (Union of Representatives) was founded with a view to representing their collective interests. Some of the 'pokrol bambu' earned a full-time wage from this work (Lev 1973a:7-8). Judges, advocates and administrative officers generally held them in low esteem because they had not been trained formally in the law, were thought out of greed to goad people into commencing proceedings as well as poaching business from qualified advocates (Lev 1973a:13-5; compare Boekhoudt 1916:345).

Native defendants in criminal cases probably felt most ill at ease, intimidated even, during the procedure, as must litigants in civil cases, though less severely so. The former in particular were at the mercy, lock, stock and barrel, of investigation and prosecution officers, but plaintiffs and defendants in

84 See art. 243 IR in conjunction with *Stb.* 1832, no. 36; compare Immink 1889:293-4, Rutgers 1911:375-6 and Winckel 1920:182. The amended, newly promulgated Inlandsch Reglement of 1926 (*Stb.* no. 559) permitted a *landraad* chairman to assign a counsel to those accused of capital crimes. The counsel could be a member of the *landraad* trained in the law, a law or Rechtsschool graduate seconded to the chairman, or any other law or Rechtsschool graduate who chose to take on this kind of case (art. 74 clause 2 in conjunction with 250 clauses 4, 5 IR). But in the event none of the above categories had any availability, no counsel was assigned (art. 250 clause 4 IR).

85 According to the census held in 1930, only 6.44% of Natives could read and write in that year. See Rutgers 1911:259. Some plaintiffs made the journey to the *landraad* in vain – upon arrival, they would discover that their claims could only be heard on a particular day (Rutgers 1911:259).

86 See Lev 1973a:4-5, 20. Defendants tried in the European courts were better off – every person accused was entitled to have an advocate assigned (art. 120 clause 2 Sv).

civil proceedings, too, were usually dependent on others' expertise from the moment of commencing a claim onwards. During the hearing proper, the distance between the court and its subjects, presumably, can only have increased. The defendant or the litigants would sit on the floor in front of the table at which were seated the European chairman, the registrar and several stern-looking *priyayi* (upper-class officials).[87]

As described above, the togaed chairman did not usually communicate directly with the subjects of the hearing; the chairman would speak, in a foreign language, to a native official, the *jaksa* for example, who would subsequently address the litigant or defendant or representative in a language they knew.[88] In the opposite direction, the native official would translate the words of the defendant or the litigants into the foreign language. The sum total of the environment (the strange, formal situation; being confronted with various upper-class people; the alien manner of speaking and of being addressed; the bewildering rules of the game applied from behind the table) must have been outlandish, verging on the surreal (compare Tamanaha 1993:109). As mentioned, Rutgers talks of Natives before the *landraad* who will '*never* [understand] a European, though he might utter exactly the same words as the *Jaksa*'; Boekhoudt (1916:340-1) mentions defendants maintaining silence throughout and Natives who, 'even when there cannot be the slightest cause for concealing the truth, have a tendency to lie to their judge'; Sibenius Trip even has a defendant feigning lunacy.[89] These are expressions of confusion, nerves, distrust and apathy, of people utterly nonplussed.[90]

However, litigants and defendants were not alone in finding the path to justice strewn with obstacles. The chairman of the *landraad*, too, encountered numerous obstructions along the way. On a daily basis he faced problems

87 The Javanese term for a higher-ranking person, (professional) elite. The role in the procedure played by each of the people at the table will presumably have been unclear to those before it. A. van den Bergh (1900:471) wondered whether any litigant or defendant would notice, should the body of members of the *landraad* be replaced with a single experienced member with an advisory function: 'Because of the added presence of Member, Jaksa and Penghulu, those before the court would consider the decision or sentence to have been made by *all of these*, just as they do now'. Compare with Lev 1976:159.

88 When interpreting, some *jaksa* would also attempt to convey the mood of the speaker, such as the chairman's ire (Besar Martokoesoemo interviewed by Daniel Lev, in Lev 1976:159).

89 'At Magelang, the following incident occurred. A defendant feigned insanity during the hearing. His reply to all questions put to him was: "Emboeh" [I don't know]. It so happened that the Raden Adipatie appeared in the pendopo and sat down next to me. I asked the Regent to put a question to the defendant and hardly had this gentleman called the defendant by his name or he raised his voice and replied respectfully "koelo" [yes], to the great amusement of everyone present. The defendant could not then continue in his role of madman and proceeded to answer properly any question put to him.' (Sibenius Trip 1905:11.)

90 Nemo 1900 provides a fine example of trifling with defendants, ignorant in the extreme of the colonial government's administration of justice.

for which his training had hardly prepared him, if at all. For example, in the Netherlands and in the European courts in the Indies, cases customarily commenced with a summons (*dagvaarding*), which required the defendant in the case to appear before the court at a specified time, at the behest of the plaintiff or the prosecutor, to answer to the explicit claims or charges set out in the document.

Both the format of a summons and the manner of serving it (in which the defendant was notified, that is) were stringently regulated. Non-compliance with some provisions could result in the nullification of the instrument.[91] But hardly any requirements were imposed on the format of the introductive petitions used to bring a case before the *landraad*, their language and content being free from even a single specification. The chairman therefore had to perform the unenviable task of perusing petitions completed in Malay or any of the regional languages, whether or not aided by the *jaksa* or a registry employee, and to translate these into legal language he could reasonably understand. In practice, according to Rutgers (1911:260), this came down to the *landraad* '[having to] make do with unclear petitions and having a stab at the case'. Claims often were wrought in the 'rigid legal forms of European procedural law', on a regular basis 'an "*intention*" came to the fore [...] that was wholly absent from the petition' and in yet other cases, the plaintiff's action was held not allowable because the petition had not been duly completed.[92]

Lawyers' typical fondness of specific formats, prescribed by law or ingrained through the force of habit, could present a considerable obstacle to efficacious justice in the daily practice of the *landraad*. Chairmen operating strictly within the scope of their legal duties and authority commonly could not but acquit the defendant or declare the case non-allowable.[93] Dyed-in-the wool jurists, boasting many years of experience in the judiciary, occasionally voiced the need for a less formal and more pro-active approach,[94] sometimes even to the extent of ignoring what was legally prescribed. An example of a

91 For more on summonses and subpoenas, see art. 1-21, 94, 97, 99-106 Rv.

92 See Redactie RNI 1910:112, Rutgers 1911:260 and Boekhoudt 1916:346, in that order.

93 An acquittal (Dutch 'vrijspraak') is a statement of the charge(s) not having been proven; not allowable (Dutch 'ontslag van rechtsvervolging') means that the claim is rejected on grounds not related to the case itself, for example non-compliance with a formality. Compare with footnote 7 and p. 110-1.

94 See the exhortation by Boekhoudt (1916:346-7) and Winckel (1927:1008) for increased pragmatism among judges whose 'requirements, in legal terms, impose too high a standard'. Boekhoudt quotes several cases, one of which relates to a civil case repeatedly declared not allowable because, for one, the plaintiff had signed the petition with a cross. Winckel's article (1927:1008) includes the following: '[T]he judge is to avoid finding fault with the format, is not to impose excessive demands on decisions made by non-jurist administrative officers, is to apply his common sense to prevent the operation of justice becoming incapacitated through contrived argument'. Both judges concluded their careers as justices at the Hooggerechtshof.

provision thus disregarded is the prohibition on putting leading or trick questions to defendants and witnesses (art. 260 IR; compare Rutgers 1911:384-5). Boekhoudt (1916:344) argues that it was simply impossible to observe this rule where Natives were concerned:

> If the truthfulness of the reply solicited can be verified properly, the due process of the law may, at times, be served better by such questions than by the rigid application of the regulations, and I have heard of *Landraad* chairmen who enjoy an excellent reputation for their work, real authorities on the Natives, that they cannot always abide by these. An example. A judge who asks a defendant: have you ever been convicted of an offence? as a rule will receive an emphatic denial. But should he ask a Lombroso-faced defendant: how many previous convictions off the police roll do you have?, the defendant, convinced that his judge sees straight through him and disposes of the means to obtain the information by another route if necessary, will reply truthfully, occasionally dumbfounding his audience with the string of sentences he mentions. Questioned next: and how many of these sentences were passed by the *Landraad*?, it will frequently become apparent that he was tried by this particular judge before. Summary judgements are then requested and thus it is established *de jure* that the defendant is a hardened criminal. Trying to find out about prior convictions without the defendant's information often is tantamount to looking for a needle in a haystack, wherefore one plainly has to make do with whatever one's got.

At face value, one could take Boekhoudt's account to express contempt for the native suspect who apparently was less deserving of procedural safeguards than his European counterpart. Upon closer inspection, though, the approach advocated by Boekhoudt and others, such as Sibenius Trip, reveals something else: an awareness of the vast divide between themselves and the colonial legal system on the one hand, and the native defendant on the other, as well as the conviction that the latter had to be reached somehow. Boekhoudt's formally disallowed trick questions constitute another language entirely – in the wider, metalinguistic sense of perspective on the world, a belief system charged with values and convictions (see Chapter II) – than the neutral, open questions the Inlandsch Reglement permitted the chairman of the *landraad* (see footnote 69). Presumably, the disallowed form of addressing Natives in court (perhaps gleaned from a *mantri-politie* (native police officer) or a *jaksa*, or acquired themselves through dealing with domestic servants) coincided much more closely with the languages and genres to which the defendant was accustomed than the formal-distant method, for which reason the former line of questioning did produce a result and the latter did not.

Other ways of reaching Natives were also practised – Boekhoudt mentions fixing his gaze on the defendant from the moment the latter entered the court and continuing to do so once he had sat down. 'Brazen defendants – some most impudent rascals, especially among the persistent offenders – [understood] from this welcome that the President was not a pushover and gradually became open to reason.'[95] Boekhoudt made use of interpreters during the hearing and Sibenius Trip, upon being appointed a circuit judge, devoted himself to further study of Javanese. He was taught at Semarang by a native teacher who had trained at the then *kweekschool* (teacher training college) at Solo, and practised on his domestic servants and on 'the little man'. During court sessions, however, he did not speak Javanese 'out of respect for my fellow members, because I was aware of the unfavourable disposition, to say the very least, caused the native officials through the use of an incorrect form in their presence'.[96]

More important than the various levels of command of language, however, is the conscientious performance of their official duties evident from the literature, as well as the embedding of that performance in a network of ties, close ones more often than not, with native and European officials from all ranks of the judicial hierarchy. Managing the staff of the registry, clarifying matters to the members of the *landraad*, actively involving them in the deliberations and heeding their decisions, numerous discussions with regents and other administrative officers, for example about the motives underpinning a particular, apparently irrational decision by the members or the conduct of a certain *jaksa* – the core values are a calm, thorough approach, the ability to relate to the indigenous society, respect for other people and a dislike of rush jobs. Sibenius Trip approvingly cites a colleague: 'justice cannot be done by the hour'.[97]

'A more rewarding post than that of *landraad* chairman is well-nigh unthinkable', Boekhoudt (1916:330) wrote. But taking into account the multitude of complaints, the critical, at times even cynical commentary and the numbers leaving the service (Boekhoudt 1916:317-8; Van Wageningen 1920:262-4), his opinion hardly reflects the consensus among chairmen. Many executed their duties by the book, others could not be bothered to improve their command of indigenous languages. To people faced with an ever-increasing pile of dossiers (containing many form mistakes) to be dealt with, a relatively formalistic attitude may have offered some relief. Seen from this perspective, various aspects

95 Boekhoudt 1916:341. The contact was maintained subsequently, too: 'For as long as a defendant persisted in his spiel to deceive the judge with fallacies, the tone remained severe. With much finger-bending and toe-curling, the defendant would gradually abandon his attitude and become susceptible to a more jovial atmosphere.' (Boekhoudt 1916:341.)

96 Sibenius Trip 1905:10. The author reports that this was also why Javanese officials were reluctant to speak their mother tongue to Europeans. Compare Immink 1889:362, Mounier 1900:154 and Fasseur 1995:133. A. van den Bergh (1900:472), too, advised against speaking Javanese during the trial.

97 Sibenius Trip 1905:10. The quote is from the circuit judge W. Tadema. W.F. Wertheim, engaged by the *landraad* at Tanjung Karang in the 1930s, mentions the 'target' of thirty cases per chairman per month (Wertheim and Wertheim-Gijse Weenink 1991:112).

of the legal process at the *landraad* must have gone entirely against the grain of the lawyer in the chairman. The manner in which native officials acquitted themselves of the investigation into offences and in which suspects were interviewed and the information obtained was recorded,[98] the ideas about due process that varied from the registrar through the *jaksa* and the members to the witnesses – many chairmen will have been aware of at least part of the daily irregularities. Their inadequate command of the language, their impotence to fathom the Natives or sheer lack of time to delve more deeply into the cases – being unable to distinguish fact from fabrication must have caused the chairmen considerable frustration. Given the above, it is only natural that many a judicial officer warmly welcomed the prospect of native *landraad* chairmen.

### *Native rechtskundigen in the colonial administration of justice*

So far, this chapter has sketched the practice of the *landraad* prior to the native *rechtskundige* appearing on the scene. To what extent did his arrival prompt changes in the communication and the relationships at the *landraad* (and other official bodies such as the *landgerecht*), both between the officials and between the judge and litigants or defendants? To what extent did his arrival herald an improvement in the functioning of those bodies?

98 In Steinmetz 1897:64-6 and Van der Linden 1910, see the paragraph entitled 'Opteekenen van verhooren door inlandsche ambtenaren' (The recording of interviews by native officials). In the same article, in a paragraph entitled 'Middelen om hun eenig inzicht in rechtszaken en eenige meerdere wetskennis te doen verkrijgen' (Means to provide them [the native officials, that is] with some insight into proceedings and some deeper understanding of the law), Steinmetz puts forward several suggestions on how to motivate these officials to improve their judicial investigations. The author says, for example, that he had 'a trainee *controleur* (controller) draw up a précis of those sections of the I.S.W. [Inlandsch Strafwetboek, Native Criminal Code] they most crucially required, arranged according to the severity of the sentence, and [dictated] this to the native chiefs'. Another tip was to supply the chiefs with the IR and the Wetboek van Strafrecht voor Inlanders (Criminal Code for Natives) in the regional language and 'to demand that the article violated be cited in the official reports of the investigation'. Finally, it was recommended that, for the most commonly committed offences (such as theft), native officials be provided with a list of questions 'they are supposed to ask themselves, the accused and the witnesses, the answers to which ought to reveal the nature of the fact, as well as any aggravating or mitigating circumstances and other necessary particulars'. The questionnaire related to theft preceded by breaking and entering, phrased in 'Malay intelligible to Native chiefs', starts thus: '1e Pekarangannja apa di pageri antero? [Is your property completely fenced in?] 2e Pager itoe, brapa pintoenja? [How many entrances does the fence have?] 3e Wektoe ada malingan, itoe pintoe apa die toetoep semoeanja; di toetoep pake bekakas apa? Wektoe kowe bangoen, apa itoe pintoe kedapet masih die toetoep saperti malemnja wektoe kowe pigi tidoer? [Were all of these entrances locked, at the time of the theft? How were they locked? When you got up in the morning, were all of the entrances locked just as they had been when you turned in for the night?]' And so forth (Steinmetz 1897:61-4).

It has been mentioned that the career of a *rechtskundige* usually began at the registry office. But it is doubtful whether the registrar welcomed this new addition to his staff with open arms – this was a Native entering the service who, though inexperienced, had a superior command of Dutch to himself, a *European* no less! This Native would but while away a period at the registry on his way up, even to the post of chairman of the *landraad*, whereas he, the registrar, had already reached the peak of his career. Moreover, it was hard to bear that the *rechtskundige* was able to discuss legal matters with the chairman on a (near) equal footing. And to top it all, the new arrival was eminently versed in the procedural law laid down in the Inlandsch Reglement – on which point the registrar could actually outshine the chairman, all the more so if the latter was inexperienced. All said and done, the introduction of the native *rechtskundige* onto the legal stage greatly undermined the position of the registrar. The same was true for the *jaksa* – not only did the *rechtskundige* possess a solid legal grounding, since childhood he had been immersed in the local languages and etiquette, having been assigned, whenever possible, to the *landraad* of his place of origin, in accordance with the official policy.[99]

The particular blend of skills combined in the native *rechtskundige*, whether employed as a deputy registrar, a member or the deputy chairman, was sure to make him a valued source of support for and 'native extension' of the Dutch chairman. Having a *rechtskundige* in the post of deputy registrar may have eliminated the need to dictate the record of the hearing. Furthermore, the linguistic prowess and legal perspective on the procedure of that same *rechtskundige* provided the chairman with a markedly less partial and therefore more reliable interpreter and translator than the *jaksa* and the registrar could ever be. Before the hearing he could assist those wishing to submit a petition

99 Some examples of *rechtskundigen* who spent (a considerable part of) their working lives in their native areas or, in the case of Sumatrans, on their native island: Soedirman (Rechtsschool diploma 1912, born at Banyumas (Central Java), appointed *a.t.b.* at Batavia and Banyumas, subsequent career involving various positions on Central Java and Madura; Mohamad Hamid (Rechtsschool diploma 1912), born at Pandeglang (West Java), *a.t.b.* at Batavia and Serang (West Java), career at Batavia and on West Java; Besar Martokoesoemo (Rechtsschool diploma 1915), born at Brebes (Central Java), *a.t.b.* at Pekalongan (Central Java), career in the judiciary of Central Java; Gondokoesoemo (Rechtsschool diploma 1917), born at Blora (Central Java), *a.t.b.* at Bojonegoro, Blora and Rembang (Central and East Java), career on Java; Soetan Kali Malikoel Adil (Rechtsschool diploma 1920), born at Priaman (Sumatra), *a.t.b.* Bukittinggi (Sumatra), career at Batavia, on West Java, Sumatra, Borneo and Madura; Boerhanoeddin (Rechtsschool diploma 1923), born at Kota Gedang (Tapanuli, Sumatra), *a.t.b.* at Bukittinggi (Sumatra), career on Java; Abdoel Gafar Wahab (Rechtsschool diploma 1925), born at Padang (Sumatra), *a.t.b.* at Bogor, career on Sumatra and Java; Rochmat Kromoatmodjo (Rechtsschool diploma 1925), born at Kebumen (Central Java), *a.t.b.* at Magelang (Central Java), career on Central Java; Joesoef Ismail (Rechtsschool diploma 1928), born at Bogor (West Java), *a.t.b.* at Bogor, career on Sumatra, East and West Java (*Orang Indonesia jang terkemoeka* 1973:54, 136, 138, 140-3, 146).

or needing to be questioned and during the hearing he could be deployed as an interpreter or as counsel to the accused.[100] The opinions of native *rechtskundigen* who were members of a *landraad* will have been taken to heart by the European chairmen much more easily than those voiced by their fellow members. In the course of his professional progress, while deputy chairman, for instance, the *rechtskundige* would gradually become familiar with the rules of conduct (languages, genres) a *landraad* chairman was expected to know. Some were fortunate in finding a European *landraad* chairman prepared and able to guide them well, others had to cope by themselves (see Van Helsdingen 1929d, Van Wageningen 1920:266-7 and Lev 1976:151). Next, a recommendation from the president, the chief prosecutor and the vice presidents of the Hooggerechtshof to the Governor General might result in an appointment to the chairmanship (art. 17 clause 2 RO).

The engagement of the first few native *rechtskundigen* in the office of *landraad* chairman was the acid test for the Rechtsschool. They seem to have passed with flying colours, in the opinion of the European jurists, at least.[101] On appeal, the decisions taken by native chairmen were either upheld or quashed and were published and discussed in the *Indisch Tijdschrift van het Recht*, as were court decisions taken by Europeans.[102] The journals that had

100 The following fragment of a letter written by a *rechtskundige* to his former teacher A. Neytzell de Wilde (1913:111-2) provides some details. It is dated several months after the writer was appointed *a.t.b.*: 'It is my pleasure to report to you, that I am entrusted with drawing up *akten van verwijzing* for the President, which, in my opinion, may be considered excellent practice for a Native *rechtskundige* who only recently left the classroom; five of these *akten* have now been approved, a few of which contained some minor corrections made by the President himself, but the nature of the charges laid he left unchanged. [...] I am, for the time being, only occupied with criminal cases, namely all those dealt with by the *landraad* under the direction of the President; during the sessions, the President permits me to keep the record of the proceedings entirely by myself – which I feel to be capable of, as I understand Javanese, maybe even have a command of it –, which I write up at home ... [...] Thus far, I have not been criticized on the point of my use of Dutch. The President also lets me present the Dutch documents to the accused or witnesses in Javanese. [...] Concerning my intercourse with both the European and the Native staff, this leaves nothing to be desired and I hope it will remain so. Unity should be observed everywhere. Amongst the members, too, I move freely.' (Letter dated March 1913.) Compare with Daniel Lev's interview with Besar Martokoesoemo, in which the interviewee states that, in his post of *a.t.b.*, he frequently assisted native defendants (Lev 1976:159).

101 Van Helsdingen 1929a:14-6, 20-1, 1929d:59-60; Lev 1976:151-2. In the memorial book, 134 (out of 202) graduates are listed as employed (or having been employed up until their death) at a court at the time the book was under production (1928-29) (*Gedenkboek Rechtsschool* 1929:xx).

102 The *Indisch Tijdschrift van het Recht* 136 (1932), for example, contains some of Wirjono Prodjodikoro's court decisions (Rechtsschool diploma 1922), in office as chairman of the Kutoarjo *landraad* (pp. 236-9: decision dated 4-4-1932, upheld by the Semarang *raad van justitie* on 10-6-1932; incidentally, Wirjono had obtained the title of master of laws at Leiden University in the meantime); by Soeparto (Rechtsschool diploma 1921) of the Surabaya *landraad* (pp. 264-6, 266-71: decisions dated 1-10-1931 and 30-7-1931, upheld and quashed, respectively, by the

previously expressed scathing criticism of the *landraden* and their chairmen (think of the *Indisch Tijdschrift van het Recht*, the *Tijdschrift voor Binnenlandsch Bestuur*, taken over by the *Koloniaal Tijdschrift* in 1917, and the *Indische Gids*) now kept quiet. The doubts about the integrity of the new chairmen, too, were proved unfounded. The *rechtskundigen* will have had quite a time of it in this respect, in the first few years at least. In the indigenous world they represented a new authority that spoke a new language, one of priorities and values of a foreign origin. Yet within the set-up of the *landraad*, with its long-embedded roles and routines, presumably they were able to carry out their work without encountering too many obstacles in their path, simply following in the footsteps of their predecessors. Their social skills, too, must have dispelled any feelings of resentment the established indigenous order (registrar, members who were not *rechtskundigen*, *jaksa*) may have harboured.

But outside of the *landraad*, either in the sphere of influence of traditional authorities and hierarchical structures or on 'open terrain', the *rechtskundige* had yet to establish his position. The first couple of meetings with high-ranking native administrative officers, who played an important role in law enforcement and in the detection of criminal offences (art. 65-72 IR), and who could bring to bear enormous influence on the apparatus of indigenous civil servants, are likely to have been especially confrontational. What, for example, was the correct form of address between a *rechtskundige* and a regent when the former came to pay his respects? Most *rechtskundigen* were employed on Java and on this island, in particular, such encounters involved two mutually exclusive world views. Speaking either of the languages that were customary outside of the big cities, Javanese (Central and East Java) or Sundanese (West Java), one automatically was drawn into a heavily stratified gamut of conventions determined by social rank. Not only was a selection required from the spectrum of languages and genres ranging from low Javanese (*ngoko*) to high Javanese (*krama*), but also (in so far as Javanese was concerned) a certain posture.[103] Language is not a neutral instrument to be adapted according to one's whim, but the reflection of an entire repertoire of familiar poses and manners,

Surabaya *raad van justitie* on 20-1-1932); by Boerhanoeddin (Rechtsschool diploma 1923) of the Jember *landraad* (pp. 278-82: decision dated 17-3-1932, quashed by the Surabaya *raad van justitie* on 1-1-1932); by Soetan Kali Malikoel Adil (Rechtsschool diploma 1921) of the Kuala Kapuas *landraad* (the decision had been taken on 26-2-1931 and was upheld by the Surabaya *raad van justitie* on 12-8-1931: pp. 289-93); and by Oerip Kartodirdjo (Rechtsschool diploma 1919) of the Bantaeng *landraad* (pp. 294-6: decision dated 3-3-1932; Kartodirdjo, too, had completed his master of laws in the meantime).

103 Quoting a former *resident* who wrote in 1891: 'The Native will remain standing in your presence provided you address him in Malay and permit him to reply in that language. But if he is required to speak with you in Javanese, he will do so sitting down, cross-legged.' (Cited by A.J. Spaan in a presentation to Delft indologists, borrowed from Fasseur 1995:134.)

entrenched views of and approaches to the world and one's fellow man. A Javanese official refusing to *jongkok* (to squat walk, that is) in the presence of the regent affronted not just the regent himself but the entire social structure he represented.[104]

From the opposite perspective, assuming the pose of subservience conflicted acutely with the norms and languages the *rechtskundige* had had drummed into him during his training. After all, as a judicial officer he formed part of a machine that was supposed to function autonomously, independently from the administration.[105] Attire, too, was a bone of contention – *rechtskundigen* wished to hold office *in European dress*, in one fell swoop 'relieving them of those expressions of courtesy they felt were unbecoming their future post and standing' (Van Helsdingen 1929a:15). In 1919 the dress code for judicial officers indeed was declared applicable to native *rechtskundigen*.[106]

The *rechtskundigen* arrived on the instructions of the government and were there to stay. The regents and other native officials who were part of the status quo will just have had to grin and bear it (Van Helsdingen 1929a:16; *De wording der Rechtsschool* 1929:49; Van Niel 1984:23-4). In the process of forging new relationships, new languages and genres came into being. To enable the meetings between *rechtskundigen* and regents, a mode of speaking must have been selected from among the extensive possibilities of the Javanese repertoire or, to keep things simple, the more egalitarian Dutch may have been spoken.[107]

104 In the first few years, regents more advanced in years, in particular, turned to the colonial government to voice their discontent about the refusal of the *rechtskundigen* to squat before them (Van Helsdingen 1929a:13-6). The government had expressed its irritation with the refusal in question. But Van Helsdingen (1929a:14) points out the principle at stake: 'He [the *rechtskundige*] realized full well the import of the issue, namely his position of a *rechtskundige*, of a future judge serving the law independently, separate from the administrative officer, that is. The issue was to maintain his independence with respect to the highest-ranking Native official. The issue was to comply with one of the very requirements perpetually impressed on him at this school, to assert one of the very character traits previously deemed non-existent in him and his entire group and the reason why Natives – more particularly, the Javanese –, being considered wanting in this virtuous courage, were declared unsuitable material for the judiciary. And precisely that important matter of principle revolved around a trifle: whether to honour the regent and show him respect in the Native fashion or in the manner of the Europeans.'

105 A comparable notion, though viewed from another angle, may be detected in the refusal on the part of Tjokrosoedarmo (leading figure in the Djawa Dipo movement that stood for the abolition of *krama* or high Javanese) to seat himself in court in the cross-legged position (*sila*) in the presence of the *jaksa* and to address the latter in high Javanese, seeing the *jaksa* was not acting as a Javanese but in the capacity of a government official (Anderson 1990a:215-6).

106 *Stb.* 1919, no. 207 in conjunction with *Stb.* 1848, no. 8. Judicial officers employed on Java and Madura were required to wear the following garb: 'black undergarments, a black outer garment, a black, wide-sleeved toga, a black cap by way of head gear, and a hanging, pleated jabot made from white cambric' (*Stb.* 1848, no. 8 art. 1).

107 Selecting the same formality level of language has become acceptable in Javanese, too; nowadays, both the *rechtskundigen* and the administrative officers would presumably speak

With the appointment of a native *rechtskundige* to the chairmanship, official languages other than Dutch, *dienstmaleis* (service Malay) and several variants of what was derogatorily referred to as 'gibberish' entered the court room – Javanese, Sundanese, Minangkabau-Malay and countless new varieties of Malay arising spontaneously from one day to the next.[108] The reliance on interpreters to communicate with defendants, litigants and witnesses is likely to have decreased but not to have become altogether redundant – bearing in mind the chairman extraordinary of the Medan *landraad* who was born on Central Java or the *rechtskundige* from Sumatra who chaired the *landraad* at Banjarmasin (Borneo), Pangkalpinang (Bangka) or Tanjungpandan (Billiton).[109] But unlike most European chairmen, the native *rechtskundige* will mostly have been able to conduct the questioning directly, unhampered by the misunderstandings the interpreter might cause. This can only have facilitated the establishment of the facts of a case and thus have benefitted greatly the due functioning of the *landraad*. Yet command of language was not a panacea here either. Of equal importance, at least, were factors such as a sense of duty, the ability to put oneself in another's shoes and a flair for networking.[110]

Though in court the native *rechtskundigen* spoke the language of those coming before it, they actually worked and thought in the Dutch languages and genres of the legal system and procedure they had internalized during their training and career to date. The focus of their work (the internal legal attitude) was not so much placed on the Javanese or Malay of the court session but on the composition (in Dutch) of the court decisions, something that only occurred *after* the trial had been concluded.[111] It was on those decisions (and

---

*krama* (*basa*) (information supplied by professor Bernard Arps on 2-4-2002; compare Anderson 1990b:132).

108 See Lev 1976:159 footnote 44. Minangkabau probably was the official language in the era of Soetan Kali Malikoel Adil (Rechtsschool diploma 1921, born at Priaman, Sumatra) as deputy chairman and chairman extraordinary of the Padang *landraad* (1927-30) or the period of time in which Abdoel Gafar Wahab (Rechtsschool diploma 1925, born at Padang) served at Sawahlunto (1927) (*Orang Indonesia jang terkemoeka* 1973:143, 136).

109 Namely Hadi (Rechtsschool diploma 1915, born at Kedungtuban (Blora, Central Java)) and the aforementioned Soetan Kali Malikoel Adil (*Orang Indonesia jang terkemoeka* 1973:141, 143). Compare with the experiences of Wirjono Prodjodikoro (1974:12, 15), first in Makassar, then in Purworejo.

110 Soesanto Tirtoprodjo (Rechtsschool diploma 1920), in the *Indisch Tijdschrift van het Recht*, argued that the *landraad* members, who were not trained in the law, were obsolete because they, as a rule, concurred with the chairman. By way of cutting costs, the requirement for including members ought to be rescinded (Soesanto Tirtoprodjo 1932:498-9).

111 On this point, see Boekhoudt (1916:336): 'The advantage of committing the decision to paper on the same day on which it was made cannot be stated often enough. Dates, the names of witnesses and places, the President can still vividly recollect everything and the deliberations, too, are fresh in his mind so that the act of writing down the decision costs less than no effort at all.'

on other procedural documents phrased in Dutch, such as *akten van verwijzing*) that the native chairmen were assessed by (fellow) *landraad* chairmen, judges at higher courts and the Department of Justice. Had they gone about establishing the facts of the case correctly? Had they presented the relevant facts in the correct manner? Were the legal considerations in assessing the facts appropriate, was the reasoning legitimate, had the correct legislation been applied, and had that legislation been applied correctly? Did the operative part (*dictum*) of the decision concur with the considerations? Finally, did the decision as a whole read like one drawn up by a European judge in respect of lay-out, terminology and formulation? The same criteria were applied to the scrutiny of court decisions taken by *rechtskundigen* as to those by European *landraad* chairmen, though given the former and possibly still current doubts about the calibre of their authors, it is probable that the decisions of *rechtskundigen* were scrutinized more stringently, at least to begin with.

From the point of view of their profession, the *rechtskundigen* drew predominantly on the intersubjective legal community of the Netherlands East Indies. Indeed, in many respects they were fully-fledged members of that community. For example, just like masters and doctors of laws, as well as notaries, they were entitled, without ballot and at a reduced rate, to join the Nederlandsch-Indische Juristen-Vereeniging (Netherlands East Indies Jurists' Society), re-established in 1913. They then received the society's publication, the *Indisch Tijdschrift van het Recht* mentioned above (Dekker and Van Katwijk 1992:9). It welcomed their contributions, be they annotations to judicial decisions or essays. 1916 saw the first annotation by a native *rechtskundige* published in the journal; the first such essay appeared in 1920.[112]

Nevertheless, the *rechtskundige* could not integrate fully into the legal community. His training had been inferior to that of the European master of laws, for example, making him ineligible for judicial posts other than those in the legal system for Natives. This was one of the obstacles to furthering his career with a post at a *raad van justitie*. Nor did the title of *rechtskundige* give access to the advocature (operating within the European courts). His salary, too, was lower than the remuneration awarded his European colleague,[113] in accordance with the original aim, which is likely to have detracted from

112 The annotation was produced by Soedjoko and dealt with the decision taken by the Surabaya *landraad* on 10-11-1915 (*Indisch Tijdschrift van het Recht* 106 (1916):166-71); the first essay was written by Soebroto ('De plaats van diefstal' [The place of theft]; art. 363 3e. Sr', *Indisch Tijdschrift van het Recht* 112 (1920):195-8). A list of essays published in the main law journals is included in Dekker and Van Katwijk 1992; a list of the court decisions these contained is included in Dekker and Van Katwijk 1993b. Also see Soeparto 1929:57.

113 See p. 83. In the course of time, lobbying to have the salaries of *rechtskundigen* raised became the main task of the Vereeniging van Inlandsche Rechtskundigen (Society of Native *Rechtskundigen*), founded at Surabaya in 1918 (Soeparto 1929).

the social status of the *rechtskundige* and also to have stood in the way of full integration – leaving aside the colonial caste system. Finally, the common background of the native *rechtskundigen*, on the one hand, and the Dutch jurists, on the other, in both cases created a kind of mutually exclusive group cohesion (in the shape of childhood memories, student days, career and social lives, and in respect of the *rechtskundigen*, also of emancipatory and nationalist sentiment).

## *Masters of laws*

Even before the first *rechtskundige* was appointed chairman of a *landraad*, in early 1925, the Rechtsschool acquired an Indies successor that did offer a university level course in law – the Rechtshoogeschool. On 28 October 1924 Governor General D. Fock performed the official opening in the Compagnieszaal (Companies Hall) of the Museum of the Bataviaasch Genootschap van Kunsten en Wetenschappen (Batavian Society for Arts and Sciences).[114] The founder and first chairman, albeit temporarily, of the Rechtshoogeschool was the renowned Amsterdam professor Paul Scholten, who, in the first half of 1924, developed a new law curriculum specifically tailored to the situation in the Netherlands East Indies and managed to find lecturers and professors to teach it.[115]

In carrying out this job, Scholten made use of the Carpentier Alting report (among other sources), compiled by the committee with the same name established in early 1919.[116] Chaired by the then president of the Hooggerechtshof, J.H. Carpentier Alting, this committee had been instructed to investigate the measures and facilities needed to make the Rechtsschool accessible to non-Natives and, with a view to increasing the number of *rechtskundigen*, to add new schools to the existing one, if required.[117] The committee extended its

[114] Hoesein Djajadiningrat 1949:5. In its early days the Rechtshoogeschool did not have its own premises. Lectures were therefore given in the building that, by sheer coincidence, had been Fock's residence (Hoesein Djajadiningrat 1949:5). Not until 1929 did the school obtain its own, newly built premises on Koningsplein West, thanks mostly to the unceasing efforts of its chairman, J. van Kan (Resink 1949:14).

[115] Van Asbeck 1949:7, 10-1 and *Mededeelingen der Regeering* 1924:228-9. The Statutes of the Rechtshoogeschool are appended to the Governor General's Decree dated 9-10-1924 no. 1 (*Stb.* 1924, no. 457). Scholten's lengthy speech to mark the occasion of the opening was published in *Opening Rechtshoogeschool* 1925.

[116] In addition to this report (to be discussed below), Scholten had at his disposal various papers on the future of higher education in the Netherlands East Indies in general, issued on the government's initiative as well as that of the private sector (Van Asbeck 1949:8-9).

[117] Gouvernementsbesluit (Colonial Government Decree) dated 4-1-1919 no. 18. The committee secretary was C.C. van Helsdingen, the members were F.J.H. Cowan, A. Heyman, H. Jelgerhuis

Fig. 15. Professors and lecturers of the Rechtshoogeschool, Batavia, 1924 (from left to right, first row, professors Hoesein Djajadiningrat, P. Scholten and J.H.A. Logemann; second row, professors B.J.O. Schrieke, B. ter Haar, F.M. Baron van Asbeck, R.D. Kollewijn and J.H. Boeke; third row (in light-color suits), E. Bessem and J. Kats; KITLV collection no. 2638)

mandate, however, addressing instead the question of how law was to be taught in the Netherlands East Indies of the future (*Verslag Commissie hervorming Rechtsschool* 1920:2-3). The report envisaged two kinds of law courses. *Scholen voor recht en administratie* (schools for law and administration), teaching law at secondary level, had to be initiated to train a comprehensive force of support staff for the country's judiciary and administration. These were

Swildens, A. Neytzell de Wilde and Z. Stokvis (*Verslag Commissie hervorming Rechtsschool* 1920:1). Several years earlier it had been suggested that admission to the school should be open to all population groups but this had not been pursued at that time. The idea was revived when notions of unification – in the areas of legislation (1918: a single *Wetboek van Strafrecht* for all population groups), education (all courses to be based on the European model and open to all population groups) and human resources (organizing posts to as great an extent as possible on a uniform, rational bureaucratic foundation and making these accessible to all population groups) – began to prevail in the Volksraad (People's Council, the colonial 'Parliament'), too (*Mededeelingen der Regeering* 1924:15). For more on the principle of unification and its rise and fall, see *Unificatie* 1921 and Van Niel 1984:36-8, 247-50.

Fig. 16. Rechtshoogeschool students, 1939 (KITLV collection no. 30637)

to be supplemented with a *rechtshogeschool* along academic lines to deliver a small nucleus of civil servants intended for the higher ranks.[118] This institution

118 *Verslag Commissie hervorming Rechtsschool* 1920:6, 11, 47. The committee did not set out with the idea of a course with academic status. Its initial plan was to establish a vocational institute of education, namely by redefining the Rechtsschool as a 'Higher Rechtsschool', to involve a more comprehensive syllabus, an extended course duration and, notably, the admission of students from all population groups (*Verslag Commissie hervorming Rechtsschool* 1920:46, 12). But the fairly limited purpose of such a school – to produce candidates for a handful of specific judicial offices – caused the committee to discard this plan and to embrace the notion of a university-level law course instead. After all, a degree course in jurisprudence would supply graduates suited to a very wide range of posts, even those outside of the practice of the law. Such an education would, furthermore, also be of interest to people seeking employment outside of the civil service (*Verslag Commissie hervorming Rechtsschool* 1920:46-7).
The committee knew itself supported by the government, should it come to arguing the case for a *rechtshogeschool*, because in June 1919 it received correspondence from the colonial government's first secretary, written on behalf of the Governor General, in which it was requested to incorporate into its recommendations the possible introduction into the Netherlands East Indies of an academic law course, to commence in 1923. By writing in these terms, the Governor General

was to offer courses in law at the same level and with the same status as the law faculties in the Netherlands and in due course was to be subsumed by a university, becoming a faculty of law itself.[119]

The proposal to found *scholen voor recht en administratie* was not taken up but the law college did come into being,[120] sounding the death knell for the Rechtsschool, which, in the proposed new organization of law courses, had become redundant. The education it had provided was neither fish, flesh

---

also backed an earlier recommendation of the same purport, made by the Director of Education and Worship (*Verslag Commissie hervorming Rechtsschool* 1920:4-5, 11). 1923 was a critical year in that the first cohort in the department of Western classical education (department A II) at the Algemeene Middelbare School (AMS, General Secondary School) was to sit its final examination. The diploma of this kind of secondary education (together with several equivalent courses) was to satisfy, as a rule, the requirements for admission to the higher education to be established (*Verslag Commissie hervorming Rechtsschool* 1920:5, 66, 97).

Finally, the committee's recommendations were inspired by efforts (to be discussed) in the Netherlands to attract more students from the Netherlands East Indies, to be achieved through setting up a special course in Indies law. In the committee's opinion, such a scheme would not be capable of meeting to a sufficient extent the increasing insistence on law courses among the indigenous population and the growing demand in the colonial government for legally trained personnel (*Verslag Commissie hervorming Rechtsschool* 1920:10). But the report also contained criticism of the very principle of the Dutch plans. Was it not so that only in the Netherlands East Indies could 'that direct contact with Indies society [...] be had, that complements the training and shapes the Native jurist?'; in their first few years in the Netherlands East Indies, the members of the committee themselves, nearly all of them lawyers educated in Holland, had experienced the lack of such knowledge and insight as problematic (*Verslag Commissie hervorming Rechtsschool* 1920:10-1). Another point of criticism concerned the practical side of studying in the Netherlands, such as the climate, the 'danger of compromising virtue and decency' and the high cost (*Verslag Commissie hervorming Rechtsschool* 1920:10-1).

119 *Verslag Commissie hervorming Rechtsschool* 1920:11, 47. The 1924 Hoger Onderwijs-ordonnantie (Higher Education ordinance) bestowed a common status on the Technische Hoogeschool (College of Technology) at Bandung, founded in 1920, and the new Rechtshoogeschool (Governor General's Decree dated 9-10-1924 no. 1, *Stb.* no. 456). It laid the foundation for a future university, for example by determining that the schools for higher education were to be designated as 'hogeschool', that a *hogeschool* was to comprise a single faculty only and that, at some point in the future, a number of *hogescholen* were to merge into a university (art. 2 clauses 1, 2 and 4). The higher education provided by the state would, for the time being, remain confined to the Faculty of Science and Technology at Bandung and the Law Faculty (still to be created at that time) at Batavia (art. 3, 8). The Carpentier Alting Committee and many other parties had, incidentally, argued for the Rechtshoogeschool to be established at Bandung (*Verslag Commissie hervorming Rechtsschool* 1920:67-8), a superior location, in the committee's opinion, not only because of its more pleasant climate but also because the Technische Hoogeschool was there, too. Furthermore, there were some plans at that time to move the Hooggerechtshof to Bandung (*Enquête hooger onderwijs* 1921:VIII, XXIII, XXXI). The establishment of the Medische Hoogeschool (College of Medicine) at Batavia, later on, was for reasons specific to that course only, such as the availability in that town of some large hospitals (*Verslag Commissie hervorming Rechtsschool* 1920:67-8).

120 In 1922, in the explanatory memorandum accompanying the 1923 budget, the government announced the establishment of the Rechtshoogeschool in 1924 (*Mededeelingen der Regeering* 1924:228).

nor fowl, on the one hand providing more than was needed for positions in the rank and file of the judiciary and on the other producing graduates that could not compete with university-trained lawyers (not in the least due to the inferior quality of their pre-Rechtsschool education). Also, the teaching at the school was overly focussed on the segregated administration of justice, which was no longer in line with the idea of unification of the legal system (*Verslag Commissie hervorming Rechtsschool* 1920:45-6, 69). Though the *scholen voor recht en administratie* did not come about, the sword of Damocles over the Rechtsschool remained. The preparatory programme began to be wound down in the academic year of 1923-1924 and on 18 May 1928, shortly after the last ever final exams, the school gates were closed for the last time. For the last few years it went by its official name of Rechtsschool (rather than Opleidingsschool voor Inlandsche Rechtskundigen) as from 1922 onwards, Foreign Orientals and Europeans were also enrolled in the course.[121] In total, some twenty students of these origins acquired the Rechtsschool diploma in the period from 1923 to 1928.[122]

The Carpentier Alting Committee had given top priority to the idea that the Netherlands East Indies, in its quest for emancipation, would benefit from noth-

[121] Governor General's Decree no. 24 dated 23-5-1922; compare *Gedenkboek Rechtsschool* 1929:86-7. The committee had initially disapproved of relaxing the admission criteria. But because the Hoger Onderwijswet (Higher Education Act) was amended to make holders of a Rechtsschool diploma henceforth eligible for a Dutch PhD, which would grant native students an unfair advantage over those from other population groups, it changed its point of view. After all, the *rechtshogeschool* it had proposed also had to be open to all population groups. Moreover, pressure was exerted from the Netherlands after the society of Chinese students in Holland, Chung Hwa Hui, had petitioned the ministers for the Colonies and of Education, Arts and Sciences to admit non-Natives to the law course in the Netherlands, namely through the diploma of the five-year Indies HBS and through allowing non-Natives, too, to take the Rechtsschool's final examination. The petition was granted by virtue of the decree mentioned above, albeit on the express proviso that non-native *rechtskundigen* were not to be eligible for the offices intended for Natives only. Notwithstanding the decree dating from 1922, one Chinese had gained the title of *rechtskundige* as early as 1920. Kan Teng Tjoan sat the final examination of the Rechtsschool as an external candidate, having completed the HBS and the first part of the notary's exam and subsequently having been granted special permission to take the exams. He, too, had been concerned only with the exemptions to be obtained upon continuing his law studies in the Netherlands (*Verslag Commissie hervorming Rechtsschool* 1920:71-2; Poeze 1986:137; *Gedenkboek Rechtsschool* 1929:92).

[122] This estimate is based on the lists of names contained in the *Gedenkboek Rechtsschool* 1929:92-7. The list of external candidates includes eleven Chinese-sounding names and six European-sounding ones (the aforementioned Miss Opperman (see footnote 42) among them). The list of 'full-time students' includes a total of three such names, two of which are Chinese – Kwee Thiam Liong and Thio Tjong Goen passed their final examinations in 1925 and 1926, respectively, the former studying at Batavia and the latter being employed as an official seconded at the Makassar *landraad* at the time of the memorial book's publication – and one of which sounds European, namely Charles Louis Nagel, who passed the final examinations in 1925 and studied at Batavia in 1929 (*Gedenkboek Rechtsschool* 1929:96).

ing less than a law course at the highest – academic – level, a course that would prepare jurists for practising law in the Indies. In other words, the course could neither be of a vocational nature (limited in scope) nor a duplicate of that in the motherland (Van Asbeck 1949:7, 10-1). The committee's report argued in favour of a number of important and innovative differences with the law course in the Netherlands. These related not only to the subjects to be taught and tested, but also to the educational methodology to be applied. Instead of being drilled for the exams by crammers, a common practice in the Netherlands, the mandatory subjects would need to be taught by expert lecturers and to be presented to the students as separate units, to be completed in the first three years of the four-year course (well before the final examinations).

The fourth year would allow elective subjects to be explored in more depth (*Verslag Commissie hervorming Rechtsschool* 1920:49). Ideally, there would be much contact between lecturers and students. The report suggests interactive lectures rather than presentations, elective lectures on special subjects (*privatissima*) (by way of a 'law laboratory') and no more than twenty-four students from any one cohort per lecturer. For the first three years, attending and actively participating in lectures and practices would be compulsory, during which time the student would be closely guided towards exams. Self-study, according to the committee an unprecedented concept in the Indies though not in the Netherlands, would need to be accommodated during the fourth and final year (*Verslag Commissie hervorming Rechtsschool* 1920:51-2). Finally, the course was to prepare the students for practising law, for which purpose the committee proposed the introduction of compulsory debating soirees and practices such as writing dissertations and defending theses (*Verslag Commissie hervorming Rechtsschool* 1920:48, 50).

The influence of the Carpentier Alting Committee was clearly present in the final design of the course. It was split into two stages and conferred the title of *meester in de rechten* onto graduating students. The first stage, lasting two years, was rounded off with the *kandidaatsexamen* (candidate's exam),[123] the second with the *doctoraalexamen* (master's exam) (Hoger Onderwijs-ordonnantie (Higher Education ordinance) art. 10). Both were divided into two parts, so that the first part of the candidate's exam was taken at the end of the first year and the second part after two years; having completed the third year, students would sit the first part of the master's exam, with the second to be taken at the end of the fourth year. The subjects tested in the candidate's exam comprised an introduction to jurisprudence (one year), constitutional and administrative law (two years), the ethnology of the Netherlands East

123 University studies in the Netherlands formerly required students to pass this mid-course examination prior to embarking on the degree stage of a course. Though more or less equivalent to a bachelor's, the *kandidaats* did not constitute a stand-alone degree.

Indies (one year), Javanese, Malay or another Indonesian language to be approved by the faculty (two years), civil law, criminal law and sociology (one year each) (Rechtshoogeschool Statutes art. 13-14). At the end of the third year, exams were taken in the subjects civil law and civil procedural law, commercial law, interethnic law, adat law, criminal law, criminal procedural law and economics. For the fourth year, a specialization needed to be chosen from the subjects of private law, criminal law, constitutional law and socio-economics (Rechtshoogeschool Statutes art. 17-20).

In 1928 the degree stage of the course was extended by one year, postponing the choice of a specialization until the end of the fourth year. The subjects taught during the third year, listed above, were henceforth covered in two years rather than one (except the subject of interethnic law), simultaneously shifting the two subjects of civil and criminal procedural law to the fourth year (*Stb.* 1928, no. 349). The 1924 Statutes still imposed Latin as a prerequisite for the master's exam in private law, but this requirement was abolished in 1930.[124] Also in that year, the admission criteria were relaxed to include the diplomas of the HBS (five years) and Algemene Middelbare School (AMS, General Secondary School)-A I and B (departments of Eastern literary studies and mathematics, respectively), as well as those of the *gymnasium*[125] and the AMS-A II (department of Western classical education).[126] Rechtsschool graduates were exempt from several of the candidate's exam subjects (art. 25 clause 1 sub 1 Rechtshoogeschool Statutes). All considered, the design of the course turned out to be eminently suited to its purpose. Some of the innovations, creating various specializations, for example, even came to be adopted in the Netherlands at a later stage and the curriculum continued as the basis of legal

124 *Stb.* 1929, no. 49. As early as 1927 this requirement was suspended by way of a temporary measure (*Stb.* 1927, no. 322). It was extended in 1928 (*Stb.* 1928, no. 349) for all who enrolled prior to or during the academic year of 1928-29. From 1930 art. 21 of the Rechtshoogeschool Statutes stipulated that a student who was not in possession of a diploma from a *gymnasium* (see footnote 125), *lyceum* (institution of secondary education including *gymnasium* and HBS) or AMS-A II department and who wished to take any of the master's exams (no longer exclusively that in private law), at his own request would be given the opportunity to demonstrate his competence in reading simple Latin prose. The lectures in Latin, then attended by just a few individuals, ceased altogether in the academic year of 1934-35 with the departure of the lecturer extraordinary in Latin, dr. P.J. Koets (*Jaarboekje Rechtshoogeschool* 1936:70). The article was removed from the Statutes in 1939 (*Stb.* 1939, no. 554).

125 Highest level of secondary school, providing classical education.

126 With a view to promoting an understanding of Roman law, the Carpentier Alting Committee had initially included Latin in the admission criteria. When it became apparent, however, that the Snouck Hurgronje Committee, established in 1919, also intended to admit students not schooled in Latin to the course in Indies Law to be founded in the Netherlands (see below), the East Indies committee dropped this criterion in 1921 (*Mededeelingen der Regeering* 1924:227; compare Van Helsdingen 1922:19-20). Compare art. 21 of the Rechtshoogeschool Statutes and art. 12-13 of the Higher Education ordinance.

education in Indonesia for decades after its independence (Van Asbeck 1949:7, 10; Mardjono Reksodiputro 1989:540-1, 1995d:201).

Scholten, in his speech on the occasion of the opening of the Rechtshoogeschool, impressed on his audience the priority to be given to method over ready knowledge. Learning by rote a 'diligently copied dictation' was beside the point entirely but learning to think for oneself was essential. He also argued the notion that a country in pursuit of new law could not do without its own centre of jurisprudence. Insight into the social balance and the prevalent attitudes was required in order to assess with any degree of accuracy whether a legal rule could gain legitimacy, such insight generally being acquirable only in the country in question (*Opening Rechtshoogeschool* 1925:14, 18-9). To conclude, Scholten pointed out the importance of truly understanding those for whom the legal rules were intended – the selfsame argument that had figured so prominently in establishing the Rechtsschool.[127]

Following Scholten's departure from the Indies in November 1924, his post of faculty chairman was taken up by J. van Kan, civil law professor-to-be.[128] The (lawyer and) former Director of Education and Worship K.F. Creutzberg was appointed chairman of the board of curators. The lecturing staff with which the Rechtshoogeschool kicked off consisted of the professors F.M. baron Van Asbeck (international law, foreign colonial law and historical development of state institutions), J.H. Boeke (economics), R.A. (Raden Ario) Hoesein Djajadiningrat (Malay, Islamic law and institutions),[129] B. ter Haar (adat law), R.D. Kollewijn (interethnic law), J.H.A. Logemann (constitutional and administrative law of the Netherlands East Indies), J.M.J. Schepper (criminal law, criminology and legal ethics) and B.J.O. Schrieke (ethnology and sociology), as well as the lecturers E. Bessem (Latin) and J. Kats (Javanese) (Resink 1974:426-30; see Fig. 15).

The Rechtshoogeschool grew into a flourishing institution. At the close of 1934, having just celebrated two quinquennia, a total of 350 students were enrolled, consisting of 199 Indonesians, 83 Europeans and 68 Chinese. The total included thirty females (*Jaarboekje Rechtshoogeschool* 1936:71). In 1926 Mohammad Nazif became the first Indonesian to be awarded a doctorate by

127 'Jurisprudence not only requires understanding rules and knowledge nor even understanding facts, it also begs empathy with the very people for whom the rules are intended. Such empathy comprises more than simple understanding. It harbours emotion. Anyone seeking to inform a people with a view to establishing law needs to be a good interpreter of that people. Here, too, love is all.' (*Opening Rechtshoogeschool* 1925:20). Compare pp. 81-2.

128 In recognition of his efforts, Scholten received a knighthood in the Order of the Dutch Lion (*Opening Rechtshoogeschool* 1925:24).

129 Hoesein Djajadiningrat, who had abandoned his law studies due to the vague career prospects (see footnote 13) and had opted for language and literature instead, by a curious quirk of fate was appointed professor at a law faculty.

the Rechtshoogeschool, his thesis having been prepared in the Netherlands and in Paris;[130] the first three master's degrees were awarded in 1928.

Several years before the first batch of indigenous students was able to enroll in the law course at Batavia, dozens of others had made their way to Leiden. The motherland had put in place various measures that greatly enhanced the appeal of reading law in the Netherlands. To begin with, from 1919, the Minister of Education, Arts and Sciences was personally allowed to exempt the holders of certain Indies diplomas from some of the exams at Dutch universities, having first sought the advice of the educational institution in question.[131] Shortly afterwards, Leiden University's Faculty of Law informed the government of the Netherlands East Indies, by telegram, of its resolution to agree to exempt native *rechtskundigen* from the candidate's exam when requested to do so.[132] Secondly, native *rechtskundigen* and secondary school leavers from the Indies were eligible for a grant (as well as reimbursement of their travel costs), provided their parents would pay the remainder of the study and living costs.[133] And thirdly, in September 1921, the Leiden University faculties of Law and of Arts and Philosophy jointly launched a new course in Indies law, which offered unconditional admission to holders of the Dutch HBS diploma (also encompassing youngsters in possession of an Indies HBS or AMS-B diploma).[134]

The course in Indies law was the first independent law course in the

130 During his studies in the Netherlands, Nazif was a board member of the Perhimpoenan Indonesia (Indonesian Society). While abroad, the police conducted an action against this society, forcing Nazif to conclude his studies elsewhere (Poeze 1986:221; compare Resink 1974:444).

131 Act dated 7-6-1919, *Ned. Stb.* no. 307. This came about by means of an amendment of art. 132 of the *Hoger Onderwijswet* (see the *Verslag Commissie hervorming Rechtsschool* 1920:7-10). Up until that time, such exemptions could only be granted through an *algemene maatregel van bestuur* (order in council), involving a lengthy and time-consuming procedure.

132 *Verslag Commissie hervorming Rechtsschool* 1920:7. The telegram sent by Leiden University was read out in the Volksraad on 2-7-1919.

133 *Stb.* 1918, no. 747; compare Fasseur 1993:402. Dutch students wishing to enter the Indies service, too, could apply for certain grants – see *Stb.* 1915, no. 737, as amended successively by *Stb.* 1918, no. 198 and *Stb.* 1921, no. 139. In *Stb.* 1922, no. 291, these decisions were revoked and replaced by a new arrangement, which allowed students put forward by a particular committee to the Minister for the Colonies to be trained up as candidates for the Indies civil service. Once the candidate's exam had been passed a grant could be allocated, though in exceptional cases a grant was awarded for the entire course (to a maximum of six years).

134 The entrance requirements for the 'ordinary' law course included a diploma from a secondary school teaching classics (or passing an equivalent state exam). On 1-9-1921 the new Academisch Statuut (Academic Statute), enacted by Koninklijk Besluit (Royal Decree) dated 15-6-1921 (*Ned. Stb.* no. 800), came into force. For the provisions relating to the Indies law course, see paragraphs 57-61. Admission of the holders of a Dutch HBS diploma to the course concerned was effected by amending art. 133 of the Hoger Onderwijswet (Act dated 1-3-1920, *Ned. Stb.* no. 105). The Act dated 11-1-1919 (*Stb.* no. 19; *Verslag Commissie opleiding rechterlijke ambtenaren* 1920:5) put the Indies HBS and AMS-B diplomas on a par with those from the Dutch HBS.

Netherlands aimed exclusively at the Netherlands East Indies. It was to satisfy once and for all the long-standing call for a sufficient number of lawyers equipped for their tasks within the Indies judiciary. It was also hoped that the new discipline would persuade students indigenous to the colony to come and study in the Netherlands (Fasseur 1993:401). In September 1919 the committee appointed by the joint ministers of Education, Arts and Sciences and for the Colonies had advised in favour of establishing the course and had designed a programme of study and examination (*Verslag Commissie opleiding rechterlijke ambtenaren* 1920:3). The committee consisted of the Leiden professors Snouck Hurgronje (chairman), G. André de la Porte and C. van Vollenhoven, their Groningen University colleague Ph. Kleintjes and the former justice at the Hooggerechtshof Boekhoudt, mentioned above.[135] The committee considered a law course that from the outset focussed entirely on the Netherlands East Indies preferable to the existing MA course supplemented by the faculty exam and the Indology exam (the latter testing the students' knowledge of the 'Indies subjects' with a view to service in the country's judiciary and administration, respectively).[136]

It took about four years to complete the course. Those who did so successfully were awarded the title of master of laws, together with the right to use this title in both the Netherlands and the Netherlands East Indies. However, contrary to the committee's recommendation, masters of Indies law were only permitted to hold offices in the judiciary or to register as advocates in the Netherlands East Indies. In 1923 the course began to admit holders of the diploma AMS-A II, too, and later still, the diploma AMS-A I was also put on a par with the HBS diploma.[137] As promised, *rechtskundigen* were admitted straight to the master's stage of the course. The rules for the allocation of grants were adapted early in 1922 in order to make students reading Indies law (bearing the title of candidate Indies judicial officer) eligible for funding, too.[138] There was, incidentally, a more general arrangement enabling indigenous youngsters wishing to study in the Netherlands, but lacking the funds to do so, to obtain free passage as well as a grant.[139]

135 Joint decision dated 18-9-1919, Chapter V, no. 46 (*Verslag Commissie opleiding rechterlijke ambtenaren* 1920:3-4).

136 *Verslag Commissie opleiding rechterlijke ambtenaren* 1920:4-5. Henceforth, graduates in Dutch law wishing to widen their options with an appointment in the Indies judiciary were required to take a supplementary exam in Indies law (Fasseur 1993:401).

137 *Ned. Stb.* 1923, no. 47 in conjunction with 428; compare *Verslag Commissie opleiding rechterlijke ambtenaren* 1920:5-6.

138 *Stb.* 1921, no. 291. The rules regarding the repayment of the grant, if any, were given in *Stb.* 1921, no. 1356.

139 *Stb.* 1918, no. 747. It should be mentioned, lastly, that, by virtue of the Opleidingsbesluit op de Indische Bestuursopleiding (Education Decree pertaining to the Indies Administration

Fig. 17. Rechtsschool graduates on the occasion of Gondokoesoemo's doctorate, Leiden, 1922 (from left to right, sitting on the floor: Sartono, Singgih and Boediarto; seated: Zainal Abidin, Iskaq Tjokrohadisoerjo, Gondokoesoemo, Hadi, Achmad, Moekiman; front row standing: Iwa Koesoema Soemantri, Koesnoen, Soedibjo Dwidjosewojo, Notosoebagijo, Soewono, Oerip Kartodirdjo, Soebroto and Alinoeddin Enda Boemi; back row standing: Soejoedi, Soetikno, Soesanto Tirtoprodjo, Gatot Taroenomihardjo, Koesoemah Atmadja, Soedirman, Sastromoeljono (names taken from Poeze 1986:164). According to Poeze (1986:164), Besar, Soemardi and Soedjono are missing in the photograph. The latter name only is not listed among the Rechtsschool alumni (from 1912 to 1922) included in *Gedenkboek Rechtsschool* 1929.) (KITLV collection no. 4534)

In the candidate's exam, students were tested on history of law, constitutional law and comparative ethnology; the master's exam covered adat law, the civil, commercial and criminal law of the Netherlands East Indies (including the law governing civil and criminal procedure), Javanese and another subject selected from a wide range, for example philosophy of law, international law, archeology and one other Indonesian language.[140] Javanese instead of Malay had been made compulsory because, the committee had argued, one or the other ought to be so and Malay (customarily used in European circles) would be relatively easy to learn in practice. Moreover, Snouck Hurgronje and his like-minded colleagues portrayed Javanese as the chief indigenous language bar none from both a numerical and a cultural perspective, a command of which would aid the acquisition of other indigenous languages such as Madurese, Sundanese and Batak.[141] In 1937 both Malay and Javanese became electives, making the language teaching at the course now bear a closer resemblance to the curriculum of the Rechtshoogeschool (Fasseur 1993:402).

Many a native *rechtskundige* grabbed the new opportunity with both hands. In 1920 eleven set sail for Leiden – all at their own expense and all having quit their jobs in the colonial government. Only two years later the number of *rechtskundigen* enrolled at Leiden University was twenty-seven. The law students admitted on their Rechtsschool diploma were preceded, in 1919, by three Indonesians with an HBS diploma who, under the old rules, had had to take a state exam prior to being admitted to the law course.[142] In the period from 1920 until 1924 a total of fifty Indonesians and ten ethnic Chinese read law at Leiden, of whom forty-seven and six, respectively, graduated. The Rechtsschool proved to be an excellent preparatory course – most *rechtskundigen* succeeded in gaining their master's within eighteen months to two years

---

Course), from 1922 graduates in Indies law were also eligible for posts in the colonial administration. This decision was revoked in 1924, however (Fasseur 1993:405-7).

140 See *Verslag Commissie opleiding rechterlijke ambtenaren* 1920:7-10. Fasseur (1993:402) points out that, here, the term 'Indonesian' is used in the State Gazette for the first time.

141 *Verslag Commissie opleiding rechterlijke ambtenaren* 1920:13-4. The committee's argument adhered to the tradition of Dutch education policy that had been followed in respect of the Netherlands East Indies since the introduction of the Cultuurstelsel (Cultivation System) in 1830. In the Indies, however, Malay was considered of equal if not greater importance to judicial officers than Javanese, which was also in accordance with a long-standing tradition.

142 The three were Soebardjo, A.A. Maramis and N.D. Pamontjak (Poeze 1989:261-2, compare with Poeze 1986:157, 163-5). They were not the first non-Europeans to have left the Netherlands East Indies to read law in the Netherlands. Oei Jan Lee, for example, obtained the master of laws title at Leiden in 1888. The first Indonesian to graduate in the Netherlands was Gondowinoto. He enrolled at Leiden University in 1910, graduated in 1918 and was awarded a doctorate 'on his theses' in the following year (at the start of the twentieth century, a thesis was not necessarily presented in writing). His brother, Noto Soeroto, having enrolled in the Leiden Faculty of Law in 1908, would not stay the course (Poeze 1989:252, 256-7, compare Poeze 1986:164-5).

Fig. 18. Batavia *raad van justitie* (presently Museum Seni Rupa dan Keramik/Fine Arts and Ceramics Museum) (www.greatmirrors.com)

(see Lev 1976:152). The first holder of a Rechtsschool diploma to do a PhD in jurisprudence was Gondokoesoemo; he arrived in Leiden in September 1920 with the first cohort of *rechtskundigen*, passed his master's exams by June 1921 and was awarded a doctorate in June 1922.[143] Some *rechtskundigen* also graduated in Dutch law or even in Dutch law only. Up until 1927, the majority completed the degree course in both Dutch and Indies law. Thereafter, nearly all native students obtained the Indies title only. Approximately fourteen Indonesians eventually graduated in Dutch law only (Lev 1976:152).

The majority of graduates enjoyed a career within the judiciary. In reality, this meant various offices at the *landraad* and the *landgerecht* as the door leading towards a judgeship at a higher European court (*raad van justitie* or Hooggerechtshof) remained firmly closed. In 1928 Koesoemah Atmadja (Rechtsschool diploma 1919, Leiden University doctorate 1922, faculty exam 1923) became the first Indonesian in the colonial era to be appointed mem-

143 These data are derived from Poeze 1989:261, 276 and 1986:163-5. Gondokoesoemo's PhD thesis was entitled *Vernietiging van dorpsbesluiten in Indië* (Quashing village council decisions in the Netherlands East Indies). For more on this work and other theses on the Netherlands East Indies defended in Leiden, see Pompe 1993.

Fig. 19. Padang *raad van justitie,* ca 1890 (KITLV collection no. 6806)

ber of a *raad van justitie,* at Padang.[144] He was one of very few indigenous judges to be employed at this level.[145] Access to these same courts was made considerably easier for those who had joined the advocature (be it for some years or a lifetime). Daniel Lev's article, based in part on his interviews with several members of this first batch of Indonesian advocates, contains a wealth of information on this group. Besar Martokoesoemo blazed a trail by starting a legal practice in Tegal in 1924 and opening a branch in Semarang a few years later (Lev 1976:153; *Orang Indonesia jang terkemoeka* 1973:54). Others followed, establishing law firms in Batavia, Bandung, Surabaya, Makassar and in other important towns in the Netherlands East Indies.

Confrères from Sumatra or other Outer Territories followed in the footsteps of the first advocates from Java. From the end of the 1920s, Chinese, too, began

144 His appointment as a member of this *raad van justitie* took effect on 2-8-1928. He had been a temporary member extraordinary since 18-11-1927 (*Regeeringsalmanak* for 1928 and 1929). He became a member of the Semarang *raad van justitie* in 1939.

145 R.P. Notosoebagijo (Rechtsschool diploma 1915, graduated from Leiden in both 1924 and 1925) was appointed judge at the Makassar *raad van justitie* in 1930; Sastromoeljono was appointed member extraordinary of the Semarang *raad van justitie* in 1937.

Fig. 20. Medan *raad van justitie*, 1937 (KITLV collection no. 50561)

Fig. 21. The judges of the Medan *raad van justitie*, 1908 (KITLV collection no. 31008)

Fig. 22. Native employees of the Padang *raad van justitie*, 1919 (KITLV collection no. 18150)

Fig. 23. Personnel of the Makassar *raad van justitie*, 1908-09 (KITLV collection no. 18081)

Fig. 24. Hooggerechtshof, Batavia, ca 1940 (KITLV collection no. 4264)

to start up firms (Lev 1976:155-6), finding ample business in the vast world of trade of their countrymen. Indonesians by and large dealt with criminal cases or civil disputes concerning land, inheritance matters and other family affairs. Their clients were Natives and Chinese, but Europeans also made use of their services. The firms operated on a maximum of six to seven advocates (Lev 1976:155, 158).

Although the new advocates enjoyed a fair measure of success, the road was not an easy one. The established order of European advocates would sooner oppose than support the newcomers (and competitors). Nor were the native and Chinese novices welcome in the existing law firms. The external opposition, partly directed against the involved nationalism of the new advocates, did contribute to a strong group sense – they all knew one another, collaborated with one another and helped out where necessary.[146]

The total number of native masters of laws graduated by 1940 from either Leiden or Batavia is estimated at 275, with an additional fifty to seventy-five Chinese. Advocates represented a clear minority, relative to both the number of indigenous jurists employed outside of the advocature and the number of European advocates – in 1942 there were 36 Indonesians, 36 Chinese and 122 Dutch advocates. The lion's share of indigenous jurists secured a position in the judicial or administrative bureaucracy. The number of native chairmen of *landraden*, in 1942, was slightly below that of Europeans holding the office, but adding the (salaried) members made for a small majority of 60 Indonesians over 56 Dutch and two Chinese; 23 native judicial officers held master's degrees.[147] The *rechtskundigen* who had not supplemented their education

[146] Lev 1976:154-5. Some mixed Indonesian-Chinese firms were founded, too (Lev 1976:164). An example of the opposition encountered by indigenous advocates was the allocation to their firms of a disproportionately large number of pro bono (non-lucrative) cases (Lev 1976:157). Hetty Wertheim-Gijse Weenink, the spouse of the future professor at both the Rechtshoogeschool and Amsterdam University W.F. Wertheim, describes the tour undertaken by her husband, in his capacity of *a.t.b.* at the Tanjungkarang *landraad*, and relates the following about A.A. Maramis, an advocate with a successful practice: 'In our small village, there were but a handful of "notables". We were required to pay each a visit, preferably in the order of their social status. The boss gave us the names. "Why is the advocate [Maramis] not mentioned?" "No, he is a Native, you mustn't go there, that is not the custom", then, noticing the stunned look on my husband's face: "You really must not go there".' They disregarded the advice and went anyway – the person in question had even been a fellow student of the couple at Leiden! 'We felt personally slighted that one of our own should be dismissed so easily.' Regarding the visit to Maramis, she wrote: 'We had a very pleasant time. While reminiscing about Leiden, he gradually began to open up and what we heard about humiliations and discrimination: we couldn't believe our ears. Being a Native, he was denied admission to the social club (though he had been club president in his Leiden days!) nor was he admitted to the swimming club. The racial barriers were so high that the indigenous high society would invite the Europeans and the Chinese to their parties on separate nights. The segregation was considered to be natural.' (Wertheim and Wertheim-Gijse Weenink 1991:110.) The separate worlds and networks in which indigenous and European advocates played out their parts are put into sharp perspective when comparing Iwa Koesoema Soemantri's memoires (2002) with those of Sinninghe Damsté (1999). Ali Sastroamidjojo, who set himself up as an advocate in Yogyakarta in 1927, was very active in the political sphere and achieved various high offices, including that of Prime Minister. He paints a picture of the cold-hearted treatment meted out to him upon being sworn in by the president of the Semarang *raad van justitie*. His political involvement with the Perhimpoenan Indonesia was well-known. His name had also been slurred by a European newspaper: 'As my name was painted in red letters, one of the Dutch newspapers, obviously trying to provoke me, stated: "Whoever wishes to ask for red advice can come to the office of the new advocate, Mr Ali Sastroamidjojo, who is a well-known criminal. He is one of the four red *inlands* students in Holland who were detained in prison in The Hague."' (Ali Sastroamijoyo 1979:47-8.)

[147] These data are derived from Lev 1976:147, 160, 1985:68, Pompe 1996:17, 25 and Fasseur 1995:145. Some fifty Indonesian and twenty Chinese jurists are thought to have acted as advocates throughout any period in the 1920s and 1930s (Lev 1976:161).

with a degree course would continue to form an ample majority.[148] Over the years, they would increasingly be looked down upon, while Leiden graduates (the smallest group) enjoyed the highest status by far.[149]

### *Nationalism, language and adat law*

> [O]ne [can] easily imagine that especially in teaching constitutional and administrative law, history and the like, it would have been downright impossible and undesirable to prevent the evaluation of government policy: *impossible*, because it is a direct consequence of the teaching method applied, *undesirable*, because not only would this erect a wall of mutual distrust between teachers and students, that would adversely affect the moral influence the former have on the latter, but primarily because this would create the impression that the government ought to be ashamed of what it does for the people of these quarters.[150]

Be they at the Rechtsschool or a university, reading law introduced the students to new texts (authoritative, often also internally persuasive) and languages. The lectures, the books and the social contact with teachers and fellow students alike, to a greater or lesser extent caused all of them to adopt new ideas and values, a new ideology and vision on man and society. New ties were forged, new communities came into being – based on friendship, academic years spent in each other's company, shared careers. Their working lives might vary enormously, with most of them working year on year in the same office, forming part of an official machine (judges and other officers of the judicature), while others led a metropolitan existence, wandering from one big city in the archipel to the next (advocates) (Lev 1976:164). Even judges and advocates who had been out of touch for many years, though, continued to be part of at least two communities, accompanied by two languages – that of former fellow students and that of the Netherlands East Indies law. If communally singing the national anthem can make visible a national bond (Anderson 1985:132), the awning of legal provisions and handbooks that canopied the majority of *rechtskundigen* and *meesters in de rechten* in their work,

148 A head count of names listed under 'pengadilan' (judicature), in particular, in *Orang Indonesia jang terkemoeka* 1973 (see footnote 48) resulted in the figure of 114 native *rechtskundigen*, 81 of whom had not yet obtained the master's degree at the time of publication (1944).

149 Lev 1976:146-7. In 1940, according to Lev, there were at least 108 Indonesians with a master of laws from Leiden University and nine more with an LL.M from Utrecht University (awarded by the Faculty of Indology established there in the mid-1920s); of the others, at least 146 had graduated from the Rechtshoogeschool (Lev 1976:147).

150 Van Helsdingen 1929c:64. The opportunity to speak freely whenever possible was considered to be a precondition for 'that form of mutual trust, that alone can be a solid foundation for the fruition of teaching oriented towards ethics' (Van Helsdingen 1929c:65).

and the languages they spoke there, constituted their professional bond.

But the law course did not present the students with texts on the law alone. Texts of a different nature, too, were circulated. Though maybe less authoritative than the lectures, they were at least equally persuasive. Reading the descriptions of the budding nationalism, one cannot fail to be struck by the sheer quantity of texts and authors mentioned. R.A. Kartini's *Van duisternis tot licht* (From darkness to light), Multatuli, Ernest Renan, Karl Marx, Gandhi – these are but a selection from the infinite range of books and names that inspired, provoked change and caused people to steer a new course. The joint 'pilgrimage' to the strange town or the faraway land (see p. 98 and Anderson 1972:18), the new courses of study and the new jobs, away from home and fixed patterns, led students and new *priyayi* to adopt new angles on society and process them into a new consciousness, new solidarities, new languages and communities that transcended the boundaries of their areas of study and work.[151]

The texts and languages of the lectures on law and those referring to a new social or national order by no means were irreconcilable. One could hate all things Western yet complete a law course in the Netherlands; one could be an active member of the Partai Nasional Indonesia (PNI, Indonesian National Party) yet be employed as an advocate.[152] The story of the law had a higher status than the actual social order. However unjust the actions of the colonial (or Indonesian) government, in the opinion of the indigenous jurists, however poor their experiences with the actual workings of the law in which they had been trained, their confidence in the story of the law was undiminished. Because of this, though, violations had all the more impact.[153]

Visions of the future, whether of an independent Indonesia or an Indies Commonwealth, translated pre-eminently into the language and the terms of the law.[154] Some of the texts and concepts bandied about by nationalists came

151 Harsja Bachtiar 1976:31-44. Ali Sastroamijoyo's depiction (1979:23) of his introduction to the Indische (Indonesische) Vereeniging (Indies/Indonesian Society) is also illustrative.

152 See Lev 1976:149, 153-8. Compare Soetan Sjahrir: 'I spoke to someone, recently, an advocate who, in the four years or so he had spent studying in Holland, had managed to amplify his prejudices, his antipathy towards all things Western and European, his fanatical hatred even' (Sjahrazad 1945:8).

153 For example, Iwa Koesooema Soemantri, in the personal memoires he compiled in the second half of the 1960s, expresses indignation not just at his unfounded exile, in 1930, but also over the procedural error committed at that time in not having a bailiff serve notice of the decision to take him into custody (Iwa Kusuma Sumantri 2002:98). The conviction of Soekarno by the Bandung *landraad*, too, was a disappointment to law students (Ali Sastroamidjojo 1979:69).

154 Noteworthy, here, is the 'flag ceremony' mentioned in the memoires of Ali Sastroamijoyo. He relates that the student members of the Indonesische Vereeniging/Perhimpoenan Indonesia in Leiden observed a custom, immediately before taking an exam, of meditating for a moment in front of the red and white flag with the buffalo head that adorned Achmad Soebardjo's sitting

straight from the lecture halls. Words spoken by C. van Vollenhoven (Leiden), B.J.O. Schrieke (Rechtshoogeschool), J.H. Boeke (Coöperatieve Commissie (Commission supervising cooperative societies), then Rechtshoogeschool) and R. Kranenburg (Leiden) resounded in the Perhimpoenan Indonesia (Indonesian Society)[155] in the Netherlands and at the youth conferences in the Netherlands East Indies (Van Miert 1995:321, 397; compare Van Niel 1984:246-7).

The influence of these mentors was reinforced by the fairly close relationships the law students had with their teachers, who would invite the students to their homes, to high tea or to while away their Saturday evenings. Professors such as Van Vollenhoven were not only held in high esteem by their students, but they were also well-liked.[156] Some were progressive in their thinking and acting, like the law lecturers among the thirteen men who called for plans to found an Indies Commonwealth, in 1930, and would publish the paper *De Stuw* (The Propeller) for several years.[157] J.M.J. Schepper, criminal law professor, wrote an article containing scathing criticism of the court's decision in the Soekarno case but was refused publication in the *Indisch Tijdschrift van het Recht*. The article was therefore published under separate cover.[158] As is evident from the above quote of Van Helsdingen, open discussion (at the Rechtsschool also taking place in the Chamber of Rhetoric) and independent thinking were encouraged, even when the subject was a sensitive one. Ideas that were too radical to Van Helsdingen's liking (which he ascribed largely to the 'Sturm und Drang' phase of the students' development), he tried to moderate through argumentation. From time to time, the professors would distance themselves from groups and opinions they considered too unbridled.[159]

---

room. The idea was 'to strengthen our will and conviction that the examination was important in the struggle for the independence of our homeland' (Ali Sastroamijoyo 1979:22).

155 The Perhimpoenan Indonesia, founded under the name of Indische Vereeniging (Indies Society) in 1908 but renamed Indonesische Vereeniging (Indonesian Society) in 1922, was a society of Indonesian students in the Netherlands. From the 1920s onwards, it gradually adopted a more radical nationalist stance.

156 De Beaufort 1954:190-2; Otto and Pompe 1989:243; Van Helsdingen 1929c:65; Wertheim and Wertheim-Gijse Weenink 1991:166-7; Lev 1976:150, 152. Compare pp. 92-3.

157 For more on *De Stuw*, see Locher-Scholten 1971, Resink 1974 and Jonkman 1971:71-3. The thirteen men were F.M. van Asbeck, F.D.K. Bosch, A.W.H. Bussink, G.W.J. Drewes, Th.A. Fruin, B. ter Haar, H.A. Idema, J.A. Jonkman, G.H. van der Kolff, A.F. de Savornin Lohman, H.J. van Mook, J.J.G.E. Rückert and E.W. Walch (Jonkman 1971:71-2). Also see Wertheim and Wertheim-Gijse Weenink 1991:153.

158 Resink 1974:434. Schepper's article was published by De Unie at Batavia, in 1931, and bore the title 'Het vonnis in de P.N.I.-zaak' (The decision in the P.N.I. case).

159 Van Helsdingen, who taught at the Rechtsschool from 1912 to 1928 and had been the acting head of school for the last two years, put it that even notions held by the students that could be branded as 'wrong impressions and fallacies' had better be discussed openly 'rather than tiptoeing round these matters, which – even when not touched upon at school – inevitably would stir the hearts and heads of the youngsters and would then work their detriment unchecked' (Van

Fig. 25. The Board of the Indonesische Vereeniging, 1923 (from left to right, Darmawan Mangoenkoesoemo, Moh. Hatta, Iwa Koesoema Soemantri, Sastromoeljono, Sartono) (*Oedaya* 1-II:65)

Education and the nature of the studies have contributed in part to the prominent role played by law students and jurists in initiatives and organizations that, in retrospect, all come under the heading of 'nationalist movement' (see Poeze 1989:263 and Resink 1974:432-5). Well-known examples are the

Helsdingen 1929c:66). He then points out that Dutch governance 'has been a blessing and continues to be so' for the Indonesians, that the government counted on the future support of the pupils in 'nurturing [the Netherlands East Indies] into greater prosperity and development' and that 'the Native society [...] for the time being is not capable of standing on its own two feet, thus needing still the guardianship of the "dominator", whose governance alone is capable of protecting the people against the self-interest of half-baked "strebers" (social climbers)' (Van Helsdingen 1929c:64). He does not seem to have taken the radical ideas altogether seriously, calling them understandable but 'it was borne in mind that young men of about twenty years of age rarely fathom the potency of their words and that for incompletely developed minds, still in their Sturm und Drang phase, slogans such as "the awakening of the East", "the Indies for the Indonesians", "the emancipation of the Natives", etc. etc. cast a powerful spell' (Van Helsdingen 1929c:65). Van Vollenhoven was an honorary member of the Perhimpoenan Indonesia and attended their meetings but ceased to do so once non-cooperation began to be advocated (compare Lev 1976:150). Nor did he want to contribute to *De Stuw* (De Beaufort 1954:144).

Perhimpoenan Indonesia in the Netherlands and the Perhimpoenan Peladjar-Peladjar Indonesia (PPPI, Society of Indonesian Students) in the Netherlands East Indies. The latter, founded in 1926, was the organization behind the second youth conference, held in Batavia in October 1928, that would go down in history as 'Sumpah Pemuda' ('Oath of the Young').[160]

By comparison with many other highly qualified professionals, law students, *rechtskundigen* and law graduates were fairly active in the more radical political organizations. Within their own group, however, those engaging in politics represented a minority. There may have been a consensus of sorts on how to shape the future state but the most suitable path towards it was a matter of severe discord. For example, some masters of laws and *rechtskundigen* favoured gradual change through legal channels. Most of the proponents of the speedier, non-cooperative method opted to practise law as advocates rather than as officers of the colonial system.

The explanation for the relationship between political leaning and career choice is twofold. Seen from one angle, a job in the colonial government was forfeit to students who had chosen to support the more radical ideas and had actively engaged in politics, often in the Netherlands, away from the colonial structure. Seen from another, it was advocates in particular who were confronted with the sharp edge of colonial reality. They were the only native jurists (barring a few officials seconded) with access to the various *raden van justitie*. Here, they met with a judicial apparatus that functioned honourably, and with a comprehensive set of provisions aimed at ensuring the integrity of the legal process, for the benefit of defendants and litigants alike. Here, too, they were respected as equal players of the law game, at the highest level at that, and were accorded the esteem due an advocate. On the downside they encountered opposition and discrimination in establishing their practices and performing their duties, being mere Natives, while watching native defendants before the *landraad* sit on the floor, dependent as they were for a fair trial on the goodwill of the 'Kangdjeng Toean' (Honorable Lord) president (Lev 1976:148-64). Such experiences probably fuelled rather than quenched the fire of their nationalist politics. Advocates' membership of a 'supra-ethnic' metropolitan culture also contributed to their relatively fervent nationalism (Lev 1976:164).

Most law students and jurists, however, did not at all, or hardly, engage in radical political groups. A large number of *rechtskundigen* and many others were in the employ of the colonial government or studied in the Netherlands,

160 For more on the Perhimpoenan Indonesia (and the Indonesische Vereeniging), see Dahm 1969:52-4 and Poeze 1986:175-9, 188-92, 209-20, 251-65; for the PPPI, see Van Miert 1995:325. Resink (1974) points out the symbolism in the date on which the Sumpah Pemuda took place, 28 October, which happened to be the foundation day of the Rechtshoogeschool.

supported by a grant, which rather limited the scope for political involvement.[161] The relationship between political leaning and career options can here be seen to function inversely. The everyday cogs of the judicial machine tended to identify with the state and were inclined towards gradual reform of the system instead of its wholesale renovation (Pompe 1996:14; Van Niel 1984:241-2). If advocates thought in terms of civil rights and procedural forms, judicial officers in a sense constituted part of (a modern day version of) the patriarchal tradition of informal arrangements and supposed powers or hierarchies of the authorities (Lev 1976:160). On occasion, nationalists and native judges opposed each other in court in the most literal sense – Sebastiaan Pompe lists several incidences of nationalists convicted by judges belonging to their own population group.[162] Some ideologies and the paths towards their realization simply did not fit within the framework of the law.

In the range of visions of the future that were advocated, a role was reserved for both law on European principles and adat law. Most jurists became interested in Dutch (Indies) law, as opposed to adat law, while still studying. Adat law may have been an integral part of the Indonesian tradition, it was also considered to be outdated and not at all suited to shaping a modern state based on the rule of law. The state-to-be, therefore, was framed in terms of European law. Following the proclamation of independence in 1945, advocates holding various administrative offices would be instrumental in the abolition of the adat law courts (Lev 1976:152, 165).

Nevertheless, it is evident from the first Indonesian Constitution, and especially from the role played in its creation by R. Soepomo, an expert in adat law, that the concepts of 'modern law' and 'adat law' were far from irreconcilable to Indonesian jurists.[163] In the nationalist movement, too, adat law held an exalted position, if only as a symbol. The impressive trilogy *Het adatrecht van Nederlandsch-Indië* (The adat law of the Netherlands East Indies) by Van Vollenhoven depicts a rich, highly-developed tradition of law that, notwithstanding enormous variation from one adat law territory (*rechtskring*)

161 Lev 1976:161-2. In 1924 the Bond van Indische Rechtskundigen (Union of Indies *Rechtskundigen*, later renamed Perhimpoenan Hakim Indonesia) was classed among the more 'moderate' groups – in contrast to the Indonesische Vereeniging, amongst others (Poeze 1986:184-5).

162 Pompe 1996:24-5. For example, in his decision dated 21-7-1934, Koesoemah Atmadja, chairman extraordinary of the Batavia *landraad*, deliberated 'that although the attainment of the "Indonesia Merdeka" will go hand in hand with the changed composition of the current government, this need not involve violence or breaking the law; that one can easily conceive of a free "Indonesia" with a polity such as that of the British Dominions or even of less independent legal entities within the Kingdom of the Netherlands' (*Indisch Tijdschrift van het Recht* 144 (1938):625).

163 Dr. R. Soepomo, LL.M, was a disciple of Van Vollenhoven. In 1940 he succeeded B. ter Haar as adat law professor. He was to play a prominent role in creating the Constitution. See, for example, Supomo 1949.

to the next, contained certain patterns that were applied throughout the archipelago, in the whole of Indonesia.[164] The second youth conference, organized by law students, in adopting the resolution stating that the Indonesian youth acknowledged a single fatherland, Indonesia, a single people, the Indonesians, and a single language, Indonesian, mentioned adat law as one of the five principles of the unity proclaimed.[165]

The latter conference is all the more interesting because the event brought together (adat) law and the national language in a new mode of thought, that of an independent Indonesia. Malay, proclaimed by the youth conference as the national language – *bahasa Indonesia* (Indonesian language, language of Indonesia) – became increasingly in vogue as the official, everyday language in the mid-1920s, when the nationalist idea began to gain momentum. Apart from being a political weapon, a symbol of the Indonesian nation and the independent state in the making, the language represented the neutral, democratic means par excellence (without *ngoko* or *krama*, that is) for reaching out to the masses.[166]

Curiously enough, indigenous jurists only connected the single national language of the future with *adat* law, on paper at least. At the 1928 youth conference, Yamin put it that adat law ought to be the national law, noted down in both Indonesian and the regional languages (Darmokondo 1981:150). In the trial issue of *Indonésia Raja* (the PPPI's publication) that was brought out in the same year, an anonymous article entitled 'Hoekoem-adat dan bahasa

164 Van Niel 1984:247-9. For more on Van Vollenhoven's school of adat law, see Otto and Pompe 1989 and De Beaufort 1954. A critical analysis of Van Vollenhoven's approach and findings is given in Burns 1999.

165 Resink 1974:443. See the report of the second youth conference, in Darmokondo 1981; also see Van Miert 1995:327-34. Muhammed Yamin, in his speech at the second youth conference, emphasized the authentic Indonesian character of adat law, which was to be respected and preserved (Darmokondo 1981:149-50; compare Mohammad Nazif 1924). The other four principles were the will (to be an independent nation), the history, the language and education (Darmokondo 1981:158; compare Resink 1974 and Van Miert 1995:330-1). For details on the interest in adat law on the part of Soekarno and his fellow nation builders, see Burns 1999:300-5. One aspect of Burns's book is the unravelling of the national (in the sense of encompassing the entire Indonesian archipelago) character of adat law (put forward in particular by the Leiden school of adat law) (see Burns 1999:223-78).

166 Groeneboer 1993:409-16; compare Dahm 1967:36-7. Organizations such as Boedi Oetomo (1908), Sarekat Islam (1912) and the Partai Komunis Indonesia (1920) had also used Malay as their official language, on the pragmatic basis that in this language their message could be communicated to people of different mother tongues (Groeneboer 1993:411). O.S. Tjokroaminoto, leader of Sarekat Islam, at times used Malay to elaborate on legal topics such as legal personality (of the Sarekat Islam society) (see Tjokroaminoto 1981). As early as 1922, the Indonesische Vereeniging also adopted Malay as the common language (Groeneboer 1993:413, also see Rapport centrale inlichtingendienst (Central intelligence agency Report) to Minister for the Colonies S. de Graaff dated 17-12-1923, in Kwantes 1978:51).

Indonésia' (Adat law and the Indonesian language) makes the same case. Indonesian ought to be the language of the adat law of those territories in which Malay is spoken and of those in which the local language is not yet suited to adat law. All other adat law territories ought to use their own local language. The author claimed that he also intended the article to prove the suitability of the Indonesian language for the expression of legal concepts.[167]

The link between adat law, on the one hand, and Indonesian (Malay) and the regional languages, on the other, may be traced back to a 1922 treatise by Van Vollenhoven, entitled 'Indonesische rechtstaal' (Indonesian legal language) (Van Vollenhoven 1922). Rather than use this term to indicate the adat law register of Malay or Indonesian, the professor used 'Indonesian legal language' to denote the aggregate languages of the regional offshoots (*kring-rechten*) belonging to the 'Indonesian law stock'. Thus, it is not the Indonesian equivalent of the Dutch or German legal language that is at issue, here, but the counterpart of what Van Vollenhoven would term the language of the Teutonic law stock or 'Teutonic legal language'. He did underline, however, the surrogate character descriptions of adat law acquired when phrased in a Western language – in which context the later texts quoted should be seen. West Javanese adat law ought to be described in Sundanese, Central Javanese adat law in Javanese, that of Aceh in Acehnese and so forth.[168]

Whether indigenous law students and jurists also linked Malay to practising the law of the *West*, in their visions of the future, is an interesting question. If they did at all, the notion is likely to have had a vague, far-off setting.[169] It is doubtful whether they identified the Indonesian language with their capacity of jurists while still under colonial rule. Even during the Soekarno trial before the Bandung *landraad* (1930) at which submitting sound legal arguments in 'bahasa Indonesia' would have had an enormous political impact, the counsel for the defence spoke *Dutch* – though Soekarno himself spoke Indonesian.[170]

167 *Hoekoem-adat dan bahasa Indonésia* 1929:9-10. Compare Soepomo's speech on the occasion of the fifth General Assembly of the Persatoean Taman-Siswa (Soepomo 1937).

168 See Van Vollenhoven (1928:173-4): 'Its discovery by Westerners is doomed to result in a surrogate. A book on adat law that is written in a Western language and is intended to introduce Occidentals amidst their European cultures to this Oriental phenomenon, is doomed to be a surrogate; the real book on adat law ought to be written by and in the East, by a Native for the benefit of his kin in the wide sense, in one of the Indonesian regional languages. Only the use, for this purpose, of the language or languages of each adat territory provides an opportunity for the test, whether or not the discovery that has been undertaken since 1783 may be deemed successful.' Van Vollenhoven is cited explicitly in *Hoekoem-adat dan bahasa Indonésia* 1929.

169 It was put to the first Indonesische Taal Congres (Indonesian Language Conference), held in 1938, that Indonesian ought to become the language of the law, as well as the language of the various representative bodies (Takdir Alisjahbana 1967:191).

170 The closing speeches of the advocates, translated into Indonesian by Garoeda Gentajoe, are included in *Sedjarah Pergerakan Indonésia 1929-1930. IV: Berisi soerat-toedoehan dan pembélaan*

Fig. 26. Soekarno and his advocates in front of the Bandung *landraad* building, 1930 (Petrus Blumberger 1931; courtesy Wolters Kluwer NV)

Perhaps this was due to a certain lack of confidence on the part of the advocates, common among most other law graduates or *rechtskundigen*, in the adequacy of their Malay for the purpose of putting forward a cogent concluding speech. At all three law courses discussed so far, indigenous languages were taught in a fairly limited fashion. As stated above, up until 1937 Leiden University (the place of study of Soekarno's advocates Sartono and Sastromoeljono) required Javanese to be taken, not Malay (from 1937, students could elect one or the other), while the Rechtshoogeschool offered a choice between Malay, Javanese

*perkara P.N.I. oléh Mr. Sartono, Mr. Sastromoeljono dan Idih Prawiradipoetra* (published by the Fonds Nasional P.P.P.K.I., not dated). The last named defence counsel was a native *rechtskundige*. Soekarno's speech is contained in Soekarno ca 1950 (Indonesian text) and 1931 (Dutch translation). As mentioned earlier in this chapter, legal representation before the *landraad* was not prescribed. The defending jurists therefore were at liberty to conduct their cases in Malay, for example, instead of in Dutch.

or another Indonesian language to be approved (usually Sundanese). Malay was rarely taught at secondary level, so the majority of jurists had had no instruction in that language.[171]

If they had been taught Malay at all, in Leiden (from 1937) or in Batavia, the classes most certainly had not focussed on the production of legal texts in that language. In any event, a good command of any of the countless forms of Malay (acquired in daily life) probably was considered to be of little or no use when faced with an audience (the chairman of the *landraad* first and foremost) that attached enormous importance to precisely formulated, grammatically correct Dutch sentences tying in with the terms and expressions of the law and the handbooks.

It should also be borne in mind that the promotion of Malay (Indonesian) by the nationalist factions in no way implied any intention of abolishing Dutch. The latter language led the way towards development, towards equality with the Europeans, thus being a weapon in the struggle (Groeneboer 1993:414-5). In this light, pondering or promoting Indonesian as a modern legal language might be inopportune. Furthermore, the multitude of publications in the Malay language on legal topics, such as translations of legislation, magazine features and columns and handbooks, seem hardly to have been taken up by the legal community in the colonial days. According to G.J. Resink, who read law at the Rechtshoogeschool in the 1930s and was to become a professor at the Universitas Indonesia, the publication, in 1915, of the Malay translation of the Wetboek van Strafrecht that applied to *all* population groups alike was an important event – the very availability of the first inclusive code in Malay, was bound to put an end to whatever objections remained to the use of that language in the context of the law. In reality, however, most jurists had nothing to do with this translation, though they could not help but notice that the counterfeit clause became printed on the bank notes in Malay, too.[172]

Finally, the lack of attention for Indonesian as the legal language of the future may be ascribed to the same perception of language that would figure

[171] Hooykaas 1949:143. G.J. Resink recollects that he and many fellow students opted for Javanese, partly because the exams were thought to be easier (interview dated 14-4-1994).

[172] Interview dated 24-1-1994; compare Groeneboer 1993:413. The publisher Volkslectuur/Balai Poestaka issued a Malay translation in 1921 (*Wetboek van strafrecht voor Nederlandsch-Indië; Kitab oendang-oendang hoekoeman bagi Hindia-Belanda*). New editions were published up until the start of the 1960s. For more on translations into Malay of legislation applying to the Netherlands East Indies and other publications on legal topics in the Malay language, see Massier, forthcoming. Curiously, as late as 1949, Hooykaas (1949:149) only referred in passing to the use of Indonesian as the language of the legal community, in dealing with the creation of legal and sociological terms and the clarity of the sentence structure; the use of Indonesian as the official language of legal education is not mentioned at all.

so largely in the literature of a later date – namely as the 'tool of the trade' for lawyers and, it follows, as taking second place to 'the law itself' (see Chapter II). In so far as law students and jurists, following in the footsteps of Van Vollenhoven and other professors, were primarily concerned with 'not losing sight of the actual case being dealt with, concealed behind and underneath the words' (Van Vollenhoven 1910:6), they are unlikely to have viewed a future substitution of the official language as more than a simple replacement of an instrument. Seen from this perspective, that which constituted the true subject of their discipline, 'the law itself', would not undergo any real change through being practised in a different language.

**CHAPTER IV**

# Indonesian as the legal language

## *A new beginning*

> Negara Indonesia ialah Negara kesatuan, jang berbentuk Republik. Kedaulatan adalah ditangan rakjat, dan dilakukan sepenuhnja oleh Madjelis Permusjawaratan Rakjat. (Undang-undang Dasar 1945, article 1.)[1]

This text, the first article of the 1945 Undang-undang Dasar (Constitution) of the Republik Indonesia, embodies the Indonesian archipelago's break with its former tradition of law. Independence had been proclaimed one day before the Constitution was approved. The text symbolizes a new, independent state and the impetus towards renewing the system of law, to consist partly of existing legal concepts and partly of new ones – a 'negara Indonesia' (Indonesian state) in the shape of a 'republik' (republic), its 'kedaulatan' (sovereignty) being exercised by a 'Majelis Permusyawaratan Rakyat' (People's Congress). Equally, the text implies that the new republic's legal predecessor, the Netherlands East Indies, that is, had been assigned to history – if only by the authors of the text.[2] But in a world in which speaking, writing and

1 The translation of the two clauses of article 1 is: (1) The Indonesian State is a unitary state in the shape of a republic. (2) The sovereignty lies with the people and will be exercised wholly by the People's Congress. The Constitution and the accompanying Preamble were approved on 18-8-1945, the day after the proclamation of Indonesian independence, by the Panitia Persiapan Kemerdekaan Indonesia (Indonesian Independence Preparatory Committee) (Muhammad Yamin 1959:399-437). The Constitution consists of a mere 37 articles, 4 transitional provisions and 2 complementary ones. It was originally intended as a temporary instrument for the independent state-to-be and the text is therefore sometimes referred to as the 'Konstitusi Proklamasi' (Constitution of the Proclamation). The text was published in *Berita Repoeblik Indonesia* II-7:45-8 (elucidation given on pp. 51-6). The above text (in the Suwandi spelling) has been copied from *Himpunan Engelbrecht* 1989:1-4.

2 Indonesian independence was only acknowledged formally on 27-12-1949, when the Netherlands transferred sovereignty to the Republik Indonesia Serikat (RIS, the Republic of the United States of Indonesia). The Republik Indonesia, founded as a unitary state, came to be one of the states (*negara*) of the new federation, the RIS. Thus, a new, federal Constitution, the Konstitusi RIS (published in *Lembaran Negara Republik Indonesia* (hereafter *LN*, State Gazette of the Republic of Indonesia) 1950, no. 3), came into force upon the transfer of sovereignty. Shortly afterwards, measures were taken to redefine the RIS as a unitary state. The amended Constitution

text play as crucial a role as that of the law, the most important innovation of all is that this is an *Indonesian* text. Indonesian is the language of this new Constitution, in accordance with article 36 of that same Constitution, stating that Indonesian is the *bahasa Negara* (language of the state).[3] The article bestowed onto Indonesian the status of a 'real' *language*, equipped it – to apply the famous phrase – with 'the army and the navy' that make a language of a dialect (see Chapter II). This was the language in which other legal texts (legislation, judicial decisions, notarial deeds and other instruments), produced by or on the authority of the Republic, would come to follow suit.

## *Consequences of the Japanese invasion*

The break, occurring in August 1945, was in actual fact the result of the adversity that had befallen the Netherlands East Indies three years earlier. Japanese troops, having rapidly gained control of southern Sumatra in February 1942, landed on Java on the 1st of March. On 8 March the Dutch commander of the Allied Forces surrendered and the last Governor General of the Netherlands East Indies, A.W.L. Tjarda van Starkenborgh Stachouwer, was taken into custody (Kahin 1952:101; Ricklefs 1988:184). Japanese occupation had become a reality. One of the first orders issued by the new rulers was to prohibit the use of the Dutch language for teaching purposes (Groeneboer 1993:437; compare Anderson 1972:19). Mid-March, most of the teaching staff of the Rechtshoogeschool, the Faculty of Arts and Philosophy (established in 1940) and the Geneeskundige Hoogeschool (College of Medicine) were arrested in their homes;[4] Soepomo, who had obtained both his master's and his PhD

became effective on 17-8-1950 as Undang-undang Dasar Sementara Republik Indonesia (UUDS, Provisional Constitution of the Republic of Indonesia) (*LN* 1950, no. 56). By virtue of art. 134, the temporary instrument was to be replaced with a permanent Constitution at the earliest opportunity (Logemann 1955:39-41). The body charged with drafting the final Constitution, the Konstituante, was unable to complete its task, however, and was disbanded by a decree (*dekrit*) issued by Soekarno on 5-7-1959. The same decree declared the Provisional Constitution to be inoperative and reinstated the 1945 Constitution (Simorangkir and Mang Reng Say 1975:3-8).

3 'Bahasa Negara ialah bahasa Indonesia'. An earlier draft still referred to Indonesian as 'bahasa kebangsaan' (national language) (Muhammad Yamin 1959:263, 269). In the elucidation it is stated that regional languages that are adequately kept up by the people (the examples provided are Javanese, Sundanese and Madurese) will also enjoy the respect and protection of the state. Article 4 of the Provisional Constitution read: 'Bahasa resmi Negara Republik Indonesia ialah Bahasa Indonesia' (The official language of the State of the Republic of Indonesia is the Indonesian language).

4 Wertheim and Wertheim-Gijse Weenink 1991:236. W.F. Wertheim, together with the librarian of the museum of the Bataviaasch Genootschap, A.J. Bernet Kempers, Soepomo and others, rescued what they could of the books of the Rechtshoogeschool by taking them to the museum (Wertheim and Wertheim-Gijse Weenink 1991:232). The Faculty of Arts, the establishment of

under Van Vollenhoven, was the only Indonesian professor to teach at the Rechtshoogeschool and, therefore, was not interned. The majority of high-ranking Dutch officials, judicial ones included, were arrested in April.[5]

The structure of society was turned on its head – white skin and the Dutch language became the hallmarks of the pariah, to quote W.F. Wertheim (1956:152). A series of provisions confined the use of Dutch, English and other Western languages to private gatherings. The ban on the Dutch press, as early as March 1942, was added to the prohibition on education in that language. In May it was decreed that shops, schools, companies and such were not permitted the use of any language other than Japanese or Indonesian for their shop signs, inscriptions and advertising (Groeneboer 1993:439-40; compare Aziz 1955:176). The Dutch designations of public services and civil service jobs and ranks were replaced with Indonesian names. In October it was determined that post written in Dutch or English would no longer be handled and that telephone conversations in those languages were prohibited.[6] No population group was allowed to speak or write Dutch or English, not even in the privacy of one's own home, nor to read books in those languages. On the instructions of the regional Kantor Pengadjaran Balatentara Djepang (Education Offices of the Japanese Army), school books in Malay (Indonesian) were 'cleansed' of all things Dutch – words and proper names in that language had to be crossed out by teachers and pupils and be replaced with Indonesian ones. Not even the term 'Belanda' (Holland, Dutch) escaped the exercise, being replaced by 'Eropah' (Europe, European). The final radio broadcast in Dutch was transmitted on 7 December 1942.[7]

---

which had been planned since the early 1920s, was opened on 4-12-1940. The execution of the plans had been stepped up when the German occupation of the Netherlands rendered the promotion of Dutch cultural interests outside of enemy territory a matter of some urgency. Although a lecturer in Dutch had been appointed, a chair in Dutch language and culture had not as yet been created, the opposite being true for Javanese and Malay. The courses comprised social sciences, Indonesian language and literature, history and ethnology (Groeneboer 1993:428-34).

5 Han Bing Siong 1998:426; compare Sastroamijoyo 1979:93 and Brugmans et al. 1960:139. Han Bing Siong, on the one hand, provides an excellent synopsis of the literature on the administration of justice during the Japanese occupation while on the other hand, having researched various primary sources, he unravels various myths that arose in the past and have been handed down ever since. For more on the internment of allied civilians, see Van Velden 1977:29-92, Han Bing Siong 1998:426, 430-1 and Keuchenius 2002:54-5.

6 Groeneboer 1993:440. Later on it was even decided that telephony in either of the languages mentioned would be terminated.

7 Groeneboer 1993:439-42; Khaidir Anwar 1985:44-5; compare Oei Tjoe Tat 1995:49. The prohibition on speaking Dutch at home seems to have failed to have an undivided effect. Although Khaidir Anwar (1985:172) speaks of people fearful of using the language even behind closed doors, Han Bing Siong remembers that Dutch continued to be spoken both at his parents' house and in the homes of all the Chinese and Indonesian friends of the family. Nor was he reprimanded for conversing in Dutch with his Chinese friends when happening upon Japanese

Outlawing the Dutch language (which continued to be spoken in private, naturally) was accompanied by various measures to promote the acquisition and use of Japanese, the future lingua franca of the Indonesian archipelago, indeed throughout the whole of Asia![8] With the new language making insufficient inroads into the country, however, Malay, or *Indonesian* (*bahasa Indonesia*) – as the language was called in the gazette of the Japanese military administration – was in practice becoming the day-to-day language used in all circumstances in which Dutch used to be applied.[9] The result was a deluge of Indonesian text and speech among all social classes and circles (barring the camps where Europeans were interned) on countless subjects that had never before been touched upon in Malay. So, together with the Japanese soldiers and the propaganda aimed at mobilizing the people for the war towards the Greater East Asia Co-Prosperity Sphere, the Indonesian language penetrated into the remotest corners of the archipelago. It was the language of official announcements, of correspondence between civil servants, of all sectors and strata of education.[10]

Jurists and law students initially experienced the Japanese invasion as a major shock, as did other members of the native elite who had had a Western

soldiers (information provided 30-10-2002). In February 1943 libraries and book shops were ordered to submit inventories. Blacklists served to force the surrender of proscribed books. The New Testament by the Nederlandsch Bijbel Genootschap (Dutch Bible Society) was the only book in Dutch permitted to be circulated (Groeneboer 1993:439-40 and Zubaidah Isa 1972:74; compare Aziz 1955:173-4), though preaching in Dutch was prohibited (Aziz 1955:173). On the point of replacing the term 'Belanda' with 'Eropah', Groeneboer (1993:437) comments that the Japanese seemed to have overlooked that, in the colonial era, 'European' was the official designation for the population group to which the Dutch belonged.

8 *Kamoes istilah* 1945:4; compare Khaidir Anwar 1985:36-7 and Aziz 1955:175. Khaidir Anwar (1985:36-42) deals extensively with the requirement to learn and use Japanese during the occupation. For more on this subject, also see Kurasawa Aiko 1990:178-92.

9 The Japanese only came to acknowledge Indonesian as an official language (*bahasa resmi*) on 29-4-1945 (Teeuw 1961:64).

10 Takdir Alisjahbana 1949:390, 1988:126-7, 1974:400; Groeneboer 1993:436-7. The term 'bahasa Indonesia' is used as early as in art. 6 of Oendang-oendang no. 14 dated 29-4-1942 in respect of the administration of justice in civil law cases, for example, and in the corresponding elucidation dated 5-6-1942 (*Oendang-Oendang Pembesar* 1942:19, 33-4). The term 'bahasa Melajoe' (old spelling), in the former text given between parentheses, was omitted by the time of the elucidation of 5-6-1942. It was also left out of the next decree concerning the administration of justice, Oendang-oendang no. 34/Osamu Seirei no. 3 dated 26-9-1942. The use of this term in the gazette, *Kan Poo*, seems to be contrary to Alisjahbana's remark that the term 'bahasa Indonesia', with its nationalist overtone, only became allowed once Japan was inevitably going to lose the war (*Kamoes istilah* 1945:6). The same is true for E.St. Harahap's unilingual reference dictionary, the title of which, *Kitab arti logat Melajoe* (literally 'book giving the meanings of Malay words' or Malay dictionary), was disallowed by the Japanese command, although *Kamoes Indonésia, jang berlainan dari pada "Kitab Arti Logat Melajoe"* (Indonesian dictionary, differing from the Malay one) was permitted (Foreword in *Kamoes Indonésia*, eighth edition, Batavia: Kolff, 1948).

upbringing. The closure of the Rechtshoogeschool meant that studying had to be shelved indefinitely and that career plans were put on a loose footing.[11] Only a couple of weeks after judicial officers and advocates were able to pick up where they had been forced to leave off,[12] the judicial and administrative machinery ground to a halt with the arrest of Dutch judges and other high officials at the end of April. Though work could be resumed shortly afterwards, the departure of so many Dutch colleagues (the top of the judiciary among them) and the arrival of Japanese officials affected one's work within the government in no small measure.[13]

Finally, the ban on Dutch language and literature, imposed step by step, hit both students and jurists (native *rechtskundigen* included). It was the language of reading, studying and writing, of communicating in the majority of situations (see Teeuw 1979:106-7). Jurists and students are bound to have felt lost, restricted in their communication and cast out socially when this language could no longer be called 'Dutch' or even 'bahasa Belanda' but, as enemy language, was dubbed 'bahasa asing' (foreign language).[14] Furthermore, the vast majority had only spent one, maybe two years studying Malay (at the Rechtsschool, the Rechtshoogeschool or at university), suddenly the tongue to be spoken in public, not by choice but of necessity (see Hooykaas 1949:143). This language, called 'Indonesian' in the new legislation, as mentioned above, also became the official language of the juridical world – used both in legisla-

11 Anderson 1972:19. Compare with Oei Tjoe Tat, forced to discontinue his studies at the Rechtshoogeschool due to the Japanese invasion: 'I felt confused and experienced a certain satisfaction in finally seeing white kneel – literally – before yellow. But reading about the brutality of the new "colonizer", I also felt fear, an anxiety that is hard to explain. Add to this my uncertainty about the future because of having to quit my course. Being totally honest, I had to admit that I'd not done badly out of the Dutch time.' ('Perasaan saya campur-aduk, diliputi semacam kepuasan bisa menyaksikan si kulit putih yang akhirnya benar-benar dibikin bertekuk-lutut oleh yang berwarna kuning. Sebaliknya, saya juga cemas akibat pernah membaca tentang kebengisan "penjajah" baru ini, kecemasan yang sulit untuk bisa dijelaskan. Belum lagi ditambah gambaran tak pasti akan masa depan saya akibat studi yang terputus. Alam bawah sadar saya sendiri mulai mengakui, bahwa sesungguhnya jaman Belanda bagi saya tidak terlalu jelek.') (Oei Tjoe Tat 1995:44, 49.) In his memoirs, Mohammad Hatta (1981:209) relates that several law students and recent law graduates offered him their services.

12 In art. 4 clause 3 of Oendang-oendang no. 1, dated 7-3-1942 (*Oendang-Oendang Pembesar* 1942:2), employees (*pegawai*) and others were ordered to return to work (see Brugmans et al. 1960:131). On 13-3-1942 the ordinary sessions of the Semarang *raad van justitie* were resumed (Brugmans et al. 1960:135-6).

13 Aziz 1955:164. The Batavia courts reopened at the end of May 1942 (Han Tiauw Hing 1948:3).

14 The term 'bahasa asing' was used in the Dutch-Indonesian lexicons included in the gazette *Kan Poo* (*Berita Pemerintah*) in 1944 (see *Kan Poo* no. 27, 2604 [1944] p. 30, containing the abbreviations 'dka' ('*d*ari *k*ata *a*sing', that is to say 'of the foreign word') and 'dba' ('*d*alam *b*ahasa *a*sing', that is to say 'in the foreign language').

tion and in court. On Java,[15] the Indonesian texts of decrees were published in the gazette called *Kan Poo* (*Berita Pemerintah*) (Government Announcements), issued twice a month from August 1942 onwards. There was also a Japanese edition, entitled *Osamu Kan Poo*.[16] (Subsequent mention of 'Kan Poo' refers to the Indonesian version.) Upon publication of new regulations, Indonesian jurists came into contact, for the first time, with official legislation terms in the Indonesian language (such as 'undang-undang' (act, statute), 'peraturan' (regulation), 'peraturan pemerintah' (government regulation)), applied side by side with terms in Japanese.[17] Everyone in court (judge, prosecutor,

15 For the sake of administration, the territory of the Netherlands East Indies was divided into three parts – Java came under the command of the 16th army (code name 'Osamu', capital Batavia, called Jakarta from 8-12-1942), Sumatra under that of the 25th (code name 'Tomi', capital Bukittinggi, previously Fort de Kock) and Dutch Borneo, Celebes and all of the islands to the east of the north-south axis through Bali and the Strait of Makassar under that of the navy ('Minseifu territory', capital Makassar) (Aziz 1955:152-60).

16 Echols 1963:38-9, nos. 242 and 246; compare Zorab 1954:27-8 and Aziz 1955:161-2. As mentioned, 'Osamu' was the code name of the 16th army, commanding Java. The Japanese edition was published once a month and exclusively contained the orders issued by the military command, whereas the Indonesian one also included official commentary, transcripts of speeches and appointments. The Indonesian edition saw 74 issues; after the Japanese surrender in September 1945 the journal appeared for a while longer under the name of *Berita Gunseikanbu* (Announcements by the Gunseikanbu – see next footnote) (Zorab 1954:27). It is not known whether the military administration of Sumatra, the 25th army, issued a gazette. In the territory controlled by the navy, legislation was published in *Koohoo* (Zorab 1954:9-10; compare Aziz 1955:162). The twenty 'undang-undang' issued in the period of March to June 1942 (prior to the first edition of the *Kan Poo*) were finally published in March 1943 in a *Kan Poo* special edition (*istimewa*). Inclusion in either the Japanese or the Indonesian version of the publication was not a condition, incidentally, for the new legislation to come into force. This merely required the Japanese original of the order to be posted on the notice board of the office of the Japanese military administration (Gunseikanbu) or of the issuing authority (for example, in case of a *syuurei* – an order issued by the head of a *syuu*, residency) (Oendang-oendang no. 40/Osamu Seirei no. 9 art. 9). If military secrets were at play, posting the legislation could be omitted (Zorab 1954:38-9). Aziz (1955:162) mentions that such legislation was published only in *Osamu Kan Poo* (the Japanese edition, that is).

17 Art. 2 Oendang-oendang no. 40/Osamu Seirei no. 9, dated 5-10-1942, specified the six categories of *gunseirei* (decrees and orders of the military administration). Two of these originated with the central military command, the Gunsireikan (the commander of the 16th army) and the Gunseikan (the head of the central administrative organization or Gunseikanbu, operating independently from the army), to be more precise. The decrees made by the former were called *Osamu seirei/undang-undang Osamu*, those made by the latter *Osamu kanrei/undang-undang pemerintah Osamu* (art. 3-4). To implement *Osamu seirei* and *Osamu kanrei* and to maintain the peace, local governors would issue *syuurei* or *peraturan syuu* (art. 2; the areas of jurisdiction of these governors, which came in the place of the former residencies, were called 'syuu'; see Zorab 1954:9). The regulations were numbered sequentially, per year, in the order of their promulgation. The decrees of the commander of the Japanese army dating from the period of March to September 1942 were referred to in *Kan Poo* as 'undang-undang' only, temporarily followed by both 'undang-undang' and 'osamu seirei' (each with its own number), and finally as 'osamu seirei' only. The army orders issued immediately following the Japanese landing, the *Osamu*

litigants, defendants and so on) was prescribed the use of either Japanese or Indonesian as the official languages. A litigant or other person involved in a hearing who spoke neither, was allowed to use Javanese, Sundanese or another language. Nevertheless, the record of the proceedings had to be composed in Japanese or Indonesian and state which language had been spoken. Court decisions and other official documents were also required to be formulated in either of these two languages, as were any items addressed to the court.[18]

Following the restructuring of the courts, non-European judicial officers could return to work in May 1942. On 7 March it had been decreed that all government institutions, the law and the legislation of the former government were to be maintained for the time being, in so far as they were in keeping with the laws made by the new military administration.[19] The internment of the Dutch officials necessitated an overhaul of the judicial system, however – of the judges and justices of the various *raden van justitie* and the Hooggerechtshof (both of which formed part of the judicial system for Europeans), only Koesoemah Atmadja, an indigenous judge, remained. Moreover, nearly half of all *landraad* chairmen and a large number of *landrechters* were removed from their posts.[20] Therefore, on 29 April 1942, an order was issued that reinstated only the courts previously intended for Natives, giving these a new Japanese and Indonesian name.

The main courts were the former *landraad*, renamed 'tihoo hooin' or 'pengadilan negeri', and the former *landgerecht*, now called 'keizai hooin' or 'hakim kepolisian'. The prosecution service dedicated to the *landraad*

*gunrei* or *ketetapan Balatentara*, are excluded from Oendang-oendang no. 40 but included in the *Kan Poo*. One of the names under which other measures taken by the central command on Java were published was 'kokuzi' (proclamations, *maklumat*) (Zorab 1954:9, 38). Decrees could also be issued by higher-ranking Japanese commanders, such as the commander-in-chief of the Southern Territories. Such decrees were not published in *Kan Poo*, however (Aziz 1955:161).

18 See Oendang-oendang no. 14 (tentang peratoeran Pengadilan Pemerintah Balatentara Dai Nippon) dated 29-4-2602 (1942) art. 6 clause 1 together with the corresponding elucidation (entitled 'Tjara mengoeroes perkara menoeroet Oendang-Oendang no. 14') sub 1 and 3, and Oendang-oendang no. 34 (Osamu Seirei no. 3) art. 8. The elucidation was included in the appendices to *Oendang-Oendang Pembesar* 1942. The text of the first law contains the term 'bahasa Indonesia (Melajoe)' (Indonesian (Malay) language), though both the elucidation and the second law have 'bahasa Indonesia' (Indonesian language) only. Special forms were produced for decisions and other court documents. Until these became available, one had to make do with either blank paper or forms left over from the Dutch colonial era that had been adapted (for example, with the phrase 'In the name of the Queen' crossed out) (elucidation sub 2).

19 Oendang-oendang no. 1, art. 3. The Semarang *raad van justitie*, for example, resumed its operations on 13-3-1942 (compare footnote 12).

20 See p. 145-6. Han Bing Siong (1998:446, 2002:320) reports that shortly before the Japanese invasion, many judicial officers' posts were left unfilled due to conscription. For this reason, simplified court procedures had been introduced.

became 'tihoo kensatu kyoku' or 'kedjaksaan pengadilan negeri'.[21] A fundamental change was made to the court system, consisting of the transfer of the jurisdiction of the *residentiegerecht* and the *raad van justitie* (that is to say, the European courts) to the *tihoo hooin/pengadilan negeri*. This court thus became the ordinary, day-to-day place where justice was administered to *all* population groups, be they Native, Chinese and other Foreign Orientals or European, with Japanese falling into the latter category on the basis of the colonial legislation retained. The same situation was effected on Sumatra.[22] The *tihoo hooin/pengadilan negeri* had a single judge and two members who were administrative officers. Cases that, under the old system, would have been heard by a *raad van justitie* required three judges. Regarding the applicable substantive law, the existing arrangement was continued – civil cases concerning Europeans and Chinese were governed by the Burgerlijk Wetboek and the Wetboek van Koophandel and those involving native litigants by adat law (barring some exceptions); criminal cases, whatever the ethnic origin of the defendants, were dealt with in accordance with the Wetboek van Strafrecht. Procedural law, too, continued to be subject to the legislation of the Dutch colonial era, namely the Herziene Inlandsch Reglement (HIR, Revised Native Code). Litigants did not have recourse to either appeal or retrial.[23]

The Osamu commander-in-chief at that time, Lieutenant General Imamura Hitoshi, had no policy of removing European citizens from everyday social life.[24] Therefore, on 26 September 1942, once a number of Japanese judges had

21 The other courts comprised the *ken hooin/pengadilan kabupaten* (regency court), the *gun hooin/pengadilan kawedanan* (district court), the *kaikyo kooto hooin/mahkamah islam tinggi* (court of appeal for Muslim affairs) and the *sooryo hooin/rapat agama* ('religious court', formerly the *priesterraad*) (Oendang-oendang no. 14/1942, art. 4).

22 Oendang-oendang no. 14/1942 art. 7 and Han Bing Siong 1998:422. The regulation that applied to Sumatra was Tomi Seirei no. 40/1943 (Han Bing Siong 1998:422). The *landgerecht* (*keizai hooin/hakim kepolisian*) already dealt with all ethnic groups but only had jurisdiction in petty crimes cases (see Chapter III). The *gun hooin/pengadilan kawedanan* and the *ken hooin/pengadilan kabupaten* continued to hear only the small claims and petty crimes of the Natives, whereas the *gumpoo kaigi* were charged with hearing certain cases related to Japanese army personnel (Han Bing Siong 1998:421). There also was a *gunritu kaigi*, a military court with the authority to try the offences listed in Osamu Gunrei no. 1 (effective from 2-3-1942) (Osamu Gunrei no. 2 dated 8-3-1942; see *Oendang-Oendang Pembesar* 1942:29-33; compare Han Bing Siong 1998:421).

23 Oendang-oendang no. 1/1942 art. 3, Oendang-oendang no. 14/1942 art. 6 clause 1, art. 7 clause 1 and art. 13; Han Bing Siong 1998:423; Zorab 1954:52-6; Kartodirdjo 1947:13. It was within the powers of the commander of the Japanese army to refer cases decided either contrary to the applicable legislation or unjustly to the *gun siho kaigi* for retrial (art. 8 clause 1). No decrees concerning this court were ever issued, however, meaning that it never actually existed (Han Tiauw Hing 1948:8). Han Tiauw Hing (1948:5) mentions that territories where the Herziene Inlandsch Reglement had not yet been implemented at the time of the Dutch surrender, continued to be subject to the Inlandsch Reglement for some time afterwards.

24 Han Bing Siong (1998:425-31), having read carefully all relevant sources including the Japanese ones, puts forward a convincing argument to support this.

become available to take up the vacancies that had arisen in the European courts, the two-tier system of law was reinstated. Oendang-oendang no. 34/ Osamu Seirei no. 3 added three *kootoo hooin/pengadilan tinggi*, one Saikoo Hooin/Pengadilan Agoeng and their corresponding prosecution departments to the existing courts. While awaiting new regulations to define the powers and the competences of these new courts, the earlier ones pertaining to the judicial organization continued to apply. This meant that the *kootoo hooin/ pengadilan tinggi* came to replace the former *raden van justitie* of Batavia (as of 8 December 1942, Jakarta), Surabaya and Semarang, while the Saikoo Hooin/ Pengadilan Agoeng revived the former Hooggerechtshof at Batavia. Thus the *kootoo hooin/pengadilan tinggi* became the normal court for Europeans and Japanese (as well as for the civil cases of Chinese), with the indigenous population retaining the *tihoo hooin/pengadilan negeri* for their everyday cases (Han Bing Siong 1998:425; Oendang-oendang no. 34/Osamu Seirei no. 3 art. 3-4). The Saikoo Hooin/Pengadilan Agoeng had a bench consisting of three justices; the level of the *tihoo hooin/pengadilan negeri* and *kootoo hooin/pengadilan tinggi* saw the introduction of a single judge.[25] The Saikoo Hooin/Pengadilan Agoeng initially was staffed by Japanese jurists only, but later on was supplemented by three Indonesian deputies who doubled as *kootoo hooin/pengadilan tinggi* judges.[26] The judges of the *kootoo hooin/pengadilan tinggi* also could sit as judges of a higher instance at the *tihoo hooin/pengadilan negeri* in their territory, instead of their first-instance colleagues. The same was truc mutatis mutandis

25 The Saikoo Hooin/Pengadilan Agoeng was empowered to determine a bench of three judges for special cases at the *tihoo hooin/pengadilan negeri* and the *kootoo hooin/pengadilan tinggi* (Oendang-oendang no. 34/Osamu Seirei no. 3, art. 4 clause 2).

26 Kartodirdjo 1947:16; Han Bing Siong 1998:427. They were Soepomo, Notosoebagijo and Sastromoeljono (Han Bing Siong 1998:427 footnote 27). Following his career in the judiciary and at the Department of Justice, Soepomo (Rechtsschool diploma 1923, Leiden PhD 1927) was appointed professor extraordinary of adat law at the Rechtshoogeschool in 1938, his post being converted into a full professorship in 1941 (*Orang Indonesia jang terkemoeka* 1973:159 and *Verslag Rechtshoogeschool* 1941:7; compare Han Bing Siong 1998:417). In April 1942 Notosoebagijo (Rechtsschool diploma 1915, graduated from Leiden in 1924-25) and Sastromoeljono (Rechtsschool diploma 1918, graduated from Leiden in 1922) were appointed chairman and judge, respectively, of the Batavia and Tangerang *tihoo hooin/pengadilan negeri*, in September 1942 they became judges of the Batavia *kootoo hooin/pengadilan tinggi* and in April 1943 justices of the Saikoo Hooin/ Pengadilan Agoeng (*Orang Indonesia jang terkemoeka* 1973:150, 154-5). Notosoebagijo had had a career in the judiciary. Upon returning from Leiden, Sastromoeljono had become an advocate and had only later joined the judiciary, as well as holding various directorships. He had been a counsel of Soekarno's when the latter was tried by the Bandung *landraad*. From 1939-40, he was a member extraordinary of the Semarang *raad van justitie* (*Orang Indonesia jang terkemoeka* 1973:156; Han Bing Siong 1998:448). M.M. Djojodigoeno (Rechtsschool diploma 1920, graduated from the Rechtshoogeschool in 1931) became a justice at a later point in time (Han Bing Siong 1998:427). After having followed a career in the judiciary, in 1941 he took up employ at the Department of Justice (*Orang Indonesia jang terkemoeka* 1973:8).

for the prosecutors/*jaksa* of the prosecution department at the *kootoo hooin/ pengadilan tinggi*. The existing substantive and procedural law applicable to the respective courts remained in force; as regards the proceedings, in practice the HIR was always applied.[27]

The option of appealing or applying for a retrial, in the ordinary sense of the word, at the *kootoo hooin/pengadilan tinggi* was suspended. These courts had the competence of the former *raden van justitie* (including that of deciding cases on appeal), and once several Indonesian judges had been appointed, such cases were indeed heard.[28] A point of reform was that the Saikoo Hooin/ Pengadilan Agoeng could retry cases in which the sentence appeared to be contrary to the law or unjust, in terms of either the grounds or the decision. It was up to the judge to determine such instances and not a *right* on the part of litigants or defendants to effect a retrial.[29]

Once Imamura had been replaced, the ostracism of the Dutch increased. Through successive measures, they were removed fully from society. Thus, the reasons for maintaining a separate court for Europeans (and their equivalents) became obsolete. By virtue of Osamu Seirei no. 21 dated 1 July 1943, the two-tier system was abolished (Han Bing Siong 1998:431). Cases formerly supposed to be heard in the first and the last instance by the Saikoo Hooin, those supposed to be dealt with in the first instance by the *kootoo hooin* (*raad van justitie*) and those formerly coming under the jurisdiction of the residency court, now had to come before the *tihoo hooin/pengadilan negeri*. All of those cases were subjected to the HIR procedures (art. 1). Other amendments to the court system worth mentioning are instructions concerning the law of evidence pertaining to criminal cases (dated 12 July 1943), the cessation of the activities of the Saikoo Hooin/Pengadilan Agoeng and its prosecution service (Osamu Seirei no. 2 dated 14 January 1944) and the introduction of a Gunsei Keizirei/Oendang-oendang Kriminil, a new criminal code (Osamu Seirei no.

27 Oendang-oendang no. 34/Osamu Seirei no. 3 art. 6-7; Zorab 1954:52; Han Tiauw Hing 1948:5.

28 Oendang-oendang no. 34/Osamu Seirei no. 3 art. 14; Kartodirdjo 1947:16; Han Bing Siong 1998:436-7; Zorab 1954:52-3. Halfway through 1944 new provisions pertaining to the appeal procedure were issued in Osamu Seihi no. 1573, to replace the Dutch colonial regulations (Han Bing Siong 1998:437 and footnote 50). European procedural law was applied by analogy with cases subject to European law should the procedural law of the HIR/IR be inadequate (Zorab 1954:52-3). For more on the judges appointed to the *kootoo hooin/pengadilan tinggi*, see Han Bing Siong 1998:436 and *Kan Poo*.

29 Art. 9; Zorab 1954:51; Han Bing Siong 1998:432-3. The procedural rules for this body were only issued in 1944, once the Saikoo Hooin/Pengadilan Agoeng had been abolished and its jurisdiction had been transferred to the *kootoo hooin*. In practice, either the aggrieved or a third party filed a petition demonstrating why the decision was unjust or contrary to the law. The judge could then grant or dismiss the petition for review (Kartodirdjo 1947:15-6; Zorab 1954:51).

25 dated 10 May 1944).[30]

The abolition of the European courts in April 1942 (and again in July 1943 following their temporary reinstatement with a handful of Japanese judges) was an inadequate solution, on its own, to the shortage of judges at the *landraden* and the *landgerechten*. The shortfall was replenished from both inside and outside of the judiciary. Judicial officers working as (salaried) members, vice chairmen or, occasionally, *jaksa* of a *landraad*, were promoted to the position of (single) judge of a *tihoo hooin/pengadilan negeri*. Recruitment began of jurists who, having completed their studies, had opted for a career other than one in the judiciary, in the advocature, for example, or with a government department.[31] In May 1943 a one-year crash course for judges was established (Sihoo Kanri Yooseizyo/Koersoes Kehakiman (Judicial Training Course)), followed by a two-year course in 1945. In view of the fact that those who completed the one-year course (May 1944 at the earliest) were initially to be employed at a court on trial and would subsequently have to pass a second exam, to qualify for a post as assistant judge, it is doubtful whether a single participant in the course ever became a judge.[32] The quality of the civil judi-

30 See Han Tiauw Hing 1948, Han Bing Siong 1998, Zorab 1954 and others. In accordance with Osamu Seirei no. 2/1944, the authority to retry was transferred to the *kootoo hooin/pengadilan tinggi*, thereby actually abolishing the Saikoo Hooin/Pengadilan Agoeng (Han Bing Siong 1998:433).

31 Some examples: Hadi (Rechtsschool diploma 1915, graduated from Leiden in 1924-25) held various administrative posts when acceding to the judiciary in 1942 (*Orang Indonesia jang terkemoeka* 1973:141). Gatot (Rechtsschool diploma 1919, graduated from Leiden in 1927) was an advocate when appointed judge (*Orang Indonesia jang terkemoeka* 1973:140) and the occupation of Moeljatno (graduated from the Rechtshoogeschool in 1936) at that time was that of registrar at the Batavia Hof voor Islamietische Zaken (Appeal Court for proceedings under Islamic Law) (*Orang Indonesia jang terkemoeka* 1973:148). Boerhanoeddin (Rechtsschool diploma 1923), Abdoel Razak (Rechtsschool diploma 1924), Abdoel Gafar Wahab (Rechtsschool diploma 1925), Rochmat Kromoatmodjo (Rechtsschool diploma 1925) and Abdulkadar Martohoedojo (Rechtsschool diploma 1926) were vice chairmen of a *landraad* when promoted to judges of a *tihoo hooin/pengadilan negeri* (*Orang Indonesia jang terkemoeka* 1973:138, 136, 146-7). Marah Abdoel Moenit (Rechtsschool diploma 1925) had been a *landraad* member (Batavia and Bogor) for many years when taking charge of the Bogor *tihoo hooin/pengadilan negeri* in 1942 (*Orang Indonesia jang terkemoeka* 1973:136), while Hilman Mangkoewidjaja (Rechtsschool diploma 1925) had been a *jaksa* before being appointed judge (*Orang Indonesia jang terkemoeka* 1973:146). Iwa Koesoema Soemantri, in exile in Makassar at the time of the Japanese invasion, was forced to learn Japanese and, some time afterwards, became the head of the local court of the first instance (*kepala pengadilan pertama*) (Iwa Kusuma Sumantri 2002:136).

32 Han Bing Siong 1998:448-50. Moreover, Han Bing Siong was not able to find any registers of graduates, although such documents were available for other courses and exams. An explanation that is not implausible is that the Japanese realized, soon after establishing the course, that a single year's preparation would be wholly inadequate for a judgeship and therefore substituted it for a two-year training (Han Bing Siong 1998:449-50). In the final year of the occupation, there possibly was an actual turnabout in judiciary appointments. Han Tiauw Hing (1948:15) claims that the Batavia/Jakarta courts were presided over by experienced Indonesian jurists, though the

ciary during the Japanese era seems to have been reasonable, with adequate regard for its independence.[33] In so far as the Kempeitai (Japanese military police) intimidated judges to obtain a certain result, several instances may be quoted of judges who stood firm even in those circumstances (Han Bing Siong 1998:441-2).

Under the Japanese, the administration of justice became an Indonesian affair altogether, not just in the first instance but also at the higher levels. At best, Japanese judges sometimes played a part in the sessions of the Saikoo Hooin/Pengadilan Agoeng and the *kootoo hooin/pengadilan tinggi*, and even then dealt with criminal cases only (Kartodirdjo 1947:10, 16). Osamu Seirei

---

*tihoo hooin* in various places seem 'to have been chaired by fairly young, inexperienced jurists, while during the final year of occupation the trials at several courts were entrusted to persons who had acquired their knowledge at one of these Koersoes Kilat (crash course), lasting approximately one year, and who had "qualified further" by serving as a registrar for a few months'. (See Lev 1973:8 and Pompe 1997:60.) Also worth mentioning is that the new 'law school' founded in 1943 encompassed a school for registrars, providing six months' training to persons in possession of the MULO diploma (Meer Uitgebreid Lager Onderwijs, More Extended Elementary Education) (Kartodirdjo 1947:17).

33 Han Bing Siong 1998:440, 442-4, 449-50; compare Kartodirdjo 1947:9, 17. Wertheim reports that, while he was detained in Batavia's Struiswijk prison for eighteen months from March 1942, the Japanese provided him and several colleagues of his choosing with the opportunity to spend one or two days a week working on translating the Dutch colonial law codes into either English, German or French. He was under the impression that this was an initiative of Soepomo's, who was thought to be employed at the Sihoobu (Department of Justice), though it is unclear in which capacity (Soepomo was only appointed *sanyo* (consultant) of this department on 4-10-1943 – see *Kan Poo* no. 28, 2603 [1943], p. 29). At a later date, Soepomo came to chair the Panitya Penjelenggara Kitab Oendang-oendang (Law Codes Editorial Committee), established on 22-1-1945. In 1947 it published a lexicon in the journal *Hoekoem*. The committee's brief was to edit and translate Dutch colonial legislation ('oendang-oendang tertoelis'). Several laws ('oendang-oendang') are supposed to have been translated (see editor's preface in *Hoekoem* 1947). Wertheim accepted the order on the basis of the good use to which such translations might be put if the Japanese 'truly intended to apply the regulations in force in daily practice' (Wertheim and Wertheim-Gijse Weenink 1991:247-8).

That judgeships were not dished out willy-nilly, for example to lay persons or the poorly qualified, seems to be confirmed by the continuation in their posts at the *keizai hooin/hakim kepolisian* in question of several native *rechtskundigen* (under the new title of 'shoki'), who in February/March 1942 were employed as *fiscaal-griffiers* at *landgerechten* (examples are Hartojo Hadipoetro, Rechtsschool diploma 1922; Darmojo Ashari, Rechtsschool diploma 1927; Moekimin, Rechtsschool diploma 1927; Hasan Nasoetion, Rechtsschool diploma 1927; Joesoef Ismail, Rechtsschool diploma 1928; Soehadi Mertohatmodjo, Rechtsschool diploma 1928; and Bagindo Sinaro Nazaroeddin, Rechtsschool diploma 1928; see *Orang Indonesia jang terkemoeka* 1973:139, 141, 143, 147, 149). That these people were not appointed to judgeships, even though they were formally qualified to hold the office of chairman of a *landraad*, is indicative of a stringent selection procedure. None of this detracts from the brutality of the police during the Japanese occupation, not in the least on the part of the Kempeitai, who frequently executed suspects without due process (Kartodirdjo 1947:9; also see Brugmans 1960:172-3). It should also be borne in mind that the Japanese authorities' treatment of the Dutch colonial legislation and the greater part of their new decrees and regulations were in violation of international law (Kollewijn and Van Dijk 1948:22-4).

no. 3/Oendang-oendang no. 34 dated 26 September 1942, determining that justice at the *tihoo hooin/pengadilan negeri* would henceforth be dispensed by a sole judge (unus judex), caused the administrative officer to become defunct at this judicial body (Han Bing Siong 1998:423-4).

In the *gun hooin/pengadilan kawedanan* and the *ken hooin/pengadilan kabupaten*, however, administrative officers kept their seats on the bench. The prosecution service at the level of the *tihoo hooin/pengadilan negeri*, too, remained staffed extensively by (former) administrative officers (see *Orang Indonesia jang terkemoeka* 1973). The position of the *jaksa* at what was once the *landraad* changed considerably, though. He became a fully-fledged officer of the prosecution service with all the authority, in the domain of prosecution, that had formerly been the prerogative of the *assistent-resident*. From an institutional point of view, too, the prosecution department of the *tihoo hooin/pengadilan negeri* (*tihoo kensatu kyoku/kedjaksaan pengadilan negeri*) was amalgamated with the (European) *openbaar ministerie* (prosecution service). Whereas at the *landraad*, the *jaksa* had ranked lower than the (*assistent-*)*resident*, at the *tihoo hooin/pengadilan negeri* he came directly under the prosecutor of the *kootoo hooin/pengadilan tinggi*, with both officials answerable to the prosecution department of the Saikoo Hooin/Pengadilan Agoeng (Saikoo Kensatu Kyoku).[34] Inversely, the incorporation of the *jaksa* then serving, most of whom had had but a limited education in law (as a rule, only the law subjects of the OSVIA curriculum), into the prosecution office and the enforcement of the HIR in the proceedings, in a way devalued the standing of the native prosecution officer who held the title of *rechtskundige* or *meester in de rechten*.

A considerable proportion of the indigenous advocates also continued to practise law during the occupation, even though the circumstances were far from advantageous.[35] The slice of the economy controlled by the Europeans vanished overnight, along with an important part of the advocature's client

34 Zorab 1954:52; art. 180 RO; Han Bing Siong 2002:319-20; compare Chapter III. As far as the *ken hooin/pengadilan kabupaten* and the *gun hooin/pengadilan kawedanan* were concerned, the civil jurisdiction of these courts, in urban communities, was transferred to the *tihoo hooin/pengadilan negeri* in 1943; their jurisdiction under criminal law fell to the *keizai hooin/hakim kepolisian* (Osamu Seirei no. 21/1943 art. 2).

35 According to Lev, the number of advocates who actively continued to practise law was twenty-two, which is just below two thirds of the total number of native advocates in 1942 (compare with p. 145-6), while several Chinese also kept up their *métier* (Lev 1976:161). Some of the jurists who worked as advocates during the Japanese occupation were A.A. Maramis (graduated from Leiden in 1924), Mohammad Roem (graduated from the Rechtshoogeschool in 1939), Sartono (Rechtsschool diploma 1922, graduated from Leiden in 1926), Oesman Sastroamidjojo (graduated from Leiden in 1934), Soetan Mohamad Sjah (graduated from the Rechtshoogeschool in 1936), Soejoedi (Rechtsschool diploma 1913, graduated from Leiden in 1924), Soenarko (graduated from the Rechtshoogeschool in 1932) and Iskaq Tjokrohadisoerjo (Rechtsschool diploma 1917, graduated from Leiden in 1925) (*Orang Indonesia jang terkemoeka* 1973:294, 296-8).

base. Advocates, too, struggled under the poor economic conditions. The content of their work had also changed – the substitution of the *raad van justitie* as the court of the first instance for Europeans and Chinese (in civil cases) with the *tihoo hooin/pengadilan negeri* forced advocates outside of their natural habitat. The comfortable, detailed provisions of the Reglement op de burgerlijke rechtsvordering (Regulations for civil proceedings) and the Reglement op de strafvordering (Regulations for criminal proceedings) were usurped by the much simpler and little known HIR. Desk jurists, employed at the ministries and other government bodies, will generally have witnessed more professional upheaval than their confrères in the judiciary. The activities of the former Raad van Nederlandsch-Indië (Netherlands East Indies Council), of the Cabinet of the Governor General, of the Algemeene Secretarie (General Secretariat), of the Volksraad and the College van Gedelegeerden (the 'management' of the Volksraad) had ground to a halt, while the ministries were undergoing major restructuring (Zorab 1954:33).

Gunseikanbu, the central machinery of the chief of staff of the occupying army, consisted of eight departments. One of these, Sihoobu (Justice Department), in a manner of speaking was the reorganized successor of the Department of Justice. It was headed by a Japanese official who was a law scholar (Zorab 1954:36). Soepomo, mentioned several times previously, was appointed consultant (*sanyo*) to this department in October 1943. The aforementioned 1944 list of prominent Indonesians on Java includes the names of several people employed at Sihoobu who had formerly worked at the Department of Justice.[36]

## *A new legal language*

The changeover from Dutch to Indonesian that indigenous jurists were coerced into by the Japanese has not as yet been explored in any detail. Nevertheless, this process is bound to have deeply affected a group of people who spoke Dutch in a professional capacity as well as in other areas of their lives. They had been taught hardly any Malay and what little they spoke

36 Han Bing Siong 1998:417. Alwi St. Osman (graduated from the Rechtshoogeschool in 1939), M.M. Djojodigoeno (see footnote 26), Notosoesanto (graduated from the Rechtshoogeschool in 1932) and Koesoemadi (graduated from the Rechtshoogeschool in 1938), for example, had spent some time at the Department of Justice. Other well-known jurists who were employed at Sihoobu for a while include Ali Boediardjo (graduated from the Rechtshoogeschool in 1937), Djokosoetono (graduated from the Rechtshoogeschool in 1938, 1938-42 Rechtshoogeschool assistant), Sahardjo (graduated from the Rechtshoogeschool in 1942), Soenarjo (Rechtsschool diploma 1923, graduated from Leiden in 1925) and Maria Ullfah Santoso Wirodihardjo (graduated from Leiden in 1933) (*Orang Indonesia jang terkemoeka* 1973:7-9, 11, 18).

had been acquired in practice – in court, at the Department or elsewhere. After all, it had always been cast as a language to be learnt in day-to-day settings. Once the jurists returned to their jobs of judges, prosecution officers/ *jaksa*, court registrars, secretaries, advocates or desk jurists, most of them, to be able to continue their professions, had no choice but to build on their knowledge of 'pasar-Maleis' ('pasar Malay'), 'dienst-Maleis' ('civil service Malay'), 'algemeen beschaafd Maleis' ('cultivated Malay'), 'verkeers-Maleis' ('Malay of modern social life') or any other special terminology they may have applied.[37] To be compelled to write and speak a language that lacked not only a clear standard (in the shape of a modern, standard grammar, for example) but also the jargon the job required, must have been felt to be in serious conflict with the professional standards of the practice of the law, in which precise, unambiguous formulation is imperative. Were jurists not supposed to ply language – to return to the familiar metaphor – as if it were a finely tuned instrument?[38]

None of which is to imply that jurists' inadequate command of Indonesian put a stop to their speaking or writing. They simply *had to*, there was no way out, though they had to make do with a language that may have been thought of as underdeveloped and possibly unfit for the law, particularly at first. They might not have used that language in their work before (in the internal legal attitude), they might have struggled without equivalents for the refined Dutch legal terminology, but they will not have been in any doubt about the lay-out and content (in a foreign language, indeed) of the text to be produced – whether an *akte van verwijzing*, an interview, a court decision, a closing speech or reports and records. Genres, 'horizons of expectations' with respect to the form and content of certain categories of text play an important role in verbal communication, but in the world of the law, it is downright laden (see Chapter II). Also, the natural habit of speaking and writing in familiar genres may have been reinforced by the continued relevance of those genres, given that the Japanese retained most colonial legislation and the better part of the judicial organization.

Without exception, from March 1942 it was on Dutch language and genres that jurists built, just as it had been Dutch texts that had guided them in the execution of their profession – legislation (HIR, Landgerechtreglement, codes of law), judicial decisions and literature (including books on adat law).[39] One

37 For more on the varieties of Malay and their role in the process of the 'koineization' of Indonesian, see Grijns 1991.

38 At the first Indonesisch Taalcongres (Indonesian Language Conference), held in Surakarta in 1938, the development of a new grammar had been one of the issues advocated (Takdir Alisjahbana 1967:191; compare Hooykaas 1939:133).

39 The court decisions taken during the Japanese era, too, frequently referred to case law and

could say that jurists, in their speaking and writing in Indonesian, found themselves propelled by their 'Dutch-language professional memory', while simultaneously relying on (or attempting to respond to – see Chapter II) sources of law phrased predominantly in Dutch. Teeuw (1955:17) has commented that the influence of Dutch on the new Indonesian language was larger because of the suddenness with which the use of Dutch was prohibited. If this is true in general, it is true to a greater extent for legal language.[40]

When using Indonesian amongst themselves, jurists may at first have felt apprehensive, shy, perhaps even giggling in the attempt.[41] But they will soon have grown accustomed to speaking and hearing that language, new and yet so familiar. Jurists engaged by a court, law firm or ministry formed part of a world that operated in Malay – they were exposed to *Kan Poo*, legislation, official announcements, newspapers and official correspondence in Malay and it was spoken in the workplace. As they let go of the colonial past, bit by bit, and acquired responsibilities that hitherto had been the province of the Dutch, the picture of a future as an independent nation began to take shape. Shyness and apprehension will have given way to feelings of self-confidence and freedom, to enthusiasm for and excitement about the new, clean slate on which to fashion a new state and a new dawn.[42] The operation of the law in a new yet familiar language in all likelihood became tinged with the words, values and meanings present in other Indonesian texts poured out over the country, in newspapers and through tannoys – speeches by Soekarno, Hatta and the other leaders of the nationalist movement. Speaking Indonesian became emblematic of solidarity, of a national identity, of independent ideas and values in the face of the oppressors past and present (see Takdir Alisjahbana 1949:390, 1988:127). Pronouncing a court decision or writing a closing speech in Indonesian, too, may have been tantamount to expressing a new existence, to shaping the new, independent entity that was to become Indonesia. To quote Teeuw (1979:105-7), the transition from Dutch to Indonesian actually set the revolutionary wheels in motion; it heralded a new

literature in Dutch (Han Tiauw Hing 1948:6, 13; Aziz 1955:163; Han Bing Siong 1998:440).

40 Compare Heeroma 1956:22 and Groeneboer 1993:461. In court, spoken Dutch continued to be used, too – this was permitted in the event of an insufficient command of Indonesian or Japanese (Kollewijn and Van Dijk 1948:24; compare Han Bing Siong 1998:440). It is interesting to compare the translation of legal genres into Indonesian, as outlined above, with the development of the law in, say, Morocco. The non-Western law (firmly rooted in Islam) in force in that country was transformed substantially through its 'representation' or 'description' in French legal genres (legislation, court decisions, legal literature and the like) (Buskens 1993).

41 Leaving aside the range of sentiments, continually having to speak Indonesian in what amounted to a public setting must have been exceptionally tiring – one was, in actual fact, forced to translate incessantly for long periods on end.

42 Henk Maier pointed this out to me. For more on the 'boost' that was given to national confidence, see Kahin 1952:102-3, 132-3.

world of text, thought and meaning.

An infinite range of legal Indonesian variants is likely to have developed before long, especially in and around the courts. Despite a degree of standardization during the colonial days, in the shape of 'algemeen beschaafd Maleis' or 'modern verkeers-Maleis' (see Grijns 1991), few jurists had invested time and effort in learning a language that was not that of their profession. There was no nationally distributed law journal that might have contributed to the uniformity of legal Malay. Also, the tripartite administration of the former Netherlands East Indies' territory impeded what centripetal forces may have exerted themselves onto the Indonesian legal discourse. No court decisions were published, nor, self-evidently, advocates' case documents; no teaching of law or writing of legal literature in Indonesian worth mentioning was available. On the other hand, within each of the three areas of Japanese military administration, the centripetal forces will have intensified at the local level in particular (see Chapter II) – simply through the extended, shared experience of communicating in Indonesian, through the general influence of Indonesian in texts held in high esteem (like certain newspapers, speeches by nationalist leaders, the publications of Balai Poestaka, study books for Indonesian and so on),[43] or even through taking classes, an activity in which many engaged.

The growing awareness that the future national language was at stake will also have promoted some form of standardization. 'Bahasa Indonesia' must have been charged with a meaning quite different from 'Malay'/'bahasa Melayu' – a 'real' national tongue requires a degree of uniformity and a norm for 'speaking properly' which may be excused in a lingua franca (such as Malay).[44] The proclamation of Indonesian as the State language (art. 36 Constitution) is likely to have induced a similar effect.

Legislative language is likely to have developed along another path, since the legislation in Indonesian, as published in *Kan Poo*, was translated from Japanese (see Pringgodigdo 1954:54). Which translators work-

43 The newspapers published during the Japanese occupation were: *Asia Raya* (Jakarta), the official organ of the Japanese propaganda service; *Pembangoen*, the successor of *Pemandangan* and *Kung Yung Po*, the successor of *Hong Po* (all in Jakarta); *Tjahaja* (Bandung); *Sinar Matahari* (Yogyakarta); *Sinar Baru* (Bandung); *Soerabaiasch Handelsblad*, renamed *Perwarta Perniagaan* on 17-6-1942; *Soeara Asia* (Surabaya) (Isa 1972:75-6). *Pandji Poestaka*, the publication of Balai Poestaka, was continued under the name of *Indonesia Merdeka*. For more on the Indonesian language press during the Japanese occupation, also see Echols 1963.

44 Several Indonesian jurists who were shown various translations, in Malay, of legislation dating from before or just after the war, commented along the lines of: 'That's still in Malay'. This response demonstrates the recognition of lingual diversity but might also conceal a normative aspect: 'That is not Indonesian, cannot be Indonesian, because a "real", national language complies with the rules'.

ing from Japanese into Indonesian were contracted for this purpose merits further research. A second issue for investigation is to what extent government institutions and publishers that, in the colonial era, had concerned themselves with publications in Malay, were involved in issuing *Kan Poo*. Balai Poestaka/Volkslectuur (People's Reading), for example, boasted over twenty-five years of experience in producing and publishing Malay (and other) translations of separate items of legislation (IR/HIR, Wetboek van Strafrecht, Rechtsreglement Buitengewesten (Legal Regulations for the Outer Territories)), the State Gazette, circulars and handbooks for civil servants. The institute also fulfilled the role of official translation agency.[45] Moreover, Balai Poestaka had contributed significantly to the development and distribution of modern, antebellum Malay (Drewes 1948:17; compare Jedamski 1997:159-72). Though it was able to stay open for business under the Japanese, initially at least, Balai Poestaka's function as a propaganda medium increased during that time. Of the five people who were first selected onto the Komisi Bahasa Indonesia (Indonesian Language Committee), three were (or had been) employed at Balai Poestaka.[46] The Poesat Keboedajaan (Cultural Centre) established by the Japanese, intended to play a pivotal role in the organization of the Indonesian culture, actually developed into Balai Poestaka's competitor.[47] It is not clear to what extent Balai Poestaka was involved in editing and publishing legislation nor indeed to what extent its publications were used to edit those Indonesian texts.

## *Terminology*

Set to be an influential new institution was the Panitia goena menjempoernakan Bahasa Indonesia (Committee for the Improvement of the Indonesian

45 Drewes 1948:16-7 and Jedamski 1992:147-51. The management of Balai Poestaka/Volkslectuur preferred to deploy the available labour in the publication of light reading in the indigenous languages. By virtue of Regeeringsbeschikking (Government Decision) no. 103/IVF dated 8-1-1921, however, the institution was encumbered with the translation of legal texts (of the State Gazette, for instance), including those required by the Hooggerechtshof and the *raad van justitie*. It assumed these tasks from the 'translator for the Malay language, specifically charged with the Batavia town service' (which function had existed since 1848), and the Surakarta translators' office (*Resultaten Volkslectuur* 1925:5 and information provided by dr. Doris Jedamski on 21-5-2002 and 23-5-2002).

46 Takdir Alisjahbana, Sanoesi Pane and Armijn Pane were (or had been) employed by Balai Poestaka. The other members first appointed were Soewandi and S. Mangoensarkoro, both of whom came from the Kantor Pengadjaran (Bureau for Education) (*Kan Poo* no. 9, 2602 [1942] :9).

47 Teeuw 1972:124. The Japanese abolished the translation agency (information provided by dr. Doris Jedamski 21-5-2002).

Language), commonly termed 'Komisi Bahasa Indonesia' (Indonesian Language Committee). It was established by the Kantor Pengadjaran (Bureau for Education) at Batavia on 20 October 1942, at the insistence of several Indonesians (*Kan Poo* no. 9/1942; compare Takdir Alisjahbana 1945:4). In Medan, too, a Lembaga Bahasa Indonesia (Institute for the Indonesian Language) was set up, early in 1943.[48] The idea behind these bodies was that the Indonesian language, for the time being the main official tongue of the military administration, ought to be rendered suitable for the numerous new subjects to which it was now being applied and, in any event, ought to be standardized. The committee's brief was to determine modern, academic and scientific terminology, to define a standard body of grammar and to issue recommendations for everyday language usage.[49]

The board of governors consisted of a Japanese called Mori (head of the Kantor Pengadjaran) in the role of chairman, two Japanese vice chairmen and two Indonesian jurists, namely Soewandi[50] (general secretary) and Takdir Alisjahbana (expert secretary).[51] In the course of time, active members of the Komisi Bahasa Indonesia were Soekarno, M. Hatta, Amir Sjarifoedin, Armijn Pane, Hoesein Djajadiningrat, Poerbatjaraka, Prijono, Agoes Salim, Sanoesi Pane, Soedjono and Soenario, among others. To carry out its tasks, the

48 This institution was established on 15-1 1943 and was to have 28 members, who met once a week for approximately one year (*Kamoes istilah bahasa Indonesia* 1946:3).

49 Takdir Alisjahbana 1945:4, 1988:127-8; Groeneboer 1993:437; Teeuw 1961:70; Takdir Alisjahbana.

50 Graduated from the Rechtshoogeschool in 1938, followed by a long career at the Department of Education and Worship (*Orang Indonesia jang terkemoeka* 1973:20).

51 After the Japanese invasion, Alisjahbana was awarded the Rechtshoogeschool's emergency diploma. He had previously been a teacher and a Balai Poestaka employee. He was also a prolific writer, frequently published. Having studied Dutch for his teaching certificate, Alisjahbana went on to read law because his future in-laws (of his second marriage; his first wife passed away in 1935) objected to his education being of a lower level than hers; her teaching qualification had been obtained in the Netherlands, his had not. She also started at a higher salary (Dfl 200 as opposed to Dfl 110). He would have preferred to study in Leiden, but Ph.S. van Ronkel, professor of Malay linguistics and literature at Leiden University, would have objected. Armed with a testimonial from G.W.J. Drewes, formerly his boss at Balai Poestaka, Alisjahbana ended up with the dean of the Rechtshoogeschool, who asked to see 'one of his best articles'. A reference provided by K.A.H. Hidding of Balai Poestaka sealed the deal. At the Rechtshoogeschool, Alisjahbana got a reputation for revering the West and for advocating the substitution of Western law for adat law, which would have caused a quarrel with Soepomo (pupil of Van Vollenhoven and professor extraordinary of adat law from 1938). When war broke out a few months before his graduation, Alisjahbana was awarded the emergency diploma (interview dated 11-4-1994). The war also put paid to his MA dissertation on legal language, supervised by W.F.C. van Hattum of the Rechtshoogeschool and A.A. Cense of the Faculty of Arts. Alisjahbana's dissertation was partly based on his research at Balai Poestaka into the language used in its translation of the Wetboek van Strafrecht. He claims that his interest in the development of Indonesian was influenced by his legal training (Takdir Alisjahbana 1976:23-4).

Komisi was divided into three sections (*seksi*), the first of which focussed on composing a grammar, the second on dictionaries and on new words emerging in daily life and the third on selecting Indonesian terms to replace Dutch ones. The latter was divided, in turn, into subsections (*seksi kecil*). Ultimately, only the terms selected by the subsections for finance, law, medicine, chemistry, and physics and natural sciences were published (Takdir Alisjahbana 1945:9).

In 1943 the Komisi acquired an office (Kantor Komisi Bahasa Indonesia) to carry out its day-to-day tasks (Takdir Alisjahbana 1945:4-5). Alisjahbana was put in charge of the office, to become a longtime pioneer of the development of the Indonesian language and terminology. The office's small staff (five employees to begin with, a sixth added later on) meant that very little could be achieved in the areas of grammar and dictionaries.[52] By contrast, the office staff and the members of the Komisi and the subsections threw themselves wholeheartedly into the production and selection of new terms. The section and subsections people met at the office on a near daily basis to discuss and approve or reject terms. The necessity of the staff to work overtime was a matter of course. The subsections comprised specialists in the field in question. The Law Subsection specialists were Soenarjo, Thaib Dalimoente, Oerip Adiwidjaja, Katjasoengkana, Samjono and Salijah.[53]

The subsections took their cues from Indonesian terms already in vogue in their particular professional field. Naturally, the experts themselves were a primary source of terms. Mailshots went out to offices and teachers, requesting lists of terms they used as well as suggestions for translating certain Dutch terms. Translations of texts were a favourite source, too. The terms collected would be discussed by the subsection, the outcome being tabled successively at the meeting of the Third Section (terminology) and the general meeting of the First, Second and Third Sections. The terms were finally decided on by the full quorum of the meeting, chaired by the head of the Kantor Pengadjaran. Lists of terms thus compiled were sent to the public services, educational institutions and teaching staff in the field. In 1944 a minor part of the terms appeared in *Kan Poo* and in newspapers.[54] After the proclamation,

52 The short lists of general Indonesian terms accompanied by an Indonesian definition that were published in the Bandung newspaper *Tjahaja* at the start of 1944 (also see footnote 43), drawn to my attention by dr. Nicole Niessen, seem to have originated with the second section (dictionaries).

53 Soenarjo (Rechtsschool diploma 1923, graduated from Leiden in 1925) and Samjono (graduated from the Rechtshoogeschool in 1942) were both employed at the Sihoobu (*Orang Indonesia jang terkemoeka* 1973:15, 18). The names of Thaib (Thajeb) Dalimoente, Oerip Adiwidjaja, Katjasoengkana and Salijah do not appear in the 1944 Japanese list.

54 Takdir Alisjahbana 1945:6-9 and interview dated 11-4-1994; *Kan Poo* no. 37-9, 2604 [1944]. One of the newspapers also publishing the Committee's terms was *Tjahaja*; in February 1944, for

Alisjahbana was to publish all of the terms approved by the Komisi Bahasa Indonesia (a total of 6,772) in *Kamoes istilah* (Dictionary of Terms, Dutch-Indonesian and Indonesian-Dutch).[55] The Komisi office developed steadily into a bulwark of Indonesian nationalism. In early January 1945, several of the office staff, Alisjahbana among them, were arrested by the Kempeitai. On 29 April, the day before their release, the Komisi Bahasa Indonesia and its office were abolished.[56] A number of institutions have continued the activities of the Komisi to the present day.

Only the tip of the iceberg of Indonesian terms that had found their way into daily life could be discussed by the Komisi Bahasa Indonesia. After the Japanese invasion, at innumerable locations and in the whole gamut of social relationships – public services, offices, schools, companies, other bodies – people had begun to speak Indonesian wherever Dutch had been customary and in each of those locations, a need for terms had become apparent. Through speaking and writing, usable ones had been found in many instances – in the shape of a Malay translation one already knew (from daily use or a book), had seen in the paper,[57] *Kan Poo* or a dictionary, in the shape of an existing term one began to apply with a slanted meaning ('sah' for 'legally binding')

example, it included short lists of Dutch-Indonesian medical terms. (I owe this information to dr. Nicole Niessen.) Sending the lists to interested parties, something mentioned by Alisjahbana during the interview cited above, seems to have been at the sole initiative of the office staff and due to their limited number can only have been small-scale. The Kantor Pengadjaran did not cooperate on this point, nor did the Japanese honour their commitment to appoint a Committee representative within each public service and office (Takdir Alisjahbana 1945:6).

55 Part I (Asing-Indonesia) is *Kamoes istilah* 1945. Part II (Indonesia-Asing) took the Indonesian terms of Part I as its point of departure for translation into the 'foreign' (*asing*) language and was issued in 1947, also at Poestaka Rakjat. The publication resulted in a fierce altercation between Alisjahbana and Prijono (Teeuw 1961:70-1). Alisjahbana quotes the following numbers of terms for each of the subjects: 493 terms for 'general/financial/domestic governance'; 605 terms for law; 3,132 terms for medicine; 867 terms for chemistry; 164 terms for administration; 521 terms for mathematics; 990 terms for the natural sciences (Takdir Alisjahbana 1945:8). The results of the Lembaga Bahasa Indonesia at Medan were published in 1946 under the title of *Kamoes istilah bahasa Indonesia*. The booklet contains a preface by Adinegoro, whose name also appears on the cover. Comparing the two works on the basis of a random sample of legal headwords, the Medan book differs considerably from that by the Jakarta Committee, both in its headwords and in its proposed Indonesian equivalents. Teeuw (1961:70) mentions a second product of the Medan institute, called 'Istilah Bahasa Indonesia', dating from around 1944.

56 Takdir Alisjahbana 1945:8 and interview dated 11-4-1994. Some time before his arrest, Alisjahbana had written a pamphlet on the future of Indonesia, which had fallen into the hands of the Japanese police (interview dated 11-4-1994).

57 Khaidir Anwar (1985:45) mentions a number of new terms that were circulated through newspapers, some of which have remained in common usage: 'kereta kebal' for 'armoured vehicle'; 'jentera' for 'machine' (in lieu of the term 'mesin' that was later approved by the Committee); 'kilang' for 'factory, mill' instead of the later, widely used 'fabrik'; 'pajak' for 'taxes' and various compounds with 'juru', such as 'juru terbang' (pilot), 'jurubicara' (spokesperson), 'juru tulis' (secretary) and 'juru masak' (cook).

or of a loan translation (a new combination made up of existing components, like 'jang takhak' for 'onrechtmatig'/unlawful or 'badan hoekoem' for 'rechtspersoon'/legal person).[58] Where no suitable Indonesian words or terms for translation sprang to mind, the Dutch term was Indonesianized (such as 'kasasi') or was simply left untranslated – because Dutch had been the customary language, the speaker or writer felt confident of being understood properly.

A wealth of terms of particular interest to jurists was to be found in sources of law (the Indonesian versions/translations of *oendang-oendang/ osamu seirei, osamu kanrei* and the like, as well as earlier court decisions stored in the archives of the court at which one worked), petitions for proceedings and other documents in the files of law firms, previous Malay translations of legislation or handbooks and so forth. The terms used in sections of laws and in (archived) judicial decisions were highly authoritative, considering the central role those sources played in a jurist's work (see Chapter II). It should be borne in mind, however, that the lion's share of legislation and court decisions dated back to the Dutch era, such sources therefore being available as Dutch texts. Regarding trends of divergence and convergence, what applies to legal language usage in general, also holds true for terms. Force of habit also played a part in this. For example, despite linguistic objections to the designations bestowed on various judicial bodies during the time of the Japanese, these have stayed the course to the present day.[59]

58 The terms are derived from *Kamoes istilah* 1945.

59 The terms 'pengadilan negeri' and 'pengadilan tinggi', used for the first time in Oendang-oendang no. 14/1942, continue to be the names of the courts of the first and the second instance in Indonesia (see Han Bing Siong 1998:417-8). In this case, habit got the better of the linguistic standard – in line with the overall meaning of *peN – an*-compounds, the Committee provided the term of 'pengadilan' as the translation of 'gerecht' in the sense of administering justice, adjudication, that is to say, to indicate a nominalized action. The linguist Anton Moeliono later voiced his objection, on many an occasion, to the use of the form 'pengadilan' for 'gerecht' in the meaning of 'court', in vain suggesting a construction like 'badan pengadilan' ('adjudication body' or 'adjudication institution', a court, that is) (*Hukum dan Pembangunan* 18 (1988):71, interview dated 13-4-1994 and A. Moeliono 2000:5, 9). It is interesting to note, here, that the *Javanese* term 'pangadilan' does bear the meaning of 'court' (see Pigeaud 1938, under 'pangadilan' and Pigeaud 1978, under 'rechtbank' (court)). 'Pengadilan' seems to have already occurred in Malay, too. In the Malay-Dutch section of the dictionary produced by L.Th. Mayer (1932), the translation given for 'pengadilan' (under 'adil') is 'rechtspraak, uitspraak, ook rechtbank, gerecht, enz.' ('administration of justice, court decision, also court and the like'). The Dutch-Malay part has as the translation of 'gerecht': 'hoekoem, madjelis hoekoem, pengadilan', whereas the term 'rechtbank' is translated as: 'madjelis bitjara, mahkamat pengadilan'. 'Undang-undang', used for a while in *Kan Poo*, during the Japanese era, as the Indonesian equivalent of *Osamu seirei*, on the one hand has become integral to the highest form of law of the Republic (*undang-undang dasar* or constitution) and, on the other, in its article 5 acquired the new, concise legal meaning of a resolution made by the President and the Dewan Perwakilan Rakyat (House of Representatives) (parallel to the UK 'act of Parliament' and the Dutch 'wet (in de formele zin)', that is to say, a resolution made

*The first Indonesian Constitution*

As stated at the start of this chapter, the preliminary Constitution ratified on 18 August 1945 ushered in a new era.[60] Here was a constitutional founding document that had not been composed by Dutch jurists, nor by Japanese ones. It had been created by Indonesian law scholars. According to Harold Munneke (1986:92-9), the Constitution performed several important functions for the new Republik Indonesia – the text was a document that formed a nation and assumed the Indonesian state's sovereignty, it embedded the authority of the state in a legal context, represented the first and, for the time being, only source of law for Indonesia's constitutional law and, finally, acted as a nation builder by appealing to citizens' sense of social solidarity. The latter occurred by referring to national symbols such as flag, language and culture, and by anchoring such symbols in the constitutional framework of the new state (art. 32, 35-6 Constitution; see Munneke 1986:95).

As the very foundation of the Indonesian state, the Preamble (*pembukaan*) to the Constitution mentioned not only the sovereignty of the people but also a national Indonesian ideology, called the Pancasila (the Five Principles). It comprises the principles of (a) nationalism (*kebangsaan*), (b) internationalism or humanitarianism (*internationalisme, peri-kemanusiaan*), (c) democracy (*kerakyatan*) through consultation and agreement (*musyawarah, mufakat*), (d) social justice and welfare (*keadilan, kesejahteraan social*) and (e) monotheism (*Ketuhanan*).[61]

by the government and the Staten-Generaal in a particular form in accordance with a procedure laid down in the Constitution).

60 See pp. 157-8. The Undang-undang Dasar, too, contained new legal terms, one of which is 'mahkamah agung' (literally something like 'great/high court'). Han Bing Siong (1998:425) suggests that the term may have been formed by combining parts of the already familiar terms 'pengadilan agung' and 'mahkamah islam tinggi'. The Draft Constitution Muhammad Yamin submitted to the Panitia Persiapan (see footnote 1), on 29-5-1945, has 'Balai Agung' in its article 24, covering both a 'Mahkamah Agung' and a 'Mahkamah Islam Tinggi' (Muhammad Yamin 1959:726). In the speech held by Yamin on the occasion of presenting the draft, however, he refers to both a 'Balai Agung' and a 'Mahkamah Tinggi' (Muhammad Yamin 1959:234). The term 'mahkamah agung' had been applied at least once before, to wit in the report covering the first year of Japanese occupation, as published in *Kan Poo* no. 14/1943 p. 4, which instance was a mistranslation of 'Saikoo Hooin' (the official Indonesian designation for this body being 'Pengadilan Agung').

61 Preamble Constitution; Muhammad Yamin 1959:61-81; compare Kahin 1952:122-6 and Dahm 1969:295, 336-50. Benedict Anderson (1990b:147-8) has pointed out the occasional use of words, in Indonesian politics, as 'amulets' – pocket-sized trinkets to carry on one's person, steeped in words and texts that express power (compare Soekarno 1964:32-3 and Dahm 1969:348-50). Soekarno, too, presented the Pancasila as if it were an amulet, the different components of which may be collapsed or unfolded – nationalism and humanitarianism collapse into the concept of 'socio-nationalism', democracy/agreement and social justice into that of

Soekarno had set forth this ideology in a speech at the Badan Penjelidik Oesaha Persiapan Kemerdekaan (Preparation of Independence Investigative Committee), held on 1 June 1945. The Badan Penjelidik had been established on 1 March 1945, had sixty members and was presided over by an Indonesian chairman, Dr. Radjiman Wediodiningrat, and two vice chairmen, one Japanese, one Indonesian. The membership was made up of leading figures from among the nationalist movement, Soekarno, Hatta, Agoes Salim, K.H. Dewantara, M. Yamin and Sartono included. Apart from the latter two, fourteen other jurists, such as Soepomo, Koesoemah Atmadja, A. Soebardjo, A.A. Maramis and Sastromoeljono, sat on the committee. It held two plenary meetings (28 May-1 June and 10-17 July) to debate matters both economic and constitutional. The official language was Indonesian – as was true for all official gatherings.[62]

On 11 July a commission to edit the Constitution (Panitia Perantjang Oendang-oendang Dasar) was appointed from among the membership of the Badan Penjelidik. It numbered nineteen (plus a member extraordinary who was Japanese), chaired by Soekarno.[63] A small subcommittee (*panitia kecil*), made up of seven people (five of whom were jurists) led by Soepomo, composed a draft constitution. Having been discussed and also looked at by a Panitia Penghaloes Bahasa (Language Improvement Committee), it was approved by the Badan Penjelidik on 16 July 1945.[64] Following its amendment, the meeting of the Panitia Persiapan Kemerdekaan Indonesia (Indonesian Independence Preparatory Committee) was to ratify this draft on 18 August 1945 (Muhammad Yamin 1959:399-437).

---

'socio-democracy'. Ultimately, socio-nationalism, socio-democracy and monotheism compress into the Indonesian concept of 'gotong royong' (mutual helpfulness, cooperation in solidarity) (Muhammad Yamin 1959:78-9; compare Kahin 1952:126). Due to being the foundation of the Indonesian State's authority, the Pancasila and the Preamble cannot be amended (Simorangkir and Mang Reng Say 1975:8; compare Munneke 1986:95).

62 Muhammad Yamin 1959:60; Kahin 1952:61; Dahm 1969:294-5. Yamin (1959:60) lists the seats at the meetings of the Badan Penjelidik. The name of A.G. Pringgodigdo, who acted as secretary jointly with a Japanese (who did not speak Indonesian) (Kahin 1952:121), does not occur on the list. Nor is it clear where the 'seven additional Japanese', mentioned by Kahin (1959:121), were supposed to have sat. The seating arrangement still has Radjiman as a vice chairman, his place next to Soeroso's, whereas the chairman's seat is empty.

63 Apart from Soekarno, the committee was made up of A.A. Maramis, Oto Iskandar Dinata, B.P.H. Poeroebojo, Agoes Salim, Achmad Soebardjo, Soepomo, Maria Ullfah Santosa, Wachid Hasjim, Parada Harahap, J. Latuharhary, Soesanto Tirtoprodjo, Sartono, Wongsonagoro, Woerjaningrat, Singgih, Tan Eng Hoa, Hoesein Djajadiningrat and Soekiman. The member extraordinary was Myano (Muhammad Yamin 1959:250-1, 60; *Orang Indonesia jang terkemoeka* 1973:112).

64 Muhammad Yamin 1959:260-70, 391-6. The members of the Panitia Penghaloes Bahasa were Hoesein Djajadiningrat, Agoes Salim and Soepomo. This was not the first Draft Constitution, as Yamin had already submitted one on 29-5-1945 (Muhammad Yamin 1959:721-8).

The specialist in adat law Soepomo left an unmistakable mark on the Constitution. He also wrote its elucidation.[65] On 31 May 1945 he made a speech at the meeting of the Badan Penjelidik in which he set out his ideas for the Indonesian state-to-be. Several parts of the Constitution can be traced back to elements presented in the speech. The core of Soepomo's thinking was that Indonesia should be modelled neither on liberalism or the Western idea of democracy, nor on the Marxist system. Instead, it ought to be given a constitutional basis in line with society's structure and ideals for the future. This particular form of government, according to Soepomo, ought to be inspired by an *integralist* state philosophy,[66] in which the state is to be viewed as an organic context in which all people, groups and component parts are closely interrelated. Thus, the state not so much represents one or more social groups but is above society, is at one with all of it. Soepomo's model was the *desa*:

> In line with the characteristics of the original Indonesian style of ordering the state, to be observed to the present day at the level of the *desa*, be it on Java, Sumatra or any other Indonesian island, the officers of the state are leaders *of the same mind* as the people and have a continuous duty to preserve the unity and equilibrum of society.[67]

Through continuous consultation, *musyawarah*, between the head of the *desa* (or the leader of the people) and the population, the former is always aware of the people's mindset. Owing to this permanent tie, he is able to do justice – here, Soepomo uses the term 'memegang adat' (Minangkabau saying), which translates into something like 'to follow the adat' – to the population's ideals and sense of justice. In such a state of unity and harmony, all people coexist as if in a family (*kekeluargaan*), in a spirit of cooperation-in-fellowship (*gotong-*

65 Logemann 1962:112. It is worth mentioning, here, that Soepomo was appointed a member of the Customs and State Institutions Research Committee (Kyuukan Seido Choosakai Setchi No Ken Tsuuchoo/Panitia (or Komisi) Menjelidiki Adat-Istiadat dan Tatanegara) on 24-9-1942. The other members were Soekarno, Hatta, Hoesein Djajadiningrat, Ki Hadjar Dewantara and Oto Iskandar Dinata (*Orang Indonesia jang terkemoeka* 1973:159, Document no. 33 in Benda, Irikura and Kishi 1965:133-5 and Kurasawa 1990:191). Research into the customs and institutions of Java was considered important for the smooth operation of the military administration on Java. In 1942 the committee advised on a number of topics, such as the official language to be used in schools (Kurasawa 1990:185).

66 Muhammad Yamin 1959:110-2; compare Logemann 1962:704. In their speeches, Soekarno, Yamin and Hatta also rejected the model of Western democracy, on which point the other members of the Badan Penjelidik concurred (Logemann 1962:704).

67 'Menurut sifat tatanegara Indonesia jang asli, jang sampai zaman sekarangpun masih dapat terlihat dalam suasana desa baik di Djawa, maupun di Sumatera dan kepulauan-kepulauan Indonesia lain, maka para pendjabat negara ialah pemimpin jang *bersatu-djiwa* dengan rakjat dan para pendjabat senantiasa berwadjib memegang teguh persatuan dan keimbangan dalam masjarakatnja' (Muhammad Yamin 1959:113).

*royong*), which concept also is at the heart of the Pancasila doctrine.[68]

One of the consequences arising from the principle of oneness of leaders and people and unity within the state, which principle (in Soepomo's thinking, too) has strong leanings towards the national socialist idea, is that civil liberties (such as freedom of association, of assembly and of speech) have no place in a constitution – inherent in the incorporation of such rights, after all, is the assumption that the state and its citizens might have opposing interests. The essential attitude of the citizen towards the state ought not to be inspired by his *rights* but by his *duties* as a member of the extended family that is society. At the insistence of Hatta, Yamin and others, who perceived the risk of degeneration into a police state, a compromise was reached whereby the Constitution determined that these rights were to be laid down in statute law (*undang-undang*) (art. 28; Muhammad Yamin 1959:299-300, 313-5, 330; compare Logemann 1962:706-7). The same train of thought casts some light on the absence in the Constitution of a provision regarding (legislation detailing) the election of the Dewan Perwakilan Rakyat (DPR, House of Representatives). From an organic perspective, whether the people's representatives are elected by the populace, appointed or designated is not of primary importance (Logemann 1962:20; compare Munneke 1986:99).

## *Retrospective of the Japanese epoch*

At the time of proclaiming Indonesian independence, the Indonesian legal community consisted of people educated in the Dutch colonial era.[69] Naturally, it was a patchwork of small groups of former fellow students, of people who had grown up together or had jointly progressed up the career ladder. Nevertheless, it was a tight community. Everyone knew everyone else, if not in person than through someone else; they spoke each other's language. Being the

68 Muhammad Yamin 1959:113; compare footnote 61 and Logemann 1962:704-5.

69 Under the heading of 'pengadilan' (justice), the aforementioned list of prominent Indonesians on Java (and Madura) has 84 *rechtskundigen* (who may or may not also have spent several years at university) and 67 masters of laws (whether or not also *rechtskundigen*), a total of 151 people trained in the law. This group held offices ranging from the presiding judge of a *tihoo hooin/ pengadilan negeri, kootoo hooin/pengadilan tinggi* and Saikoo Hooin/Pengadilan Agoeng, through registrar at any of those bodies or judge at a *landgerecht, fiscaal-griffier* at a *keizai hooin/hakim kepolisian* to various judicial posts in the Vorstenlanden (Principalities, found in Central Java). In addition to the jurists, the heading mostly covers the *jaksa* employed by the various institutions on Java and Madura that have been mentioned. As nearly all Indonesian judicial officers with a master's degree resided on these two islands – out of this group numbering twenty-three, Pompe (1996:25) places one on Sumatra and one on Celebes – elsewhere, the Japanese rulers probably appointed primarily native *rechtskundigen*, advocates and other jurists operating outside of the judiciary (compare footnote 32).

indigenous privileged, they had all studied in Batavia or in the Netherlands, even, had been taught the legal profession, had had careers in the judiciary, the advocature or the colonial government. Education and career had disengaged them, socially and lingually, from whatever their traditional (Javanese, Minangkabau, Makassarese) background, had entranced them with the story and the language of the law. They had witnessed Justice at work, meting out equality before the law; faced with the representatives of the ancient indigenous elites, they had *personally* made a stand for the law. Yet they had also experienced what it meant to be Natives under the colonial system, to a greater or lesser extent had been active in emancipatory or nationalist groups and had lived through the social revolution provoked by the Japanese occupation. And now before them, the dawn of the independent Republik Indonesia.

In the history of law of the archipelago, the proclamation of Indonesian as the national language signified a new path to be embarked upon. Countless new, authoritative texts such as legislation, judicial decisions and legal literature, would be formulated and published in Indonesian from then on. The law game, the translation of authoritative texts into the language of the case in hand (see Chapter II), would be played in a new language, taking the 1945 Constitution as its first and most important authoritative source. The law would be democratized in that legal texts would no longer be accessible exclusively to a few speakers of Dutch. As a legal language, Indonesian had not yet won itself a memory, a history. No older Indonesian legal texts resounded in the Indonesian words of the Constitution, words that had become charged heavily with politics and nationalism, predominantly, during the preceding years. In the course of time, the words, sounds and texts of the new language would construct a personal memory and acquire their 'own' meanings, a significance determined by Indonesian texts.

The Constitution heralded an era in which Indonesian alone would be the official language of the legislator, the court and the law faculty. But although this was a Constitution in which an authentic-Indonesian ideology of state was given legal shape, Dutch did not become obsolete overnight. Article II of the Constitution's Transitional Provisions maintained all existing offices of state and regulations until such a time as they would have been replaced in accordance with the Constitution.[70] Thus, a sizeable body of Dutch texts retained its authoritative status in Indonesian law. Even if the authors of the Constitution had decided to reject the legacy of past laws, however, the Dutch

70 'Segala badan Negara dan peraturan jang ada masih langsung berlaku selama belum diadakan jang baru menurut Undang-undang Dasar ini.' The constitutions of December 1949 (the RIS Constitution) and August 1950 (the Provisional Constitution of the new unitary state), that followed one another in rapid succession, also contained such a clause: see art. 192 and 142, respectively, of the constitutions mentioned (see *Himpunan Engelbrecht* 1989:28, 47).

language would have continued to figure largely for some time to come. Formal language barriers in verbal communication, in speaking, listening, writing and reading, are mostly observed in public, outwardly. The lingual memory, the internally persuasive texts from the past, the genres in which one has come to view and express society and work – these have formed over many years and cannot simply be erased by the proclamation of a new state and a new national language. Politically correct or not politically correct, they are part of the lifelong development of a person's identity.[71]

Actually, to the first generation of Indonesian jurists and *rechtskundigen*, the Indonesian words of the new Constitution did have a legal history, albeit consisting of *Dutch* texts and words. When writing, reading and interpreting the text, not only the words of Soekarno and the other nationalists played a role but also those – in Dutch – of the lectures on constitutional law and of the books by R. Kranenburg,[72] as well as those by C. van Vollenhoven and B. ter Haar on adat law. When writing and perusing the constitutional articles on the judiciary, too, their education and experience as judicial officers – in Dutch – will have exerted themselves, whether or not consciously, whether or not voluntarily. For jurists, these two different lingual identities – the new Indonesian identity and the Dutch professional identity – did not clash in the slightest. However 'Indonesia asli' (authentic Indonesian) the new Constitution may have been, even the jurist Soepomo conceived of it in a wider framework, cast in Dutch terms for the time being – a rule of law that enabled Indonesia to participate in the modern world and a system of law and justice second to none of the modern countries (Supomo 1949:48). Seen from this wider, legal perspective, what matters is that the law game is played by the rules and not in what language the rules are formulated or discussed.

71 It is interesting to note, here, the idea expounded by Mohammad Koesnoe, professor at the Surabaya Universitas Airlangga, in a 1991 article. According to Koesnoe (1991:125), pursuant to article 36 of the 1945 Constitution, 'the Dutch legal language cannot and may not be perpetuated as the national legal language'. In his opinion, maintaining and developing the legal language and traditional legal doctrine in the areas of the Wetboek van Strafrecht and the Burgerlijk Wetboek was contrary to the Indonesian rule of law. Koesnoe (1991:123-6) therefore viewed the gradual being taken up of unofficial translations as a proper, natural process. In view of the fact that such translations were being used as if they were the original, official texts of the codes, they had the status of unwritten law in the shape of *books of authority*. The main objection to Koesnoe's argument is that this interpretation of art. 36 of the Constitution is very far-fetched, indeed! It is highly improbable that the authors of the Indonesian Constitution intended an article on language to bear a meaning such that it would negate almost entirely art. II of the Transitional Provisions (concerning the retention of existing legislation). Compare footnote 213 on Moeljatno.

72 Well-known books by Kranenburg are *Algemeene staatsleer* (Haarlem: Tjeenk Willink, 1937) and *Het Nederlandsch staatsrecht* (Haarlem: Tjeenk Winnink, two volumes, 1924-25). The Indonesian translation of the former was reprinted several times, with the 1955 translation by Tk.B. Sabaroedin seeing its tenth reprint in 1986 (*Ilmu negara umum*, Jakarta: Pradnya Paramita).

The communication and work of the legal elite in office was conducted in an awareness of a joint reference structure consisting of Dutch texts (and English, German and French ones, though to a lesser extent), as well as meanings and values phrased in Dutch. At issue were, on the one hand, the informal languages and genres of mutual relations and friendships and, on the other, those of one's specialization within the law, part of which retained their official status by virtue of the constitutional provision mentioned above. Indonesian university-trained lawyers and *rechtskundigen* interpreted even newly-produced Indonesian texts and words in the light of Dutch-language legislation, judicial decisions and handbooks and of the (partly joint) education and career in that tongue. In communication among themselves, the Dutch language and texts always hovered in the background, to be recalled with a single Dutch word, whether or not placed in brackets. For many, speaking and interpreting Indonesian is bound to have felt, for quite some time, like translating from and into Dutch.[73] All said and done, the legal community's position of power and its language and texts emerged from the Japanese era mostly unscathed.

### *The practice and development of the law in the 1950s*

Major changes were made to the practice of the law in the 1950s. Shortly after the transfer of sovereignty, the restructuring of the judiciary was undertaken – 1950 and 1951 saw the promulgation of legislation concerning the unification of the judiciary.[74] On the one hand, judicial bodies in which administra-

73 The various speeches held during the meetings of the Badan Penjelidik and the Panitia Persiapan also contain many a Dutch word or phrase, whether or not in parentheses (see Muhammad Yamin 1959). An interesting analogy for the language transition is the changeover in the legal tender from guilders to euros in the Netherlands. The value or meaning most people ascribed to a guilder in daily life was determined by the price of certain goods or services, all of those prices together forming the reference framework that determined the value of the currency unit in everyday life – this is how much a loaf of bread costs, this is how much a bottle of milk sets you back and so forth. The euro lacked this framework at first – there was no standard against which to judge the cost of a loaf of bread or a bottle of milk in euros, to know what is dear and what is cheap. Because of this, many people developed the habit of translating the euro price into an amount in guilders, since the value of the latter is known. Over time, a standard price in euros will be internalized for all manner of goods and services, meaning that euros themselves have acquired a value. In the new Republic, jurists were accustomed to communicating and thinking in Dutch (guilders). Therefore, initially at least, Indonesian texts (euros) were 'translated back' into Dutch – sometimes literally so, as many legal texts could be retraced to a Dutch text (either on paper or in the author's mind). Because legislation in the Dutch language (accompanied by a large body of case law and literature) was retained, by and large, the legal elite in actual fact was able to continue to work in Dutch (to think in guilders instead of euros).

74 The relevant legislation was UU Darurat no. 18/1950 (*LN* no. 27), UU no. 1/1950 (*LN* no.

tive officers played a role (such as magistrate's, regency and district courts) were abolished and the phasing out of the indigenous administration of justice (*inheemse rechtspraak*) was on the horizon (UU Darurat (Emergency Act) no. 1/1951 art. 1; see Chapter III). On the other, the patchwork of judicial bodies in the archipelago was being transformed, on paper at least, into an orderly system of *pengadilan negeri* (courts of first instance), *pengadilan tinggi* (courts of appeal) and a Mahkamah Agung (being the highest instance, charged with cassation and with monitoring the lower courts, among other tasks). Realizing this transformation, however, made much larger demands on the Republic than it could afford, whether in personnel, transport facilities, various material provisions or hard cash. Though the unification, rather than being a rushed project, was implemented steadily over nearly a decade, Pompe describes its consequences for the dispensation of justice as not far short of disastrous, if only initially.[75] The government had bitten off more than it could chew, a situation aggravated by the country's continuing poor economic performance. A picture is painted of judges without a court, house or transport, of courts devoid of desks, chairs and typewriters, bereft, even, of roofs and sanitation.[76] It would take until the 1970s and 1980s for the state judicial system to be implemented with uniformity throughout the Republic (Pompe 1996:149-52).

The above also affected the composition of the judiciary. Whereas the higher offices of both the judiciary and the prosecution service could be staffed by 'the old guard',[77] the number of jurists available for the *pengadilan negeri*

30) and UU Darurat no. 1/1951 (*LN* no. 9). For more on unification policy, see Lev 1973b:23-37, Pompe 1996:140-58 and Han Bing Siong 1998:420.

75 'It hardly is an exaggeration to say that the unification of the judiciary initially at least had a pretty disastrous impact on the administration of justice in Indonesia. It confronted the Indonesian state with unprecedented institutional problems that required massive investments in terms of both human and financial resources to be resolved. As a result, the judicial organisation came close to physical disintegration, from which it did not even begin to recover until well into the 1970s.' (Pompe 1996:140.)

76 Pompe 1996:141-5. Typewriters were essential to the operation of the judiciary as documents had to be typed to be granted legal validity (Pompe 1996:143).

77 Pompe (1996:321-2) divides the judges who have served at the Mahkamah Agung since the Proclamation into three generations. The first consisted of the jurists of the 'old guard', still educated in the Netherlands East Indies and/or the Netherlands. Up until 1968, the entire bench of the Mahkamah Agung was made up of members of this group. The last two (Subekti and Abdurrachman) vacated their posts in 1974. The second generation Pompe calls the 'generation of the fiftiers'. Nearly all of its representatives studied law at either the Universitas Indonesia or the Universitas Gadjah Mada shortly after independence. Many of these entered the judiciary before the demise of the parliamentary democracy in 1957. Of this generation, the first appointments to the Mahkamah Agung were made in 1968. As their numbers decreased, too, the few remaining began to refer to themselves as 'the last of the Mohicans'. The third group is the 'new generation'. The justices classed as belonging to this generation were not trained (entirely) in the

and *pengadilan tinggi* to be established in numerous locations (in lieu of the indigenous administration of justice) was wholly inadequate (Lev 1973b:24-6, 31-2). To make things worse, following the transfer of sovereignty the Dutch judges once again were made to quit their posts, this time for good.[78] To swell the ranks, it became commonplace in the 1950s, especially in the Outer Territories where the majority of new courts had been established, to appoint judges considerably less well-qualified than their predecessors – the judges at former adat law courts, people who had been registrars before the war, recent law graduates and people who had completed part of their law course or secondary school only, as well as others with a scant understanding of the law.[79] Many had but a limited understanding, if any, of the legal meaning system and the complex terminology of the law. All of them lacked the years of training that had until then preceded an appointment to a judgeship, consisting of drafting court decisions and other procedural documents and of thorough practice in learning to think and write like a jurist, like a judge. Disregarding the guidance they received in the shape of corrections of their decisions by higher judges, many of the newcomers operating far from the big cities performed their task in relative isolation. And having to make do without so much as a good legal periodical at that time, they had 'no contact at all with what [went] on in the world of the law'.[80] From a legal point of view, scores of court decisions made by new judges were below par (Pompe 1996:338-9).

The discrepancy in education and experience from one judge to the next caused the judiciary to become divided into several groups, with the legal elite

1950s, are alumni of different universities and, more often than not, only acceded to the judiciary during the Orde Baru (New Order). This generational classification, that may also be applied to jurists other than the judges at the highest court of justice, is useful within the scope of this work because of its synchronicity with the waning command of Dutch and the waxing proficiency in Indonesian (Pompe 1996:341-2).

78 For more on the sidelining of Dutch civil servants, see Meijer 1994:166, 169-76. Compare Wirjono Prodjodikoro 1974:33.

79 The statistics used by Lev show that, in 1959, a mere 158 of the 500 judges held a law degree from a university or the Rechtsschool (Lev 1965a:183, 1973b:26; Pompe 1996:34). In an attempt to alleviate the staff shortage, students who had passed their candidate's exam (*kandidat/sarjana muda*) at the UI were admitted to the judiciary or the prosecution service, to be trained as judges or prosecutors on the job (Supomo 1953:10). The same opportunity was provided for those who had obtained their baccalaureat (*baccalaureat hukum*, abbreviated to Bc.Hk., see also footnote 126) at the Universitas Gadjah Mada. Lamya Moeljatno, for example, was employed in the early 1950s as a prosecutor and a judge, following her achievement of a baccalaureat in criminal law and various other positions at the court (interview dated 23-2-1993). The situation as regards lower ranking court personnel, such as registrars, was downright critical. For example, for want of qualified staff, the registrar's duties were carried out by guards without any legal grounding whatsoever (Pompe 1996:142).

80 Pompe 1996:374-5. According to Ko Swan Sik, at the start of the 1950s, it was still hoped that the law journal *Hukum* would continue to be published (information provided on 26-11-2002).

at the top of the ladder, those who had graduated from or completed at least part of a law course but lacking practical experience a few rungs lower, and the judges with neither training nor experience at the bottom. Though some newcomers participated in the legal meaning system, thus becoming part of the established legal community to some extent, the majority fell outside of it entirely. As long as the community retained its power base in the Ministry of Justice, the court system and the law courses, it maintained its position as 'the priestly caste to whom all others resort for knowledge about law', to quote Tamanaha (1993:190). But with the older jurists leaving the profession, over the years, and making way for a steadily growing influx of jurists graduated from Indonesian-language law faculties, the meaning system and indeed the position of the legal community itself came under threat.

The influx of underqualified judges and the inadequacy of the facilities with which judges were supposed to work (see Pompe 1996:142, 145) adversely affected the status and the standing of judges and, correspondingly, of the law itself and of other legal professions, such as the advocature. But pressure was also brought to bear by a more fundamental mechanism. To quote Lev, over the years, the balance of power shifted away from the judiciary and towards the political system (Lev 1972:257-61, 267-8, 303-6; Soetandyo Wignjosoebroto 1994:208-9). No sooner had the proclamation been made or it became apparent that the judiciary's position in the new state was far less invulnerable than it had been in the Dutch era. The first major political case brought before the Mahkamah Tentara Agung (the High Military Court, made up of military staff as well as the chairman and the members of the Mahkamah Agung), in 1946, tried general Sudarsono and his fellow accused. They had been charged with conspiring to kidnap Soetan Sjahrir, the Prime Minister, and several other people. Some of the accused were associates of President Soekarno's so, throughout the trial, the latter pressured the chairman of the tribunal, Koesoemah Atmadja, to exercise leniency.[81] Koesoemah Atmadja withstood the coercion but the interference by the President on this occasion harbingered the growing pressure to which the judiciary would become subjected, in terms of its position and operation. The status of the judiciary (and thus the facticity of the law – see Chapter II) was undermined gradually in countless ways,[82] which directly diminished the power of the judiciary, according to Pompe:

[81] Pompe 1996:28. An account of the facts of this case, that came to be known as 'the 3rd of July affair', together with the political manoeuvres surrounding it, is given by Anderson 1972:370-409.

[82] Pompe (1996:28, 30-2) provides examples ranging from the decreasing prominence of the seating at state banquets allocated to the president of the Mahkamah Agung to the special remuneration status of judges being whittled away.

> Judicial status immediately reflects upon the place and role which the state is prepared to bestow upon the courts. The respect with which judges are treated is a significant indication of how important courts in general are viewed in the political system. Indeed, the political symbolism of status and respect are of particular relevance to the judiciary. Unlike government or parliament, this weakest of government powers really has no other instruments through which it can make its power felt, aside from the respect with which it is endowed. There is a highly intimate relationship between the status of judicious office and the power which it can exercise. It is this which makes its occupants particularly concerned in upholding their public dignity and susceptible and vulnerable to public scoffs.[83]

With time, both the government and private enterprise came to shun the courts (Lev 1965b:298-300). The relationships between the cogs of the court machinery, too, had changed beyond recognition since the colonial days. Iwa Koesoema Soemantri, one of the accused in the case of Sudarsono, exemplifies this in his memoirs, in which he elaborates upon the unseemly conduct, in his opinion, of the representative of the Prosecution Service, Prosecutor General Tirtawinata, towards the justices.[84] This example is significant, because in the 1950s a fierce conflict would ensue, with status and prestige at stake, precisely between judges and public prosecutors (*jaksa*). Although both judges and prosecutors aimed to have their (poor) salaries increased, the judges also meant to prevent the salaries of the prosecutors being put on a par with their own.[85] Not only did they bring into play their extended training and the greater burden of work and responsibility they faced (for example, it was the judge rather than the prosecutor who was authorized to draw up

83 Pompe 1996:30. Bear in mind the importance of acceptance of the 'facticity' of the institutional order of the law. See Chapter II.

84 Iwa quotes the objection raised by Gatot Taroenamihardja, his counsel (and fellow Rechtsschool alumnus, though not of the same cohort, as well as his fellow student at Leiden), to Tirtawinata's conduct: 'The Prosecutor General has lost track and seems to think he is delivering his closing speech. It is not customary for a prosecutor general to vent his anger and display his sentiments during the investigation and the questioning, and to make statements that are an insult to the accused and to his feelings. The defence protests vehemently in the name and on behalf of the accused against the Prosecutor General's conduct and respectfully requests the President to ensure that this unconscionable behaviour is not repeated. I have decades of experience as an advocate at the highest court of justice, and am excellently informed of the regulations pertaining to order and of the conventions to be applied with respect to the judge. Never in all my days have I witnessed a member of the prosecution office who could not muster the respect for the court to stand up when putting forward his argument or making a point. Equally, I am loath to conduct this case in a manner not in keeping with the position of the Bench/the President.' (Translated from: Iwa Kusuma Sumantri 2002:268.)

85 For more on the war of the wallet between judges and the prosecution office, see Lev 1965a:176-90 and Pompe 1996:31-6.

the charges),[86] they also invoked the special status the judiciary had been accorded in the Trias Politica doctrine, namely as the third, independently functioning power. The Persatuan Djaksa (Union of Public Prosecutors), on its part, objected that the work load of prosecutors, too, had increased substantially and that the position of the prosecutors in the justice system had changed beyond recognition since the olden days.

Inspired by the Revolution's ideal of equality, the prosecutors intended to consign the paltry role they had played in the colonial justice system firmly to history (Pompe 1996:31-6). They were no longer answerable to the officers of the administration of the interior and they intended their remuneration to reflect this. The argument that the educational attainment of judges was higher than that of prosecutors was far less impressive than before, now that the judiciary, too, employed people without either a degree or any legal experience. Moreover, an increasing number of law graduates opted for a career in (the upper echelons of) the prosecution service.[87] The political tide, in which the executive gained more and more ground, worked in the prosecutors' favour. Their revolutionary service records, far more glowing than the judges' (many of whom had sided with the Dutch in the years from 1945-1949), also seem to have stood them in good stead.[88] In 1955 the salaries of judges and prosecutors were brought on a par (Pompe 1996:35).

The position of advocates became even more precarious than that of judges (Lev 1972:269-71). Although a comparatively large number had played an active role in nationalist groupings during the colonial days, from a political perspective they took a back seat once sovereignty had been transferred. Whereas many continued to participate in government and political parties throughout the 1940s and 1950s,[89] in terms of numbers they formed but a small minority in the new political set-up. The advocates' disadvantage was

[86] See Chapter III. The responsibility for drawing up the charges would only be transferred to the prosecutors in 1961 (pursuant to UU no. 15) (Pompe 1996:34).

[87] Pompe 1996:34. In 1959, 69 out of the 870 prosecutors are thought to have held the master of laws degree or the title of *rechtskundige* (Lev 1965a:183).

[88] Pompe 1996:34. Pompe (1996:27-9) points out that of the 23 masters of laws who were already judges at the time of the Japanese invasion, a bare nine supported the Republic in 1948. Judges had chosen the other side under enormous pressure from the Dutch and because of the exasperating economic conditions that resulted from the Dutch blockade (compare Wirjono Prodjodikoro 1974:28-9). Han Bing Siong (1998:419) claims that many judges did not opt to defect – it simply ensued from the steady gain of territory by the Dutch (also see the information provided on 30-10-2002).

[89] Lev (1976:166) mentions Sartono (chairman of Parliament), Iskaq Tjokrohadisoerjo (Minister of Finance), Ali Sastroamidjojo (Prime Minister twice), Besar Martokoesoemo (Secretary General at the Ministry of Justice), Lukman Wiriadinata (Minister of Justice and active member of the Partai Sosialis Indonesia), Jody Gondokusumo (Minister of Justice and active member of the Partai Rakjat Nasional (National People's Party)) and Soenarjo (Minister for Foreign Affairs).

exacerbated by their relative inability to speak the language of the electorate (Lev 1976:166). Professionally, too, lean years lay ahead for the advocature. This is ascribed predominantly to the position Indonesian advocates originally held in the legal establishment and in the economy, and to the legal and economic changes since independence. For example, unlike Dutch and Chinese advocates, they had never had a firm footing in the thriving economy of their population group. And in the new era, the existing (primarily Dutch and Chinese) private economic structures, rather than being dismantled through the efforts of jurists, were toppled by corruption and nationalization (Lev 1976:167). Moreover, from a professional point of view, Indonesian advocates had not ever really established any rapport with the indigenous community, which had preferred to contract the more informal and less costly legal services of the *pokrol bambu*.[90]

Finally, the greater part of their natural environment had been destroyed with the abolition of the *raden van justitie*.[91] The growing marginalization of the law and the judicial machinery, especially from 1959 onwards, meant that the work dried up even more. Whereas judges and prosecutors formed part of the state apparatus and could merge with the new political and legal reality, the independent advocature was left to its own devices. More so than the former two categories of jurists, advocates were heavily dependent on the perpetuation of the old institutional and legal values (Lev 1976:167-9; compare Wirjono Prodjodikoro 1974:27-8).

A significant problem facing both practising jurists and those engaged in law teaching was the very limited accessibility of important sources of law such as legislation and court decisions.[92] Very few copies of the official *Lembaran Negara Republik Indonesia* (State Gazette of the Republic of Indonesia) were printed (with great tardiness) and even then, it contained only *undang-undang* (acts), *peraturan pemerintah* (government regulations) and certain *keputusan presiden* (presidential decrees).[93] Prior to the war, judges had been able to peruse a substantial number of court decisions in the monthly *Indisch Tijdschrift van het Recht*, but the 1950s saw a mere fraction of court decisions published in the (sporadically issued) law journal *Hukum* (Pompe 1996:374-5; compare Churchill 1992:12). Especially the judges at the *pengadilan negeri* in the rural areas, far removed from any colleagues, let alone experienced

90 Lev 1976:167-8; compare Chapter III. For more on the *pokrol bambu*, advocates and their client catchments, see Lev 1973a in particular.

91 Lev 1976:168, also see p. 170.

92 For extensive information on this point, see Churchill 1992.

93 Churchill 1992:5. The basis in law for the *Lembaran Negara* (*LN*) is UU no. 2/1950. Legislation issued by the Republik Indonesia in the period 1945-49 was made public by being posted up (Peratoeran Pemerintah (hereafter PP, Government Regulation) no. 1/1945 art. 2), though a part was published in the *Berita Repoeblik Indonesia*.

ones, thus lacked the professional guidance from which novice judges had benefitted in the past (Pompe 1996:374-5). The limited availability of authoritative texts, to many jurists and the general public alike, also degraded the law game, which now could not be played by the book (see Chapter II). At the same time, less access to these sources caused legal certainty to decline and increased the public's lack of faith in its proper operation (see Churchill 1992:2).

## *A legacy in Dutch*

The transfer of sovereignty also changed the lingual aspect of Indonesian law. Indonesian, having stood side by side with Dutch as the official languages in large areas of the archipelago that had remained under Dutch control, became the single official language of the new state.[94] New Indonesian legislation and court decisions would see the light of day in that tongue only. From now on the 'outside', the formal side of the law was in the Indonesian language, which circumstance affected the thinking and communicating of all jurists (see Chapter II). The situation now differed from that of 1942, when the Japanese ousted the Dutch and their language from public life in a relatively short time span, and also from that when Indonesian was proclaimed to be the official language of the Indonesian Republic by virtue of the 1945 Constitution. Unlike those situations, in which the future was blurred by uncertainty as to the return of the Dutch, for some more than others, this change was final – the Dutch government had gone and so had its language! The position of all who used Dutch, professionally or otherwise, suddenly changed. No matter that Dutch remained the tongue of the Indonesian elite, it was no longer the official language of the political powerhouse. Dutch belonged to the colonial dominator, the conservative forces and thus, in a sense, was politically suspect.[95] Jurists, too, became increasingly isolated,

94 Art. 4 Konstitusi RIS and UUDS. On 6-11-1945 H.J. van Mook announced that Indonesian would henceforth be the official language, to stand side by side with Dutch (Groeneboer 1993:447-9). The coexistence of two official languages came about as a matter of course only in those regions that came to be governed by the Dutch. The areas held by the Republik Indonesia maintained Indonesian as the single official language. In 1948 Indonesian became the official language of the federal state of East Indonesia (instituted by the Dutch) (Meijer 1994:312 footnote 69). According to Meijer (1994:280-1, 312 footnote 69), in January 1950 an act was passed that confirmed the status of Indonesian as the official language. This act resulted in Indonesian also being adopted as the language of the country's administration and before long radio programmes were almost exclusively broadcast in that tongue. It is not clear to which act Meijer refers (compare footnote 101).

95 That the Indonesian elite, Soekarno himself in actual fact, frequently still spoke Dutch *among themselves* does not detract from this.

now that the umbilical cord that had linked them with Dutch law and Dutch universities, and that had ensured a steady supply of new Dutch-speaking jurists, had been severed.[96]

Despite the transition to Indonesian as the official language, the dominance of Dutch within the established legal community by no means ended. This was also true for a large share of the political and social elite of Indonesia. Many of its members had Dutch as their first or main language.[97] It formed part of their identity and social conduct and shaped their standards and values, in a manner of speaking. Even after independence, speaking Dutch was seen as a status symbol, the mark of breeding and learning.[98] Jurists' training, moreover, had been in Dutch so the language was integral to their professional identity and ability. The meaning system in Dutch that had united them since the early days of their training was not yet to be replaced by one in Indonesian.[99] For example, as had been the case both under the Japanese and in the 1945 Constitution, the constitutions of December 1949 (the RIS Constitution) and August 1950 (the Provisional Constitution of the new unitary state), rapidly succeeding one another, retained the legislation that was predominantly in the Dutch language (see footnotes 2 and 70). Also, with the near absence of law books and journals for a considerable length of time, one could only rely on Dutch materials in this respect, too. To practise law by the standards that had prevailed before the war, a thorough receptive proficiency in Dutch continued to be the minimum requirement. And for all in charge at the Ministry of Justice and in the legal professions, Dutch represented a kind of 'primeval' language of the law – it had been the language used in their initiation into the law, of the texts in which they had looked for answers to their questions and on which they had based new legal texts. To jurists, speaking and writing Indonesian must have been like translating from Dutch, as commented earlier (see pp. 214-7). Some judges and others in legal professions with no command of Dutch took lessons (given the time and energy), either because they thought Dutch necessary to the adequate execution of their

96 Which is not to say that Indonesian students ceased to attend Dutch universities once the transfer of sovereignty had taken place. On the contrary, no less than 889 Indonesians graduated from a Dutch higher education institution in the academic year of 1952-53 (Munadjat Danusaputro 1953:78).

97 Information provided by Daniel Lev on 19-6-2002. The famed advocate and professor Sudargo Gautama (Gouw Giok Siong) recollects conversing primarily in Dutch during the 1950s, both among friends and in his firm (interview dated 8-3-1994).

98 Information provided by Daniel Lev on 19-6-2002; Groeneboer 1993:462-3.

99 Lev (1973b:13) points out the lack of an alternative and, therefore, the absence of anyone to implement such an alternative. Though this passage specifically refers to the motives of the nationalist leaders halfway through 1945, the reason stated applied equally to 1949 and 1950. For the various reasons for maintaining existing legislation and institutions, see Lev 1973b:13-4.

duties or because they wanted to improve their chances of promotion.[100]

To safeguard adequate future access to the sources of law, several measures ought to have been taken. It would have helped, for instance, had the subject of Dutch been maintained at secondary schools for a longer period of time, if only for pupils intending to read law (see Han Bing Siong 1998:447 and Wertheim 1956:326). This and this alone might have ensured that generations of jurists to come would still have been able to fulfil one of the basic requirements of their profession – to consult old legislation, judicial decisions and literature. Moreover, a reasonable understanding of Dutch (if only receptive), of the sources of law in the Dutch language and of the legal meaning system (by and large in Dutch) among jurists might have forestalled the profusion of Indonesian translations of Dutch legal terminology that had the potential to lead to a linguistic hotchpotch of Babel-like proportions. This was exceedingly important, as terms in a legal meaning system are of crucial significance. Being 'compressed texts' themselves, as it were, containing layer upon layer of meaning, terms are the main points of navigation and road signs in legal discourse, the hinges between articles of law, court decisions and legal textbooks.

The Indonesian legal elite of the 1950s had at its disposal a refined, complex repertoire, a veritable tapestry of terms and definitions – in *Dutch*. Then, anyone with legal ambitions simply had to internalize those terms and definitions. Were newly trained Indonesian jurists still to command the old legal language and terminology, the legal community would have retained a joint frame of reference, in the shape of the established legal meaning system, 'behind' any unclear Indonesian terms or synonyms, so to speak. In the course of time, colonial legislation could have been replaced with new laws in the Indonesian language. A doctrine and a body of court decisions could have ensued. Dutch could gradually have been phased out.

The reality was different. In the space of a few years, Dutch all but vanished from primary and secondary education.[101] In part at least, this may

[100] Information provided by Daniel Lev on 19-6-2002. Lev interviewed numerous Indonesian jurists towards the end of the 1950s and in the early 1960s and relates that even among those who did not want to learn Dutch, it was a matter of form to display several Dutch books (preferably including the Engelbrecht legislation reader) on their desks or bookshelves (information provided on 19-6-2002).

[101] Meijer 1994:281-2 and 313, footnote 78; Harimurti Kridalaksana 1974:43; Groeneboer 1993:456-8. Compare *Hoger onderwijs* 1953:13-4. In 1950 the (then federal state) Republik Indonesia made Indonesian the official language of education (UU no. 4/1950 art. 5). According to Han Bing Siong (2004:588), this law in all probability was designed particularly for the *daerah pulihan* or recovered areas (areas which had only recently joined the Republic). In 1954 this law was announced to apply to all of Indonesia (UU no. 12/1954). At the start of the academic year of 1952-53, Dutch language and literature, instituted in February 1949 with the primary aim of preparing teachers for Indonesian secondary education, was abolished as a main course of study

have been the result of the Dutch legacy, language included, increasingly becoming a political hot potato. Alternatively, the policy opposing the Dutch language that dated from the time of the Revolution (and earlier, from the Japanese era) may simply have carried on (Han Bing Siong 2004:588). Notions of phasing the transition from a Dutch to an Indonesian education system met with staunch resistance from politicians (Meijer 1994:280; compare Madong Lubis 1954:94-5). Nor did Takdir Alisjahbana's campaign to continue the subject of Dutch (for law teaching, research and other purposes), to carry out a wholesale translation of Dutch (and other foreign language) literary and scientific books, and to instigate a rigourous policy in respect of developing the Indonesian language and terminology[102] sustain any success. Opposed to Alisjahbana there were others, the Yogya professor in criminal law Moeljatno for one, who wanted to abandon as soon as possible the Dutch sources of law and literature (the Dutch language, all said and done) as the single point of reference and advocated the earliest Indonesianization of the law.[103] Even if there had been a political will to maintain Dutch somewhat longer, however, it is doubtful whether the intention could have been realized – on the one hand, there simply were not enough teachers of Dutch for the rapidly growing number of secondary schools and on the other, Dutch teachers were leaving Indonesia.[104]

As a consequence of the abolition of Dutch in primary and secondary schools, new cohorts of law students, many of whom had not acquired Dutch

at the UI (Groeneboer 1993:433). Nevertheless, several secondary schools continued to use Dutch up until 1957. These schools came under the auspices of the Stichting Nederlands Onderwijs in Indonesië (Foundation for Dutch Education in Indonesia, established in 1950). The prohibition on education in the Dutch language eventually put an end to these schools (Groeneboer 1993:460-3; Willems 2001:182-3).

102 Alisjahbana considered the terminology to be key to the development of Indonesian into a fully-fledged national language. Indonesian ought to be adequate to express anything other languages were capable of expressing. It was for this reason that he advocated translation of the most important foreign-language literature into Indonesian (interview dated 11-4-1994). Apart from the political opposition this ambitious plan encountered, the Indonesian government also had insufficient means at its disposal to carry it out. Not surprisingly, therefore, the Universitas Nasional Alisjahbana founded later on was to include a special Pusat Penerjemahan (Translation Centre) (interview dated 11-4-1994). For more on his condemnation of government policy during the period of 1949-51, see Takdir Alisjahbana 1988:129-30, 158, 172-7.

103 Moeljatno 1954:4, also see Moeljatno 1981:26-7; interview with Han Bing Siong dated 28-11-1996.

104 Meijer 1994:282. On this point, Han Bing Siong says that large numbers of Indonesians had such an excellent command of Dutch that they could have been deployed as teachers (information provided on 22-10-2002). To counter this argument, the majority of these people presumably had not trained as teachers or did not relish teaching. In addition, one could ask whether their number was adequate for the onrush of law students that developed particularly from 1957 onwards (see footnote 158).

at home either, could barely (having taken a course, for example) or not at all study the authoritative texts of Indonesian law. This predicament was exacerbated by the snail's pace with which these texts were being replaced. By the end of the 1950s, the major Netherlands East Indies items of legislation – the Burgerlijk Wetboek, Wetboek van Koophandel and Wetboek van Strafrecht as well as the Herziene Indonesisch Reglement and the Rechtsreglement Buitengewesten – were still in force. In the areas of practising and teaching law, however, the need for Indonesian translations of these items and the terms they contained was increasingly asserted. Translations of the terms could be found fairly easily in the extensive store of daily practice – from lectures, legislation, fellow students or colleagues, a law book in Indonesian (a rare occurrence, initially), a dictionary or any of the rapidly growing number of (unofficial) Indonesian translations of legislation. On the other hand, neither attempts by the Komisi Bahasa Indonesia nor subsequent public or private initiatives to effect a manner of standardization through the distribution of Indonesian lexicons (contradicting each other,[105] at times) achieved any success worth mentioning.[106] Many students and jurists were not aware of the lists. And even if they knew of their existence, they would often prefer Dutch terms (whether or not Indonesianized or inserted in brackets after the Indonesian ones), their own translations or the terms acquired during their training.[107] The result was a thriving heterogeneity of terms in legal texts,

105 Comparing *Kamoes istilah* 1945 with the lexicon of the Panitya Penjelenggara Kitab Oendang-oendang published as a supplement to the first edition of *Hoekoem* (1947) (see footnote 33), for example, different translations may be found for 'beklaagde' (accused): '[si] tertoedoeh' and 'terdakwa'; 'dagvaarding' (summons): 'soerat dakwa' and 'soerat goegat/soerat toentoetan'; 'terechtzitting' (trial): 'sidang [pengadilan]' and 'persidangan'; 'hoger beroep' (appeal): 'apél/pandjatan perkara' and 'naik peradilan'; 'bekentenis' (confession): 'pengakoean salah' and 'pengakoean'; 'gedaagde' (defendant): 'terdakwa' and 'tergoegat'; and 'rechtspraak' (administration of justice): 'pengadilan hakim' and 'peradilan'.

106 For a survey of the successive government bodies engaged in standardizing the terminology, see Johannes 1972:101-22, A. Moeliono 1981:17-9, 33-6.

107 Harjadi Hartowardojo 1972:1, interviews with Mardjono Reksodiputro on 2-3-1994, Lamya Moeljatno and Soerastri Isminingsih Djojodipoero on 23-2-1993 and Soetojo Prawirohamidjojo on 20-2-1993, and information provided by Daniel Lev on 19-6-2002. The first jurist to obtain a PhD (in 1955) for a thesis in Indonesian, Gouw Giok Siong (renamed Sudargo Gautama), derived his terms from daily language usage or coined new terms himself (interview dated 8-3-1994). The Dutch and Indonesian terms for his specialization in law, namely 'interrechtsordenrecht' (also known as 'conflictenrecht' or conflict law) and 'hukum antar tata hukum' – encompassing both international private law and interethnic law (especially developed in the legal literature of Indonesia) – came from his mentor G.J. Resink (information provided by Han Bing Siong on 22-10-2002). Mochtar Kusumaatmadja, the second jurist to write a thesis in Indonesian, too, produced many terms for the areas of the law on which he was the first to write in that language, being international law, maritime law and warfare law (interview dated 27-4-1994). According to Ko Swan Sik, who studied law during the early 1950s and worked as an advocate from 1957 to 1965, legal terminology developed fairly rapidly during that decade in legal practice, too (inter-

which matter for concern was raised as early as at the 1954 Kongres Bahasa Indonesia (Kuntjoro Purbopranoto 1954:106-7, 110-1).

Responding to the growing need for translations of Netherlands East Indies legislation was left entirely up to private initiative (see Pompe 1996:340-1). New editions of the Balai Poestaka translations of the Wetboek van Strafrecht and the Herziene Indonesisch Reglement were published and from 1950 onwards the Engelbrecht legislation readers came also to include Indonesian translations of these codes and of various other items of legislation, as well as translations into Dutch of several new Indonesian acts.[108] Some translations undertaken by police officers also appeared on the market.[109] This was no coincidence, as the call for translations came primarily from the quarter of officers charged with the detection and investigation of crimes (police officers, prosecutors, administrative officers) to begin with.[110] Jurists themselves initially did not make use of published translations, apart from the occasional search for an Indonesian translation of a particular term, but translated their own materials ad hoc.[111] With time, however, law students came to consult the translations on an increasingly regular basis, followed at some point by jurists, too.[112] The use of the various translations and their gradual canoniza-

view dated 20-6-2001). Actually, the 'production' of legal terms by the successive terms committees took considerably longer than that in areas like biology or chemistry (interviews with Anton Moeliono dated 5-3-1993 and 13-4-1994). Yet the subjects of sociology, history and philosophy saw the definition of even fewer terms (Rudjiati Muljadi 1976).

108 1960 saw the publication of the 18th edition of the Balai Pustaka translation of the Wetboek van Strafrecht, edited by A.W. Djumena and in 1950 the same publishers brought out the 12th edition of the translated HIR. The final reprint of the Engelbrecht readers, originally published by Sijthoff Pers, presumably rolled off the press in 1971 ('s-Gravenhage: Van Hoeve).

109 Examples are the legislation reader (*Himpunan undang-undang umum; Ringkasan*, Bogor: Politeia [1956]) and translations of the HIR (published by Schenkhuizen (1956) and Politeia (1954, 1960, 1969, 1975) in Bogor) by the chief of police Karjadi, as well as the Wetboek van Strafrecht translation by the retired deputy chief of police Soesilo (Bogor: Politeia, ca 1950, 1965, 1971, 1980, 1989).

110 Moeljatno, too, was said to have originally had prosecutors in mind when translating the Wetboek van Strafrecht in the early 1950s. His work was first published in 1959 (interview with Lamya Moeljatno dated 13-2-1994).

111 According to S. Gautama, for one. He confessed to primarily having used Subekti's translation of the Burgerlijk Wetboek (also see footnote 215), adding his own rectifications (interview dated 8-3-1994). Translations had found their way into court, however. Lamya Moeljatno (the widow of the professor cited) tells of a difference of opinion with a prosecutor, in the early 1950s, on how to interpret a particular article of the Wetboek van Strafrecht/Kitab Undang-undang Hukum Pidana. The prosecutor based his view on an Indonesian translation whereas she was using the original Dutch text (interviews dated 23-2-1993 and 13-2-1994).

112 From the end of the 1950s, judges increasingly made use of translations and in the 1960s Subekti's BW translation is said to have served many a judge. In his capacity of judge, professor Sudikno Mertokusumo initially translated from the Dutch himself though later on he also began to rely on published translations (interview dated 22-2-1993).

tion stimulated the heterogeneity of legal terminology.[113]

While one may safely assume that even official translations of colonial legislation, commissioned by the government, that is, would have seen little usage among jurists, teachers and students, such works might have encouraged a degree of standardization of terms and expressions.[114] The failure on the part of the Ministry of Justice to take action on this point may partly be ascribed to the government's lack of interest in the Dutch legacy. Its attention focussed on new legislation, away from the remnants of the colonial regime.[115] Large-scale translation projects as advocated by Alisjahbana and others met with nationalist, anti-colonial resistance, not to mention with a lack of resources such as the people and the funding to undertake the project.[116] The government had to restore order to much in disarray and the language of the law hardly belonged to the priorities. Many a jurist (judges, advocates, prosecutors, law faculty lecturers) welcomed the opportunity to supplement an oft meagre income by fashioning and publishing translations of legislation themselves. And as Western law – in fact, the law in general – and the legal community came to be viewed increasingly as a hindrance rather than a help in the course of the 1950s, the political elite may even have welcomed the fading away of one of the main attributes of that community.

Despite the above, at least one university initiative was developed to arrive

113 A random selection of examples will suffice here. 'Burgerlijke vordering' (civil law claim) in art. 118 clause 1 of the HIR is given as 'tuntutan perkara perdata' in *R.I.J.B./H.I.R.* 1954 (Karjadi), whereas *Kitab2 undang2 Republik Indonesia* 1954 (Engelbrecht) provides 'tuntutan perdata'; 'in eerste aanleg' (in the first instance) (art. 118 clause 1) is translated as 'buat pertama kali' and 'dalam tingkat pertama'; 'eiser' (plaintiff) (art. 124) as 'orang jang mendakwa' and 'sipenggugat'; 'gedaagde' (defendant) (art. 125) as 'orang jang didakwa' and 'sitergugat'; 'vonnis' (court decision) (art. 128) as 'keputusan hukum' and 'keputusan hakim'; and 'eis in reconventie' (cross claim) (art. 132a clause 1) as 'pendakwaan kembali' and 'tuntutan melawan'. 'Samenloop' (concursus) (art. 63-71 WvS) is given as 'gabungan tindak-pidana' in *Kitab2 undang2 Republik Indonesia* 1960 (Engelbrecht) and as 'perbarengan' in *Kitab Undang2 Hukum Pidana Indonesia* 1969 (Moeljatno, first published 1959); 'overmacht' (force majeure) (art. 48) as 'berat-lawan' and 'daya paksa'; 'moord' (murder) (art. 340) as 'pembunuhan berancang' and 'pembunuhan dengan rencana'. Finally, scrutinizing various terms included in the Burgerlijk Wetboek, 'zaken' (goods, property) (art. 499) is translated as 'benda' in *Kitab himpunan perundang-undangan* 1957 (Husin) whereas *Kitab Undang2 Hukum Perdata* 1957 (Subekti and Tjitrosudibio) has 'kebendaan'; 'onroerende zaken' (real estate) (art. 506) as 'benda-tetap' and 'kebendaan takbergerak'; 'bezit' (possession) (art. 529) as 'kedudukan-berkuasa' and 'milik'; and 'eigendom' (property) (art. 570) as 'milik-mutlak' and 'hak milik'. Compare with Van Dievoet 1943 for the successive Dutch translations of articles of law in French at the start of the nineteenth century.

114 Even then, proficiency in Dutch would have been indispensable – official translations, too, would have been embedded in a body of older legislation, case law and literature predominantly in the Dutch language.

115 Interview with Purnadi Purbacaraka dated 5-3-1993.

116 Although the Ministry of Education, Teaching and Culture did instigate the translation of 360 books covering all branches of science (*Hoger onderwijs* 1953:13).

at an Indonesian counterpart of a Dutch code. In 1954 professor Moeljatno published part of the Wetboek van Strafrecht/Kitab Undang-undang Hukum Pidana in an Indonesian version (Moeljatno 1954:3-20). Contrary to the various *translations* of the Code that had already been issued and that to his mind were overly literal, the sentences in this *naskah* (original, new source text) were said to be syntactically Indonesian and therefore generally intelligible even to those with no knowledge of Dutch. Ratifying this text as an official law text would finally make a code available in the national, official language and simultaneously facilitate the development of theories in Indonesian. In turn, this would allow the Dutch literature and body of case law in respect of criminal law to be phased out. Moeljatno's suggestion fell on deaf ears, however, presumably because colleagues viewed the Indonesian text proposed simply as an interpretation of the source document, consequently providing plenty of scope for discussion.

In general, though, it can be argued that the Dutch legal legacy received very little attention in the 1950s. There was no government policy on legal language, nor did the legal professions generate initiatives to tackle the language issue – jointly lobbying the government, for example, to save Dutch as a pre-university subject. No doubt those in the legal professions were preoccupied by more pressing matters, like their suddenly precarious political and social status and the drying up of their incomes. Also, the prevalent notions of language and law (the instrumental language approach) are likely to have contributed to some people's consideration of 'language', per definition, as of secondary importance. From this perspective, it did not present an insurmountable problem that new generations of jurists would have to make do with (diverging) translations of original legislation.[117]

All said and done, one wonders whether the legal elite were to any degree aware of the problem in the making. They had never experienced Dutch texts as a problem themselves; they knew no legal reality other than that of the meaning system in which they had jointly been raised.[118] They had always understood each other in Dutch or, if using some other language, in a common awareness of a frame of reference in Dutch. While surrounded mostly by their peers, at work in and around the country's legal centres, they cannot

117 For example, a judge interviewed as late as 1996, after an age of changed circumstances and priorities, claimed that the sudden absence of Dutch presented no problem 'as long as translations like Subekti's are available'. Another jurist argued emphatically in favour of an approach to the law along the lines of the exact sciences (as opposed to the humanities) and, consequently and in line with the instrumental notion of language, that legal language should above all be clear and business-like (see Chapter I).

118 See Lev (1965b:287): 'Quite apart from the constitutional maintenance of existing legislation, most Indonesian judges, advocates, and other servants of the law were inclined to operate the legal system as they knew it, even when it began to break down'.

have perceived that the meaning system and accompanying attunement that characterized the manner in which they carried out their profession was at variance with those of many of the newcomers (Tamanaha 1993:151; compare Chapter II). It must have been difficult to put themselves in the shoes of young jurists and inadequately trained judges and fathom the reality in which they worked and the problems they faced. To imagine practising law in the void left by the rich and nuanced tapestry of Dutch and the texts in that language may be likened to imagining one's jumping over one's own shadow.

It was also a leap into the unknown. Neither a doctrine nor legal literature in Indonesian existed as yet and therefore, neither did jurists who had 'become lawyers in that language' (see Chapter II). The future of a legal system in the Indonesian language was uncertain. Doubts about the language were being voiced. Was it suitable for the law? Could the Dutch sources be translated into Indonesian at all? Were the Indonesian translations reliable?[119] And so the legal elite continued to focus on the Dutch language and texts and, when necessary and concordant with the concrete situation, to produce Indonesian translations and select legal terms themselves.[120] The work of jurists who lacked or had a limited command of Dutch was treated with suspicion and the use of incorrect translations or their absence altogether was sometimes blamed for the failing legal system.[121]

With time, the numbers of jurists 'on the wrong side of the tracks' in terms of language and education swelled rapidly. For a long time, many of the old guard must have experienced speaking Indonesian as some kind of façade, with their Dutch reality taking place in between brackets (whether or not explicitly). Well into the 1950s, legislation might be formulated in Dutch before being translated into Indonesian and promulgated.[122] From the perspective of legal development, too, the leading jurists set a firm course in this period in the shape of authoritative judicial decisions and ministerial policy

119 See Chapter I, as well as information provided by Daniel Lev on 19-6-2002. Lev has it that, nowadays, the same questions are asked in Malaysia, where attempts are made to designate Malaysian as the official legal language.

120 Interviews with Purwoto Gandasubrata on 11-9-1996, Han Bing Siong on 28-11-1996, S. Gautama on 8-3-1994 and Soetojo Prawirohamidjojo on 20-2-1993. It should be borne in mind, here, that Dutch legal terms are highly system-linked (see Chapter II). Jurists and their professions are mutually bound by an entire network of Dutch terms, 'compressed texts', concealing interrelated theories, articles of law and paragraphs from legal handbooks. The use of this Indonesian term or that (as proposed by the Ministry of Justice, for example) instead of the Dutch ones, left this network intact.

121 Information provided by Daniel Lev on 19-6-2002; Pompe 1996:342.

122 Busthanul Arifin (1976:78) gives UU no. 1/1950 concerning the Mahkamah Agung as an example. In the 1950s J.R.H. Mager, officer of the colonial government turned Republik Indonesia, was engaged in translating draft acts composed in Dutch (information provided by Drs Jerry Mager on 4-6-2003).

– to elaborate on colonial law and, if necessary, to adapt it (Pompe 1994:10-1, 19), in the language and on the foundations with which they were familiar. Dutch items of legislation supplied various models for new Indonesian ones (Busthanul Arifin 1976:78; compare Pompe 1994:19). For the time being, the tightknit old guard, encompassing both the legal professions and the law faculties, were firmly at the helm.[123]

### *Legal education in the 1950s*

The law courses offered in the Republik's infancy must be discussed for two main reasons. First, training law students would make an important contribution to the germination of the country's legal future. The meaning system to be shared by new generations of jurists, the languages and genres to bind them together and the terms to be applied – they were all rooted in the training jurists had received. Secondly, the law faculties represented the location par excellence for the development of a law doctrine in Indonesian, of a version in the Indonesian language of the story of the state under the rule of law and of the various areas of law. New Indonesian handbooks might mature into authoritative texts, not only in the setting of law teaching and research, but also in the practice of law. Such texts might become significant centripetal forces in developing the discourse – in Indonesian – of legal literature, legislation and case law.

The 1950s are characterized by a disproportionate increase in law students, initially in terms of their number per course but as of 1954 also in the amount of law faculties opened within new state universities. Up until then, only two state universities had existed, namely the Jakarta-based Universitas Indonesia (UI) and the Universitas Gadjah Mada (Gama or UGM) at Yogyakarta.[124] Their origins could not have been more different. The Gama was firmly rooted in republicanism. It was officially opened on 19 December 1949 as the successor to several higher education institutions, some of them private, on the territory of the first republic. One private insti-

123 Pompe (1996:321-34) sketches the various networks that played a role within the body of Mahkamah Agung judges over many years.

124 Until mid-1955 the official name of the university of Jakarta was Universit*et* Indonesia and that of Yogyakarta Universit*it* Negeri Gadjah Mada. By virtue of UU no. 10/1955, the terms *universitet*, *universitit* and *universiteit* used in names were replaced by *universitas*, and *fakulteit*, *fakultet* and *fakultit* by *fakultas*. Apart from the law colleges in Jakarta and Yogyakarta, from 1952 onwards the UI also had a Faculty of Law at Makassar and the Gama at Surabaya. In Padang, there was a private higher education institution that taught law and Yogyakarta and Surakarta had a Universitas Islam Indonesia, the Law Faculty of which was located in Surakarta (Supomo 1953:14 and *Hoger onderwijs* 1953:10-2).

tution subsumed by the Gama was the Balai Perguruan Tinggi Gadjah Mada (Gadjah Mada University), founded in the first few months of 1946 and comprising law and arts faculties.[125] The Universitas Indonesia, established on 2 February 1950, was still founded formally in the 1946 Hoger Onderwijs-ordonnantie. On 11 December 1950 its Faculteit der Rechtsgeleerdheid en Sociale Wetenschappen (Faculty of Law and Social Sciences) became the Fakultas Hukum dan Pengetahuan Masjarakat. Contrary to its Yogya counterpart, this Faculty had both republican and colonial roots – not only did it succeed the Faculteit der Rechtsgeleerdheid en Sociale Wetenschappen of the Universiteit van Indonesië (University of Indonesia), founded in 1947, but also the republican Perguruan Tinggi Ilmu Hukum (Law College) at Jakarta, established in the same year. Tracing the lineage back further, its forebear was the Rechtshoogeschool.[126]

Both universities became swamped with students. The UI especially attracted large numbers of students, ex-army for instance, from the territories of the former Republic.[127] The roll of the Gama grew nearly tenfold

125 For more on the history of the Gama, see *Zeven jaar Republik Indonesia* 1952:140-9, Liz Wiwiek 1989a and *Hoger onderwijs* 1953:9-10. For the UI, see Liz Wiwiek 1989b, *Hoger onderwijs* 1953:10-1, Supomo 1953 and Resink 1974:439-40. The Gama was regulated by PP no. 37/1950.

126 The 1946 Hoger Onderwijs-ordonnantie was published in *Stb.* 1947, no. 47. Undang-undang Darurat no. 7/1950 charged the Minister of Education, Teaching and Culture with taking measures to align the UI more closely with the national policy on education. The measures were allowed to depart from the Hoger Onderwijs-ordonnantie, if need be (Supomo 1953:4-5). The Universiteit van Indonesië was founded on 12-3-1947 as the successor to the Nood-Universiteit van Indonesië (Emergency University of Indonesia), established in 1946. The republican Perguruan Tinggi Ilmu Hukum (Law College), operating in Batavia alongside the Universiteit van Indonesië, was founded in 1947 by Soediman Kartohadiprodjo, one of J.H.A. Logemann's students. The latter institution had few students (information provided by Mardjono Reksodiputro on 19-11-2002) and lectures are said to have been held in the homes of the professors (information provided by Han Bing Siong). It was formally acknowledged that the origins of the UI Law Faculty lay in the Rechtshoogeschool in 1972, when the latter's foundation day of 28 October was adopted as the Faculty's birthday (Resink 1974:446-7). Apart from the different roles played by the Dutch language at the UI compared to the Gama (discussed below), the structure of the course also differed. At the Gama, a 'baccalaureat' programme (*tingkat pengadjaran baccalaureat*) had already been implemented (see PP no. 37/1950 art. 4 clauses 3, 16, 21 and compare with footnote 79), when the UI still offered the colonial stages of foundation course (*propaedeuse*), candidate's and master's exams. The universities also differed in their capacity to appoint non-Indonesian citizens, who were only eligible for extraordinary or associate posts at the Gama (PP no. 37/1950 art. 22 clause 3 in conjunction with clause 1 sub b, c), whereas in the first half of the 1950s, the majority of ordinary chairs and lectureships at the UI were held by Dutch citizens, some of whom had transferred from the Universiteit van Indonesië (Supomo 1953:6-7). Halfway through that decade, the Law Faculty was staffed mostly by Indonesian professors (Supomo 1953:7).

127 Interview with Ko Swan Sik dated 20-6-2001; *Hoger onderwijs* 1953:14; Utrecht 1991:172. Thousands of Indonesians from Yogyakarta descended on the new capital, many of whom hoped to secure a position in the new civil service (Meijer 1994:166).

between 1949 and 1952.[128] The onrush was all the more problematic because the universities were now poorly resourced. There was a shortage of lecture halls (especially the Gama) and libraries, but above all, of properly qualified teaching staff (*Openbare bibliotheken* 1953:22-3; *Hoger onderwijs* 1953:10, 14; compare Wertheim 1956:326). In the colonial days, a wholly insufficient number of Indonesian scholars had been trained to take up the new lectureships and professorships. Of the few who were qualified, a considerable number were engaged in parliament or held posts at the ministries (*Hoger onderwijs* 1953:13). The then Minister of Education Abu Hanifah managed to thwart a 1950 bill to substitute all Dutch professors for Indonesian ones. The universities struck a gentlemen's agreement allowing Dutch professors to be contracted for another decade.[129] But many lecturers were also appointed who were inadequately qualified to teach, at least not at the level prevailing prior to the Japanese invasion (Han Bing Siong 1998:446). The academic year of 1951-1952 saw the first appointments of teaching assistants who had passed the candidate's exam (Supomo 1953:7-8; see Chapter III). Due to the lack of lecture halls, the hords of students attended their lectures in 'shifts', taking place in the morning, afternoon and evening.[130]

Keeping hold of the Dutch lecturers thus was crucial to the survival of higher education. Their presence ensured that Dutch continued to be used at university. As late as 1950, all lectures but one at the UI Law Faculty were still held in Dutch, almost exclusively by Dutch professors.[131] Strong pressure was exerted from the nationalist quarter, however, to indonesify the body of lecturers and to banish Dutch at the earliest opportunity. In 1951 a ministerial decree was issued allowing the government to appoint professors without involving the Faculty, although the University Chancellor did need to be consulted (Supomo 1953:4). In connection with the restyling of the UI Faculteit der Rechtsgeleerdheid en Sociale Wetenschappen as the Fakultas Hukum dan Pengetahuan Masjarakat, on 11 December 1950, the following year several Dutch professors were replaced by Indonesians.[132] With respect to the

128 In November 1949, 463 students were enrolled. Three years later the roll counted no less than 4,457 (*Hoger onderwijs* 1953:10). The UI had 6,854 students at the end of 1952, 857 of whom at the Fakultas Hukum dan Pengetahuan Masjarakat. Students at the Makassar Law Faculty numbered 63. Also in 1952, eight students obtained their master of laws degree from the UI (Supomo 1953:14).

129 This applied especially to the technical faculties (Meijer 1994:281; compare Supomo 1953:7-9).

130 Also, many members of staff were only available to lecture after office hours (*Hoger onderwijs* 1953:14).

131 The lecturer teaching in Indonesian was sociology professor T.S.G. Moelia (information provided by Han Bing Siong on 22-10-2002).

132 Interview with Han Bing Siong on 28-11-1996 and information provided by Han Bing Siong on 22-10-2002. The newly employed Indonesian professors were Djokosoetono, Satochid

language used in lectures, the requirement for Dutch professors to teach in Indonesian from the start of the 1950-1951 academic year was rescinded due to its unfeasibility.[133] But things were different from one faculty to the next and at each location. Partly due to the appointment of new Indonesian professors (who taught in Indonesian), for example, Dutch soon all but disappeared from the lecture halls of the UI Faculty of Law. Only the Dutch professors who remained continued to use that language.[134]

Once Indonesian had become the common language of the Perguruan Tinggi Ilmu Hukum in Jakarta and the (private) Balai Perguruan Tinggi Gadjah Mada in Yogyakarta for some years, barring the odd interval, the language eventually gained currency in law teaching, too.[135] Before long, most

---

Kartanegara, Soediman Kartohadiprodjo, Koesoemadi Poedjosewojo and Hazairin (information provided by Ko Swan Sik on 26-11-2002).

133 Meijer 1994:281. The government later suggested that English be used as a temporary, emergency solution. Foreign lecturers were enrolled in special courses in Indonesian (*Hoger onderwijs* 1953:13).

134 At the UI these were H.Th. Chabot, P.N. Drost, G.J. Held, W.M.E. Noach and R.F. Beerling (information provided by Ko Swan Sik on 26-11-2002 and Han Bing Siong on 24-9-2004). Professor G.J. Resink, who had taken Indonesian nationality, also continued to lecture in Dutch. His students had been asked to choose between Dutch and poor Indonesian and in any event, for his specialist areas of law there was no literature in Indonesian (interviews with Resink on 24-1-1994 and Han Bing Siong on 28-11-1996).

135 As far as teaching law in Indonesian at an earlier date is concerned, the one and two-year courses for judges taught in Malay/Indonesian have already been mentioned (see p. 167 and footnote 32). Iwa Koesoema Soemantri speaks of teaching the subject of international law, in 1943, at the Asrama Indonesia Merdeka, founded by the Japanese (Iwa Kusuma Sumantri 2002:146). Four decades earlier, at the end of the nineteenth century, law had been taught in Malay for some years at the Magelang Hoofdenschool. Legal subjects were added to the curriculum in 1893, by way of experiment. Dutch as the language of instruction was simultaneously replaced by Malay and Javanese because the heavy investment in education in Dutch had not produced the desired result in terms of command of that language (Groeneboer 1993:204). The law teacher there was P.L.A. Collard, a former *landraad* chairman. In his first year at the Hoofdenschool, he still taught in Dutch but would subsequently change nearly altogether to Malay (*Algemeen verslag inlandsch onderwijs* 1901:73). In 1896-97 he published a two-part textbook, written in Malay, on the Wetboek van Strafrecht and the Inlandsch Reglement. The introduction contained a summary of areas of law, of Netherlands East Indies legislation and of judicial organization (*Roekoen-roekoen hoekoem jang lakoe di tanah Hindi-Belanda, pertama-tama di poelau Djawa dan Mendoera*, Batavia: Albrecht & Co, 1896-97). Exam results over the period 1893-97 do not reveal major problems with law teaching – the results are said to be 'satisfactory', in the sense that the students had shown 'to have acquired sufficient knowledge' in the subjects mentioned (as far as the subject of jurisprudence is concerned) and about the general and regional administration of the Netherlands East Indies (for the subject of constitutional and administrative law) (*Algemeen verslag inlandsch onderwijs* 1901:83). In 1899 it was nevertheless decided to change back to Dutch as the use of Javanese or Malay 'was detrimental to the education in general *and to that in the principles of law in particular*' (*Algemeen verslag inlandsch onderwijs* 1901:61). The use of Malay as the language of instruction was generally considered to be counterproductive to the aim of ensuring that future civil servants would have a thorough command of Dutch, valued enormously not only by the govern-

examinations were held in Indonesian.[136] The transition was by no means all plain sailing, neither for the lecturers nor for the students. Some professors, Indonesians among them, were apprehensive of the uncharted territory and experienced considerable trepidation of expressing themselves in Indonesian (interview with Resink dated 24-1-1994). Students who had not been taught Malay or Indonesian at school barely coped with the lectures in Indonesian held by certain professors. At the UI in particular, the influx of hordes of students with little or no command of Dutch meant that university life no longer took place in a common language.[137]

During that period the variants of Indonesian that were current at the universities diverged widely. Ask ten people who studied in those years about the Indonesian of lectures, law textbooks or legal practice and you will get ten different descriptions. A common answer is that the language written and spoken by most lecturers and other jurists at that time was 'not yet good Indonesian' but rather 'typically 1950s Indonesian', 'Malay' ('bahasa Melayu', 'Malay from the Dutch time', 'Malay from the olden days') or 'pasar Malay'.[138] Or regionally coloured designations are provided. In particular, a distinction is made between the Malay spoken by people originally from Java ('Javanese pasar Malay', 'Javanese, actually, which means Malay with lots of Javanese words', 'the Indonesian of a Javanese') and those originally from Sumatra ('Indonesian influenced by the regional language', 'bahasa Melayu Riau', 'high Indonesian').[139] A third characterization, intertwined with the other two, relates to the influence of Dutch (whether or not surmised) on the language usage. In this respect, common expressions are 'translated Dutch',

---

ment but also by pupils' parents (*Algemeen verslag inlandsch onderwijs* 1901:7-8; see Groeneboer 1993:204-5). The experiment of teaching law was followed by the Bandung and Probolinggo Hoofdenscholen, renamed OSVIA in 1900, but these only ever taught in Dutch and, in actual fact, tightened the admission requirements in terms of command of Dutch (see Chapter III).

136 In accordance with art. 17 of PP no. 37/1950, the Gama was permitted to hold exams in other languages if the faculty in question considered it necessary to do so. Giving lectures in a language other than Indonesian was only allowed in special circumstances and required the Minister's permission (art. 25 clause 1); compare with the interview with Hajati Suroredjo (UI 1951-57) dated 25-4-1994.

137 Ko Swan Sik (UI 1948-53) relates that the influx of Indonesian students from the Javanese interior had an enormous impact on him and dramatically changed his opinion – gaps in his understanding of colonial history were filled in and he began to see the other side of the story. Yet there was a certain bond between him and the other students, who had still been trained in Dutch, as well as with the older jurists trained before the war (interview dated 20-6-2001).

138 Interviews with Han Bing Siong on 28-11-1996, Hartono Soerjopratikno on 23-2-1993, Lamya Moeljatno on 23-2-1993, Soerastri Isminingsih Djojodipoero on 23-2-1993, Soetojo Prawirohamidjojo on 20-2-1993, Emmy Pangaribuan on 12-2-1994, Liem Goan Hwie/Robby Liem on 19-2-1994 and Retnowulan Sutantio on both 23-2-1994 and 29-4-1994.

139 Interviews with Han Bing Siong on 28-11-1996, Ko Swan Sik on 20-6-2001 and Purwoto Gandasubrata on 11-9-1996.

'bahasa terjemahan' ('translations language'), 'Indonesian with a Dutch sentence structure', 'Indonesian still strongly reminiscent of Dutch' or 'hardly intelligible without knowing Dutch'.[140]

Despite the classifications not being calibrated scientifically, they are most revealing. After all, people do not construct their lingual utterances from abstract, equiform units gleaned from dictionaries and grammar books. They elaborate on the store of lingual memory and repertoire acquired throughout their life spans, in whichever language that process took place (see Chapter II). The lingual memory that guided lecturers at the Law Faculty when expressing themselves in Indonesian, consisted substantially of *non*-Indonesian texts (not composed in 'bahasa Indonesia', that is), such as Dutch (childhood, university, career), 'pasar Malay' (town, shops) and, if a native speaker of an Indonesian language, languages such as Javanese, Sundanese, Makassarese, Minangkabau-Malay or any other variant of Sumatran Malay. The interviewees ostensibly had recognized traces of those other languages in their lecturers' Indonesian (or reckoned that they had done so). Whatever the case may be, they had experienced that Indonesian as sufficiently divergent to classify it differently.

> Just how divergent is evident from Han Bing Siong's story. Han (UI 1950-56), who had not learnt Indonesian at school, recalls that he had no trouble at all understanding the Indonesian spoken by most of his lecturers – which he puts down to his command of both Dutch and Javanese, feeling these languages to reverberate in the Indonesian spoken. The Indonesian of the Sumatran professor Hazairin (which Han classified as 'high Indonesian') was utterly lost on him, however. He 'could not understand a word' and, in 1951, even considered quitting his course because of this. (Interview dated 28 November 1996.)[141]

Although it did not take long for Indonesian to become the main official language of the law faculties, Dutch continued to play a prominent part here, too. As has been said for those practising law, the bigwigs, the cream of the academic staff, had been educated in Dutch and had (partly) worked in that

140 Interviews with Han Bing Siong on 28-11-1996, Mardjono Reksodiputro on 2-5-1994, Lamya Moeljatno on 23-2-1993 and Resink on 24-1-1994.

141 Han Bing Siong pondered dropping out in 1951 because of Hazairin's lectures. Han attempted unsuccessfully to note down the sounds he perceived. Pronunciation, grammar and terminology – each was problematic. Hazairin taught Islamic and adat law and Han felt that part of the problem was due to his language being laced with words of Arabic origin. Six months of reading *Pedoman* (a newspaper with a reputation for quality and good language usage) on a daily basis, dictionary in hand, helped him to remove the obstacle, or so he said (interview dated 28-11-1996 and information provided on 19-6-2003). Ko Swan Sik, who had enrolled at the UI in 1948 and benefitted from a year's *sekolah dasar* (primary school) and regular reading of Indonesian texts, confirms that Hazairin's lectures were hard to follow (interview dated 20-6-2001).

language. Many students had also learnt Dutch during their childhoods, either at home or at school. Outside of lectures, students conversing with fellow students or lecturers, or lecturers conversing amongst themselves, by and large might still (commonly) speak Dutch.[142] Yogyakarta, however, differed in one important respect from the other cities providing higher education. The Gama was the offspring par excellence of the 1945 Republik Indonesia, a thriving memento of the Revolution.[143] Since the foundation of the Gama's private predecessor, in 1946, Indonesian had self-evidently, as it were, been the institution's formal language so that by the time of the transfer of sovereignty, part of the staff boasted some experience in lecturing in that language. On occasion, principles might tip the balance between speaking Dutch or Indonesian – a celebrated professor like Moeljatno, for example, who had been educated in Dutch, always spoke Indonesian, even to Dutch colleagues.[144] Finally, the students who graduated from secondary schools in republican territory in the second half of the 1940s had not had the benefit of Dutch as both a subject and school language (see Groeneboer 1993:447, 456). It should be noted, however, that this territory was relatively small (Han Bing Siong 2004:588). Therefore, a considerable number of students at the UI and the Makassar Law Faculty had still been exposed to education in Dutch. Many a UI lecturer was inexperienced in lecturing in Indonesian.[145] Owing to these factors, proficiency in Dutch declined much more rapidly among Gama students than among those studying at the UI and, to a lesser extent, at the Makassar Faculty.[146] Speaking Dutch nevertheless continued to be regarded

142 Interviews with Retnowulan Sutantio on 23-2-1994, Purwoto Gandasubrata on 11-9-1996, Han Bing Siong on 28-11-1996 and Hartono Soerjopratikno on 23-2-1993.

143 Although plans were made to move the Gama to Jakarta and merge it with the UI, when the former became state-owned, they were discarded, not in the least due to the special role Yogyakarta had played in the Revolution. The state university Gadjah Mada was established on 19-12-1949, which date commemorated the Dutch attack on Yogyakarta and the people's resistance exactly one year before (Liz Wiwiek 1989a; compare *Zeven jaar Republik Indonesia* 1952:143, 147-9).

144 Interview with Han Bing Siong dated 28-11-1996. Moeljatno's assistant Roeslan Saleh, too, was said to be anti-Dutch (interview with Sahetapy dated 18-2-1994). At the UI, it was mostly professor Hazairin who was known for his stance against the Dutch and their language (interview with Retnowulan Sutantio dated 23-2-1994). Notwithstanding his convictions, he concluded the oral examination of Han Bing Siong in the subject of adat law, conducted in Indonesian, with the Dutch phrase: 'Mijn complimenten, U hebt een vier' ('My compliments, you have got a four [nowadays, the equivalent of a first]') (interview dated 28-11-1996).

145 Groeneboer 1993:449; information provided by Han Bing Siong on 22-10-2002; Pompe 1996:341-2; interviews with Liem Goan Hwie/Robby Liem on 19-2-1994, Retnowulan Sutantio on 29-4-1994 and Purwoto Gandasubrata on 11-9-1996. The statements about the UI could equally apply to students at the Surabaya Law Faculty. This Faculty came under the sphere of influence of the Gama, however (see note 124). All the lecturers, for example, had originally worked at the Gama (interview with Sahetapy dated 18-2-1994; Han Bing Siong 2004:588).

146 Interviews with Sahetapy on 18-2-1994 and Liem Goan Hwie/Robby Liem on 19-2-1994.

as prestigious, generally, and even in Yogya, being able to quote articles of law in Dutch was considered conducive to high exam marks.[147] At least until the end of the 1950s, Dutch courses, whether held at the university or somewhere else, were very sought after by law students.[148]

It has been pointed out, above, that the jurists-to-be of that time ought to have possessed at least a thorough receptive command of Dutch,[149] necessary because the sources of law were formulated in Dutch and legal literature was available nearly exclusively in that language. The latter *continued to be* mostly in Dutch – large sums of money were spent into the early 1950s on importing Dutch books, subsidized mostly by the Netherlands,[150] while relatively few books in Indonesian of any size or comprehension worth mentioning were published.[151] One reason for this was that lecturers enjoyed but a meagre salary. Lecturers who had nothing but their salaries were forced to spend a substantial portion of their time supplementing their income through other work, leaving none for research and publishing.[152] Another reason for the scant number of Indonesian publications was that an important prerequisite for research, being the availability of books and journals, became increasingly difficult to satisfy – books were in scarce supply and their prices rose rapidly, not in the least as a result of monetary policy (Supomo 1953:16; Meijer 1994:158-9). Finally, some jurists had a particularly high threshold to publishing in Indonesian or there may have been other, personal reasons as to why some lecturers did not publish much.[153]

147 Interview with Sahetapy dated 18-2-1994 and information provided by Daniel Lev on 19-6-2002.

148 Interviews with Mardjono Reksodiputro on 1-6-2001, Saleh Adiwinata on 26-2-1993, Ateng Syafrudin on 1-3-1993 and Sahetapy on 18-2-1994. According to Han Bing Siong, the subject of Dutch language was added to the UI curriculum as late as 1957. It was taught by the then renowned Taman Siswa teacher Mohamed Said. Notwithstanding the growing anti-Dutch sentiment in the political sense, this very popular subject was taught well into the 1960s (interview dated 28-11-1996 and information provided on 22-10-2002; compare interview with Mardjono Reksodiputro dated 2-3-1994).

149 Han Bing Siong recollects this requirement being stipulated, in so many words, when he was a student (interview dated 28-11-1996).

150 The trade agreement between the Netherlands and Indonesia, reached early in 1950, details Dfl 3,500,000 for the export of books destined for Indonesia; in May 1950 a sum was added to this amount and by 1951 the export of Dutch books reached Dfl 70,000,000 (Meijer 1994:280, 313; also see the interview with Hartono Soerjopratikno dated 13-2-1994). German and English books, too, were occasionally set (interviews with Hartono Soerjopratikno on 13-2-1994, Mardjono Reksodiputro on 2-3-1994 and Han Bing Siong on 28-11-1996).

151 See footnote 116 regarding the government initiative of translating Dutch academic literature. It is not clear whether any law books resulted from this initiative.

152 Interview with Han Bing Siong dated 28-11-1996; Utrecht 1991:97-8, 172.

153 Resink (1974:447-8) comments as follows: 'The lecturers' academic industry is in decline because not only do foreign books and journals now trickle in compared to the steady flow before the war, not only do the language of the law, of jurisprudence and of lecturing require

All of the above had a profound effect on the students and on the quality of their training. While the student demand for material in Indonesian picked up speed, the lecturers of necessity set little else but Dutch literature.[154] But the scarcity of decent libraries, the rising cost of books and the increased demand from the waves of new students meant that these texts were not readily available to all and sundry either. Even a legislation reader like the Engelbrecht, that was mandatory exam material at the UI, was beyond the means of most students and new legislation was not published regularly or in full.[155] Students could purchase some books with vouchers funded by Unesco and other foundations and institutions (some of them private), but were supposed to pay for the remainder out of their own pockets.[156] In addition, the declining proficiency in Dutch resulted in severely impoverished education – the percentage of students for whom text in Dutch was intelligible at all fell steadily. The impoverishment went hand in glove with what became known as the 'dictation culture'. Owing to the pressure on their time in preparing their sessions, many lecturers failed to keep up their reading, resulting in the gradual transformation of lectures and exams into routines. In the course of time, many a lecture deteriorated into an annually repeated recitation, that simultaneously gained in status as the exclusive study material for the exams.

primal formulation, but also because education and the formation of an educated class are given a higher priority by the fledgeling state than research, which, moreover, can also be very costly'. An example of a 1950s professor who published very little, due to factors on a personal level, is the renowned Djokosoetono (graduated from the Rechtshoogeschool in 1938). He had left the Gama in favour of the UI in 1950, following the transfer of sovereignty (Resink 1974:440-1). W.F. Wertheim, who had had the pleasure of being Djokosoetono's mentor and had appointed the latter to an assistantship immediately upon his graduation, describes him as a shrewd jurist (Logemann even referred to him as 'our college's most prized possession'), though smitten with phobiae and anxiety, including exam fear (Wertheim and Wertheim-Gijse Weenink 1991:154). Though exceptionally erudite in various areas of law, he feared being attacked on the substance of his work. Therefore, but a handful of publications bear witness to his stretch as professor of constitutional law (and lecturer in numerous other subjects) (Resink 1974:441; interview with Han Bing Siong dated 28-11-1996). That Djokosoetono of all people should have published so little was all the more regretful because, also having been dean of the Fakultas Hukum dan Pengetahuan Masjarakat for many years, he commanded great authority and was much-loved, thus being an important role model (interview with Han Bing Siong dated 28-11-1996).

154 Interviews with Ko Swan Sik on 20-6-2001, S. Gautama on 8-3-1994, Sri Soemantri Martosoewignjo on 28-2-1993, Hajati Suroredjo on 25-4-1994, Sahetapy on 18-2-1994, Andi Hamzah on 15-4-1994, Sudikno Mertokusumo on 22-2-1993 and Hartono Soerjopratikno on 13-2-1994.

155 Interviews with Mardjono Reksodiputro on 2-5-1994, Hadiman Djukardi on 4-2-1994, Retnowulan Sutantio on 23-2-1994, Girindro Pringgodigdo on 26-2-1994, Resink on 24-1-1994 and Han Bing Siong on 28-11-1996.

156 Interviews with Retnowulan Sutantio on 23-2-1994 and Mardjono Reksodiputro on 2-5-1994; Supomo 1953:21. Books were also known to be bought collectively, to be divvied up by drawing lots (interview with Liem Goan Hwie/Robby Liem dated 19-2-1994).

Eventually, students were hardly tested on the mandatory literature, by and large in Dutch, and could pass their exams simply by learning questions and answers off by heart. Students and assistants would type up the (Dutch or Indonesian) dictations, then have them stencilled and distributed, usually turning a coin in the process. Partly because of the scarcity of books, a flourishing trade in dictation stencils ensued.[157]

From 1954 onwards, numerous public and private universities sprung up, some of them nominational. After the law faculties of Surabaya and Makassar were swallowed up by the Universitas Airlangga (UNAIR) in 1954 and the Universitas Hasanuddin (UNHAS) in 1956, respectively, the 1950s saw the establishment of new state universities in Padang (Universitas Andalas, 1956), Bandung (Universitas Padjadjaran, or UNPAD, 1957) and Medan (Universitas Sumatera Utara, or USU, 1957).[158] This meant that there were even fewer lecturers to go round. Part of the shortage was relieved by creating 'flying

157 Han Bing Siong 1998:446-7; interviews with Han Bing Siong on 28-11-1996, Resink on 15-4-1994, Soetojo Prawirohamidjojo on 19-2-1994, Sahetapy on 18-2-1994, Hajati Suroredjo on 25-4-1994, Emmy Pangaribuan on 12-2-1994 and Mardjono Reksodiputro on both 2-3-1994 and 1-6-2001. Mardjono, enrolled at the UI from 1955-61, recounts that T.M. Radhie, the future head of the BPHN, earnt himself the nickname 'the dictator' with his dictations. He was said to have an excellent command of several languages and to be adept at translating from the Dutch (interview dated 1-6-2001). A common method of preparing for exams was offered by *tenteergroepjes* (mock exam groups) (interview dated 1-6-2001). Djokosoetono, mentioned above (see footnote 153), had already acquired a reputation as a *tenteerder* (mock examiner) when still at the Rechtshoogeschool (Oei Tjoe Tat 1995:37-8). It is interesting to wonder to what extent the primary and secondary education of the lecturers had impacted on this 'dictation culture'. See Wertheim's memoirs: 'Student delegations repeatedly came to request that I speak more slowly, however. I got the impression that they much preferred to have their lectures dictated to them, so that they could learn the material by rote!' (Wertheim and Wertheim-Gijse Weenink 1991:156.)

158 Since 1954 the following state universities have been founded: Universitas Airlangga (UNAIR) in Surabaya (PP no. 57/1954); Universitas Hasanuddin (UNHAS) in Makassar/Ujung Pandang (PP no. 23/1956); Universitas Andalas in Padang (PP no. 24/1956); Universitas Padjadjaran (UNPAD) in Bandung (PP no. 37/1957); Universitas Sumatera Utara (USU) in Medan (PP no. 48/1957); Universitas Lambung Mangkurat in Banjarmasin (PP no. 41/1960); Universitas Sriwijaya in Palembang (PP no. 42/1960); Universitas Diponegoro (UNDIP) in Semarang (PP no. 7/1961); Universitas Syiah Kuala in Banda Aceh (Keppres no. 161/1962); Universitas Cendrawasih in Jayapura (Keppres no. 389/1962); Universitas Nusa Cendana in Kupang (SK Menteri Pendidikan Tinggi no. 111/1962 in conjunction with SK Presiden no. 67/1963); Universitas Udayana in Denpasar (Keppres no. 19/1963); Universitas Pattimura in Ambon (Keppres no. 66/1963); Universitas Nusa Cendana (Keppres no. 67/1963); Universitas Jenderal Soedirman in Purwokerto (Keppres no. 195/1963); Universitas Brawijaya in Malang (Keppres no. 196/1963); Universitas Mataram in Mataram (Keppres no. 257/1963); Universitas Jember in Jember (Kepmen Perguruan Tinggi no. 151/1964); Universitas Sam Ratulangi in Manado (Keppres no. 277/1965); Universitas Tanjungpura in Pontianak (Keppres no. 278/1965); Universitas Lampung in Bandar Lampung (Keppres no. 73/1966); Universitas Jambi in Jambi (Keppres no. 148/1966); Universitas Sebelas Maret in Surakarta (Keppres no. 10/1976); Universitas Tadulako in Palu (Keppres no. 36/1981); and Universitas Bengkulu in Bengkulu (Keppres no. 17/1982).

lecturers' (who taught at several universities and travelled from one to the other by plane) (Utrecht 1991:109-10), whereas the remainder of the vacancies was filled by unqualified staff (see Han Bing Siong 1998:447).

The factors mentioned contributed to a reality of reading law that was very different from that which was prescribed. Officially, students were required to work their way steadily through a reading list that consisted primarily of sound though somewhat antiquated Dutch books. Law faculties such as that of the UI supposed students with an inadequate command of Dutch to redress their shortcoming themselves by taking a course. The problem of the foreign-language sources of law was also tackled in the actual lectures – assistants clarified the Dutch texts and terms in Indonesian.[159] The idea was that with the growth of the body of Indonesian legislation and legal literature, the dominance of the Dutch language and texts would wane.

The reality was very different. Hard-working students who already knew Dutch or who managed to gain a sufficient understanding of that language during their studies would actually work their way through the reading list, provided they could get hold of the books. If these students additionally had the good fortune of studying at a university with a half decent academic staff and library (like the UI and the Gama), upon receiving their degrees, they could actually look back on law education of quality. Yet as early as the 1950s, the great majority of law students studied under conditions that were a far cry from those mentioned. As has been said, good lecturers and books were in short supply, although the established law faculties were not too badly off, by comparison. But increasing numbers of students had no knowledge of Dutch and thus could not access at first hand the major works on law and the main body of legislation and case law. Their insight into the nuanced terminology relating particularly to substantial and formal criminal, civil and commercial law not only came to them second hand (in translation, through explanations during lectures) but of necessity also in an incomplete format. Whereas at the start of the 1950s, Indonesian translations of legislation were used only by prosecutors and police officers and the available Indonesian books, commonly abridged, initially were either banned by the law faculties or condoned purely as introductory material, with time an increasing number of future jurists came to depend on those sources.[160] And all considered, let's

159 Interviews with Sahetapy on 18-2-1994 and Liem Goan Hwie/Robby Liem on 19-2-1994. Mardjono recollects that in his day (1955-61), students would gather after a lecture to go into the content of and the terms used in the lecture in Indonesian and at times also to discuss books (interview dated 1-6-2001 and interviews with Retnowulan Sutantio on 29-4-1994 and Limahelu on 19-2-1994).

160 A well-known series dating from the 1950s consisted of concise introductions to various areas of law published by Wirjono Prodjodikoro, president of the Indonesian Supreme Court in the 1950s and 1960s and later also holding a chair. Han Bing Siong says that the Wirjono series

not forget the inclination of students – throughout the world – to cut as many corners as possible and get their degrees in the shortest possible time. Given the discrepancy between the officially prescribed substantial reading list and the exam questions that were increasingly derived from the lecture dictations, which path would most students have trodden? In this climate, lecturers who continued insisting on applying the standards of yore to the literature requirements and the stringency of the exams became the exception and were pressured from all sides to toe the line.[161]

Several of the above factors hold true in a wider context than just law courses in Indonesia. Dutch students reading law or other subjects, too, try and skimp on their reading. And in the Netherlands, too, law students are familiar with tried and tested means (mock exams, crammers) of ensuring good exam results.[162] What was different about the Indonesian situation was that the gradual emaciation of the study material and the exams reduced students' knowledge of the law to a motley collection of thin Indonesian texts. Both the very foundation of the legal system in force, a body of legislation, case law and literature largely formulated in Dutch, and the key to access it, a complex terminology, thus remained mostly hidden from the new jurists leaving the law faculties. Of decisive importance was the declining command of Dutch – an unstoppable process in both a political and a practical sense. The availability of Indonesian translations in some cases was of secondary importance – what mattered most is that, contrary to the principles of the law game, future jurists would no longer be able to consult a sizeable part of the

---

was not taken up by students when he was at university (interview dated 28-11-1996). Mardjono claims that when he was a student, the series served as an introduction to certain areas of law, followed by Soekardono's books (taking commercial law as an example), with Dutch books serving the purpose of deepening the students' understanding (interview dated 2-3-1994). Incidentally, rather than the series mentioned, it was L.J. van Apeldoorn's *Inleiding tot de studie van het Nederlandse recht* (first published in 1932) that was used by way of general introduction to the law and jurisprudence (interview 1-6-2001). Han Bing Siong remembers that his lecturers only ever mentioned – in passing, at that – a single Indonesian translation (of A.H.M.J. van Kan's *Inleiding tot de rechtswetenschap,* first published in 1920), though Mardjono occasionally consulted an item of legislation in translation and Girindro Pringgodigdo (UI, 1957-64) used translations to gain a better understanding of the Dutch text (interviews with Mardjono on 2-5-1994, Girindro on 26-2-1994, Purwoto Gandasubrata on 11-9-1996, Retnowulan Sutantio on 23-2-1994, Ateng Syafruddin on 1-3-1993 and Liem Goan Hwie/Robby Liem on 19-2-1994). In the absence of translations in print, in the 1950s, some students are said to have produced their own translations of legislation (Soetojo Prawirohamidjojo dated 20-2-1993). A UNAIR law lecturer blamed the tardiness of many 1950s students on the poor quality of most translations of legislation (interview with Liem Goan Hwie/Robby Liem dated 19-2-1994).

161 Han Bing Siong 1998:446-7 and interview dated 28-11-1996.

162 See Jansen 1991:567-8, for instance, on the role played by dictations and crammers in the nineteenth century.

authoritative texts of their legal system.[163] And even though people not initiated into the legal meaning system had been entering the legal professions since the start of the 1950s, the development of the law courses turned what had been a trickle into a spring tide.

As has been said of the legal professions, for the time being, the top brass (chairs, deaneries) at the law faculties, too, were jurists who had been raised in Dutch and who communicated mostly in Dutch among themselves.[164] Most took it for granted that students should also know that language and those who did not, simply were not taken seriously.[165] The 1950s saw the last cohorts of jurists who spoke excellent Dutch, particularly so at the UI, and who referred to themselves as 'the last of the Mohicans' (Pompe 1996:341). A rift developed between the members of that group and those with an inferior or no command of Dutch.[166] Neither on the Dutch side of the schism nor among the academic staff was 'language' really seen as an issue; there was no concerted nationwide action to arrive at Indonesian standard translations and terms[167] and criticizing someone else's Indonesian, style or word choice, was not good form. 'It was not on', says Han Bing Siong, 'we were all in the same boat, making the best out of a bad job', and if a colleague came out with poor or unclear Indonesian, 'you could guess what was meant'.[168] At that time, though, the Dutch frame of reference and meaning system to which Han refers was shared by his entire group, but growing numbers of newly qualified jurists were excluded from it. The transition to Indonesian had to

163 See Han Bing Siong 1961a:51-2 and Chapter II. It is frequently assumed that translations of legislation are perfectly good substitutes for their originals; see, for example, a statement made by Minister Sahardjo at the start of the 1960s: 'Guided Democracy Minister of Justice Sahardjo was "surprised" that students no longer read Dutch and said that then assuredly they studied Dutch in informal classes. Anyway, said he, they can use Indonesian translations of the old laws.' (Pompe 1996:342.)

164 Han Bing Siong remembers a time when a lecturer at the UI who did not speak Dutch was the exception rather than the rule. The handful of such people possessed at least a thorough receptive command of the language (interview dated 28-11-1996).

165 Information provided by Daniel Lev on 19-6-2002.

166 See the information provided by Daniel Lev on 19-6-2002. Han Bing Siong's fellow student Purwoto Gandasubrata comments that students who did not know Dutch were 'less at ease', 'more passive' – they were unable to join in (interview dated 11-9-1996).

167 See pp. 197-9 and the interview with Han Bing Siong dated 28-11-1996. Legal literature, however, did at times raise the issue of language. See Kusumadi Pudjosewojo 1959:36-7, for example. Also see *Hoger onderwijs* 1953:13 on the exigency for technical terms, especially at the law faculties. In the field of terminology, professors in different disciplines and at the various faculties developed their own schools (see pp. 218-9). The lists compiled by successive terms committees or other official bodies were either not known or not applied (interviews with Sahetapy on 18-2-1994, Han Bing Siong on 28-11-1996 and F. Limahelu on 19-2-1994). Han Bing Siong preferred to find his own Indonesian terms though he might consult Moeljatno's work or court decisions published in *Hukum* 'for the very tricky ones' (interview dated 28-11-1996).

168 Interview with Han Bing Siong dated 28-11-1996.

be made sooner or later, but it was extraordinarily hard to take that step into the unknown.[169] Seen from this perspective, an initiative such as Moeljatno's, to create a code of law in Indonesian, is comparable to a swimmer's desperate attempts to pull clear of a strong current. Effecting a smooth transition required a hands-on approach. The failure to instigate this was to have serious consequences for decades to come.

### *'... adalah sangat gezocht ...'*[170]

Reviewing the 1950s, one can say that the upper echelons of the legal world still primarily spoke Dutch. The Dutch language was the thread that held together the meaning system of the legal community, the dome of texts encasing the legal world and the communication between the legal top guns. Even where Indonesian was spoken or written, Dutch was never far off – for example in the shape of single words, that often were placed in parentheses but sometimes not, as in the quote that heads this section.

The descriptions of Indonesian given above, such as 'translated Dutch', 'Indonesian with a Dutch sentence structure' and 'Indonesian very reminiscent of Dutch', also inherently express the proximity of Dutch. Moreover, the designations prompt associations with a stage in the acquisition of a new language, being the 'translation stage'. Here, typically, one attempts to put into the words of the new language whatever one was accustomed to saying in the old one. Only once the next stage is reached does one realize that the tendency to translate must be overcome. Each language is characterized by its own way of expressing and dealing with man and his environment so that, when learning a new language, one must also learn, in that language, what to say and what not to say (Becker 1992). The different descriptions indicate that the Indonesian of the jurists in question, seen through the eyes of today's, had not yet reached that later stage.

[169] For example, when Han as a lecturer in criminal law was charged in 1957 with creating a syllabus and exam papers, he dropped the Dutch book by D. Simons (which he considered outdated), and once again prescribed other Dutch textbooks, by D. Hazewinkel-Suringa and W.F.C. van Hattum (interview dated 28-11-1996). As late as the 1970s, some study guides still contain titles (recommended or mandatory, even) that also occur in the 1936 *Jaarboekje Rechtshoogeschool*, for example. By and large the law faculties' curriculum would remain unchanged from that of the Rechtshoogeschool until the beginning of the 1980s (Mardjono Reksodiputro 1989:540-1).

[170] This phrase is derived from a 1957 decision by the Jakarta *pengadilan negeri*, discussed in Pompe 1994:9-10. The full passage quoted by Pompe (1994:10) reads: '[H]ukum adat didalam gugat ini adalah sangat gezocht', or: '[I]n this claim, [the application of] adat law is very contrived'. Pompe (1994:10) claims that the legal world in Indonesia in de period 1949-59 is characterized by the frequent use of Dutch words.

There are several major differences between just any student of, say, English as a foreign language and a 1950s Indonesian jurist wanting to speak and write good Indonesian. First, the student of English is likely to kick off with a grammar and a dictionary, as is the custom when learning a foreign language. Indonesian law students and jurists, however, probably made much less use of such texts. Supposedly, they viewed standard Indonesian only partly as foreign – after all, the great majority already knew some form of Malay. Moreover, anyone employed is likely to have had to rely on picking up Indonesian on the job rather than learning the language with the aid of traditional teaching materials. Contrary to subsequent generations, that progressed through primary and secondary education using grammar books such as Takdir Alisjahbana's, the jurists and law students of the early 1950s had to make do without the unifying influence of such works.[171] This is not to infer that they were not at all familiar with Alisjahbana's book or that they did not apply other criteria for 'good Indonesian'; compared to the position of the student of English, however, they probably naturally used a wider range of variation and instinctively interwove the new language with more familiar ones like Dutch.[172]

The second difference is that whereas a learner of English can draw on many speakers of what is generally considered to be good, standard English (the well-known examples being BBC newscasters; those who speak Oxford or the Queen's English), the Indonesian students reading law and the jurists of that day had hardly any examples of lecturers or colleagues with a good professional reputation who *additionally* spoke and wrote standard Indonesian. The speaking and writing of respected advocates and judges

171 Alisjahbana's grammar (*Tatabahasa baru bahasa Indonesia*) was first published in 1949 (Jakarta: Pustaka Rakjat) and saw its 29th (much edited) edition in 1975. The defeat of 'language conservatism' at the 1954 Kongres Bahasa Indonesia should also be mentioned here. This school of teachers and writers of textbooks, mostly from Sumatra, of old had shaped the Malay of Balai Poestaka to an important extent (and inherently also the development of the 'general standard of Indonesian'). They advocated rooting the development of Indonesian language usage and grammar in the tradition of the Sumatran varieties of Malay. At the conference, those in favour of the liberalization of language and grammar won the day, however (Khaidir Anwar 1985:108-20).

172 See pp. 205-6. Yardsticks for 'good Indonesian' could be the language used in a newspaper or journal or by a particular author (interviews with Han Bing Siong on 28-11-1996, Mardjono Reksodiputro on 14-4-1994 and Liem Goan Hwie/Robby Liem on 19-2-1994). 'Good Indonesian' seems to cover both the usage of the language in compliance with a certain general, official standard and usage experienced as unambiguous. Han Bing Siong mentions the newspaper *Pedoman* as an example of a publication with a reputation, in those days, for using 'good Indonesian'. Just how personal this perception was, is apparent from Han's scathing criticism of his own Indonesian ('poor Indonesian', 'translated Dutch' and 'barely intelligible without also knowing Dutch') (interview dated 28-11-1996), whereas another jurist, a student in the 1950s, rates Han's language usage, together with that of another Yogya criminal law professor, as shining examples of 'good Indonesian' (interview with Liem Goan Hwie/Robby Liem dated 19-2-1994).

(as well as professors) will nevertheless have been emulated by more junior colleagues (and students), even if the example did not qualify as standard or 'good' Indonesian.

Thirdly, people learning English have the option of immersing themselves for six months or longer in an English-speaking environment, like the United Kingdom or the United States, to improve fluency, understand conventions and rid themselves of the constraints of their own native language. To learn Indonesian, however, Indonesian jurists could not and did not want to rid themselves of their 'own language' – Dutch – as the knowledge and texts in their heads happened to be in Dutch and continued to be crucial to practising and teaching law. As regards the former, the specific, lingual behaviours of jurists played a role, too. Many of the Indonesian jurists who held leading positions at the Ministry of Justice and in the judiciary and the advocature from the start of the 1950s onwards, were jurists to the core. On arriving at work, they would switch automatically to the internal legal attitude, beaming, in a sense, to a reality separate from that of non-jurists. Maintaining an iron grip on the professional activities of the jurist, this attitude, together with the corresponding cognitive style, thus represented the primary drive mechanism for the production of legal texts (see Chapter II and Tamanaha 1993:151).

At issue here was practical knowledge that was necessary for practising law but could not easily be put into words (see Chapter II). Grammar books and lexicons belonged to another world, the domain of the outsiders, at best being useful on the odd occasion, or in retrospect (to refine texts). The initiated already had an entire repertoire of authoritative texts and lingual forms at their disposal, which they applied to internal communication and to the legal texts they produced for each other and for the outside world. Modifications in accordance with a general linguistic standard would hardly be welcomed by this closed discourse community – the powerful inclination to create routines, as well as the strong attachment to fixed forms, on the one hand led to a harking back to existing languages and genres, in Indonesian (Malay) or Dutch,[173] and on the other to a clutching onto new forms, whether or not in standard Indonesian, no sooner had these found acceptance. In the latter case, 'translated Dutch', rather than pointing at the perpetual proximity of Dutch, indicates fossilized forms in which Dutch formulations and expressions can still be perceived.

173 It is interesting to note that as early as Undang-undang no. 1/1945, the common Dutch trio of expressions 'overwegende (considering) [...]; gelet op (in view of) [...]; heeft besloten: vast te stellen (has decided: to be determined) [...]' (in translation: 'menimbang: [...]; mengingat: [...]; memutuskan: menetapkan [...]') is present, which formulation did not occur in the legislation of the Japanese period (Koesnodiprodjo 1951:21; compare Pompe 1994:20).

Finally, the pressure on the law and the legal system that increased as the 1950s progressed possibly exerted a conservative influence on the language usage in legal circles. Language is not a tool that you can pick up and put down, it is part and parcel of a person's most personal possessions and represents particular values and social attitudes. When put under pressure from the outside, such a personal attribute probably becomes cherished, a token of steadfastness and of closing ranks.

The factors discussed serve to explain why, in the 1950s, the influence of Dutch and Dutch texts on texts in the 'new language' of Indonesian, was relatively strong and why the effect of Dutch on legal language usage has remained considerable ever since. It is also feasible that the continuing import of Dutch in the sphere of law studies in particular (where the propensity to create routines was less entrenched than in environments where law was practised) delayed the natural trend towards the standardization of Indonesian, compared to other sectors of society – if the 'own', familiar language and texts in that language retain their importance, speaking and writing the new language will forever have a voluntary feel.[174] Using the new language is reminiscent of producing translations – it is random, in a way, and volatile; it can be replaced by a new translation as long as the 'source', as it were, remains available.

It should be pointed out that the Dutch language and texts were not omnipresent. Before long, numerous new laws and regulations in legal areas such as constitutional and administrative law were introduced to replace their Dutch predecessors, whether in full or in part.[175] Here, a new academic discourse could develop on the basis of Indonesian texts containing new, Indonesian terms and definitions. Dutch did not disappear overnight from these subcategories of the law, either – here, too, lecturers whose upbringing had been in Dutch; here, too, literature that was largely Dutch – yet the frame

174 Nor did a jurist's low opinion of his own Indonesian need to present an obstacle to frequent publishing – see the condemnation by Han Bing Siong (who published prolifically) of his language usage (footnote 172). This may be ascribed to everyone being in the same boat, but because the legal meaning system remained principally Dutch, presumably the predicament lasted longer here than in other sectors. Compared to those other sectors, in law one's proficiency in Indonesian did not matter much, especially when addressing one's immediate colleagues. The relative informality also is borne out by a comment made by Purwoto Gandasubrata during a conversation: 'At first, it was just as well that the legal language had not yet been standardized because it meant that making a lot of mistakes did not matter, really. You simply put the Dutch term in brackets after the Indonesian one.' (Interview dated 11-9-1996 and interview with S. Gautama on 8-3-1994.)

175 Examples are the new legislation in the fields of health and safety at work (Undang-undang Kerja (Labour Law) dated 20-4-1948 no. 12 in conjunction with UU no. 1/1951), the Mahkamah Agung (UU no. 1/1950), economic crimes (UU no. 7/Drt/1955) and the resolution of labour disputes (UU no. 22/1957).

of reference ceased to be wholly Dutch. Some of the new concepts no longer bore straightforward translation back into Dutch.[176] In the plethora of situations in the practice and the teaching of law in which Indonesian became the everyday language of communication spoken by jurists or students amongst themselves and with one another, Indonesian terms, expressions and formulae came into use. In the course of time, they developed their own 'meaning genealogy' in the Indonesian tongue and their own nuances, now no longer rooted in Dutch words and texts.

New centripetal forces gradually gained a foothold in the legal language usage and a multitude of fixed forms in Indonesian ensued – at law faculties, in courts, prosecution offices, law firms, government departments and other institutions where jurists and jurists-to-be had the whip hand.[177] At law courses, the language used by professors for lectures, dictations or books had a strong impact on that spoken or written by the students, on study-related subjects at least. The Indonesian jargon deployed by the professors usually was chosen carefully so that the students learnt their trade on the basis of those terms and, depending on the lecturers' input and the students' zeal and knowledge of Dutch, also the corresponding Dutch ones. The Indonesian terms were not supplied as single units, though – they came integral to lectures and books, shrouded in formulae and expressions that might or might not be characteristic of a particular lecturer, defined and correlated with other terms. As the 'dictation culture' gained momentum, so the professor's application of exactly the right terms and definitions increased in importance. Thus, several schools could spring up in a single area of law – the students of Satochid Kartanegara's (criminal law, UI), for example, used different terms and expressions pertaining to criminal law than Moeljatno's (criminal law, Gama). With Satochid, Moeljatno and others, such as Djokosoetono, teaching at several higher education institutions and with the sphere of influence of the UI and the Gama extending beyond Jakarta and Yogyakarta, respectively, the language they plied could ripple on in ever

176 For example, Kuntjoro Purbopranoto (1954:102-3) points out that terms such as 'daerah istimewa' (special territory) and 'desa' (desa, village) contained in the Indonesian general law pertaining to regional governance (UU no. 22/1948) cannot simply be translated back into the terminology of the former Decentralisatie-Besluit (Decentralisation Decree) (*Stb.* 1905, no. 137), the Bestuurshervormingswet (Reform of Government Act) (*Stb.* 1922, no. 216 in conjunction with no. 179) or the Inlandsche Gemeente-ordonnantie (Native Council ordinance) (*Stb.* 1906, no. 83).

177 Kuntjoro Purbopranoto (1954:106-7) exemplifies the heterogeneity of the Indonesian terminology in official documents. Purwoto Gandasubrata, who set out on a career in the judiciary in 1956, recollects that the Indonesian in which the registrars phrased the records of the court proceedings diverged widely to begin with but displayed a tendency towards greater uniformity as time went by (interview dated 11-9-1996).

increasing circles.[178] Popular publications such as Wirjono Prodjodikoro's series (see footnote 160) and the model books by Gouw Giok Siong/Sudargo Gautama also grew into major centripetal forces at law courses and wherever law was practised.[179]

A student's adoption of his mentor's terms and expressions meant one thing if that student also knew Dutch, and quite another if he did not. The former might acquire the term 'perikatan', for example, knowing this term to translate as 'verbintenis' (obligation, contract), whereby 'verbintenis' is defined in certain articles of the Burgerlijk Wetboek and discussed in various literature. The latter student, however, would acquire 'perikatan' as a standalone term (perhaps at the start of the treatise or the book accompanied by some other translations of which the professor disapproved and possibly also by the Dutch term that failed to sink in). The student would know that a certain book or particular chapter of the translation of the BW he used, had something to say about this 'perikatan' (provided, of course, that the translation actually used that term instead of an alternative). Therefore, which articles of law and literature the student would associate with 'perikatan' depended on the Indonesian terms (translations) he happened to know. The same was true of all terms in the legal lexical set of which 'verbintenis' is but one. By comparison with the former, Dutch-speaking student, he had a limited awareness of the contract law meaning system, and only a partial understanding of legal concepts and their interconnectedness.[180] The abundance of synonyms in circulation obscured areas of law such as civil law, which still had a Dutch taxonomy. To some extent, this holds true to date. The state of affairs in the early 1990s, as sketched by a Gama professor, can only have been accumulating since the 1950s.

> As an example, the professor provides the concept of 'overeenkomst' (agreement), nowadays commonly translated as 'perjanjian'. Should he ask his students what

[178] Moeljatno taught at the Gama, the UNAIR and the Universitas Islam Indonesia; Satochid and Djokosoetono not only lectured at the UI but also at the Perguruan Tinggi Hukum Militer (Army Law College, originally called Akademi Hukum Militer) and the Perguruan Tinggi Ilmu Kepolisian (Police Training College) (interviews with Mardjono Reksodiputro on 2-3-1994 and 14-4-1994; also see Resink 1974:441). In addition, the older universities exerted a certain influence on universities elsewhere (see footnote 124 and the interview with Mardjono Reksodiputro dated 14-4-1994).

[179] Compare with the interviews with Mardjono Reksodiputro on 2-3-1994 and 14-4-1994. In 1956-57 Gouw Giok Siong brought out three model collections entitled *Tjontoh-tjontoh kontrak-kontrak, rekes-rekes dan surat-surat resmi sehari-sehari* (Jakarta: Keng Po).

[180] Criticism of particular legal terms in Indonesian (translations), too, can either derive from the critic's knowledge of the Dutch term followed by his disapproval of the translation, or from his lecturers having advocated a different Indonesian term (this option does not preclude the critic's knowledge of the Dutch term). See Busthanul Arifin 1976:83-4.

> a 'perjanjian' is, he will be told a definition [based on lectures and literature]. But should he ask next how the concept of 'perjanjian' is defined in the BW, they will be unable to answer because the most popular translation of the BW – that by Subekti and Tjitrosudibio – has 'persetujuan' for 'overeenkomst', not 'perjanjian'.[181]

Some jurists also became aware of the different frames of reference, the different 'meaning genealogies' – the short one being Indonesian and the long one being largely Dutch – from another angle. Legal scholars, especially those working on areas of law in which Dutch legislation was still in force and corresponding Indonesian terms often were translations, sometimes were called upon to indicate expressly that an Indonesian term was *not* a translation but a *new* concept, with a new meaning. Thus, Moeljatno emphatically refuted as a translation of the Dutch 'strafbaar feit' one of the key terms of his criminal law theory, the 'perbuatan pidana' (literally 'criminal act/deed'). In contrast with the terms 'peristiwa pidana' and 'tindak pidana' used for 'strafbaar feit' elsewhere, 'perbuatan pidana' is a new Indonesian concept somewhat similar to the Anglo-Saxon 'criminal act'.[182] This tied in with his previously mentioned initiative to underpin criminal law with fixed legislation in the *Indonesian* language. However, in the literature and in daily practice, this crucial difference between translation and new concept was and is often overlooked, so that 'perbuatan pidana' has become tarred with the same brush as the other two terms mentioned and is more or less dealt with as if it were a translation of 'strafbaar feit'.[183] This not only clouds the criminal law discourse, it also uproots the term 'perbuatan pidana' from its foundation in

[181] Interview with Sudikno Mertokusumo on 5-5-1994. The term 'perjanjian' is only used from the 25th edition of Subekti's translation onwards (see footnote 215) (*Kitab Undang-undang Hukum Perdata* 1992:xi).

[182] Moeljatno 1980:37-9; compare Moeljatno 1954:5-6. According to Han Bing Siong (2004:587), Moeljatno's line of reasoning, too, had been influenced by his teachers and by W.F.C. van Hattum in particular.

[183] Kuntjoro Purbopranoto objected to Moeljatno's 'translation' on the basis that it did not always make clear how Dutch terms were translated. For instance, Moeljatno translated the phrase 'Geen feit is strafbaar [...]' (No fact is punishable [...]) contained in art. 1 of the Wetboek van Strafrecht with 'Tidak seorang boleh dipidana [...]'. Translated back into Dutch, Moeljatno's phrase literally means something like 'No-one may be punished [...]' (Kuntjoro Purbopranoto 1954:101). In the end, in the translation of the Wetboek van Strafrecht published by the BPHN (*Kitab Undang-undang Hukum Pidana* 1983), the term 'perbuatan pidana' eventually was replaced with 'tindak pidana' (vertaling), which was more politically correct (interview with Lamya Moeljatno dated 13-2-1994). At a later date, the same term (supposedly coined by the UI professor Satochid Kartanegara) was chosen for use in the draft act of the new Criminal Code, because it happened to be more widely known (interview with Mardjono Reksodiputro dated 2-3-1994). Despite the above, it ought to be borne in mind that this 'perbuatan pidana' continued to form part of the old system of concepts in respect of the Wetboek van Strafrecht/Kitab Undang-undang Hukum Pidana.

the Indonesian language. Indonesian terms originating with new, Indonesian legislation are less at risk in this respect because their legal-textual foundation is set in stone. Taking into account that Dutch legislation continued to be a source of inspiration even after the transfer of sovereignty and that the frame of reference of the legal top dogs was mostly in Dutch, however, the chance of original Indonesian being translated 'back' into Dutch (by misconception) could not altogether be ruled out.

As noted before, the topic of language was not paid much explicit attention to in the 1950s, neither by practising nor by teaching jurists. Although many Indonesian introductions to law dealt (and deal) with the terminology of the area of law that is its subject, with any Dutch terms and their preferred Indonesian equivalents, the Indonesian legal language and the role played by Dutch in the law are hardly touched upon.[184] Notable exceptions are the preliminary advice on the Indonesian language in legislation and government, written by A.G. Pringgodigdo (professor at Yogyakarta and Surabaya) and Kuntjoro Purbopranoto for the 1954 Kongres Bahasa Indonesia held at Medan.[185] Pringgodigdo's piece provides an extensive chronology of the use of Dutch and Indonesian in a juridical context in the Netherlands East Indies and Indonesia.

In the context of this work, Kuntjoro's advice is more interesting as he explored several problems the Indonesian legal language faced and expounded on how these ought to be resolved, in his view. His approach is highly precursory to that adopted two decades later at the Simposium Bahasa dan Hukum, also taking place in Medan.[186] Staying with the theme of the conference, the Indonesian language, the main problem of the law in day-to-day practice – the gradual disappearance of proficiency in Dutch among

184 In his introduction, Kusumadi Pudjosewojo (1959:36-7) briefly discusses legal language (*bahasa hukum*). Kusumadi draws attention to the discrepancy between the language of court decisions and legislation and that of daily usage. He also points out that the Indonesian legislation or legal language is still in a development stage and trying to discover a style of its own ('mentjari gajanja sendiri'). He proceeds to comment on the as yet unfixed terminology, the lion's share of which consists of translations of Dutch legal terms, and on the obvious influence of Dutch that is evident from the sentence structures. The Indonesian legal language thus still reflects the conceptual realm of Dutch law rather than its own, according to Kusumadi. The articles by Soetan Mohamad Sjah have already been mentioned (Chapter I).

185 The programme and preliminary recommendations for and the conclusions drawn by this conference were published in *Medan Bahasa* 4 (1954), nos. 7-8. The two advisory documents put forward by Pringgodigdo and Kuntjoro Purbopranoto are both entitled 'Bahasa Indonesia didalam (resp. dalam) perundang-undangan dan administrasi' (Kuntjoro Purbopranoto 1954 and Pringgodigdo 1954).

186 See Chapter I. Some of the phrasing was repeated at the later conference, amongst which the notion that jurists ought to use 'normal Indonesian' and that the legal language *is part and parcel* of the common language (Kuntjoro Purbopranoto 1954:96, 110; compare Chapter I).

law students and jurists – is sidestepped, to focus on the development of an Indonesian legal language and particularly on that of an Indonesian legal terminology. Kuntjoro draws extensively on work by adat law specialists like Van Vollenhoven and Ter Haar, which is logical given his broad interpretation of the concepts of 'law' and 'legal language' – to him, 'Indonesian law' envisages a law system that ties in with the rich and pluriform Indonesian tradition of law; 'legal language' spans not only all written juridical language but also that which is unwritten and forms part of the non-codified law (Kuntjoro Purbopranoto 1954:99). The document's leitmotiv, that Kuntjoro derives from a formula by Ter Haar, is the desire for 'purified legal language' ('gezuiverde rechtstaal').[187] The raw materials for such a legal language should first and foremost be delved from the original sources of indigenous Indonesian law and language; new terms based on foreign languages would only be permitted should the excavation prove fruitless. He rejects the method advocated by the Ministry of Education, Teaching and Culture, for one, to arrive at Indonesian terms through translating Dutch ones, via Western thinking, that is, rather than to search directly in the Indonesian language sources. According to Kuntjoro (1954:102), such a tactic bears a risk of introducing elements into the Indonesian law system that are quintessentially alien to it.

> When using Indonesian for legislation purposes, the prime consideration is the selection of sentence structures and terms that agree with, or in any event are not contrary to, Indonesian legal institutions in general. To be able to understand this matter, we must study the sources of our own law and, if need be, cultivate these so as to find terms that are fitting, in the sense of being in keeping with the ideal of justice and the concept of law of the entirety of the Indonesian nation. (Kuntjoro Purbopranoto 1954:103.)

Referring particularly to administrative language, Kuntjoro (1954:105-7) emphasizes the importance of unambiguous contents and of applying a precise form; he points out the heterogeneity of terms and expressions, diverging sentence structures (translated from the Dutch) and unclear language usage.

It is evident from the conclusions of the conference's section on legislation and administrative language that the frequent use of Dutch terms and the multitude of Indonesian synonyms were the main topics of discussion. It was argued that a state committee should be instituted to correct the language used in (draft) legislation, where necessary, and to monitor the application of fixed terminology; that professors and legal practitioners should meet regularly to work towards ensuring the uniformity of legal terminology; and that

[187] Kuntjoro Purbopranoto 1954:99. Ter Haar already had proposed that adat law terms be applied to a 'purified indigenous adat-law language' (Kuntjoro Purbopranoto 1954:98).

the government in its legislation should also aim at uniformity of terminology and spelling.[188] Neither Kuntjoro's advice to nor the conclusions of the conference, however, addressed the question of why Indonesian jurists spoke and wrote as they did (for example, how had the influence of Dutch taken on such proportions?) and of how their language use could be changed (to what extent could the influence of Dutch be stemmed?).

The focal point, which, as stated, anticipates the dominant perspective at the future Simposium Bahasa dan Hukum and behind the various government initiatives, was legal language as a new, detached structure, as a large-scale national project that should first and foremost be authentically Indonesian. The fact that the armature of this structure was foreign in part and that the main contractors had long been used to a construction technique that had originated abroad was ignored, just as the transition from Dutch to Indonesian would also be largely ignored at the 1974 conference. Woven into this approach is the notion that language (abstract, a-historic) can be adapted, kneaded into shape, 'tweaked' as the jurist pleases – the same notion that came to dominate the discourse on legal language at a later date.[189]

### *The demise of a legal community: 1959-1965*

The preceding paragraphs explain in some detail how and why the prewar configuration of the legal community, state legal system and legal meaning system could continue its existence more or less unscathed by the transfer of sovereignty. Also, the processes have been pinpointed that inescapably would come to jeopardize the community and its meaning system as the years went by – in particular the falling standards of legal education and the declining knowledge of the Dutch language among jurists. Political developments in the second half of the 1950s catalysed these processes and dealt the legal community a blow in the very heart of its being – the legal system. Examining the political turmoil of this period in any detail would go far beyond the scope of this study. Suffice it, here, to spotlight two of its aspects that immediately stand out – the abolition of parliamentary democracy and the anti-Dutch policy.

188 Conclusions of Section B, determined on 1-11-1954 by Soehardjo Soerjobroto and Achmad Bastari and included in the *berita-atjara* (record of the proceedings) of 2-11-1954 by the ad hoc Committee of the Kongres Bahasa Indonesia. As regards the establishment of a state committee, the section envisaged broadening the remit of the committee/s that, pursuant to art. 145 of the Provisional Constitution of 1950, was/were charged with ensuring the harmonization with the Constitution of all legislation in force at the time of the Constitution taking effect.

189 Compare Kusumadi Pudjosewojo (1959:37), who concludes his paragraph on legal language by commenting that 'when researching the law in general but Indonesian law in particular, language, too, is an instrument that should not be ignored'.

The transition to the new method of governing that was designated 'demokrasi terpimpin' ('guided democracy') was a gradual one. In the course of the 1950s, dissatisfaction with the parliamentary system increased hand over fist. The successive cabinets, falling one after the other,[190] were divided amongst themselves, rendering them impotent to tackle effectively the nation's gigantic problems such as economic crisis and persistent regional disturbances. Jakarta's political scene was known for its elbow work, its old boy network and its corruption. Government bodies and society at large became politicized and divided (Ricklefs 1988:230-44). Many, the army included, were riled by the rise of the Partai Komunis Indonesia (PKI, Indonesian Communist Party), that grew increasingly influential in both national politics and society as a whole, though particularly so in the country.

These were the circumstances under which Soekarno, whose powers had been curtailed to no small degree since the 1945 proclamation, returned to the helm and from 1957 to 1959 introduced a series of measures that ultimately would lead to the abolition of parliamentary democracy. In the spring of 1957 he announced the changeover to guided democracy, a form of governance that would tally more closely with the features that distinguished Indonesia. Following an uprising against central government in East Indonesia, martial law was declared and a *kabinet karya* (business cabinet) was formed, headed by the independent Djuanda Kartawidjaja. This cabinet was advised by a Dewan Nasional (National Council), the members of which represented 'functional groups' (students, farmers, labourers, women, intelligentsia, religious groups and so forth) rather than political parties.[191]

But the political and economic troubles got the better of the new cabinet and the army, too. An attempt was made on Soekarno's life and a national conference aimed at reunifying Jakarta and the dissident regional army factions proved futile. Meanwhile, both the PKI and the army manoeuvred into positions of greater power and influence (Ricklefs 1988:247-9). Another source of tension became manifest at the end of 1957, when the United Nations voted on a resolution calling upon the Netherlands to resume negotiations over New Guinea. Prior to the vote, steadily increasing pressure had been brought to bear on the UN and the Netherlands to accept the resolution – the Indonesian government had warned repeatedly of far-reaching measures against the Netherlands, anti-Dutch rallies had been held, Dutch households

190 The period of September 1950-March 1957 saw no less than six cabinets. In April 1957 Soekarno appointed the first of his *kabinet karya* (business cabinet) (Ricklefs 1988:225-47). For a complete record of the Indonesian cabinets during the period fom 1945 to 1965, see Finch and Lev 1965.

191 Ricklefs 1988:242-3, 246-7. From October 1959 cabinets were no longer answerable to parliament (Dahm 1969:333).

had been looted and the Dutch generally were becoming increasingly intimidated. When the resolution was rejected, on 29 November 1957, an explosion of anti-Dutch actions ensued. Dutch companies, trading offices and banks, in the eyes of many *the* symbol of the continued colonization of Indonesia, were seized one after the other by trade unionists. Though opposed to this form of action because of its extensive economic consequences, the Indonesian government found itself faced with a fait accompli so that in May 1958, when the Dutch government once again declared itself in favour of retaining New Guinea, it took the step of formally nationalizing nearly all Dutch interests.[192] Publications and education in the Dutch language became prohibited, and Dutch citizens without employ were ordered to leave the country. The events led to a near exodus of all Dutch, however.[193]

More anti-Dutch measures followed. The effects on both the economy and the infrastructure were disastrous. The takeover of the Koninklijke Paketvaart Maatschappij (KPM, Royal Parcel Shipping), for example, resulted in the loss of three quarters of all sailings between islands, causing the price of rice and other goods to double in no time at all (Meijer 1994:587; Ricklefs 1988:249). In addition to having to cope with such new economic setbacks, the government had, by this time, also been confronted with a new political opponent in the shape of the Pemerintah Revolusioner Republik Indonesia (PRRI, Revolutionary Government of the Republic of Indonesia), proclaimed on Sumatra in February 1958 (Ricklefs 1988:250-2). Calls to effect the changeover to a guided democracy, to a president governing with a strong hand, became amplified. Soekarno declared himself in support of the plan put forward by the army General A.H. Nasution, to rescind the 1950 Provisional Constitution and reintroduce the 1945 Constitution. This was not surprising as the latter, rather than being based on notions of a liberal, Western-style democratic state, sanctioned an integralist state philosophy that conferred near-unlimited powers on the president (compare with p. 182). The plan was submitted to the Konstituante (Constituent Assembly), the body that had been engaged in drafting a new, permanent Constitution since 1956, made up of representatives elected from amongst the political parties. The poll in the Assembly failed to endorse the plan by the required majority, however, prompting Soekarno to decree its dissolution on 5 July 1959 and to re-enact the 1945 Constitution. Thus Guided Democracy had come to pass.[194]

192 Ricklefs 1988:249-50; Meijer 1994:575-81. Compare with Wertheim 1956:326-8. The banks were only nationalized in 1959-60 (Meijer 1994:601).

193 Meijer 1994:583, 588, 592, 616; Groeneboer 1993:463. By June 1958, 34,000 people had left; halfway through 1959, a little over 6,000 remained in Indonesia (Meijer 1994:592, 620). For more on the anti-Dutch measures, also see Willems 2001:146-54.

194 Ricklefs 1988:252-4; Dahm 1969:330-3. The Dewan Nasional was also dissolved. In its stead,

One feature of the Guided Democracy era (1959-1965) was an all-pervasive and ever more radical ideologizing of the state machinery and of Indonesian society. The official ideology, known by the double-barrelled acronym 'Manipol-USDEK', emphasized revolutionary spirit, social justice and the 'indonesification' of the administrative system.[195] It emanated from the view that the Indonesian Revolution was incomplete, as a just and affluent society had not yet ensued, federalist forces still jeopardized the unitary state and, to top it all, Indonesia was under threat of political, military, economic and financial opportunism from domestic and foreign factions. In the days of parliamentary democracy (borrowed from the West!), Indonesia had lost sight of the spirit of the first Constitution, Soekarno claimed, and the country had descended into political bickering, armed conflict and corruption.

The resurrection of the 1945 Constitution would instigate a democracy aligned more closely with the Indonesian society than the current model, on a liberal foundation. A guided democracy would protect the weak from the strong, for example, would reach decisions unanimously and through consultation rather than simply going by the majority, and would guarantee the stability of the country's administration for five years, given the limited powers of parliament.[196] Fervent chauvinism, focus on the authentically Indonesian, fierce rejection of Dutch interests and influences in Indonesia (New Guinea, corporate interests) and, more generally, abhorrence of all things Western, were the recurrent themes of the government's ideology and policy from the end of the 1950s (Soetandyo Wignjosoebroto 1994:210).

Self-evidently, the developments described above had an enormous impact on the rule of law in force and on the legal community, whose colonial and Dutch-language roots were cast in a bad light by the new spin. The ban on Dutch literature – books (legal ones, too) were burnt, even – further marginalized the primary literature for most areas of law.[197] The replacement of the

a Dewan Pertimbangan Agung (Supreme Advisory Council) was established, in accordance with article 16 of the 1945 Constitution. A Dewan Perantjang Nasional (National Planning Council) was founded, too (Ricklefs 1988:254). Various documents and speeches dating from the period prior to the decree are included in Muhammad Yamin 1959:487-702.

195 Ricklefs 1988:255. 'Manipol' was short for 'Manifesto Politik' (Political Manifesto), the designation of the speech Soekarno held on 17-8-1959, in which he had clarified the ideology of guided democracy. The acronym 'USDEK' (Undang-undang Dasar 1945, Sosialisme ala Indonesia, Demokrasi Terpimpin, Ekonomi Terpimpin, Kepribadian Indonesia) was added in 1960 and represented 'Constitution of 1945, Indonesian-style Socialism, Guided Democracy, Guided Economy, Indonesian Authenticity' (Ricklefs 1988:255).

196 Soekarno 1959:665-71. The last clause was based on art. 7 of the 1945 Constitution, granting the President and the Vice President a term of office of five years (and leave to stand for re-election) (Soekarno 1959:669-70).

197 Interviews with Ph.M. Hadjon on 12-9-1996 and Iskandar Oeripkartadinata on 17-4-1994 and information provided by Daniel Lev on 19-5-2002.

Constitution was of more fundamental importance, however. Although in the 1950s the role played by politics and ideology and their inherent languages and standards (power, loyalty, corruption and the like) had gained the better of the legal language and standards (procedures, impartiality) (compare with Lev 1972:257-61, 304-5), the legal professions nevertheless had possessed an ideological basis, in a manner of speaking, in the parliamentary democracy – this being the form of government (after the Dutch model) with which Indonesian jurists had become familiar during their studies and from which model the Indonesian system had borrowed to a substantial degree.[198] The abolition of parliamentary democracy and the re-enactment of the revolutionary Constitution now formally acknowledged the actuality of a politicized and ideologized society.

The languages of the revolutionary leader and those of the jurist contradicted each other in every respect. The leader, focussed on the future, required ample elbow room to act on whichever situation presented itself, whereas the jurist placed enormous store on consistency and predictability, by acting in keeping with precedent.[199] The jurist's actions were driven by books (sources of law, textbooks, legal theory), while it was incumbent upon the true revolutionary, to quote Soekarno, to *un*learn 'textbook thinking'.[200]

198 Compare with Daniel Lev (1972:305): 'During the early 1950's, the parliamentary system tended to promote symbols favorable to the "rule of law", even as existing legal processes were being strained, because the language of parliamentarism and the language of formal law were closely related"'.

199 Lev 1972:261. Soekarno's political theory was clearly reminiscent of the nineteenth century German movement 'Rechtshistorische Schule', though. Peter Burns (1999:292-308) sets out how Soekarno and other Indonesian jurists were influenced by this movement, with which they became familiar through the Leiden school of adat law.

200 For example, see the speech on the occasion of the plenary session of the Konstituante, held on 22-4-1959, entitled 'Res Publica, sekali lagi Res Publica!' (Soekarno 1959), in particular pp. 697-8, 700. The following passage especially expresses most eloquently the 'atextual' aspect of the revolution: 'Ja, kataku: – tinggalkan "textbook-thinking". Revolusi tidak mengenal "text", dan memang tidak ada satu revolusipun jang menurut "text". ... Semua bangsa jang baru sadja mengindjak alam kemerdekaan, semua bangsa jang berada dalam pintu gerbang pembangunan dan konsolidasi-nasional besar-besaran, harus memetjahkan beberapa persoalan pelik, jang harus dipetjahkan menurut tuntutan keadaan-keadaannja *sendiri*. Kemerdekaan bangsa-bangsa di Asia dan Afrika membawa norma-norma baru didunia sekarang ini, baik dilapangan ekonomi atau sosial, maupun dilapangan politik. Mau tidak mau, senang atau tidak senang, norma-norma baru itu harus diterima oleh banga-bangsa lain sebagai suatu realitet. "Menurut text" atau "tidak menurut text", – itu bukan persoalan jang kita hadapi. Persoalan kita ialah "baik atau tidak buat revolusi kita", – "baik atau tidak buat rakjat Indonesia". Sesuai atau tidak dengan kepribadian kita, sesuai atau tidak dengan amanat penderitaan kita. Marilah kita dalam memikirkan dan memadjukan norma-norma baru itu tidak selaku mendjiplak dan membuntut sadja. Marilah kita mentjari dan menemukan kepribadian kita sendiri!' ('Yes, I say: Let go of that "textbook-thinking". There isn't any "textbook" for a revolution, and there isn't any revolution that goes according to the textbook. . ... Every nation that enters the world of freedom for the first time,

Jurists thus became branded the epitome of conservative, reactionary even, an impossible group to involve in a revolution (Lev 1965b:191, 1972:260-1; Soetandyo Wignjosoebroto 1994:215-9). The 'basic story' of the rule of law (*negara hukum*), the 'framework story' that enveloped the professional thinking of jurists, turned the law in force and the specialists that operated it into obstacles to Soekarno's revolutionary policy. Nevertheless, even revolutionary policy cannot be moulded in any legitimate manner without law, without legal institutions and without their constituent languages and genres. The law and jurists therefore had to be converted into entities that could contribute to rather than impede the new order.

Thus, the development of a new, national system of law, to be rooted in authentic, Indonesian traditions and principles, became a key policy issue. The law in force was spurned as typically the product of the former foreign oppressor, sodden with Western (liberal, individual) ideas and values.[201] In 1960 the Madjelis Permusjawaratan Rakjat Sementara (MPRS, the Provisional People's Congress) determined that the new Indonesian legal system should reflect Indonesian reality and be partly based on adat law, in the colonial era already the designated term for the original Indonesian legal tradition.[202] According to the Lembaga Pembinaan Hukum Nasional (LPHN, National Law Development Institute), established in 1958, the national law ought to contain an element of 'help thy neighbour' (*kegotongroyongan*), to serve to protect the community and to oppose colonialism, imperialism and feudalism.[203] New legislation in connection with land, Undang-undang Pokok Agraria (UUPA, Basic Agrarian Act), was issued in 1960, making obsolete a large part of Book II of the Burgerlijk Wetboek. The new act put paid to the racial division that had been characteristic of agrarian law up until that time (rights in accordance with the BW for Europeans and with adat law for Indonesians) and its elucidation states that it is based on adat law.[204]

every people that takes the first step towards a large development and wants to establish itself as a nation, is confronted with many complex problemens that can only be resolved by focusing on what is needed in the specific situation. The independence of nations in Asia and Africa brings with it new norms, not only politically, but also economically and socially. Whether others want this or not, whether others like this or not, the new norms will have to be accepted as reality by other nations. "Following the textbook" or "not following the textbook" – this is not important. What is important for us is: "Is it good for our revolution or not?" "Is it good for the Indonesian people or not?" Is it in harmony with our identity, with the mandate of our suffering? In setting the new norms and trying to achieve them, let us not behave like imitators or followers. Let us seek our own identity and find it!" (Soekarno 1959:700.)

201 Jaspan 1965:255-6; Soetandyo Wignjosoebroto 1994:210-2, 218; Lev 1972:260-1; Pompe 1996:38.

202 Soetandyo Wignjosoebroto 1994:211; Pompe 1994:13; compare with Chapter III.

203 Soetandyo Wignjosoebroto 1994:215-6. For more on the LPHN, see Lev 1965b:292.

204 Soetandyo Wignjosoebroto 1994:212-5; Lev 1965b:290. For more on adat law as the source

New symbols were introduced. In 1960 the blindfolded Lady Justice, the symbol of impartiality and objective consideration, was replaced with the waringin or banyan tree, the tree with the splayed canopy, underneath which justice was done in days of yore, a symbol known to all Indonesians. An inscription below the tree reads 'pengayoman', a word of Javanese origin denoting something in the vein of 'protection, shelter'. The symbol fitted in with traditional Javanese values and attitudes towards the law, according to which the ruler of a community in father-fashion shelters his subjects from injustice (Lev 1965b:282, 1972:299-300). A second measure aimed at indonesifying the law and its practitioners was taken in 1962; it consisted of disallowing law graduates from Indonesian universities the use of the title of 'meester in de rechten' (Mr.). Instead, they had to call themselves 'sarjana hukum' (S.H.).[205] At a later date, the black judge's robe was abolished in favour of the revolutionary camouflage uniform, worn by all government officers of the day (Pompe 1996:42-3).

Once again, the professional integrity of jurists was tested. But this time round, their position was more precarious than in colonial times – now, their adversaries included the leadership of central government and its ideology (compare with Chapter III). In so far as the authoritative and internally persuasive texts of their law studies had held their own, they now came under greater pressure than ever from the changing social climate with its incessant influx of new authoritative texts coloured by different words and values. Prominent jurists like Sahardjo, Astrawinata (the successive ministers of Justice) and Wirjono Prodjodikoro (president of the Mahkamah Agung and included as a cabinet minister in that capacity by Soekarno) increasingly assumed the language of the Guided Democracy. Soekarno's comment about the unsuitability of jurists for revolutionary purposes, at a 1961 conference of jurists, met with Wirjono's riposte that this would only hold water if there was no such thing as 'revolutionary law'.

In subsequent debates and publications attempts were made to reinterpret certain principles of law and items of legislation so as to ally them with the

---

of the new property law, see Soetandyo Wignjosoebroto 1994:212-5, Lev 1965b:290 and Burns 1999:306-7.

205 Pursuant to Keppres no. 265/1962 dated 20-8-1962. The application of the Dutch title was considered out of keeping with the basic principles of the Indonesian state. The ban was aimed specifically at those graduating from the Universitas Indonesia, whose conferment of the title of 'meester' derived its legitimacy from the 1946 Hoger Onderwijs-ordonnantie. In practice, though, the title was also used by graduates from other universities (information provided by Han Bing Siong on 19-6-2003). Graduates who had read law at a Dutch university were advised to use 'S.H.' in lieu of 'meester'. Eventually, the use of the title 'sarjana hukum' by graduates from all Indonesian law faculties would be laid down in the new higher education legislation. At a later date, some jurists resumed their title of 'meester'.

Guided Democracy ideology and the Manipol-USDEK. For example, at gatherings held in 1962 and 1963, the then Minister of Justice Sahardjo suggested that the Burgerlijk Wetboek and the Wetboek van Koophandel were not to be equated with legislation issued by the Republik Indonesia. These codes, promulgated for the benefit of Europeans and, to an extent, Chinese and other 'foreign orientals', were the product of a system of legal pluralism contrary to the Indonesian Constitution. Therefore, the BW and WvK would have to be viewed, henceforth, as still being in force, though downgraded from act to unwritten law (Han Bing Siong 2002:321-3). Sahardjo's theory was picked up on in Surat Edaran Mahkamah Agung (SEMA, Supreme Court Circular Letter) no. 3/1963, of September 1963, that declared the court in support of the view that the Burgerlijk Wetboek, designed to serve the interests of the former colonizers, merely laid down unwritten law. From then on, the authorities in general and judges in particular would be given more leeway to disregard articles they considered no longer in keeping with the current state of affairs. Finally, the Mahkamah Agung invalidated eight articles it found to be contrary to the Constitution.[206]

To the close of the Guided Democracy epoch, judges at courts of the first instance would treat the code as a 'rechtsboek' (book of law).[207] Even jurisprudential debate became tainted by political and ideological standards and values. For example, it was pointed out that a certain article that had criticized particular court decisions and items of legislation ran the risk of besmirching the good name of the government and its apparatus, and contempt was expressed for those who based their opinions on *Dutch* or *Leiden* jurists, as the case might be.[208]

Gradually, the pressure on the judiciary to toe the line was increased. Principles like the independence of the judiciary were now deemed reactionary and counterrevolutionary. Members of the judiciary were required to be 'hakim revolusi' ('revolutionary judges'), instruments of the Revolution, and thus to cast their decisions in the mould of the highest ideal, that of the

206 SEMA no. 3/1963 is included in *Himpunan Engelbrecht* 1989:597-9.

207 Han Bing Siong 2002:323, compare with Lev 1965b:291-4 and Soetandyo Wignjosoebroto 1994:218-23. Incidentally, the idea of converting the BW into a guideline (*pedoman*) predated 1963 – for example, Kusumadi Pudjosewojo reported the subject having been discussed at an official faculty meeting (presumably of the UI) as early as 1952 (Kusumadi Pudjosewojo 1952:14). Translated into Bakhtin's terminology, what actually took place is that the status of the legal text and its meaning are interpreted in the light of a language, a text, an argument originating outside of the law, yet at the same time not acknowledged by the law. Here, the authoritative text is dialogized and forfeits its authoritative status; the rule of law and its languages and argumentation are marginalized and rendered ineffective.

208 Moeljatno 1960:12, 26, quoted in Han Bing Siong 1961b:108-9 and information provided by Han Bing Siong on 22-10-2002. Compare with Han Bing Siong 1998:447.

Revolution. They were supposed to try favourably those committed to the Revolution, deal harshly with its enemies and interpret the law creatively (Lev 1965b:298; Pompe 1996:42-3; Soetandyo Wignjosoebroto 1994:223). The final act in these developments brought new legislation, promulgated in 1964 and 1965, concerning the Mahkamah Agung and the judiciary – the curtain fell on the separation of powers (Trias Politica) and judges were directed to effect the truth, as embodied in the Pancasila and Manipol-USDEK, in their decisions. Also, presidential intervention in the course of justice was authorized, for example when the Revolution demanded it or for important reasons in the public interest.[209]

The legal community could not but be affected by the deteriorating climate and the upsurge in political and ideological rhetoric. In fact, whereas a combination of circumstances had enabled them more or less to resist adversity in the past, things had now changed dramatically. To list the most invasive development first, the very foundation of the law, the very acknowledgement of the 'facticity' of the legal institutional order (see Chapter II), was called into question – directly, through the orations on the importance of 'revolutionary law', and indirectly, through sidelining the courts and negating the generally accepted notions of their role and place in society.[210]

Secondly, that which for most of the established legal order was the main professional language, namely Dutch, together with the primary legal texts in that language, was relegated to the shadows and declared politically suspect. Intense pressure was applied to adopt the political language of the Guided Democracy and to live by different professional values than those instilled at university and on the job; as mentioned earlier, prominent personages at important legal institutions like the Mahkamah Agung and the prosecution service 'betrayed the side'. Major legal professional bodies, such as the association of judges, gave the symbol of the waringin their seal of approval and incorporated it into their emblems.[211] Corruption gradually spread through-

[209] Pompe 1996:38, 43; Han Bing Siong 1998:425. According to art. 19 of UU no. 19/1964 concerning the judiciary, the President could intervene in judicial matters for the benefit of the Revolution, the virtue of the State and the Nation, and any interests of society of the utmost importance. For more on the procedure in such an instance, see art. 23 of UU no. 13/1965 concerning the Mahkamah Agung.

[210] Compare with Pompe (1996:36): 'The salary debate and subsequent direct power contests really were just the prelude of a process in which generally accepted values and ideas on the place and role of courts were questioned, consciously ignored and deliberately violated with ever greater frequency and insistence. It pushed the boundaries of the debate outwards as the judges were compelled to explain, justify and defend what hitherto were essentially truisms, in no need of justification.' Cast into the terminology of Chapter II: outsiders pulled up a seat at the legal game board and took part in the game at will, while even the official players no longer always abided by the rules.

[211] Lev 1976:168-9. By exception, according to Lev (1976:168-9), advocates retained the symbol

out legal practice, at first tainting only the prosecution service, then, from the end of the 1950s, also the courts, which phenomenon was to become rampant as time went on (Pompe 1996:344-5; Lev 1972:268, 1965a:196-7). Professionally speaking, advocates fell on even harder times than before and they, too, succumbed to temptation (Lev 1976:168, 1972:259-60).

Thirdly, the 'dome of authoritative texts' in whose safety the legal elite had long basked, suffered structural damage. The new agrarian legislation, for example, engendered much uncertainty about land rights that were not converted into rights consistent with that act before 1970. The demotion of the BW from formal source of law to directive, by the president of the Mahkamah Agung, induced uncertainty about the actual status of the code (was he authorized to take such a measure?) and also about its successor, if any (exactly how was the BW to be interpreted in a 'creative' and politically correct manner?).[212]

Fourthly, the cream of the 'old guard', the jurists that had held the key positions at the Ministry of Justice, in legal practice and in law teaching up until that time, had to one by one step down to make way for younger jurists, whose training in the law had been of a different nature and whose work experience was more limited than their own. And some of these 'youngsters' were much more eager to dance to the new political tune (see Soetandyo Wignjosoebroto 1994:218).

Simultaneous to the above, the quality of the country's law courses continued to decline, to the detriment of the legal professions. Even though Dutch books were still essential to acquiring a thorough understanding of most areas of law, even though books in Indonesian were few and far between, the anti-Dutch policy accelerated the process of de-dutchifying law teaching in favour of its Indonesianization. Whereas knowledge of Dutch had been seen as desirable for a course in law, if only tacitly so, several professors now dismissed it as wholly unnecessary.[213] Though lacking any formal-legal

---

of the scales of justice, though interestingly, the organization of public prosecutors adopted an emblem sporting a pair of scales (Surat Keputusan Menteri Djaksa Agung dated 2-1-1961, published in *Suara Persadja* 1, 1961:23-4; this decision was drawn to my attention by Han Bing Siong on 22-10-2002).

212 Soetandyo Wignjosoebroto 1994:223; Pompe 1994:11-5; Lev 1965b:294. Pompe (1994:12-3) classes the period in Indonesian law from 1959 to 1966 as an era of severance and chaos – the legislator intended to sever the tie with colonial law but ended up in a halfway house instead. Here, the old colonial provisions and those laid down in the new Indonesian legislation alloyed to produce chaos.

213 In 1963 Moeljatno, the Gama professor whose name has been mentioned, repeatedly refuted that studying law was impossible without knowing Dutch. He claimed that not only was this fallacious – were there not plenty of examples of jurists who had no command of Dutch but acquitted themselves of their tasks more than satisfactorily? – it was also dangerous in that lecturers of that opinion might be tempted in their work to draw on nothing but familiar literature,

status,[214] new Indonesian translations of legislation, produced by lecturers and professors, soared in popularity.[215] Anyone wishing to study the authentic texts now had a job finding an Engelbrecht or other Dutch legislation reader.[216] Meanwhile, the education system continued to expand. The seven state universities in 1957 were joined by double that number between 1960 and 1965 – even though the existing ones were already struggling with insufficient staff and resources (compare with footnote 158). With law being one of the cheaper disciplines, thus having a fairly low access threshold, the law faculties in addition became swamped by many poorly motivated students who had opted for law for want of a viable alternative (Utrecht 1991:172; interview with F. Limahelu dated 19-2-1994). Finally, the steady marginalization of the courts within the state system also affected the students. Intent on a good income and on clout, students increasingly pursued a career in the prosecution service rather than with the judiciary (Lev 1972:267-8).

The factors mentioned combined to produce a rapid decrease in judicial competence from the end of the 1950s (Pompe 1996:338-9). Other bench marks, too, were lost. For example, judicial decisions had traditionally been annotated by judges more senior in age or rank and a 'conduite' (record of conduct), assessing the judge's work on quality and quantity, had been kept. In the course of the 1960s, however, this tradition came to an end (Pompe 1996:220-2). The advocature was tried more severely under Guided Democracy than at any other time since the Japanese had left. Their services

in the Dutch language, that is. They would therefore be unlikely to come up with innovative ideas, derived from other foreign literature, as their contribution to national law development (Moeljatno 1981:26-7). Pompe (1996:342) has 1959 as the year of the abolition of Dutch as a mandatory subject.

214 On the other hand, the status of translations of the BW may have altered in the eyes of the proponents of its dispossession once the code had been demoted to the realm of non-legal, 'unwritten' law (Han Bing Siong 2002:221-3). Koesnoe (1991:127) takes the view that legislation translations are unwritten law taking the form of authoritative books (compare with footnote 71).

215 Interviews with Liem Goan Hwie/Robby Liem on 19-2-1994, Ateng Syafruddin on 1-3-1993 and F. Limahelu on 19-2-1994. The best-known translations of codes produced by jurists and brought onto the market from the end of the 1950s are *Kitab Undang2 Hukum Perdata* 1957 (by Subekti and Tjitrosudibio), *Kitab Undang2 Hukum Pidana* 1959 (by Moeljatno), *K.U.H.D. (Kitab Undang-undang Hukum Dagang) & P.K. (Peraturan Kepailitan)* by Siti Soemarti Hartono (Yogyakarta, 1959) and *Kitab undang-undang perniagaan; Wetboek van koophandel* by Koesnoen (Bandung: Sumur Bandung, [1959]). Also in those days, a common aid for people who had been educated in Dutch was the dictionary published by H. van der Tas, first issued in 1956 and reprinted in 1961 (*Kamus hukum Belanda-Indonesia*, Jakarta: Timun Mas, 1961). During an interview, Resink recalled that professor Subekti's translation of the BW sold over a hundred thousand copies in no time at all – to Subekti's own great surprise! Resink also claimed that the translation of the BW was popular with the Chinese, to whom that code applied (interview dated 24-1-1994).

216 Interview with Ph. Hadjon dated 12-9-1996.

were in minimal demand and few new advocates presented themselves at the bar. Those practising barely survived, managing on a handful of profitable cases, perhaps, or on other sources of income (Lev 1976:166-8). Though their position had deteriorated overall since the Japanese invasion, their presence in court (no longer required by law) was now anathema to judges and prosecutors alike, who regarded it as an unwelcome check on their work – blighted by incompetence or corruption (Lev 1972:269-70).

The years preceding and during Guided Democracy gradually tightened the noose around the established legal community, the bulwark of jurists who had pulled the strings of the state legal system and of law teaching since the colonial days and who had not yet yielded to the new ideology. The traditional way of 'thinking and doing law' had become so isolated from the present-day reality that the internal legal attitude and its intrinsic routines lost ground hand over fist. The dominance of the common frame of reference – words, meanings, values – that had determined the legal community's conduct had to be relinquished. Adjacent to yet also intersecting the old 'basic story' of the law, a new reality had manifested itself, one that opposed that story and refused staunchly to budge or bow down. In the not so distant past, older jurists had been aware that their attitudes towards and knowledge of law and society were supported by the 1950 Provisional Constitution, the parliamentary democracy and the factuality of the Trias Politica doctrine. But the new Constitution together with the curtailment and subsequent abolition of the parliamentary democracy and the separation of powers had pulled the rug out from under those attitudes and had turned their know-how into an anachronism.

When the legal system was invalidated, so was the essence of their monopoly on understanding the law and thus their power base. In years gone by, they had been safe in the knowledge that their professional frame of reference was shared by generational peers in key positions in legal practice, in law policy making and in education. Now, their numbers at those posts were dwindling and they became outnumbered by the collective of younger jurists whose notions, legal know-how and frame of reference were different to theirs and by peers who had yielded to the prevailing ideology. Fitting the developments into Ugo Mattei's classification of law systems, one might say that Indonesia underwent a transition from an autonomous system controlled by professional jurists (rule of professional law) to a system dominated by political intervention (rule of political law).[217]

The events also put an end to the hegemony of the community's profes-

[217] Mattei 1997:23-35. The legal systems of developing countries are commonly dominated by political intervention or traditions of a religious or secular nature (Mattei 1997:27-40, compare with Otto 2000:8).

sional languages and genres – older jurists' customs of internal communication and of developing and formulating legal texts (legislation, court decisions, arguments) and handbooks, no longer qualified per definition as the language usage norm for legal practice and law studies. The old guard probably found itself compelled to relinquish piece by piece its old, predominantly Dutch frame of reference, used to address audiences of peers, having to target instead younger jurists whose language was Indonesian. No longer could the deviant manner of looking, reasoning and communicating, practised by recent graduates and people employed in judicial functions (judges, prosecutors) who were not legally qualified, be dismissed as mistakes made by beginners, poor or lay jurists – now the older jurist was inferior and forced to adapt.[218] A quote from an interview with an advocate of the old school, held by Daniel Lev in 1967, illustrates the altered relationship:

> Judges know little about the law now and care less. I must be one of the only advocates who still writes full briefs, citing books and relevant court decisions. But when I recently presented such a brief to court, the judge, a younger man, complainingly asked [me] why [I] had to submit all that crap and why didn't I write a short brief to make everything easy.[219]

This lamentation not only exemplifies to what extent the languages of older and younger jurists had grown apart but also the latter's doing away with the professional 'lingual behaviours' of the former, their rejection of the languages and genres that had long been the norm.

The anti-Dutch tack, the demise of the intersubjective legal community and the rise to power of a new generation of jurists pushed Dutch and the

218 Tamanaha's descriptions of the Micronesian law system provide excellent material for comparison (see Tamanaha 1993). In the situation he describes, the legal community, consisting of American jurists and Micronesian ones educated in the US, called the shots and Micronesian judges and non-jurists involved in the process of legislating had hardly any grip on either the procedure or the outcome. Nor did unusual 'twists and turns' in court decisions by non-jurists affect the internal legal attitude of the jurists when at work: 'In sum, when interacting with non-lawyer Micronesian legal actors, for the most part Expatriate lawyers continued to engage the internal legal attitude without alteration. The exception was interaction with the few judges like [R.] who operated in the legal system but in so unlawlike a manner that the internal legal attitude was not invoked at all. Otherwise, the major difference was a persistent doubt which was usually suppressed and did not interfere with the internal legal attitude once engaged. The grip of the internal legal attitude is so compelling that it is almost habitually invoked when stepping into the legal arena, creating its own reality even in the face of insistent contradiction.' (Tamanaha 1993:151, also see pp. 148-50 and 154-60.) This state of affairs is distinct from that in Indonesia in 1966 in that the latter's legal system, the power base of the legal community, had altered and that the influence of those whose methods of reasoning and formulating were unusual (compare with the non-jurists in Micronesia) had surpassed that of the legal community.

219 The interview was held on 20-7-1967 and is cited in Pompe 1996:339. Compare with Lev 1972:288.

sources of law in that language into the background, reserved for occasional communication between older jurists,[220] and allowed the Indonesian language and texts to advance. For jurists of the old guard, too, Indonesian as a professional language gained in importance – because of their improved proficiency in that tongue over time and hearing and using it more frequently themselves; because Dutch texts were ousted increasingly from daily practice and their lingual memory 'indonesified'. Many older jurists' progress into the next 'phase of learning' Indonesian, that following the 'translation phase' mentioned above, is likely to have coincided with this period. For practical reasons (like using the same texts as their younger colleagues, avoiding the need for translation, the shorter supply of Dutch books) and induced by the declining professional standard during this time, as well as by the thought that 'what matters in the end is the concept, not the language' (compare with Chapter I and II), this generation of jurists, too, began to use Indonesian texts even when expressly contrary to the ground rules of the law. In their circle, too, non-authentic translations of colonial legislation became increasingly popular even though, as has been said, in legal terms these had no merit whatsoever.[221] Generally speaking, at the end of the 1950s, the theme of 'language', if an item on jurists' agendas at all, was pushed aside by ever more pressing everyday problems.[222]

Something that was lost along with Dutch was what may be termed a 'unity of consciousness' (compare with Anderson 1990b:124) that had characterized the legal elite up until that time. The jurists who came to occupy whatever top positions in legal practice, at the Ministry of Justice and in law teaching at the end of the 1950s (some young, some old), no longer shared a legal meaning system and a basic legal language. The extent to which this jurist or that was still familiar with the old meaning system varied considerably and with the greater number of law faculties, the courses taken had become increasingly diverse, as had the languages, the ways of reasoning and arguing, and the doctrines they had made their own during their studies.[223]

220 Information provided by Daniel Lev on 19-6-2002.

221 Compare with Koesnoe 1991:125-7. Purwoto Gandasubrata remembers that, to begin with, he would translate Dutch articles of law himself whenever necessary but later on used translations published by Moeljatno and Subekti, for example. Such translations came in handy, according to Purwoto, and because their authors were professors who could be trusted to have checked and double-checked their work, one need not doubt the quality of the translation (interview dated 11-9-1996). As a rule, judges' use of legislation in translation rose sharply throughout the 1960s (interview with Sudikno Mertokusumo dated 22-2-1993).

222 Information provided by Daniel Lev on 19-6-2002. The Komisi Istilah, comprising a jurisprudence section, continued its activities, however, until its funding was cut off in 1966 (Rudjiati Muljadi 1976:58-9).

223 The dissimilarity between jurists who trained at different universities, in this case the UI and the Gama of the 1950s, is illustrated poignantly by a Mahkamah Agung justice who was

Major Dutch primary texts for a range of areas of law no longer were held in common by the jurists fulfilling the key posts; even the 'basic story' of the law (compare with Chapter II) had not been acquired in one and the same language, the same terms and definitions. Yet neither the legislator nor the LPHN, law academia or judges were able, for the time being, to present a generally acceptable blueprint for a future national system of law. Long-standing differences of opinion (regarding the role of adat law or of Islam, for instance) continued to dominate the legal debate. In politics, the ideological tide was so exceedingly unfavourable to the law and its actors that no blueprint of any kind could have been developed (Lev 1965b:287, 290-2, 297-307). The road was long to a new, uniform law course, that focussed on a new, national system of law primarily based on texts in the Indonesian language. Whereas the jurists had in halcyon days been educated in one language and one meaning system only, new jurists graduated into an eddy of heterogeneous words and meanings.

The processes described above came to pass gradually, invisibly. The practical consciousness that steers everyday actions, speaking and writing among them, cannot usually be expressed readily. On the face of it, much of the old order was retained – the Dutch language and Dutch texts continued to figure prominently in the lives of many jurists;[224] the curricula at the law facul-

interviewed by Pompe (1996:342) in 1994: 'The relationship between Universitas Indonesia and Gadjah Mada graduates at the Mahkamah Agung is not always fluent and on the contrary sometimes quite strained. I find my Gadjah Mada brethren on the bench poor at debating. They tend to hold on to pre-set positions and do not allow open discussion. It may have something to do with the Javanese influence on Gadjah Mada. The entire philosophy of Universitas Indonesia is more outward looking and focussed on foreign law, whilst Gadjah Mada is more inward looking and nationalist.' In terms of languages and genres (see Chapter II): learning a particular language goes hand in hand with learning a new repertoire of behaviours, including one's attitude towards others. Anyone who had been accustomed to using Dutch and consulting Dutch literature at university, had also acquired the accepted ways of dealing with other people's ideas (whether or not these agreed with their own), of social contact, and of debating with lecturers and fellow students and the like that are inherent in that language and that literature. Indonesian was in its infancy and therefore possessed a more limited repertoire of languages and genres that, just like Javanese, called for different social conventions. Javanese played a role in more environments than just at the Gama, though. Han Bing Siong recollects that (high) Javanese, with all the trimmings of its etiquette, was the common language of social gatherings of lecturers in the home of professor Djokosoetono (to whose 'anak mas' (favourite students) Han Bing Siong belonged) (interview dated 28-11-1996). In this context, the comments of C.F.G. Sunaryati Hartono on the upsurge of euphemisms in the Indonesian legal language are also noteworthy (*Eufemisme dalam bahasa hukum* 1997).

224 To date, all initiatives to establish official translations of colonial legislation have been worsted by the habit of criticizing or, contrariwise, praising this legislation translation or that (or terms used in them) – often taking the Dutch source text as the starting point for the assessment. For the record, criticisms may simply be copied from the lecturer who originally voiced it or be uttered exclusively to create the impression that one speaks Dutch, without the Dutch

ties remained largely unchanged (for quite some time to come) (Mardjono Reksodiputro 1989); many continued to regard the idea of the state under rule of law as the point on the compass by which they set their sails (Pompe 1996:47-9; Lev 1976:168-9); judges continued to interpret the Burgerlijk Wetboek (whether or not as a 'guideline') in the same manner as before (Lev 1965b:294-5) and even the Basic Agrarian Act, though ostensibly rooted in adat law, only thinly veils Western legal principles.[225] Yet below the surface, the inevitable, irreversible shift from Dutch to Indonesian picked up speed in the period from 1959 to 1965. By the close of this period, Indonesian had won both the battle and the war. To quote a retired judge: 'Court decisions used to be based on thinking Dutch but the younger generations of judges think bahasa Indonesia'.[226] The shift from Dutch to Indonesian, from meaning system to meaning heterogeneity, from intersubjective legal community to jurists with different bodies of knowledge, attitudes and languages, is also reflected in the language and terms applied to legal texts – in acts and court decisions, conclusions and handbooks, notarial deeds and records of proceedings. As a result, the subject of heterogeneous language and terminology came to be raised ever more frequently from the 1960s onwards, usually as a separate project, while the historical, subtler transitions remained largely obscured.

---

text actually being ready knowledge. A comment made by one of the lecturers interviewed, that knowledge of Dutch is required 'to formulate accurately' and that Indonesian is a 'language for sentiment' rather than method, also bears witness to the continuing orientation on Dutch and Dutch texts. Another interviewee lecturer praised the 'logika Belanda' ('Dutch logic') of certain authors.

225 Soetandyo Wignjosoebroto 1994:212-3. Whichever ideology a jurist championed, he or she would neither be able to fully shed the authoritative texts in force in the colonial days nor the content of his or her studies (Lev 1965b:306).

226 Interview with Purwoto Gandasubrata dated 11-9-1996. Another apt metaphor was supplied by Mardjono Reksodiputro who related that since the 1970s Dutch books had steadily been replaced by Indonesian ones 'that cannot any longer be translated back so easily' (interview dated 2-3-1994, compare with pp. 214-6). None of which is to say, of course, that the Dutch-language past had actually been effaced. The metaphor of coral, of the quirky growths come about through varying historic conditions (compare with Chapter II) also holds true for legal genres. For example, all manner of recently enacted Indonesian legislation, such as in the area of criminal trial procedure, bears witness to earlier legislation and literature. The texts of old have found their way to the legislation jurists of now, too, both in the recognizable, written form, whether in Dutch or in an Indonesian translation, and in a less familiar form, transferred through the lectures and syllabi of lecturers who appropriated those texts in various ways. (The draft Criminal Code, too, is littered with similarities with the old colonial legislation and modern Dutch law: see Lancée 2001.) Moreover, the historical link between Indonesian and Dutch law, as well as the improved relations between the two nations, have led Indonesian jurists to peruse modern Dutch legislation from time to time (for example, see the legislation pertaining to environmental law and the courts).

## CHAPTER V

# Conclusion

*The 1974 conference revisited*

Legal language has been a bone of contention in both linguistic and legal circles in Indonesia for several decades. Apart from the criticism levied at the unintelligibility to the layman of legal texts, expressed throughout the ages in countless languages, the specific faults found in Indonesian legal language lie in the general ambiguity of its usage, the heterogeneity of terms and expressions and the failure of legal texts to comply with the rules of Indonesian grammar ('un-Indonesian' long sentences, aberrant syntax, mistakes in spelling and punctuation). The Indonesian government has taken numerous measures to combat such shortcomings. To date, however, these have failed to produce the results anticipated, as is apparent from the persistent complaints (see Chapter I).

At the end of the first chapter, the modest scope of the measures is mentioned as the first reason to explain the lack of success. The second reason, the type of initiative taken by the government, is also discussed. One wonders whether the people and institutions concerned had gauged correctly the nature and causes of the problems. For example, dispensing with the legal heritage in the Dutch language seemed to take a much higher priority in the range of legal language issues than is evident from the literature or the measures applied. A political motive may be behind this, though the neglect also seems to have some basis in the theoretical approach that was taken, mostly implicitly. The dominant metaphor applied in relation to the phenomenon of 'language' is that of an instrument – the language is subservient to the jurist's practising the law. In this model, language is isolated, detached, as it were, from both user and context. And in doing so, the history (in the Dutch language) of Indonesian law and its language, too, take second place.

This book seeks to explain why the dissatisfaction with Indonesian legal language usage has continued for so long. The actual shortcomings of that usage are pinpointed, along with their origins. To achieve this, first the notion of language as an instrument had to be dismantled and substituted for one in which language takes centre stage as a form of human behaviour (*languaging*). This approach no longer defines 'doing law' as acting *by means of* language, but as a *lingual* activity based on and resulting in texts (Chapter II). A description is given of the history of the Indonesian legal community and its language during the era of the Netherlands East Indies (Chapter III) and in the Republik Indonesia (Chapter IV). The book closes with the conclusions below.

The main recurrent complaint about Indonesian legal language usage, voiced both during and after the 1974 Simposium Bahasa dan Hukum, is the lack of uniformity of language and terminology (including the criticism that the language used does not comply with the official standard). This should be seen as a reflection of the yearning for a new 'unity of consciousness',[1] a new legal community and a new common language. Up until the 1960s, the elite of Indonesian jurists had had access to a communal framework of 'basic legal language', texts and terminology, enabling its members to perpetuate their 'imagined community'. They had internalized the same texts, albeit from different editions, and maybe not worded identically or stated in different languages (the story of the rule of law and Trias Politica, and major theories within the various areas of law); they had become thoroughly familiar with the same authoritative texts (legislation, case law), had learnt to think and write like lawyers (through solving cases during their studies and, more importantly, during their careers) and had been able to keep up with significant developments in the law and changes to authoritative texts by means of their job-specific channels (journals, conferences) and texts (journals, state publications).

The above is not to say that the meaning system and basic legal language were not subject to change before the 1960s. On the contrary, like languages and meanings everywhere, their stability and homogeneity were but relative and formed part of a world in which a plurality of communication streams intersected continuously and entwined in continuing processes of change. New authoritative texts (legislation, books, landmark court decisions) were incorporated into the legal canon and old ones were abandoned. New social languages, including some classed as belonging to other national or regional tongues, came to play a role in the legal discourse while others went out of fashion. The arrival of hordes of students who were not speakers of Dutch, in the 1950s, caused a large-scale influx of Indonesian, Javanese and other social languages into the legal discourse, which until then had predominantly taken place in the Dutch language. These new social languages mostly came in the

1 See pp. 236-7. What goes for Indonesian jurists, goes for the entire Indonesian nation-state – see Nico Schulte Nordholt (2001:883): 'If Indonesia wants to continue as a nation-state, then it will be of the essence to reach a new consensus on the national identity, on what "to be Indonesian" means'.

shape of 'hybrids' (*campuran*) of national and regional languages and dialects. Yet despite such major linguistic innovation and change to the body of legal texts, the communal framework consisting of the basic legal language and legal texts and terminology initially was not lost.

During the Guided Democracy epoch the chain of continual innovation, dating back to the days of the Netherlands East Indies, was interrupted. A combination of factors is to blame. To begin with, the Dutch language became marginalized in these years, inevitably taking down with it the texts in that language – the very key to the legal meaning system for future lawyers. Precious years were wasted in which a more gradual transition to a system of law and the teaching of law, both primarily in the Indonesian language, might have been realized. Moreover, the body of authoritative texts that enabled the legal community to play the game by the rules was affected to a considerable degree.[2]

Next, jurists from among the ruling elite, who held key positions in the legal establishment and upheld the rules, were replaced with people who were more susceptible to the political elite's languages and texts. So, while the law became politicized, outsiders interfered in the administration of justice; corruption spread like wildfire, so that the very raison d'être of the law and the legal community – accepting the facticity of the law, acknowledging the law game and respecting its outcomes – was undermined. Once the Orde Baru had dawned and the resurrection of the rule of law had become a priority issue in its manifesto for the future, the small group of older jurists with a common, primarily Dutch, basic language had lost its leading position as a community. The dividing line usually present between jurists switched on to the internal legal attitude and non-jurists had sundered the community of jurists itself.

The legal community of the old, more or less stable legal system from before the Guided Democracy had disintegrated, leaving in its wake diverse groups of jurists in a world in which the position of the law was far from secure. The heterogeneity in training, experience, attitudes and values manifested itself in a heterogeneity of language and terminology, the main theme of the 1974 conference.

2 The government could have ensured the availability of a sufficient number of jurists with receptive command of Dutch in the future, too; it could have enacted Indonesian translations to substitute the main codes; and it could have been more resolute in developing policies, in collaboration with the organizations of the legal profession and the law faculties, aimed at a greater degree of standardization of language usage and terminology. While one can easily imagine such policies not having been put into place without guided democracy, either, the government had now let the last opportunity to do so slip through its fingers.

*The Orde Baru (1966-1998)*

The continuation of the complaints about the language of the law and the legal terminology in the days of the Orde Baru[3] may be attributed to the fact that the problems outlined above became magnified rather than solved during that period. 1997 saw the publication of extensive research, commissioned by the World Bank, into the state of affairs of the law in Indonesia. The report concludes that its condition, at the end of the previous century, is nothing short of deplorable.[4] The standard of the law courses, for example, has generally taken a dramatic downturn since the 1970s due to the sharp rise in student numbers, among other reasons.[5] The law faculties try and cope with an acute shortage of lecturers, while the lecture halls, packed with 250 or more students, lend themselves only to teaching by means of lectures and are not suitable for more intensive forms of instruction (*Law reform in Indonesia* 1997:61). The programme, run largely by lecturers who are inadequately trained and lack sound practical experience, is fairly biased towards the teaching of theory (of abstract legal rules, for example), whereas the practical skills needed to apply the theory are hardly touched upon.[6]

Thus, skills such as legal thinking and writing for concrete situations, practised in the Netherlands, for instance, through solving endless cases or through writing texts such as pleas or notes on court decisions, in Indonesia are practised rarely, if at all. A substantial part of the documentation is outdated; this, combined with poor availability, is responsible in part for the failure of many students to become familiar with carrying out thorough research

3 See Chapter I, footnote 80. During interviews conducted in 1993 and 1994, there were concerns that the language and terminology lacked uniformity, that a fixed legal language, a standard so to speak, was left wanting and that the language was 'still being developed' (interviews with Saleh Adiwinata on 26-2-1993, A. Zainal Abidin on 3-5-1994, Siti Ismiati Yenie on 6-5-1994, Moerdiati Soebagyo on 18-2-1993 and Hamid Attamimi on 30-4-1994).

4 See *Law reform in Indonesia* 1997. According to Mochtar Kusumaatmadja, principal advisor to the research project, the state of affairs of the law was 'desperate but not hopeless' (*Law reform in Indonesia* 1997:159-60).

5 At the start of the 1990s, the number of law students graduating at both state and private universities was estimated at approximately 13,000 per annum. 26 state and more than 180 private universities existed at that time (*Law reform in Indonesia* 1997:5, 48; also see Pompe 1996:146-8). For comparison's sake: in 1972 Lev (1972:275) estimated the *total* number of Indonesian jurists, since the 1920s, to have obtained qualifications in law at the Dutch universities, the Rechtshoogeschool and the main Indonesian law faculties at just over 5,000. It is not clear, incidentally, what Lev meant by the 'main law faculties'. Compare Pompe 1996:339-42 and Bedner 2000:297.

6 The second difference with the earlier teaching is that the lectures for the first-year students, the actual introduction to the profession, that is, used to be given by the faculty hot shots. Later they came to be taught increasingly by assistants, meaning that the students lost out on an important kick-start to their professional zeal (information provided by drs. Jan van Olden 14-4-2003).

into texts such as legislation, court decisions and professional literature, the very basis for writing legal texts. Access to important literature is hindered further by the increased scarcity, since the 1970s, of a command of Dutch.[7] The problem is far from solved by the prescription of literature in English by increasing numbers of lecturers who spent a finishing year in, say, the United States – often, the command of English, too, leaves a lot to be desired.[8] Also, the culture of dictation still seems to prevail (see Chapter IV). The sum total of the above is that the majority of jurists fail to master the first requirement for 'doing law', namely the production of texts in relation to a concrete case, as based on authoritative texts. They are incapable of writing a logical, well-founded legal recommendation.[9] The successive attempts undertaken since the 1970s to create a course tailored to the law in practice seem to have had little result.[10]

[7] It should be mentioned, here, that the Engelbrecht legislation reader, containing mostly colonial legislation and Dutch translations of Indonesian legislative texts, was last reprinted in 1971 (presumably).

[8] *Law reform in Indonesia* 1997:66; Pompe 1996:340-2; interviews with Kartini Muljadi on 23-4-1994, Hartono Soerjopratikno on 13-2-1994, Mardjono Reksodiputro on 2-5-1994, Hajati Suroredjo on 25-4-1994, Emmy Pangaribuan on 12-2-1994, J.E. Sahetapy on 18-2-1994 and F. Limahelu on 19-2-1994. From the 1960s onwards, though more particularly since the dawn of the Orde Baru, growing numbers of Indonesian jurists began to take up (crash or extended) refresher courses in the United States and other Anglo-Saxon countries. Among the jurists later to become lecturer, Mochtar Kusumaatmadja was one of the first to do so, followed by Mardjono Reksodiputro, Sahetapy, Muladi, Barda Nawawi Arief (the two mentioned last currently hold chairs as professors at the UNDIP at Semarang) and others. The United States was mostly popular with jurists training to be advocates (information provided by Daniel Lev on 10-10-2002 and Mardjono Reksodiputro on 19-11-2002). Lev ascribes this popularity to the attraction exerted by the American advocature (activist, highly paid), the influence of American commerce on Indonesia and the ensuing demand for advocates familiar with English and American law, and to the reputation of the United States as a superpower (information provided on 10-10-2002).

[9] *Law reform in Indonesia* 1997:61, 65-6, compare Mardjono Reksodiputro 1989:542, Churchill 1992:4 and Chapter II. Leaving their dissertations aside, many students are never required to write any sizeable text. Ph.M. Hadjon, talking about his student days (UNAIR 1967-73), mentioned the phenomenon of the 'sarjana hukum kurang skripsi' (more or less 'master of laws less dissertation'), when referring to students who abandoned their studies just prior to writing their dissertation (consequently, just prior to obtaining their degree) (interview dated 12-9-1996; *Law reform in Indonesia* 1997:61). Also relevant in this context is the custom of setting multiple choice exams (interviews with Retnowulan Sutantio on 23-2-1994 and Siti Ismiati Yenie on 6-5-1994).

[10] *Law reform in Indonesia* 1997:64. In the 1997 report it is pointed out that the doctrinal aspects of a law course ought to be given priority during the first phase, level S-1 (baccalaureat, comparable to a bachelor's) resulting in the title of *sarjana hukum*, and that the wider socio-legal approach, traditionally rated more highly, only ought to be emphasized thereafter (S-2 or *magister hukum* level, comparable to a master's). According to the report, jurists cannot 'find' the law in concrete situations; they are unable to carry out their work properly because the doctrine was neglected during their studies. The 1994 curriculum, although aimed to a greater extent at instilling the basic skills needed to practise law than previous curricula, did not as yet yield any noticeable improvement (*Law reform in Indonesia* 1997:166-7). A summary of the successive curriculum

The quality of law courses and of the work undertaken by the legal profession is also hampered, in general, by the continued confusion as to which legislation (the single most important attribute of the law game) is in force and the lack of easy access to that legislation. There are more than a few instances of new Indonesian legislation being implemented without clarifying to what extent the colonial legislation remained in force.[11] Moreover, the initiatives taken to create reliable, publicly accessible legal documentation systems (for legislation, court decisions) have had limited success to date. Getting hold of a reliable text version of legislation is still a difficult task. For example, the official *Lembaran Negara* (State Gazette) and *Tambahan Lembaran Negara* (Supplementary State Gazette), that contain the main legislation and accompanying elucidation, are published at irregular intervals and are hard to obtain (*Law reform in Indonesia* 1997:90, 101, 167; Churchill 1992). Court decisions are seldom published and even then are selected on vague criteria. Command of Dutch among jurists in Indonesia has now all but vanished, putting the official texts of major legislation and other sources of law firmly beyond the reach of the majority.[12] Yet however detrimental the lack of a national system or legal resource centre, the near absence of interest in adequate documentation among the various law professions is of much greater concern (*Law reform in Indonesia* 1997:90-1).

It is self-evident that the deficiencies in the training of many jurists are reflected in the quality of the teaching of future generations of jurists as well as in the legal work undertaken in both the public and the private sector. The

reforms at the law faculties is provided by Mardjono Reksodiputro (1995d:203-8). Mardjono also headed the World Bank research.

11 Examples are the new land legislation of 1960, the 1963 circular by the Mahkamah Agung relating to the Burgerlijk Wetboek (see Chapter IV) and the Marriage Act of 1974 (UU no. 1/1974). In a court decision by the *pengadilan tinggi* of Jakarta in 1967, SEMA no. 3/1963 by the Mahkamah Agung relating to the BW was judged not to be binding. This decision was hardly publicized, however (Pompe 1994:17-8 and Gouw Giok Siong 1968:102-4). According to Pompe and Gouw Giok Siong, this led to a continuous feeling of uncertainty about the BW. Nevertheless, with the arrival of the Orde Baru, the courts are said to have reverted immediately to the application of the BW as a fully-fledged legal code (Han Bing Siong 2002:323). The Marriage Act is ambiguous on the point of unions between people of different religions (Pompe 1988).

12 Pompe 1996:340-2, compare Chapter IV. At the Indonesian Supreme Court, too, Dutch has become a thing of the past. According to Purwoto S. Gandasubrata, president of the Supreme Court in the 1990s and law student at the UI in the early 1950s, Dutch was still being spoken during the deliberations of that body under the presidency of Oemar Seno Adji (1974-81). Subsequently, a mixture (*campuran*) of Dutch and Indonesian was used (interview dated 11-9-1996). Retnowulan Sutantio, who was a justice during the last decade of the twentieth century and had graduated in the same year as Purwoto, reckons that roughly three quarters of the justices with a seat on the Supreme Court at the beginning of the 1990s retained a receptive command of Dutch. Nearly all of these justices retired halfway through that decade (interview dated 23-2-1994).

selection procedure is usually inadequate, as is any subsequent training in the daily practice.[13] Owing to the poor pay offered by government institutions (judiciary, prosecution service, Ministry of Justice, other departments and state universities), the lion's share of jurists opt for a career in the private sector (law firms, companies). Therefore, the government is faced with a shortage of jurists and those who do present themselves cannot be relied upon to be the cream of the crop. Complaints abound about the standard of work of many jurists employed at the ministerial departments (for example, the *biro hukum* or legal bureaus of the various ministries, the BPHN and the Directorate of Legislation of the Ministry of Justice), and as regards the judiciary, complaints in the same vein have even been extended regarding the justices of the Mahkamah Agung. Many judges are insufficiently knowledgeable about the law and, also, their decisions frequently show evidence of a highly un-lawlike methodology – much of their work lacks the painstaking attention to detail that is emblematic of jurists.[14]

This un-lawlike approach and lack of interest in the reliable provision of information on the law may be ascribed in part to the slant of law courses towards theory. Many Indonesian jurists who currently practise law lack the method of routinely solving concrete cases on the basis of certain authoritative texts, the authority of which is generally accepted. Their courses only managed to teach the law as a set of facts, as ready knowledge, while omitting to push students into the crucial, indispensable even, next step, the internalization of a *manner of thinking and acting* (making use of the ready knowledge).[15] Only part of the criticism voiced concerns the skills gap of most jurists, however. Much graver – and much more widely applicable, namely to *all* legal actors, operating in both the public and the private sector

13 *Law reform in Indonesia* 1997:5. Advocates and notaries are formally required, for example, to gain a certain amount of experience before they are awarded the papers necessary to put their respective professions into practice. There is no proper yardstick, however, to measure the experience actually acquired. To be eligible for a judgeship or prosecution post, law graduates must first pass an exam set by the Ministry of Justice and the Prosecutor General's Office and then complete a one-year course (*Law reform in Indonesia* 1997:48-9). Finally, in the administrative justice, too, the record of conduct has fallen into disuse as a measure to be considered when promoting a judge (Bedner 2000:251-3, compare Chapter IV).

14 *Law reform in Indonesia* 1997:8, 57, 60, 77-80, 82-3, 163-4, 169; Pompe 1996:338-40; Bedner 2000:241-9. Because of the difficulty in attracting enough candidates for judgeships, the administrative courts established in the 1990s have taken to appointing *griffiers* instead (Bedner 2000:245-6).

15 This also casts some light on the belief of some judges that a visit to a library might betray a gap in one's knowledge. After all, a judge should already know everything there is to know. If court decisions are discussed during lectures, these serve primarily to illustrate the application of legislation, not the reasoning of the judge that caused him to arrive at his decision (*Law reform in Indonesia* 1997:61). It must be borne in mind, however, that judges are not usually known to be exhaustive in their motivations (interview with Mardjono Reksodiputro dated 2-3-1994).

– are the many complaints about violations of the professional code of ethics. There are many examples of advocates intent on winning using whatever means necessary, of judges who fail to take cases seriously, of procedures that lack transparency, of prosecutors who tamper with evidence and of wholesale corruption going right to the top of the judicial hierarchy (*Law reform in Indonesia* 1997:6-7, 50, 56, 158, 169; Pompe 1996:343-8; Bedner 2000:283-99). And public faith in the law and in its practitioners is not helped by the failure of the professional societies to discipline the offenders (*Law reform in Indonesia* 1997:6, 53, 158, 169).

We have come full circle to the issue of professional integrity, to upholding and defending the 'veracity', the 'facticity' of the story that is the law – the very foundation of the rule of law. Violations of the professional code not so much evidence inadequacy to play the game by the rules but a sheer inability, an unwillingness, even, to play the game at all. For instance, the political circumstances under which jurists were required to operate during the Orde Baru hardly represented an improvement on those of the Guided Democracy era. Although the restoration of the state under rule of law and of an independent judiciary had formed part and parcel of the aims of the various groups who supported Soeharto's coup d'état, it only took a couple of years for the new regime to settle in and dash all hope for change. By virtue of Act no. 14 of 1970, the Ministry of Justice (the Executive in its wake) retained extensive control over the functioning of the judiciary. In so far as the judicial system had safeguarded a vestige of independence, the politics of patronage practised by Minister of Justice Oemar Seno Adji over the next few years whittled away the remains.[16]

In the course of time, a powerful, militarized bureaucratic regime with strong army ties was built up that left no room for an independent judiciary nor, accordingly, for the law game.[17] Just as the state under rule of law had been subordinated to the Revolution in the days of Guided Democracy, the new doctrine now elevated the Pancasila (open to a multitude of interpreta-

[16] Lev points out that Indonesian judges, in their capacity of *pegawai negeri* (civil servants), traditionally do not possess a strong sense of operational independence in relation to the executive (Lev 1978:55-6, compare Chapter IV). Seen from this perspective, the judges of the administrative courts (*pengadilan tata usaha negara*) shoulder a fairly heavy burden – they risk incurring the loathing of civilians as well as of (colleague) civil servants. According to Adriaan Bedner, administrative judges are sometimes accused of antipatriotism, which is reminiscent of the above remarks in respect of the epoch of Guided Democracy (Bedner 2000:246 and Chapter IV).

[17] See Lev (1999:6): 'With the army as its foundation, the New Order regime was powerful enough to ignore all reform proposals that intended in any way to impose constraints upon it. Once efforts at reform failed, then conditions worsened in all state institutions. Courts, prosecution, police, most bureaucratic offices, having lost any genuinely autonomous status linked to law, now sank more and more deeply into corruption.' Also see Tristam Moeliono 2000:2.

tions) to the position of highest source of all law; under the Orde Baru, democracy was said to be a 'Pancasila democracy' (*demokrasi Pancasila*).[18] Institutions like the Lembaga Bantuan Hukum (LBH, Institute for Legal Aid), that not only provided legal aid to the poor but also drew attention to the need for socio-economic and political reform, were sabotaged in no small measure.[19]

The refutation of the facticity of the law story – by the regime as well as by many litigants and jurists[20] – was a trap that sprang on each attempt to reform the law or improve the law courses. All said and done, initiatives to enhance the game and its requisites (such as the body of authoritative texts and access thereto) or to step up the training of the players (legal education) are fairly pointless and not likely to generate much enthusiasm if the board can be upset at random or outsiders can fix the match. It was no coincidence that the 1997 report argued in the first place for an unequivocal declaration of intent by President Soeharto himself, to be pronounced at the anniversary celebrations of Indonesian independence, that would straightforwardly express the government's political will to reform the law. Nothing short of such a declaration (with the potential to be both authoritative and internally persuasive), combined with the establishment of a new institution, directly answerable to the President, with unlimited powers in the area of law development, could effect the reform of law courses, institutions and, above all, the administration of justice, it was thought (*Law reform in Indonesia* 1997:159-61).

One could say that, during the epoch of the Orde Baru, too, the story of the law (the law game) failed to bring together into a community the jurists of the various legal professions and the different generations.[21] An intersubjective legal community usually owes its position of power and, consequently, its very existence to a common meaning system and a common language, founded on the specialized knowledge of the state legal system that was acquired while studying law. In the Soeharto era, though, the system crumbled, causing jurists to lose the object of their common focus. A catalyst for this process was the rapid erosion of the exalted position of the academic legal world, the flagship of freedom of expression and, in a sense, the guardian of the legal

18 See Lindsey 1999, Fitzpatrick 1999, Todung Mulya Lubis 1999 and Bourchier 1999. Compare Chapter IV.

19 Ricklefs 1993:297; Lev 2000:326-7; *Law reform in Indonesia* 1997:7, 88-9, 158, 165, 169.

20 To litigants' minds, the inefficacy of the law is confirmed by the near impossibility of enforcing judgements passed (Butt 1999; *Law reform in Indonesia* 1997:143). Their lack of faith in the judge's decision finds some expression in the trend of lodging an appeal as a matter of course in case of an unfavourable outcome (*Law reform in Indonesia* 1997:169; Pompe 1996; Bedner 2000).

21 See Bedner (2000:297): 'Law graduates do not leave law school with a clear shared body of norms and orientations, and due to the limited flow of information between lawyers this does not develop during their professional lives'.

community's conscience.[22] Overall, a climate was created that allowed centrifugal forces to intensify and centripetal ones to diminish.

From the descriptions in the 1997 World Bank report, one can glean a sore lack of cooperation, coordination and cohesion of conduct, on the one hand, and an abundance of self-interest on the other – on the parts of both individual jurists and professional groups and institutions.[23] It is mentioned, for instance, that cooperation between the various professional bodies (regarding law development, among other issues) and between the law faculties and practising jurists (in connection with the requirements to be imposed on law courses) was wholly absent. Moreover, contact between professional organizations and government bodies or between the private sector (advocature, legal advice practices, notaries, trade and industry) and the public one (departments, judiciary, prosecution service) was said hardly to occur.

The situation described for the production of legislation is most revealing – the different government departments by and large ignored the agreement to cooperate and coordinate with the Ministry of Justice, or more particularly its Directorate-General for Law and Legislation and the BPHN, while the sections within those departments dedicated to drafting legislation, the legal bureaus, in reality were only marginally involved. The private sector and the general public were not consulted about the legislative process at all (*Law reform in Indonesia* 1997:58, 77-80, 82-3, 88, 95-7, 99). In this climate, in which the law story was denied its higher plane, its role of ethical framework, self-interest and personal gain ruled. Advocates and judges who took bribes or otherwise bent the official rules of the game, were screened by rather than disciplined by the law. Many jurists were keepers turned poachers – the law, said the World Bank report, had become merchandise, had degenerated into an industry with a profit motive.[24]

The measures proposed in the report read like a cry for unity, for a united front. Government departments were advised to heed the importance of coordinated cooperation between themselves, the Ministry of Justice, the prosecu-

22 Jan van Olden drew my attention to this.

23 Sutandyo Wignyosoebroto 1977, pp. 26-8 in particular. Some of these professional organizations are: Persatuan Advokat Indonesia (PERADIN, Indonesian Society of Advocates); Ikatan Advokat Indonesia (IKADIN, Indonesian Union of Advocates); Asosiasi Advokat Indonesia (AAI, Indonesian Association of Advocates); Himpunan Penasehat Hukum Indonesia (HPHI, Indonesian Society of Legal Advisors); Asosiasi Konsultan Hukum Indonesia (AKHI, Indonesian Association of Legal Consultants); Perhimpunan Sarjana Hukum Indonesia (PERSAHI, Indonesian Society of Jurists); Ikatan Hakim Indonesia (IKAHI, Indonesian Union of Judges) and Persatuan Jaksa (PERSAJA, Society of Public Prosecutors) (*Law reform in Indonesia* 1997:55).

24 *Law reform in Indonesia* 1997:8, 157, 169. Sources of law and other legal documentation, too, were often treated as merchandise rather than as information that ought to be publicly accessible (see Tristam Moeliono 2000:3 and Churchill 1992). Lev (2000:328) points out that many advocates' interest in legal and political reform diminished as their practices grew more profitable.

tion service, the professional organizations and any other institutions involved in creating legislation or maintaining the law (*Law reform in Indonesia* 1997:68, 71, 74-5). Various sectors of the world of jurists were called upon to cooperate, for example on the teaching of law and on restoring public confidence in the law and its practitioners (*Law reform in Indonesia* 1997:58, 88). The individual jurist, too, was addressed – self-interest was contrasted with the moral duty of each to side with his clients and to oppose social injustice resulting from the legislation in force (*Law reform in Indonesia* 1997:165). What we have, here, is an invitation to reinstate the facticity of the law: 'Demonstrate that the rule of law is alive and well', is what is actually being said here, 'respect the law and endeavour to realize the guiding principle inherent in it'. The call for unity is most apparent in the case made for a national law journal. Such a publication, containing analyses of events, opinions, legislation and court decisions, could bring together the different segments of the legal community. It ought to constitute a forum for debate, at national level, between scholars and practitioners of the law, law students and graduates, the public and private sectors and jurists in Jakarta and in the provinces.[25]

### *The post-Suharto era*

> The simplest strategy would be to foster the development of an intersubjective legal community made up of members not trained in the U.S. legal tradition. Exclusion of U.S. trained lawyers, expatriate as well as Micronesian, from participation as members in the legal system would be a necessary aspect of this strategy, thereby creating a vacuum of knowledge and eliminating the existing assemblage which insures continuity with the U.S. legal tradition. Automatically, this would result in a break from the existing legal meaning system, even if all the laws on the books remain the existing body of transplanted laws. These laws on the books would simply take on different meanings, internally consistent within the new legal meaning system of the new intersubjective legal community, though far different from how they are now interpreted. (Tamanaha 1993:195.)

The Orde Baru ended when Su\oeharto relinquished the presidency in the year following the publication of the World Bank report. Important steps towards restoring the rule of law have been taken since. For example, new laws regulating the balance of power have been implemented, and in June 1999 a fair and democratic general election was held.[26] The Komisi Hukum Nasional

[25] *Law reform in Indonesia* 1997:90-1. The report considered the BPHN publication *Hukum Nasional* not to fulfil this role (*Law reform in Indonesia* 1997:90). The case made for comprehensive publication of the body of court decisions may be taken in the same vein (*Law reform in Indonesia* 1997:162-3).

[26] Of the new legislation worthy of mention are the laws in respect of the political parties

(National Law Commission), answerable directly to the President, has been founded and has developed a programme to reform the legal establishment,[27] the Komisi Ombudsman Nasional (National Ombudsman Commission) has been established (Keputusan Presiden (Keppres, Presidential Decision) no. 44/2000), the Constitution has been amended[28] and a cautious start has been made with cleansing the judiciary and other government institutions of individuals known to have engaged in corruption.

However, nearly five years after power changed hands and under the third President, no less, of the post-Suharto era, the reform machinery seems to have ground to a halt. For example, the Mahkamah Agung may have undergone a cleansing exercise but in the remainder of the judicial apparatus, corruption is still rife.[29] Judges trying some of the kingpins of the Orde Baru regime, army personnel accused of crimes against humanity (East Timor, Aceh, Irian Jaya/Papua) and bankers and businessmen suspected of corruption have found it difficult not to buckle under the enormous pressure brought to bear on them by outside parties with an interest in the outcome of the case.[30] Moreover, due to the failure to root out corruption altogether, the intrinsic value of court decisions is blighted by the continued difficulty in

---

(UU no. 2/1999), the general elections (UU no. 3/1999) and the Majelis Permusyawaratan Rakyat (MPR, People's Congress) and DPR (UU no. 4/1999). For more on the 1999 election and the political parties standing, see Pompe 1999b.

27 The Commission was established by virtue of Keppres no. 15/2000. Details of the Commission's activities may be found on www.komisihukum.go.id.

28 The amendments to the 1945 Constitution were passed during the sessions of the MPR held on 19-10-1999, 18-8-2000, 9-11-2001 and 10-8-2002. The Constitution now specifies that Indonesia is a state under rule of law (art. 1 clause 3); that the President and Vice President may not serve for more than two terms running (art. 7); that the *daerah* (regions) possess a much greater degree of autonomy in relation to Jakarta than before (art. 18A-B, 22C-D); that the members of the DPR, the DPRD (the houses of representatives of the regions), the Vice President and the President are to be elected by means of direct, general, free, honest and just elections (art. 22E); and that the judiciary is an independent power (art. 24 clause 1). Also, a chapter concerning fundamental human rights has been included (chapter XA, art. 28A-J). Interestingly, the Constitution itself now imposes a requirement of integrity on judges ('harus memiliki integritas') (art. 24A clause 2, referring to the justices on the Mahkamah Agung) – compare with Chapter I.

29 The special UN researcher Dato Param Cumaraswamy described the state of affairs he encountered in July 2002 as follows: 'I didn't realize that the situation could be as bad as what I've seen' (*Jakarta Post*, 22-7-2002). Indonesian Corruption Watch, in its report on what was tellingly called the 'court mafia', stated that many courts did not deal in justice but in hard cash. Apart from judges, the report said, police officers, registrars, advocates, employees of the prosecution service and jailors were also involved in corruption (*Jakarta Post*, 23-7-2002).

30 Public dissatisfaction with these kinds of practices is expressed, for example, in the articles 'What is so fishy about Akbar Tanjung's case?' (*Jakarta Post*, 6-9-2002), about the case against the Golkar leader and chairman of parliament Akbar Tanjung, and 'Kita perlu bertindak cepat mengembalikan wibawa hukum' (*Kompas*, 9-8-2002), about the case against the PT (Perseroan Terbatas, Limited Liability Company) Asuransi Jiwa Manulife Indonesia (AJMI).

having sentences executed.[31] The problem is that it takes many years to alter the existing institutional role patterns and relationships (of and between parliament, the government and the judiciary, for instance), as well as the professional attitude of jurists in the various institutions and professions.[32] Thus, the position of this state institution or that in relation to other institutions may have been strengthened on paper by a new law or government regulation, it does not necessarily follow that the institution in question applies its new powers – the old bulwarks of power within the state bodies and the existing routines of negotiating and reaching agreements have far from vanished upon the new law taking effect.[33]

Ever since the 1960s, it has not been possible for a new legal community or legal meaning system to come into being in Indonesia. Precisely due to the absence of a conceptual framework that encompasses all jurists, for the time being there are no circumstances conducive to the generation of a new common language. Therefore, the complaints of heterogeneity, deviation from the standard and ambiguity persist (see Chapter I). The measures taken since 1974 in the area of legal language and terminology hardly detract from this statement. Particularly those aimed directly at creating uniformity or at standardizing the legal usage, such as the dictionaries produced to this effect and the lectures in Indonesian, go wide off the mark. Such means are intended to exert external influence on the speaking and writing of jurists. Dictionaries indeed are capable of instilling a certain uniformity, through their reference function.[34] They play but a modest role, though, in the day-

31 Butt 1999 provides excellent insight into the execution of sentences.

32 Pompe 1999b:22-8. Lev (1999:8) sketches a gloomy picture of Indonesia after Suharto: 'The institutional base of the state is a shambles; nearly every institution meant to be of service to society has been destroyed, trusted by no one, filled with corruption, and bearing a reputation that must be overcome. The national bureaucracy, the regional *pamong praja*, the courts, the prosecution, the police, the parliament, the MPR, the entirety of the executive have no reason to expect public support.' For information about the passivity of the judiciary during the Reformasi, see Pompe 1999a. Minister of Justice Muladi warned the judiciary that the Reformasi involved not only changes to the law but also to professional attitudes (Pompe 1999a:73).

33 Pompe describes the role assumed by parliament during the preparation of the new laws regulating the balance of power as that of a 'serving hatch' rather than that of an actor. The decision-making process, rather than taking place in parliament, in reality was negotiated between the leaders of the main political parties, most of whom were members of the cabinet. One observer noted that members of parliament systematically shunned their responsibilities, refused to make decisions and let themselves be guided by 'a well-nigh infinitely greedy opportunism aimed at personal gain' (Pompe 1999b:26).

34 All the more so when the dictionaries are thorough pieces of work, produced by or at the instigation of official bodies that jurists consider to be authoritative, and provide not only keywords and translations but also insight into the connections between the host of synonyms and homonyms. Termorshuizen-Arts 2003 deals extensively with legal dictionaries and with the way in which lexicographical items in the field of the law would ideally be laid out.

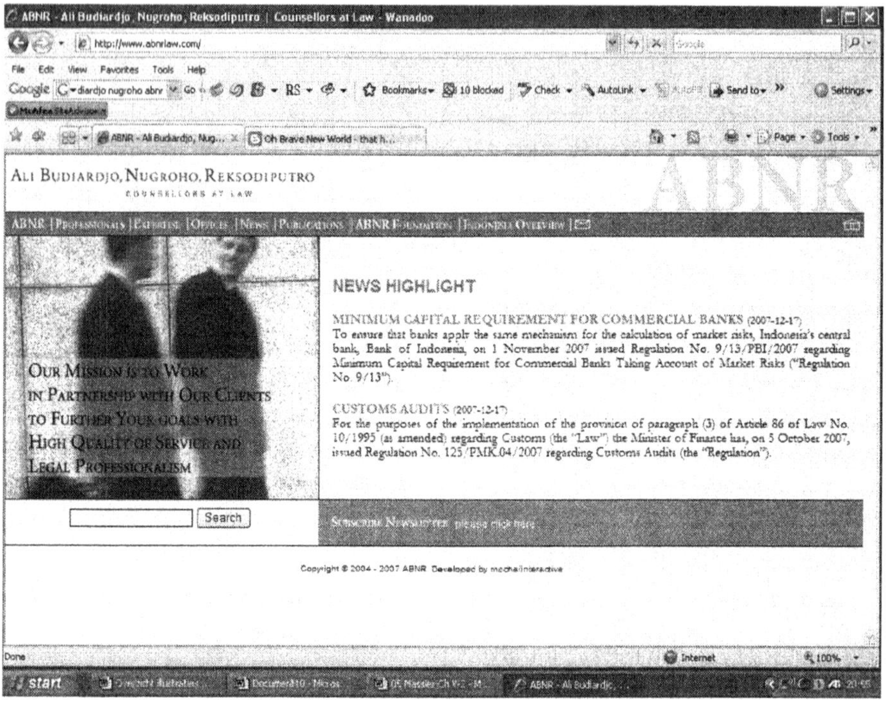


Fig. 27. Website Law Firm Ali Budiardjo, Nugroho, Reksodiputro (courtesy ABNR)

to-day speaking and writing. Equally, courses aimed at improving students' command of (standard) Indonesian should not raise one's expectations.[35] Throughout the careers of newly qualified jurists, the language usage of colleagues established in the profession and the various genres in vogue in the daily practice will influence their speaking and writing to a much greater extent than their university language classes.[36] The professional elders, as

[35] On this point, also see Maier 1997:688-95.

[36] Just as was argued in the conclusions of the Simposium Bahasa dan Hukum and various articles, several jurists interviewed expressed their unconditional support for standard Indonesian as the norm for legal usage (interviews with Kartini Muljadi on 2-3-1993 and 23-4-1994, Hajati Suroredjo on 25-4-1994, Sudikno Mertokusumo on 5-5-1994 and Mardjono Reksodiputro on 2-3-1994). Frequent transgression of the rules of standard Indonesian in jurists' professional usage might partly be related to the relative indifference with which Indonesian is applied in general, even by the elite. There are no social sanctions on speaking or writing poor Indonesian (Steinhauer 1981:12-3). At the 1975 seminar on national language policy, it was argued that sanctions ought to be imposed in cases clearly requiring the standard version (*Politik Bahasa Nasional* 1975:185). Also, students who excelled in Indonesian received hardly any merits. The marks for

well as teachers and authors of legal textbooks, thus bear a particular responsibility (compare pp. 29-30).

One could say, generally speaking, that the remedies aimed specifically at the language of the law tackle the symptoms rather than cure the illness. Measures that tie in with the routines innate in legal speaking and writing would be more efficacious. The formal substitution of major legislation in the Dutch language, still in force, with Indonesian translations, for example, might be able to contribute significantly towards the uniformity of legal terminology.[37] Although this would not result in acts and regulations that fit in seamlessly with a new system of national legislation, it would alleviate the problematic situation arising from the majority of Indonesian jurists' inability, at the present time, to consult the official, Dutch version of important pieces of legislation – particularly in the area of private law – and the consequence of having to use various, unauthorized translations (see Churchill 1992:32-3). It would replace the 'quicksand' of the Indonesian law with a solid foundation and could represent a step in the process of generating new legislation on an Indonesian basis. The ideal of producing a translation to everyone's liking needs to make way for the realization that the availability of a fixed, clearly defined body of authoritative texts is one of the quintessential features of a state under rule of law.[38]

Jurists need to bear in mind that translations, like any other text, leave room for interpretation according to various concrete applications. A disadvantage of such a measure would be that the (Dutch) language connection between the current legislation, on the one hand, and the older jurisprudence and literature, on the other, is severed, though the latter two sources of law are no exception in being hardly ever consulted in their original language,

---

the subject of Indonesian hardly played a role in the assessment of students. Furthermore, a good command of Indonesian is never listed as a job requirement, although foreign languages are (I Gusti Ngurah Oka 1975:70-1, also see Anton Moeliono 1975:37-8). Moeliono (2000:4-5) also points out that the lingual heterogeneity emanates (among others) from the fact that written language varieties (*ragam bahasa*) to many people do not serve as a model. The heterogeneity, that seems to occur within the Indonesian elite, too, ties in with the image of the *prismatic society*, the concept employed by Fred W. Riggs to describe the development process of many previously colonized countries (Riggs 1961:2, 1964:13-5).

37 This has already been argued by Tasrif (1975:15), Busthanul Arifin (1976:9, 12), Padmo Wahjono (1983:206-7, 213) and others. Also see Moeljatno's ideas about Indonesian criminal law (Chapter IV). Compare with Frans Winarta 2000:2-3, 5.

38 Indonesian jurists have always had a tendency to adhere to a particular translation and to reject all others – whether because they consider that translation best or because the *guru* recommended it (see Chapter IV). If new translations are to be produced, it is advisable not to translate literally or word by word. The notion that the more literal the translation, the more accurate and faithful to the source text the product, is a myth – the meaning of a text is *always* greater than the sum of the dictionary components. In other words, a text *never* has a 'literal meaning'. For more on this subject, see Steiner 1975:277-8 and Shen 1989:219-35. Also see Termorshuizen-Arts 2003:30-1.

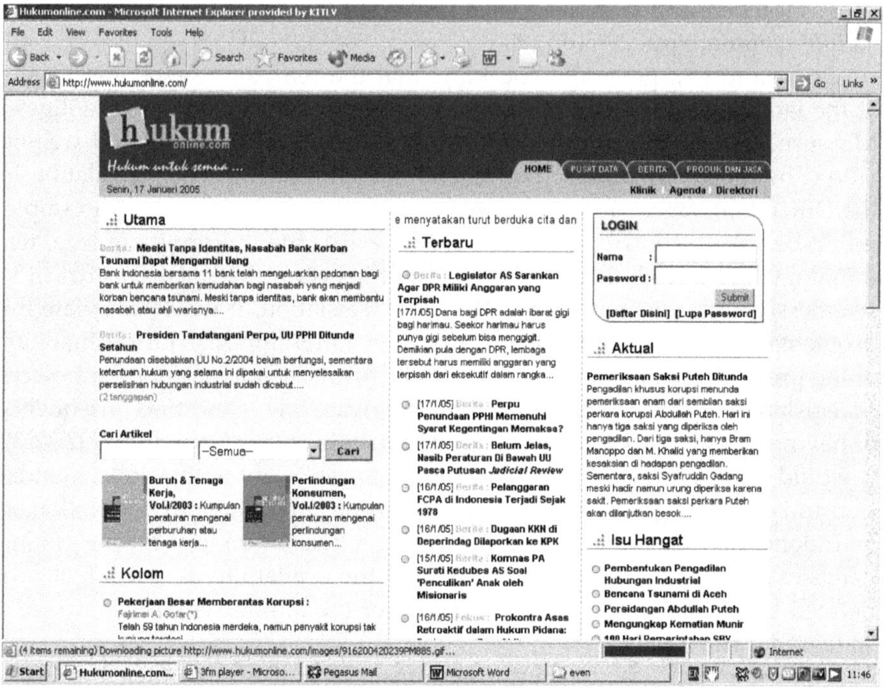


Fig. 28. Website HukumOnline (courtesy HukumOnline/Ibrahim Assegaf, S.H.)

either. The last few decades have already seen the translation into Indonesian of major handbooks, and other sources of law in Dutch have begun to be opened up. These initiatives merit continuation, with a crucial role reserved for jurists who know Dutch and are interested in the Dutch estate.[39]

The development of legal usage in Indonesia is likely to gain the most impetus, however, from measures that do not take themes such as 'bahasa' (language) or 'peristilahan' (terminology) as their remit but concentrate on 'hukum' (law) instead. One such measure would be to provide public access to not only the laws and regulations in the Dutch language but to *all* legislation currently in force and to other authoritative texts (such as court decisions and public registers) (see Churchill 1992). Initiatives that make use of the new, cheap and easily accessible medium that is the internet (www.hukumonline.

[39] The Erasmus Taalcentrum/Pusat Bahasa Belanda Erasmus in Jakarta is an excellent gauge for this interest (see www.erastaal.or.id). The centre has been providing courses in Dutch at various locations in Indonesia since 1981 and has links with the universities that teach Dutch, whether as a course or a (compulsory or elective) subject, for example as part of reading law.

com, for instance), seem to be steps in the right direction. They contribute to the visualization of a clearly defined, set body of authoritative texts, the most important attribute of the law game.

Also to be continued, with might and main, are the initiatives to reform the teaching of law. Law students must be instructed in the law that is currently applicable and in addition be taught the ins and outs of the actual legal profession – the production of texts within the framework of an imagined reality that is based on authoritative texts and rooted in the legal community. In the long run, the power of persuasion of the law story must find expression in professional integrity.[40] One is encouraged by the constancy with which some Indonesian jurists and other professionals, even in times of severe adversity, have stood firm in testifying to and demonstrating their belief in the facticity of the law.[41] The idea of the rule of law is undergoing a revival that finds favour even with younger jurists, as evidenced by the establishment of organizations like the Masyarakat Transparansi Indonesia (MTI, Indonesian Society for Transparency, www.transparansi.or.id), the Pusat Studi Hukum dan Kebijakan Indonesia (PSHKI, Indonesian Research Centre for Law and Policy), the Lembaga Kajian dan Advokasi untuk Independensi Peradilan (LeIP, Indonesian Institute for the Study and Stimulation of the Independent Administration of Justice, www.leip.or.id) and the Indonesian Corruption Watch (ICW, www.antikorupsi.org). Whether or not the state under rule of law can truly be restored, whether or not the gamut of new organizations merely herald a new phase of fragmentation of the profession, will depend on the political choices made and concrete measures taken by the government and other official bodies in the years to come.

As it becomes possible, step by step, to play the law game by internationally accepted rules, Indonesians from among the various legal professions and in different places are bound to engage with one another in the system of law and its future. The centripetal forces will gain momentum and the centrifugal ones will diminish. The growing common beliefs and the reawakening faith in the law will better enable jurists to tune into each other's wavelengths and to translate the multitude of languages and notions into a wider, common framework, which eventuality also is conducive to the shaping and realizing of ideals and plans regarding a new national system of law and leg-

40 Compare with pp. 124-5. In a report produced on behalf of the United States Agency for International Development (USAID), legal adviser Patricia Kendall (2000:11) points out that a handful of students educated abroad can have a substantial impact: 'There is no substitute for significant exposure through education to societies strongly rooted in the rule of law. Of course, there is no immediate – if ever – measurable impact for such programs, but the ripple effect from contributions of one master's degree student may well equal or exceed the training provided by funding a half dozen seminars and workshops.'

41 See Lev 1976, 1978, 2000 and Pompe 1996:47-9, for example. Also see chapters III and IV.

Fig. 29. Website Universitas Brawijaya Law Faculty, Malang (courtesy Universitas Brawijaya Law Faculty)

islation.[42] Though a more gradual process than the radical scenario sketched by Tamanaha,[43] here, too, texts and terms derived from various epochs and languages (Indonesian, Dutch, English) will be interpreted within the framework of an increasingly consistent, Indonesian-language meaning system. Jurists will construct a new, joint lingual and textual history. With time, a new

42 Busthanul Arifin also linked the standardization of the legal language to the creation of a system of law on a national, Indonesian foundation (see Chapter I). He paid no attention, however, to the impact of the political marginalization of the law and the corruption within the legal world, that is to say, to the intervention of non-players in the game and the instability of the game board. Compare with Lev (1965b:306): 'The real transformation of the legal systems of former colonies depends largely on the formation of new ideals which will impel the law in fundamentally different directions from those of the colony'.

43 The strategies outlined by Tamanaha, one of which is given at the beginning of this section, aim to sever the link between the Micronesian tradition of law and American legal thinking so as to close the gap between the wholly autonomous operation of the Micronesian system of law and civic society (Tamanaha 1993:195-6).

basic legal language will develop.[44]

There is, however, a precondition for the above scenario. Jurists must be prepared to play the law game with integrity. To do so, they must be able to rely on the recognition and acceptance of the facticity of the law by colleagues, the powers that be and civilians alike. The justification for that reliance depends entirely on the choices of the main political actors, now and in the future. In turn, these actors will have to renounce their intervention in the law game, leaving it in the hands of the jurists.[45] The present aversion to the corruption and arbitrariness of the Orde Baru hopefully will continue to propel the reformation. And apart from internal lobbying for change by individuals and organizations, whether or not official, international developments, too, are able to provoke change – think of the globalization of trade, politics, human rights and so forth. Moreover, in the international arena, the story of the law has been accepted as authoritative for a very long time.

All in all, extensive change is required in many areas, including the society-wide turnabout of the mentality of civilians, jurists and politicians. The reformers of the law and the political set-up will have to possess a great deal of tenacity to bring all this about. But no matter how long the process, no matter how arduous the task, the restoration of the rule of law in Indonesia requires it.[46] Only once Indonesia has regained its credibility as a state under rule of law, can Indonesian jurists be confident that their texts matter, that their words count.

44 It would be a worthwhile undertaking to track the development of legal language usage in Malaysia over the next few decades. Attempts have been made for some time to add Malay to English as the official languages of the law. Daniel Lev has pointed out the resemblance between the objections to the use of Malaysian put forward by ethnic Indians and Chinese as well as Malaysians and those voiced against Indonesian as legal language (primitive, unsuitable and the like). It would stretch the imagination of many a Malaysian jurist to learn that Indonesian is actually used for this purpose (information provided on 26-6-2002).

45 This fits in with Mattei's classification (see p. 234). Otto (2000:8-10) summarizes the main forces that oppose the emergence of autonomous systems of law, being tradition, politics, economic strategies of conduct and the government apparatus.

46 In 1993 Lev wrote: 'It bears repeating that neither legal aid nor the wider NGO movement in Indonesia has generated enough power to compel state leadership to concede or compromise towards genuine constitutional reforms. Political power, resting firmly on a military-bureaucratic alliance, remains quite differently oriented. But ideologically the idea of constitutionalism has been solidly entrenched, fed in part by memories of the parliamentary years but also by the interests of influential social groups in a more restrained, accountable, and accessible political system. It is likely to persist and to sustain a long struggle, without a final outcome but [with] many compromises, adjustments, and adaptations in a recognizably Indonesian political evolution.' (Lev 2000:330, also see 326-9.)

# Bibliography

*Interviews*


Achadiati Ikram, Prof.dr. (10-2-1993)
Ananda Aviati, Ms. (28-4-1994)
Andi Hamzah S.H., Dr. (15-4-1994)
Arief Sidharta S.H., Dr. (16-4-1994)
Asep Iwan Iriawan S.H. (29-4-1994)
Asis Safioedin S.H. (19-2-1993)
Ateng Syafrudin S.H., Prof.dr. (1-3-1993)
Churchill JD, Gregory (25-4-1994)
Datja Patoppoi S.H. (4-5-1994)
Emmy Pangaribuan S.H., Prof. (12-2-1994)
Etty Haryati Djukardi S.H. (4-2-1994)
Gautama, Prof.mr.dr. Sudargo (8-3-1994)
Girindro Pringgodigdo S.H., LLM (26-2-1994)
Hadiman Djukardi S.H. (4-2-1994)
Hadjon S.H., Prof.dr. Ph.M. (12-9-1996)
Hafni Sjahruddin S.H. (29-2-1994)
Hajati Suroredjo S.H. (25-4-1994)
Hamid S. Attamimi S.H., Prof.dr. A. (9-2-1993, 25-1-1994, 30-4-1994)
Han Bing Siong, Mr. (28-11-1996)
Hartono Soerjopratikno S.H. (23-2-1993, 13-2-1994)
Husni Hasbullah S.H., Frieda (10-2-1993)
Iskandar Oeripkartadinata S.H. (17-4-1994)
Kartini Muljadi S.H. (2-3-1993, 23-4-1994)
Ko Swan Sik, Prof.mr.ddr. (20-6-2001)
Koesnadi Hardjasoemantri S.H., ML, Prof.dr. (11-2-1994, 5-5-1994)
Kumariah S.H., Dr. (16-4-1994)
Liem Goan Hwie/Robby Liem S.H. (19-2-1994)
Limahelu S.H., Prof.dr. Frans (19-2-1994)
Mardjono Reksodiputro S.H., MA, Prof. B. (2-3-1994, 2-5-1994, 1-6-2001)
Maria Sumardjono S.H., Prof.dr. (11-2-1994, 20-4-1994)
Mochtar Kusumaatmadja S.H., Prof.dr. (27-4-1994)
Moeliono, Prof.dr. Anton M. (5-3-1993, 26-2-1994, 13-4-1994, 10-5-1994)
Moeljatno S.H., Lamya (23-2-1993, 13-2-1994)
Moerdiati Soebagyo S.H. (18-2-1993)

Pasmans, Drs. Loek (10-5-1994)
Pattileuw S.H., U.R. (4-5-1994)
Purnadi Purbacaraka S.H., Prof.dr. (5-3-1993)
Purwoto Gandasubrata S.H. (11-9-1996)
Resink, Prof.mr. G.J. (24-1-1994, 15-4-1994, 11-5-1994)
Retnowulan Sutantio S.H. (11-2-1993, 23-2-1994, 29-4-1994)
Retta H.I. Hutagalung (28-4-1994)
Rochmat Soemitro S.H., Prof.dr. (2-2-1994)
Rusli Effendy S.H., Prof.dr. (4-5-1994)
Sahetapy S.H., Prof.dr. J.E. (18-2-1994)
Saleh Adiwinata S.H., Prof. (26-2-1993, 18-4-1994)
Siti Ismiati Yenie S.H. (6-5-1994)
Soelaeman Bachtiar Adiwidjaja, Drs. (26-2-1993, 3-2-1994)
Soerastri Isminingsih Djojodipoero S.H. (23-2-1993, 13-2-1994)
Soetojo Prawirohamidjojo, Prof.mr. R. (20-2-1993, 19-2-1994)
Souhoka S.H., M.H., Dr. Maarten L. (16-2-1994)
Sri Soemantri Martosoewignjo S.H., Prof.dr. (28-2-1993, 8-5-1994)
Sudikno Mertokusumo S.H., Prof.dr. (22-2-1993, 5-5-1994)
Sumardjono S.H., MPA, Prof.dr. Maria (22-2-1993)
Sunaryati Hartono S.H., Prof.dr. C.F.G. (15-2-1993, 14-4-1994)
Sunaryati Hartono S.H., Prof.dr. C.F.G., Made Sudiarsih S.H. and Agus Anwar S.H. (29-1-1994)
Takdir Alisjahbana, Prof.mr. St. (11-4-1994)
Teeuw, Prof.dr. A. (20-11-1996)
Wila Candrawila Supriadi S.H., Dr. (16-4-1994)
Zainal Abidin S.H., Prof. (3-5-1994)

## *Bibliography*

Affandi, Hernadi
1994 'Persoalan bahasa hukum dan perkembangannya di Indonesia', *Bisnis Indonesia*, 28-10-1994.

Ahmad, Sabaruddin
1976 'Sebuah tinjauan tentang penggunaan bahasa Indonesia dalam dunia hukum', in: *Simposium Bahasa dan Hukum; Diselenggarakan dalam rangka kerjasama BPHN dan FH USU pada tg. 25 s/d 27 Nop. 1974 di Medan/Prapat*, pp. 87-103. Jakarta: Binacipta.

Aiko, Kurasawa
1990 'Japanese educational policy in Java, 1942-1945', *Journal of the Japan-Netherlands Institute* 2:178-92. [Papers of the Dutch-Japanese Symposium on the History of Dutch and Japanese Expansion, in memory of the late Professor Nagazumi Akira, Tokyo and Kyoto, 9-14 October 1989.]

*Algemeen verslag Inlandsch onderwijs*
1901 *Algemeen verslag van het Inlandsch onderwijs in Nederlandsch Indië lopende over de jaren 1893 t/m 1897, met aanhangsel betreffende de jaren 1898 en 1899.* Batavia: Landsdrukkerij.

Algra, N.E. and H.R.W. Gokkel
1985 *Fockema Andreae's juridisch woordenboek.* Vijfde druk. Alphen aan den Rijn: Samson.

Alisjahbana, St. Takdir
1945 'Pendahoeloean', in: *Kamoes istilah. Djilid I: Asing-Indonesia,* pp. 3-9. Djakarta: Poestaka Rakjat.
1949 'The Indonesian language; By-product of nationalism', *Pacific Affairs* 22:388-92.
1967 'The modernization of the Indonesian-Malay language in the 19th and 20th century', in: St. Takdir Alisjahbana (ed.), *The modernization of languages in Asia,* pp. 181-210. Kuala Lumpur: The Malaysian Society of Asian Studies.
1974 'Language policy, language engineering and literacy in Indonesia and Malaysia', in: Joshua A. Fishman (ed.), *Advances in language planning,* pp. 391-416. The Hague: Mouton.
1976 'Bahasa hukum; Beberapa sumbangan pikiran menuju ke arah pembentukan dan pemakaian bahasa yang baik', in: *Simposium Bahasa dan Hukum; Diselenggarakan dalam rangka kerjasama BPHN dan FH USU pada tg. 25 s/d 27 Nop. 1974 di Medan/Prapat,* pp. 21-36. Jakarta: Binacipta.
1988 'Tumbuhnya bahasa Indonesia dan soal2nya', in: St. Takdir Alisjahbana, *Dari perjuangan dan pertumbuhan bahasa Indonesia; Kumpulan esai 1932-1957,* pp. 125-30. Jakarta: Dian Rakyat. [First published in *Pembina Bahasa Indonesia,* August 1949.]

Alwi, Hasan et al. (eds)
2000 *Bahasa Indonesia dalam era globalisasi; Pemantapan peran bahasa sebagai sarana pembangunan bangsa.* Jakarta: Pusat Pembinaan dan Pengembangan Bahasa.

Anderson, Benedict R.O'G.
1961 *Some aspects of Indonesian politics under the Japanese occupation, 1944-1945.* New York: Cornell University.
1972 *Java in a time of revolution; Occupation and resistance, 1944-1946.* Ithaca/London: Cornell University Press.
1985 *Imagined communities; Reflections on the origin and spread of nationalism.* Reprint. London: Verso. [First published 1983.]
1990a 'Sembah-sumpah; The politics of language and Javanese culture', in: Benedict R.O'G. Anderson, *Language and power; Exploring political cultures in Indonesia,* pp. 194-237. Ithaca/London: Cornell University Press. [First published 1984.]
1990b 'The languages of Indonesian politics', in: *Language and power; Exploring political cultures in Indonesia,* pp. 123-51. Ithaca/London: Cornell University Press. [First published 1966.]

André de la Porte, G.
1933 *Recht en rechtsbedeeling in Nederlandsch-Indië; Handleiding bij de beoefening van het Nederlandsch-Indische privaat- en strafrecht.* Tweede, herziene druk. The Hague: Belinfante.

Anwar, Khaidir
1985 *Indonesian; The development and use of a national language.* Second printing. Yogyakarta: Gadjah Mada University Press.

Arifin, Busthanul
1976 'Pokok-pokok ceramah dalam Symposium tentang Bahasa dan Hukum, yang diselenggarakan oleh LPHN pada tanggal 25 s/d 27 Nopember 1974 di Medan', in: *Simposium Bahasa dan Hukum; Diselenggarakan dalam rangka kerjasama BPHN dan FH USU pada tg. 25 s/d 27 Nop. 1974 di Medan/Prapat*, pp. 77-86. Jakarta: Binacipta.
1997 'Bahasa hukum kita', *Mimbar Hukum* 31:68-70.

Asbeck, F.M. van
1949 'Paul Scholten en de Rechtshogeschool', in: *Gedenkboek uitgegeven ter gelegenheid van het vijf en twintig jarig bestaan van het rechtswetenschappelijk hoger onderwijs in Indonesië op 28 october 1949*, pp. 7-13. Groningen/ Djakarta: Wolters.

Asser-Hartkamp
1989 *Mr. C. Asser's handleiding tot de beoefening van het Nederlands burgerlijk recht. Deel 2: Algemene leer der overeenkomsten.* Achtste druk, bewerkt door A.S. Hartkamp. Zwolle: Tjeenk Willink.

Aziz, M.A.
1955 *Japan's colonialism and Indonesia.* 's-Gravenhage: Nijhoff.

Bachtiar, Harsja W.
1972 'Kata penutup', in: Djajanto Supra and Anton J. Lake (eds), *Seminar Bahasa Indonesia 1972; Puntjak Pass, 2-3 Maret*, pp. 235-8. Flores: Nusa Indah.
1976 'The development of a common national consciousness among students from the Indonesian archipelago in the Netherlands', *Majalah Ilmu-ilmu Sastra Indonesia* 6, 2:31-44.

Badan Pembinaan Hukum Nasional
1989-90 *Laporan II Tim Penyusunan Kamus Hukum Perdata.* [Jakarta]: Badan Pembinaan Hukum Nasional, Proyek Peningkatan Kodifikasi Hukum Nasional.
1990-91 *Laporan akhir Tim Penyusunan Kamus Hukum Perdata; Kebendaan: Van zaken.* [Jakarta]: Badan Pembinaan Hukum Nasional, Proyek Peningkatan Kodifikasi Hukum Nasional.
1994-95 *Laporan akhir pembakuan istilah hukum; Umum.* [Jakarta]: Badan Pembinaan Hukum Nasional.
1995-96 *Laporan akhir pembakuan istilah hukum; Umum.* [Jakarta]: Badan Pembinaan Hukum Nasional.

Badudu, Yus
1983 'Masalah pengembangan bahasa Indonesia sebagai bahasa hukum', *Hukum dan Pembangunan* 13:223-32.

Badudu, J.S. (ed.)

[1996] *Analisis dan evaluasi tentang perkembangan 25 tahun penggunaan bahasa hukum.* Composed under the supervision of J.S. Badudu. Jakarta: Badan Pembinaan Hukum Nasional, Departemen Kehakiman.

*Bahasa hukum harus lugas*

1997 'Bahasa hukum harus lugas', *Kompas Online*, 1 November.

Bakhtin, Mikhail M.

1996 *The dialogic imagination; Four essays by M.M. Bakhtin.* Edited by Michael Holquist, translated [from the Russian] by Caryl Emerson and Michael Holquist. Tenth (paperback) printing. Austin: University of Texas Press. [First published in English 1981; first published in Russian 1975.]

1996a 'Discourse in the novel', in: M.M. Bakhtin, *The dialogic imagination; Four essays by M.M. Bakhtin*, pp. 259-422. Austin: University of Texas Press. [First published in English 1981, in Russian 1975.]

1999 *Speech genres and other late essays.* Translated by Vern W. McGee, edited by Caryl Emerson and Michael Holquist. Seventh paperback printing. Austin: University of Texas Press. [First published in English 1986, in Russian 1979.]

1999a 'The problem of speech genres', in: M.M. Bakhtin, *Speech genres and other late essays*, pp. 60-102. Austin: University of Texas Press. [First published in English 1986, in Russian 1979.]

1999b 'The problem of the text in linguistics, philology, and the human sciences; An experiment in philosophical analysis', in: M.M. Bakhtin, *Speech genres and other late essays*, pp. 103-31. Austin: University of Texas Press. [First published in English 1986, in Russian 1979.]

1999c 'Toward a methodology for the human sciences', in: M.M. Bakhtin, *Speech genres and other late essays*, pp. 159-72. Austin: University of Texas Press. [First published in English 1986, in Russian 1979.]

Beaufort, Henriëtte L.T. de

1954 *Cornelis van Vollenhoven, 1874-1933.* Haarlem: Tjeenk Willink.

Becker, A.L.

1988 'Attunement; An essay on philology and logophilia', in: P.V. Koskrity (ed.), *On the ethnography of communication: The legacy of Sapir; Essays in honor of Harry Hoijer 1984*, pp. 109-45. Malibu: Published for the UCLA Department of Anthropology by Undena Publications.

1992 'Silence across languages; An essay', in: C. Kramsch and Sally McConnell-Ginet (eds), *Text & context; Cross-disciplinary perspectives on language study*, pp. 115-23. Lexington, Mass.: Heath.

Bedner, Adriaan Willem

2000 *Administrative courts in Indonesia; A socio-legal study.* [Leiden]: n.n. [PhD thesis Universiteit Leiden.]

Benda, Harry J., James K. Irikura and Koichi Kishi (eds)

1965 *Japanese military administration in Indonesia; Selected documents.* New Haven, Conn.: Southeast Asia Studies, Yale University.

Benda-Beckmann, Keebet von
1984 *The broken stairways to consensus; Village justice and state courts in Minangkabau.* Dordrecht: Foris. [KITLV, Verhandelingen 106.]

Bergh, A. van den
1900 'Iets over de landraden; Een woord naar aanleiding van de voordracht van Mr. D. Mounier in het Indisch Genootschap te 's-Gravenhage op den 30en Maart j.l.', *Recht in Nederlandsch-Indië* 74:463-75.
1902 'Inlandsche rechtspraak', *Recht in Nederlandsch-Indië* 78:237-46.

Bergh, G.C.J.J. van den
1979 'Preadvies', in: G.C.J.J. van den Bergh, *Recht en taal; Preadvies Prof.Mr G.C.J.J. van den Bergh en Prof.Dr Jan M. Broekman*, pp. 1-76. Deventer: Kluwer.
1994a 'Inleiding; Jacob Israël de Haan (1881-1924) en de rechtstaal', in: G.C.J.J. van den Bergh, *De taal zegt meer dan zij verantwoorden kan; Een keuze uit de verspreide rechtskundig-signifische geschriften van Mr. Jacob Israël de Haan*, pp. ix-lix. Nijmegen: Ars Aequi Libri.
1994b *Geleerd recht; Een geschiedenis van de Europese rechtswetenschap in vogelvlucht.* Derde druk. Deventer: Kluwer.

Boekhoudt, W.
1916 'Een afscheidsgroet aan de jongeren onder mijne oud-collega's', *Indisch Tijdschrift van het Recht* 107:317-52.

Boeto
1929 'Het rijk der Barbaren', in: *Gedenkboek uitgegeven ter gelegenheid van de opheffing der Rechtsschool in 1928*, pp. 76-8. Weltevreden: Kolff.

Bongenaar, Karel E.M.
1992 Dutch support for the development of legislation in Indonesia; Some considerations with respect or with reference to a development project. The Hague: n.n. [Manuscript, 12-11-1992.]

Booth, Dwayne C.
1986 'Freedom of interpretation; Bakhtin and the challenge of feminist criticism', in: Gary Saul Morson (ed.), *Bakhtin; Essays and dialogues on his work*, pp. 145-76. Chicago: University of Chicago Press.

Bourchier, David
1999 'Positivism and Romanticism in Indonesian legal thought', in: Timothy Lindsey (ed.), *Indonesia; Law and society*, pp. 186-96. Sidney: The Federation Press.

Broekman, Jan M.
1979 'Preadvies', in: G.C.J.J. van den Bergh, *Recht en taal; Preadvies Prof.Mr G.C.J.J. van den Bergh en Prof.Dr Jan M. Broekman*, pp. 81-111. Deventer: Kluwer.

Brugmans, I.J. et al. (eds)
1960 *Nederlandsch-Indië onder Japanse bezetting; Gegevens en documenten over de jaren 1942-1945.* Franeker: Wever.

Budiarto, M.
2000 'Kegiatan pembakuan istilah, penyusunan, kamus, dan tesaurus hukum di Indonesia'. Paper, Seminar Access to Legal Information; Language, Dictionaries, Databases, Jakarta, 22-23 August.

Burns, Peter J.
1999 *The Leiden legacy; Concepts of law in Indonesia.* Jakarta: Pradnya Paramita. [Originally PhD thesis James Cook University, North Queensland, 1995.]

Buskens, Léon
1993 'Islamic commentaries and French codes; The confrontation and accomodation of two forms of textualization of family law in Morocco', in: Henk Driessen (ed.), *The politics of ethnographic reading and writing; Confrontations of Western and indigenous views*, pp. 65-100. Saarbrücken: Breitenbach.

Butt, Simon
1999 'The *eksekusi* of the *Negara Hukum*; Implementing judicial decisions in Indonesia', in: Timothy Lindsey (ed.), *Indonesia; Law and society*, pp. 247-57. Sidney: The Federation Press.

Churchill, Gregory
1992 *The development of legal information systems in Indonesia; Problems and progress to date.* Leiden: Van Vollenhoven Institute for Law and Administration in Non-Western Countries.

Clark, Katerina and Michael Holquist
1984 *Mikhail Bakhtin.* Cambridge, Mass.: Harvard University Press.

Cohen Stuart, J.W.T.
1907 'Oprichting van Inlandsche rechtscholen in Indië', *De Indische Gids* 29, II:1325-53.

Cooray, L.J. Mark
1985 *Changing the language of the law; The Sri Lanka experience.* Quebec: Les Presses de l'Université Laval.

Cover, Robert M.
1986 'Violence and the word', *Yale Law Journal* 95:1601-29.

Dahm, B.
[1969] *Sukarno and the struggle for Indonesian independence.* Translated from the German by Mary F. Somers Heidhues. Revised and updated edition of *Sukarnos Kampf um Indonesians Unabhängigkeit.* Ithaca, [N.Y.]: Cornell University Press.

Damian, Eddy and Robert N. Hornick (eds)
1971 *Bibliografi Hukum Indonesia 1945-1972.* Bandung: Lembaga Penelitian Hukum dan Kriminologi (UNPAD).
1974 *Bibliografi Hukum Indonesia 1945-1972.* Edisi ke-2. Bandung: Lembaga Penelitian Hukum & Kriminologi, Fakultas Hukum, Universitas Padjadjaran.

Danusuputro, Munadjat
1953 'Enige aantekeningen betreffende het onderwijs', *Indonesisch Bulletin* 8-7, pp. 75-84.

Darmokondo, S.K.
1981 'Kongres pemoeda2 Indonesia; Lahirnja "Soempah Pemoeda", 1928', in: A. Zainoel Ihsan and Pitut Soeharto, *Aku pemuda kemarin di hari esok; Kumpulan tulisan asli, lezing, pidato tokoh Pergerakan Kebangsaan, 1913-1938*, pp. 138-58. Jakarta: Jayasakti.

Deenik, A.C., G.H.H. Zandvoort and R. Sadikin
1929 *Gedenkboek uitgegeven ter gelegenheid van de opheffing der Rechtsschool in 1928.* Weltevreden: Kolff.

Dekker, Albert and Hanneke van Katwijk
1992 *Nederlands-Indische rechtsliteratuur; Register op de verhandelingen in het Indisch Tijdschrift van het Recht (1849-1950) en de Mededelingen van het Documentatiebureau voor Overzees Recht (1950-1958).* Leiden: KITLV Uitgeverij.
1993a *Recht en rechtspraak in Nederlands-Indië.* Leiden: KITLV Uitgeverij.
1993b *Nederlands-Indische jurisprudentie; Register op de geannoteerde rechtspraak in het Indisch Tijdschrift van het Recht (1849-1950) en de Mededelingen van het Documentatiebureau voor Overzees Recht (1950-1958).* Leiden: KITLV Uitgeverij.

*De wording der Rechtsschool*
1929 'De wording der Rechtsschool', in: *Gedenkboek uitgegeven ter gelegenheid van de opheffing der Rechtsschool in 1928*, pp. 35-52. Weltevreden: Kolff.

Dianggoro, Wiratmo
[1996] 'Peran BPHN dalam pembinaan bahasa hukum', in: J.S Badudu (ed.), *Analisis dan evaluasi tentang perkembangan 25 tahun penggunaan bahasa hukum*, pp. 49-51. Jakarta: Badan Pembinaan Hukum Nasional, Departemen Kehakiman.

Dievoet, E. van
1943 'Over de taal en den vorm van het Nederlandsch Burgerlijk Wetboek', in: *Album René Verdeyen*, pp. 337-50. Bruxelles: Manteau.

Dik, S.C. and J.G. Kooij
1979 *Algemene taalwetenschap.* Utrecht/Antwerpen: Het Spektrum.

Dissel, J. van
1913 '"Koerang terang"', *Koloniaal Tijdschrift* 2:55-7.

Djabarudi, Slamet
1992 'Bahasa hukum', *Forum Keadilan*, 14 May, pp. 62-3.

Djajadiningrat, Achmad
1936 *Herinneringen van Pangeran Aria Achmad Djajadiningrat.* Amsterdam: Kolff.

Djajadiningrat, Hoesein
1949 'Ter inleiding', in: *Gedenkboek uitgegeven ter gelegenheid van het vijf en twintig jarig bestaan van het rechtswetenschappelijk hoger onderwijs in Indonesië op 28 october 1949*, pp. 5-6. Groningen/Djakarta: Wolters.

Djamin, Awaloedin
1972 'Penggunaan bahasa dalam komunikasi resmi dibidang administrasi', in: Djajanto Supra and Anton J. Lake (eds), *Seminar Bahasa Indonesia 1972; Puntjak Pass, 2-3 Maret*, pp. 48-62. Flores: Nusa Indah.

Dore, John
1995 'The emergence of language from dialogue', in: Amy Mandelker (ed.), *Bakhtin in contexts; Across the disciplines*, pp. 151-76. Illinois: Northwestern University Press.

Drewes, G.W.J.
1948 *Van Maleis naar basa Indonesia.* Leiden: Brill. [Inaugural speech Leiden University.]

Driessen, Alfons Johan
1897 *Schets der werkzaamheden in strafzaken van den Nederlandsch-Indischen ambtenaar van het openbaar ministerie op Java en Madoera.* Amsterdam: Brinkman. [PhD thesis Universiteit van Amsterdam.]

Drucker, Henri L.
1916 *De Nederlandsche rechtstaal.* 's-Gravenhage: Belinfante. Two vols.

Dunné, J.M. van
1974 *Riskante rechtsvinding.* Deventer: Kluwer. [Inaugural speech Erasmus Universiteit Rotterdam.]
1988a *De magie van het woord; Juristen en hun omgang met teksten.* Arnhem: Gouda Quint. [Foundation day speech Erasmus Universiteit Rotterdam.]
1988b 'De taal van het Nieuw BW', in: W.M.J. Bekkers et al., *Meesterlijke taal; Over taal en taalgebruik in het recht*, pp. 29-45. Zwolle: Tjeenk Willink.

Echols, John M.
1963 *Preliminary checklist of Indonesian imprints during the Japanese period; March 1942 – August 1945.* New York: Cornell Modern Indonesia Project.

Eemeren, F.H. van, R. Grootendorst and F. Snoeck Henkemans
1997 *Handboek argumentatietheorie; Historische achtergronden en hedendaagse ontwikkelingen.* Groningen: Nijhoff.

Een Javaan
1907 'Inlandsche landraadvoorzitters', *De Locomotief*, 26 October.

Effendi, S.
1974 'Lembaga Bahasa Nasional dan pengembangan bahasa Indonesia', in: *Politik bahasa nasional; Laporan praseminar 29-31 Oktober 1974.* Jakarta: Lembaga Bahasa Nasional. [Compilation of papers, not consecutively paginated.]

Emerson, Caryl
1986 'The outer word and inner speech; Bakhtin, Vygotsky, and the internalization of language', in: Gary Saul Morson (ed.), *Bakhtin; Essays and dialogues on his work*, pp. 21-40. Chicago: University of Chicago Press.

*Enquête hooger onderwijs*
1921 'Enquête betreffende het hooger onderwijs in Nederlandsch-Indië, gehouden door eene commissie, ingesteld op initiatief van het Bataviaasch Genootschap voor Kunsten en Wetenschappen', in: *Notulen van de Algemeene en Directievergaderingen van het Bataviaasch Genootschap van Kunsten en Wetenschappen*, lixi-clxxi. [Extra supplement.]

Erawaty, A.F. Elly and J.S. Badudu (eds)
1996 *Kamus hukum ekonomi Inggris-Indonesia.* Jakarta: Komponen Pengembangan Hukum Ekonomi Proyek ELIPS.

*Eufemisme dalam bahasa hukum*
1997 'Eufemisme dalam bahasa hukum kurang tepat', *Kompas Online,* 16 October.

Fasseur, C.
1993 *De indologen; Ambtenaren voor de Oost, 1825-1950.* Amsterdam: Bert Bakker.
1995 *De weg naar het paradijs en andere Indische geschiedenissen.* Amsterdam: Bert Bakker.

Finch, Susan and Daniel Lev
1965 *Republic of Indonesia cabinets, 1945-1965.* Ithaca, NY: Modern Indonesia Project, Southeast Asia Program, Department of Asian Studies, Cornell University.

Fitzpatrick, Daniel
1999 'Beyond dualism; Land acquisition and law in Indonesia', in: Timothy Lindsey (ed.), *Indonesia; Law and society,* pp. 74-96. Sidney: The Federation Press.

Franken, H.
1985 *InLeiden tot de rechtswetenschap.* Met medewerking vanf P.W. Brouwer et al. Derde druk. Arnhem: Gouda Quint.

Gaakeer, Jeanne
1998 *Hope springs eternal; An introduction to the work of James Boyd White.* Amsterdam: Amsterdam University Press.

*Gedenkboek Indonesische Vereeniging*
[1924] *Gedenkboek 1908-1923.* ['s-Gravenhage]: Indonesische Vereeniging.

*Gedenkboek M.O.S.V.I.A.*
[1929] *Gedenkboek M.O.S.V.I.A. 1879-1929; Uitgegeven ter herdenking van het 50-jarig bestaan der middelbare opleidingsschool voor inlandsche ambtenaren te Bandoeng.* [Composed by A.C. Deenik, G.H.H. Zandvoort and R. Sadikin.] [Bandoeng]: [M.O.S.V.I.A?], Vorkink.

Giddens, Anthony
1997 *The constitution of society; Outline of the theory of structuration.* Fifth paperback reprint. Cambridge: Polity Press. [First published 1984.]

Gobée, E. and C. Adriaanse (eds)
1957 *Ambtelijke adviezen van C. Snouck Hurgronje 1889-1936. Eerste deel.* 's-Gravenhage: Nijhoff.

[Gonggrijp, G.L.]
1944 *Brieven van Opheffer aan de redactie van het Bataviaasch Handelsblad.* Nieuwe en herziene uitgave onder auspiciën van de Vereeniging 'Oost en West', derde druk. Maastricht: Leiter-Nypels. [Letters written under the pen name 'Opheffer'.]

Gouw Giok Siong
1968 'De rechtsontwikkeling in Indonesië na de souvereiniteitsoverdracht (slot)', *Weekblad voor Privaatrecht, Notaris-ambt en Registratie* 99:101-4.

Grijns, C.D.
1991 'Bahasa Indonesia avant la lettre in the 1920s', *Papers in Austronesian linguistics* 1:49-81.

Groeneboer, Kees
1993 *Weg tot het Westen; Het Nederlands voor Indië, 1600-1950.* Leiden: KITLV Uitgeverij. [Verhandelingen 158.]

Groot, G.R. de
1988 'Vertaalproblemen', in: D. Kokkini-Iatridou et al., *Een inleiding tot het rechtsvergelijkende onderzoek,* pp. 94-102. Deventer: Kluwer.

Haase, W.F.
1907 'Inlandsche landraadvoorzitters; Non tali auxilio', *De Locomotief,* 23 October.

Hadi
1929 'Uit het vereenigingsleven op de Rechtsschool', in: *Gedenkboek uitgegeven ter gelegenheid van de opheffing der Rechtsschool in 1928,* pp. 67-9. Weltevreden: Kolff.

Halim, Amran
1972 'Edjaan jang disempurnakan dan perkembangan ilmu bahasa', in: Djajanto Supra and Anton J. Lake (eds), *Seminar Bahasa Indonesia 1972; Puntjak Pass, 2-3 Maret,* pp. 140-157. Flores: Nusa Indah.

Han Bing Siong
1959-60 'Aneka warna hukum pidana; Berkenaan dengan diundangkannja Undang2 No. 73, 1958', *Hukum* 1959, 5-6:31-53 and *Hukum dan Masjarakat* 1960, 1:53-66.
1961a 'Menindjau beberapa sumber-pengenal jang ada daripada Kitab Undang-undang Hukum-Pidana', *Hukum dan Masjarakat* 3-4:51-79.
1961b 'Dasar-dasar pengetahuan tata hukum Indonesia dari ilmu hukum pidana Indonesia; Sanggahan terhadap Professor Mr Moeljatno', *Medan Ilmu Pengetahuan* 2:103-56.
1998 'The Japanese occupation of Indonesia and the administration of justice today; Myths and realities', *Bijdragen tot de Taal-, Land- en Volkenkunde* 154:416-56.
2002 [Review of] Daniel S. Lev, *Legal evolution and political authority in Indonesia; Selected essays* (The Hague, 2000), *Bijdragen tot de Taal-, Land- en Volkenkunde* 158:317-27.
2004 [Review of] A.W.H. Massier, *Van recht naar hukum; Indonesische juristen en hun taal, 1915-2000'* (Privately published, 2003), *Bijdragen tot de Taal-, Land- en Volkenkunde* 160:585-8.

Han Tiauw Hing
1948 'Overzicht van de rechtspraak tijdens de Japanse bezetting', *Mededelingen van de Chung Hwa Fa Lu She Hui (Chinese Juristen Kring) te Batavia* 1-4:1-16.

Hartono, C.F.G. Sunaryati
1979 *In search for new legal principles.* Bandung: Binacipta.

Hartowardojo, Harjadi S.
1972 'Pembinaan bahasa Indonesia sebagai bahasa moderen; Sebuah sanggahan', in: *Simposium Peristilahan; Jakarta, 2-3 Desember 1972.* [Jakarta]: [Lembaga Bahasa Nasional]. [Compilation of symposium papers in typescript, not consecutively paginated]

*Hasil Seminar Hukum Nasional Keempat*
1980 *Hasil Seminar Hukum Nasional Keempat, 1979/Report of the Fourth National Law Seminar, held in 1979.* [Jakarta]: Badan Pembinaan Hukum Nasional.

Hatta, Mohammad
1981 *Indonesian patriot; Memoirs.* Edited by C.L.M. Penders. Singapore: Gunung Agung.

Heeroma, K.
1956 'De erfenis van het Latijn', in: *Algemene aspecten van de grote cultuurtalen,* pp. 5-26. Den Haag: Servire.

Helsdingen, C.C. van
1922 'De nieuwe juridische opleiding in Nederland', *Indisch Tijdschrift van het Recht* 114:1-28.
1929a 'Rede [...], gehouden bij de opheffing van de Rechtsschool op 18 mei 1928', in: *Gedenkboek uitgegeven ter gelegenheid van de opheffing der Rechtsschool in 1928,* pp. 9-22. Weltevreden: Kolff.
1929b 'De Rechtsschool en de neutraliteit', in: *Gedenkboek uitgegeven ter gelegenheid van de opheffing der Rechtsschool in 1928,* pp. 70-5. Weltevreden: Kolff.
1929c 'De geest van het onderwijs op de Rechtsschool', in: *Gedenkboek uitgegeven ter gelegenheid van de opheffing der Rechtsschool in 1928,* pp. 63-6. Weltevreden: Kolff.
1929d 'Onderzoek naar de prestaties der afkomelingen der Rechtschool', in: *Gedenkboek uitgegeven ter gelegenheid van de opheffing der Rechtsschool in 1928,* pp. 59-60. Weltevreden: Kolff.

Hesselink, Linus
1992 *Geloven op gezag; Over de prikkel tot kritiek in het juridisch onderwijs.* Kluwer: Deventer. [PhD thesis Universiteit van Amsterdam.]

Hidayana, Irma
2002 'Bahasa hukumku melambung tinggi', *Jentera* 1 (August):96-104.

Hijma, Jac. and M.M. Olthof
1988 *Compendium van het Nederlands vermogensrecht; Leidraad voor het NBW met verwijzingen naar het BW.* Derde druk. Deventer: Kluwer.

*Himpunan Engelbrecht*
1989 *Himpunan peraturan perundang-undangan Republik Indonesia; Disusun menurut sistem Engelbrecht.* Jakarta: Ichtiar Baru-Van Hoeve.

Hirschkop, Ken
1989 'Introduction; Bakhtin and cultural theory', in: Ken Hirschkop and David Shepherd (eds), *Bakhtin and cultural theory,* pp. 1-38. Manchester: Manchester University Press.

*Hoekoem-adat dan bahasa Indonésia*
[1929] 'Hoekoem-adat dan bahasa Indonésia', *Indonésia Raja*, specimen copy, pp. 7-10.

Hofhuis, H.F.M.
1988 'De taal van de rechter', in: W.M.J. Bekkers et al., *Meesterlijke taal; Over taal en taalgebruik in het recht*, pp. 51-63. Zwolle: Tjeenk Willink.

Hogendorp, Dirk van
1799 *Bericht van den tegenwoordigen toestand der Bataafsche bezittingen in Oost-Indië en den handel op dezelve*. N.p.: n.n.

*Hoger onderwijs*
1953 'Opvoeding, onderwijs en cultuur; Hoger onderwijs', *Indonesisch Bulletin* 6:9-15. [Originally published in *Indonesian Affairs*.]

Holquist, Michael
1996 'Introduction', in: M.M. Bakhtin, *The dialogic imagination; Four essays by M.M. Bakhtin*, pp. xv-xxxiii. Austin: University of Texas Press.

Hond, Bas den
2002 'Het Engels is van iedereen', *Trouw*, 29 August. [Interview with Marc van Oostendorp.]

Hooykaas, C.
1939 'Modern Maleisch, zijn verspreiding, bruikbaarheid en toekomst', *Koloniale Studiën* 23-5:405-38.
1949 'Het onderwijs in Indonesische talen aan de Rechtshoogeschool en Juridische Faculteit in verleden, heden en toekomst', in: *Gedenkboek uitgegeven ter gelegenheid van het vijf en twintig jarig bestaan van het rechtswetenschappelijk hoger onderwijs in Indonesië op 28 october 1949*, pp. 143-9. Groningen/Djakarta: Wolters.

Husein, Yunus and Retno Sunggingsari
1980 'Catatan riset; Laporan penelitian pembakuan istilah hukum', *Hukum dan Pembangunan* 10:532-6.

Idema, H.A.
1938 *Leerboek van het landraad-strafprocesrecht in zaken van misdrijf*. Leiden: Brill.

Immink, A.J.
1882 *De regterlijke organisatie van Nederlandsch-Indië*. 's-Gravenhage: Stemberg.
1889 *De regtspleging voor de inlandsche regtbanken in Nederlandsch-Indië. Eerste deel*. Batavia: Van Dorp.

Isa, Zubaidah
1972 *Printing and publishing in Indonesia, 1602-1970*. N.p.: n.n., Ann Arbor, Michigan: University Microfilms International. [PhD thesis Indiana University, Bloomington, Indiana.]

Israël de Haan, Jacob
1994 *De taal zegt meer dan zij verantwoorden kan; Een keuze uit de verspreide rechtskundig-significhe geschriften van Mr. Jacob Israël de Haan*. Verzameld en ingeleid door Govaert C.J.J. van den Bergh. Nijmegen: Ars Aequi Libri.

*Jaarboekje Rechtshoogeschool*
1936 *Jaarboekje der Rechtshoogeschool te Batavia, 1936.* Batavia: Landsdrukkerij.

Jansen, C.J.H.
1991 'De verhouding tussen wetenschap en praktijk in de juridische opleiding van de 18e en 19e eeuw', *Nederlands Juristenblad* 66:564-71.

Jaspan, M.A.
1965 'In quest of new law; The perplexity of legal syncretism in Indonesia', *Comparative Studies in Society and History* 7:252-66.

Jedamski, Doris
1992 *Die Institution Literatur und der Prozess ihrer Kolonisation; Entstehung, Entwicklung und Arbeitsweise des Kantoor voor de Volkslectuur 'Balai Poestaka' in Niederländisch-Indien zu Beginn dieses Jahrhunderts.* Münster: Lit. [Originally PhD thesis Hamburg, 1990.]
1997 'De taalpolitiek van Balai Poestaka', in: Kees Groeneboer (ed.), *Koloniale taalpolitiek in Oost en West; Nederlands-Indië, Suriname, Nederlandse Antillen, Aruba,* pp. 159-83. Amsterdam: Amsterdam University Press.

*Jentera*
2002 *Jentera; Jurnal hukum.* Edisi 01, August.

Johannes, H.
1972 'Ejaan jang disempurnakan dan pengembangan istilah-istilah ilmiah', in: Djajanto Supra and Anton J. Lake (eds), *Seminar Bahasa Indonesia 1972; Puntjak Pass, 2-3 Maret,* pp. 93-124. Flores: Nusa Indah.

Jones, Russell
1976 'Indonesia; Language and nation-building', in: George W. Keeton and Georg Schwarzenberger, *The year book of world affairs* 30:190-204. London: Stevens [for] the London Institute of World Affairs.

Jonkers, J.E.
1940 *Het vooronderzoek en de telastelegging in het landraad-strafproces.* Groningen/Batavia: Wolters.

Jonkman, J.A.
1971 *Het oude Nederlandsch-Indië; Memoires van mr. J.A. Jonkman.* Assen: Van Gorcum.

Kahin, George McTurnan
1952 *Nationalism and revolution in Indonesia.* New York: Cornell University Press.

*Kamoes istilah*
1945 *Kamoes istilah. Djilid I: Asing-Indonesia.* [With a preface by St. Takdir Alisjahbana.] Djakarta: Poestaka Rakjat.

Kartodirdjo, R.O.
1947 'De rechtspraak op Java en Madoera tijdens de Japansche bezetting 1942-1945', *Tijdschrift van het Recht* 156:8-21.

Kendall, Patricia
2000 'The course of legal system reform in Indonesia under President Wahid; The first 120 days'. [Report on behalf of USAID.]

*Kesimpulan Seminar Hukum Nasional ke III*
1974 *Kesimpulan Seminar Hukum Nasional ke III, 11-15 Maret di Surabaya.* Jakarta: Lembaga Pembinaan Hukum Nasional.

Keuchenius, Frans D.
[2002] *Herwonnen jaren; Terug naar 1942-1946.* [Zutphen]: [Grafitel.]

*Kitab himpunan perundang-undangan*
1957 *Kitab himpunan perundang-undangan Negara Republik Indonesia. Djilid I.* [Partly translated from the Dutch by K.H. Husin.] Djakarta: Kementerian Penerangan.

*Kitab Undang2 Hukum Perdata*
1957 *Kitab Undang2 Hukum Perdata.* Diterdjemahkan oleh R. Subekti dan R. Tjitrosudibio. Djakarta: Pradnya Paramita.

*Kitab Undang2 Hukum Pidana*
[ca. 1969] *Kitab Undang2 Hukum Pidana.* Diterdjemahkan oleh Moeljatno. Tjetakan ke-6. Jogjakarta: Seksi Pidana Universitas Gadjah Mada.

*Kitab Undang2 Hukum Pidana Indonesia*
1960 *Kitab Undang2 Hukum Pidana Indonesia.* [Diterdjemahkan] oleh A.W. Djumena. 18th, revised edition. Djakarta: Balai Pustaka.

*Kitab2 undang2 Republik Indonesia*
1954 *Kitab2 undang2, undang2 dan peraturan2 serta Undang2 Dasar Sementara Republik Indonesia; De wetboeken, wetten en verordeningen benevens de Voorlopige Grondwet van de Republiek Indonesië.* Uitgegeven door W.A. Engelbrecht, bewerkt door E.M.L. Engelbrecht. Leiden: Sijthoff.
1960 *Kitab2 undang2, undang2 dan peraturan2 serta Undang2 Dasar 1945 Republik Indonesia; De wetboeken, wetten en verordeningen benevens de Grondwet van 1945 van de Republiek Indonesië.* Uitgegeven door W.A. Engelbrecht, bewerkt door E.M.L. Engelbrecht. Leiden: Sijthoff; Bruxelles: Manteau.

*Kitab Undang-undang Hukum Perdata*
1992 *Kitab Undang-undang Hukum Perdata; Burgerlijk wetboek.* Diterjemahkan oleh R. Subekti dan R. Tjitrosudibio. Cetakan keduapuluh lima. Jakarta: Pradnya Paramita.

*Kitab Undang-undang Hukum Pidana*
1983 *Kitab Undang-undang Hukum Pidana; Terjemahan resmi oleh Tim Penerjemah Badan Pembinaan Hukum Nasional.* BPHN: Sinar Harapan.

Koesnodiprodjo (ed.)
[ca. 1951] *Himpunan undang2, peraturan2, penetapan Pemerintah Republik Indonesia 1945.* Djakarta: Seno.

Koesnoe, H. Moh.
1991 'Pemahaman dan penggarapan hukum kodifikasi dalam kalangan praktek dan teori hukum kita dewasa ini', *Varia Peradilan* 73:123-36.

Kollewijn, R.D.
1955 *Intergentiel recht; Verzameling opstellen over intergentiel privaatrecht.* 's-Gravenhage: Van Hoeve.

Kollewijn, R.D. and R. van Dijk
[1948] *Staatsrecht en rechterlijke organisatie van Indonesië in overgangstijd.* N.p.: n.n. [Typescript.]

Konsorsium Ilmu Hukum
1991 *Laporan studi penataan fakultas, jurusan dan program studi pada perguruan tinggi dalam bidang ilmu hukum.* Jakarta: Direktorat Jenderal Pendidikan Tinggi, Departemen Pendidikan dan Kebudayaan.

Kridalaksana, Harimurti
1975 'Tata cara standardisasi dan pengembangan bahasa nasional', in: *Politik bahasa nasional; Laporan seminar, Jakarta 25-28 Februari 1975*, pp. 42-52. Jakarta: Lembaga Bahasa Nasional.

Kusumaatmadja, Mochtar
1976 'Kata sambutan Menteri Kehakiman pada Simposium "Bahasa & Hukum", tanggal 25 Nopember 1974 di Medan', in: *Simposium Bahasa dan Hukum; Diselenggarakan dalam rangka kerjasama BPHN dan FH USU pada tg. 25 s/d 27 Nop. 1974 di Medan/Prapat*, pp. 7-13. Jakarta: Binacipta.

Kwantes, R.C.
1978 *De ontwikkeling van de nationalistische beweging in Nederlandsch-Indie; Bronnenpublicatie. Tweede stuk: Medio 1923 – 1928.* Groningen: Wolters-Noordhoff.

Lancée, Laura
2001 *Nederlandse vertaling van het Ontwerp wetboek van Strafrecht van de Republiek Indonesië (versie 1999).* Vertaald [en van commentaar voorzien] door Laura Lancée. Leiden: Centre for International Legal Cooperation.

*Law reform in Indonesia*
[1997] *Law reform in Indonesia; Diagnostic assessment of legal development in Indonesia (IDF Grant No. 28557). Volume I.* Prepared by Ali Budiardjo, Nugroho, Reksodiputro (in cooperation with Mochtar, Karuwin and Komar) and Cyberconsult. Jakarta: Cyberconsult/Siber Konsultan.

*Lembaran Negara*
1950- *Lembaran Negara Republik Indonesia.* Djakarta: Sekretariat Negara R.I./ Departemen Penerangan.

Lev, Daniel S.
1965a 'The politics of judicial development in Indonesia', *Comparative Studies in Society and History* 7:173-99.
1965b 'The lady and the banyan tree', *American Journal of Comparative Law* 14:282-307.
1972 'Judicial institutions and legal culture in Indonesia', in: Claire Holt (ed.), *Culture and politics in Indonesia*, pp. 246-318. Ithaca: Cornell University Press.
1973a 'Bush lawyers in Indonesia; Stratification, representation, and brokerage'. Berkeley: University of California. [Working Paper no. 1, Berkeley, UC Law and Society Program.]
1973b 'Judicial unification in post-colonial Indonesia', *Indonesia* 16:1-37.
1976 'Origins of the Indonesian advocacy', *Indonesia* 16:135-69.
1978 'Judicial authority and the struggle for an Indonesian *rechtsstaat*', *Law and Society Review* 12:37-70.
1985 'Colonial law and the genesis of the Indonesian state', *Indonesia* 40:57-74.

1999 'Reformasi?' [Opening speech seminar Montreal, 10-5-1999.]
2000 'Social movements, constitutionalism, and human rights', in: Daniel S. Lev, *Legal evolution and political authority in Indonesia; Selected essays*, pp. 321-36. The Hague: Kluwer Law International. [First published 1993.]

Linden, M.L.M.
1911 'De Inlandsche landraadvoorzitters', *Indisch Tijdschrift van het Recht* 97:22-9.

Lindsey, Timothy
1999 'From rule of law to law of the rulers – to Reformation?', in: Timothy Lindsey (ed.), *Indonesia; Law and society*, pp. 11-20. Sidney: The Federation Press.

Locher-Scholten, E.B.
1971 'De Stuw, tijdsrekening en teken des tijds', *Tijdschrift voor Geschiedenis* 84:36-65.

Logemann, J.H.A.
1955 *Het staatsrecht van Indonesië; Het formele systeem*. Derde herziene druk. 's-Gravenhage/Bandoeng: Van Hoeve.
1962 *Nieuwe gegevens over het ontstaan van de Indonesische grondwet van 1945*. Amsterdam: Noord-Hollandsche uitg. mij.

Loth, M.A.
1984 *Taal en recht; Een kleine methodologie*. Arnhem: Gouda Quint.

Lubis, Madong
1954 'Bahasa Indonesia didalam pergaulan sehari-hari', *Medan Bahasa* 4-7/8:89-95. [Preliminary advice Kongres Bahasa Indonesia II, Medan, 28 October – 2 November.]

Lubis, Mochtar
1972 'Penggunaan bahasa dalam pers', in: Djajanto Supra and Anton J. Lake (eds), *Seminar Bahasa Indonesia 1972; Puntjak Pass, 2-3 Maret*, pp. 63-70. Flores: Nusa Indah.

Lubis, Todung Mulya
1999 'The *Rechtsstaat* and human rights', in: Timothy Lindsey (ed.), *Indonesia; Law and society*, pp. 171-85. Sidney: The Federation Press.

Mahadi
1976 'Hukum sebagaimana tercermin dalam pepatah/pribahasa di beberapa daerah', in: *Simposium Bahasa dan Hukum; Diselenggarakan dalam rangka kerjasama BPHN dan FH USU pada tg. 25 s/d 27 Nop. 1974 di Medan/Prapat*, pp. 37-50. Jakarta: Binacipta.

Mahadi and Sabaruddin Ahmad
1979 *Pembinaan bahasa hukum Indonesia*. [Jakarta]: Binacipta.

Mahadi et al. (eds)
1975 *Simposium Bahasa dan Hukum di Medan dan Parapat; Diselenggarakan oleh FHUSU, Medan/BPHN Jakarta tg. 25-27 Nop. 1974*. Medan: Fakultas Hukum (FH) dan Pengetahuan Masyarakat, Universitas Sumatera Utara (USU).

Maier, H(endrik) M.J.
1985 *Fragments of reading; The Malay Hikayat Merong Mahawangsa.* Alblasserdam: Kanters.
1993 'From heteroglossia to polyglossia; The creation of Malay and Dutch in the Indies', *Indonesia* 56:37-65.
1997 '"We are playing relatives"; Riau, the cradle of reality and hybridity', *Bijdragen tot de Taal-, Land- en Volkenkunde* 153:672-98.

Massier, Ab (A.W.H.)
forthcoming 'Translations of colonial law into Malay and Indonesian; An introduction'.

Massier, Ab and Marjanne Termorshuizen-Arts (eds)
2000 *Indonesisch-Nederlands woordenboek privaatrecht.* Leiden: Koninklijk Instituut voor Taal-, Land- en Volkenkunde (KITLV). Six vols.

Mattei, Ugo
1997 'Three patterns of law; Taxonomy and change in the world's legal systems', *The American Journal of Comparative Law* 45:5-44.

Mayer, L.Th.
1932 *Practisch Maleisch-Hollandsch en Hollandsch-Maleisch handwoordenboek; Benevens een "kort begrip der Maleische woordvorming en spraakleer".* Vijfde druk. 's-Gravenhage: Van Dorp.

*Mededeelingen der Regeering*
1924 *Mededeelingen der Regeering omtrent enkele onderwerpen van algemeen belang (april 1924).* Weltevreden: Landsdrukkerij.

Meijer, Hans
1994 *Den Haag-Djakarta; De Nederlands-Indonesische betrekkingen 1950-1962.* Utrecht: Het Spectrum.

Mellinkoff, David
1990 *The language of the law.* Seventh printing, paperback edition. Boston: Little, Brown and Company. [First published 1963.]

Miert, Hans van
1995 *Een koel hoofd en een warm hart; Nationalisme, Javanisme en jeugdbeweging in Nederlands-Indië, 1918-1930.* Amsterdam: De Bataafsche Leeuw.

Moeliono, Anton M.
1975 'Ciri-ciri bahasa Indonesia yang baku', in: *Politik bahasa nasional; Laporan seminar, Jakarta 25-28 Februari 1975,* pp. 33-40. Jakarta: Lembaga Bahasa Nasional.
1976 'Asas dan kaidah umum bahasa Indonesia dan pembinaan bahasa umum', in: *Simposium Bahasa dan Hukum; Diselenggarakan dalam rangka kerjasama BPHN dan FH USU pada tg. 25 s/d 27 Nop. 1974 di Medan/Prapat,* pp. 14-20. Jakarta: Binacipta.
1981 *Pengembangan dan pembinaan bahasa; Ancangan alternatif di dalam perencanaan bahasa.* Jakarta: Djambatan.
1984 *Santun bahasa.* Jakarta: Gramedia.
1989 'Bahasa Indonesia dalam akta notaris', *Media Notariat* 4:239-48.

2000 'Bahasa dan peristilahan dalam konteks hukum dan perundang-undangan'. Paper, Seminar Access to Legal Information; Language, Dictionaries, Databases, Jakarta, 22-23 August.

Moeliono, Tristam

2000 [No title.] Paper, Seminar Access to Legal Information; Language, Dictionaries, Databases, Jakarta, 22-23 August.

Moeljatno

1954 'Usul tentang naskah Kitab Undang-undang Hukum Pidana dalam bahasa Indonesia', *Hukum* 1:3-20.

1960 *Benarkah ada kekeliruan terhadap hukum jang berlaku dilapangan hukum pidana bertalian dengan Undang-undang th. 1946 No. 1 dan Undang-undang tahun 1948 No. 73?* [Djogjakarta]: Fakultas Hukum Universitas Gadjah Mada. [Foundation day speech 21-12-1960.]

1980 *Azas-azas hukum pidana.* [Reprint.] [Jogjakarta]: Gadjah Mada University Press.

1981 'Segi hukum dari perbuatan yang mengakibatkan matinya orang', in: *Kuliah umum di F.K.I.P. Muhammadiyah Surakarta, pada tanggal 7 Maret 1964 [dan] kuliah umum di U.I.I. Yogyakarta, di Purwokerto, pada tanggal 12 September 1963,* pp. 25-49. [Reprint.] Djogjakarta: Gadjah Mada University Press.] [Public lecture U.I.I. Djogjakarta, Purwokerto, 12-9-1963.]

Morson, Gary Saul

1986 'Who speaks for Bakhtin?' in: Gary Saul Morson (ed.), *Bakhtin; Essays and dialogues on his work,* pp. 1-19. Chicago: University of Chicago Press.

Morson, Gary Saul and Caryl Emerson

1990 *Mikhail Bakhtin; Creation of a prosaics.* Stanford, Calif.: Stanford University Press.

Mounier, D.

1900 'Iets over de landraadvoorzitters op Java en Madoera; Onder meer hunnen rechtspraak als alleensprekend rechter', *Verslagen der algemeene vergaderingen; Indisch Genootschap, 's-Gravenhage,* pp. 141-64. The Hague: Het Genootschap.

Muljadi, S.W. Rudjiati

1974 'Pengantar ketua Proyek Pengembangan Bahasa dan Sastra Indonesia dan Daerah pada Praseminar Politik Bahasa Nasional', in: *Politik bahasa nasional; Laporan praseminar 29-31 Oktober 1974.* Jakarta: Lembaga Bahasa Nasional. [Compilation of papers, not consecutively paginated. ]

1975 'Pengantar; Seminar Politik Bahasa Nasional', in: *Laporan seminar, Jakarta 25-28 Februari 1975,* pp. 4-7. Jakarta: Lembaga Bahasa Nasional.

1976 'Lembaga Bahasa Nasional serta hasil pekerjaan Komisi Istilah khusus di bidang hukum', in: *Simposium Bahasa dan Hukum; Diselenggarakan dalam rangka kerjasama BPHN dan FH USU pada tg. 25 s/d 27 Nop. 1974 di Medan/Prapat,* pp. 58-62. Jakarta: Binacipta.

Munneke, Harold F.

1986 'Indonesië op zoek naar zijn constitutionele identiteit', *Civis Mundi* 25:92-9.

Nasoetion, Andi Hakim
1972 'Penggunaan bahasa dalam ilmu pengetahuan', in: Djajanto Supra and Anton J. Lake (eds), *Seminar Bahasa Indonesia 1972; Puntjak Pass, 2-3 Maret*, pp. 39-47. Flores: Nusa Indah.

Natabaya, H.A.S.
2000 'Bahasa Indonesia dalam wacana hukum', in: Hasan Alwi et al. (eds), *Bahasa Indonesia dalam era globalisasi; Pemantapan peran bahasa sebagai sarana pembangunan bangsa*, pp. 301-8. Jakarta: Pusat Pembinaan dan Pengembangan Bahasa.

Nazif, Mohammad
[1924] 'Het nationale recht', in: *Gedenkboek 1908-1923*, pp. 64-72. [The Hague]: Indonesische Vereeniging.

Nemoo
1900 'Pak Redjo of de slingerpaden van het recht', *Tijdschrift voor het Binnenlandsch Bestuur* 19:359-62.

Neytzell de Wilde, A.
1913 'De opleidingsscholen voor Inlandsche ambtenaren en Inlandsche rechtskundigen op Java', *Verslagen der algemeene vergaderingen van het Indisch Genootschap* 1913-14, pp. 69-112.
1929 'Aanvang en einde; Eenige herinneringen en indrukken', in: *Gedenkboek uitgegeven ter gelegenheid van de opheffing der Rechtsschool in 1928*, pp. 27-34. Weltevreden: Kolff.

Oei Tjoe Tat
1995 *Memoar Oei Tjoe Tat, pembantu Presiden Soekarno*. Jakarta: Hasta Mitra.

*Oendang-Oendang Pembesar*
1942 *Oendang-Oendang dari Pembesar Balatentara Dai Nippon; Nomor 1 sampai 20*. Betawi: Dai Nippon Gunseibu.

Oka, I Gusti Ngurah Oka
1975 'Pembinaan pengajaran bahasa Indonesia', in: *Politik bahasa nasional; Laporan seminar, Jakarta 25-28 Februari 1975*, pp. 54-73. Jakarta: Lembaga Bahasa Nasional.

Olivier, Nic
1994 'The 1993 Constitution and the languages of South Africa'. Paper, Conference [on] the Culture of Multilinguality, Unisa, Pretoria, 3/5-2-1993. [Including references to 1994 constitutional amendments.]

Omar, Abdul Hamid Bin
1991 'Ucapan dasar di Seminar Bahasa Malaysia Badan Kehakiman', *Malayan Law Journal* 60:xiii-xv.

*Openbare bibliotheken*
1953 'Openbare bibliotheken', *Indonesisch Bulletin* 5:19-23. [First published in *Indonesian Affairs* 1952, 5-6.]

*Opening Rechtshoogeschool*
1925 *Opening der Rechtshoogeschool te Batavia op 28 october 1924*. Batavia: Volkslectuur.

*Orang Indonesia jang terkemoeka*
1973 *Orang Indonesia jang terkemoeka di Djawa*. [Tjetakan oelang.] Djakarta: Gunseikanbu. [Originally published (stencilled) 1944.]

Otto, J.M.
1992 'Recht in ontwikkelingslanden; Object en benaderingswijzen', in: Societas Iuridica Grotius (ed.), *Eruditia ignorantia; Vijftien opstellen bij het vijftiende lustrum van Societas Iuridica Grotius en de vierhonderdentiende geboortedag van Grotius*, pp. 95-119. Arnhem: Gouda Quint.
2000 *Reële rechtszekerheid in ontwikkelingslanden.* [Leiden: Universiteit Leiden.] [Inaugural speech Leiden University.]

Otto, J.M. and S. Pompe
1989 'The legal Oriental connection', in: Willem Otterspeer (ed.), *Leiden Oriental connections 1850-1950*, pp. 230-49. Leiden: Brill.

*Panduan penyusunan kamus bidang ilmu*
1993 *Panduan penyusunan kamus bidang ilmu.* Jakarta: Departemen Pendidikan dan Kebudayaan.

Peters, A.A.G.
1993 'Recht als kritische discussie', in A.A.G. Peters, *Recht als kritische discussie; Een selectie uit het werk van A.A.G. Peters*, pp. 209-38. Arnhem: Gouda Quint.

Piepers, M.C.
1884 *Macht tegen recht; De vervolging der justitie in Nederlandsch Indië. Eerste gedeelte.* Batavia: Van Dorp.

Pigeaud, Th.
1938 *Javaans-Nederlands handwoordenboek.* Groningen: Wolters.
[ca. 1978] *Nederlands-Javaans handwoordenboek.* [Reprint.] Groningen: Wolters-Noordhoff. [First published 1948.]

Pilon, J.B.R.J.F.
1920 'Achterstand bij de landraden en hoe daaraan een einde te maken', *Indisch Tijdschrift van het Recht* 112:30-7.

Poeze, Harry A.
1986 *In het land van de overheerser; I: Indonesiërs in Nederland, 1600-1950.* Tweede druk. Dordrecht/Cinnaminson: Foris.
1989 'Indonesians at Leiden University', in: Willem Otterspeer (ed.), *Leiden Oriental connections 1850-1950*, pp. 250-79. Leiden: Brill.

*Politik bahasa nasional*
1974 *Politik bahasa nasional; Laporan praseminar 29-31 oktober 1974.* Jakarta: Lembaga Bahasa Nasional. [Compilation of papers, not consecutively paginated. ]
1975 *Politik bahasa nasional; Laporan seminar, Jakarta 25-28 Februari 1975.* Jakarta: Lembaga Bahasa Nasional.

Pompe, S. (Sebastiaan van Hoeij Schilthouwer Pompe)
1988 'Mixed marriages in Indonesia; Some comments on the law and the literature', *Bijdragen tot de Taal-, Land- en Volkenkunde* 144:259-75.
1993 'A short review of doctoral theses in the Netherlands-Indies accepted at the Faculty of Law of Leiden University in the period 1850-1940', *Indonesia* 56:67-88. [Including a list of PhD theses composed by C. de Waaij-Vosters.]

1994 *De doorwerking van het Nederlandse recht in Indonesië; Over een stervend lichaam en een levende geest.* Leiden: Oosters Genootschap in Nederland. [Lecture 10-12-1991.]

1996 *The Indonesian Supreme Court; Fifty years of judicial development.* [PhD thesis Universiteit Leiden.]

1997 'The effects of the Japanese administration on the judiciary in Indonesia', in: Peter Post and Elly Touwen-Bouwsma (eds), *Japan, Indonesia and the war; Myths and realities,* pp. 51-63. Leiden: KITLV Press. [Verhandelingen 173.]

1999a '"Absen dari Reformasi"; The Indonesian judiciary in the face of history', *Indonesian Law and Administration Review* 5-1:73-81.

1999b *De Indonesische algemene verkiezingen 1999.* Leiden: KITLV Uitgeverij.

Pringgodigdo, A.G.

1954 'Bahasa Indonesia didalam perundang-undangan dan administrasi', *Medan Bahasa* 4-7/8:52-8. [Preadvies Kongres Bahasa Indonesia II, Medan, 28 October – 2 November.]

Prodjodikoro, Wirjono

[1974] *Kenang-kenangan sebagai hakim selama 40 tahun mengalami tiga zaman.* Jakarta: Ichtiar Baru.

Pudjosewojo, Kusumadi

1952 'Undang-undang Dasar Sementara, peraktek hukum, teori hukum dan peladjaran hukum', *Hukum* 3:8-17.

1959 *Pedoman peladjaran tatahukum Indonesia.* [Second printing.] [Jogjakarta]: Penerbitan Universitas.

Purbacaraka, Purnadi and Soerjono Soekanto

1983 'Pendidikan hukum dan bahasa hukum', *Hukum dan Pembangunan* 13:233-9.

Purbopranoto, Kuntjoro

1954 'Bahasa Indonesia dalam perundang-undangan dan administrasi', *Kongres Bahasa Indonesia Tahun 1954 di Medan,* pp. 96-114. [*Medan Bahasa* 4, 7-8.]

*Pusat Pembinaan dan Pengembangan Bahasa*

1991 *Pusat Pembinaan dan Pengembangan Bahasa.* Jakarta: Pusat Pembinaan dan Pengembangan Bahasa, Departemen Pendidikan dan Kebudayaan.

*Rechtswezen*

1919 'Rechtswezen', in: *Encyclopaedie van Nederlandsch-Indië; Derde deel: N – Soema,* pp. 558-75. 's-Gravenhage: Nijhoff; Leiden: Brill.

Redactie RNI

1910 'Naschrift', *Recht in Nederlandsch-Indië* 95:106-13.

*Regeeringsalmanak*

1865-1942 *Regeeringsalmanak voor Nederlandsch-Indië.* Batavia: Landsdrukkerij. [Also published as *Regerings-almanak voor Nederlandsch-Indië.*]

Reinsma, M. and R. Reinsma

1976 '"De vrouw in wier lichaam zich eerstbedoeld leven ontwikkelt", of Zestig jaar Nederlandse rechtstaal', *Nederlands Juristenblad* 26:857-72.

Reksodiputro, Mardjono
1989 'Pendidikan hukum di Indonesia; Sebuah catatan', *Hukum dan Pembangunan* 19:538-49.
1995a 'Arah perubahan pendidikan tinggi hukum di Indonesia', in: *Pembaharuan pendidikan tinggi hukum di Indonesia dalam menghadapi tantangan abad ke-21; Kumpulan karangan*, pp. 1-16. Jakarta: Konsorsium Ilmu Hukum, Departemen Pendidikan dan Kebudayaan.
1995b 'Laboratorium hukum dalam pembaharuan sistem pendidikan hukum', in: *Pembaharuan pendidikan tinggi hukum di Indonesia dalam menghadapi tantangan abad ke-21; Kumpulan karangan*, pp. 67-76. Jakarta: Konsorsium Ilmu Hukum, Departemen Pendidikan dan Kebudayaan.
1995c 'Meningkatkan penelitian hukum untuk menghadapi tantangan abad ke-21', in: *Pembaharuan pendidikan tinggi hukum di Indonesia dalam menghadapi tantangan abad ke-21; Kumpulan karangan*, pp. 77-87. Jakarta: Konsorsium Ilmu Hukum, Departemen Pendidikan dan Kebudayaan.
1995d 'Pembinaan pendidikan tinggi hukum dalam pembangunan jangka panjang kedua (PJPT II)', *Hukum dan Pembangunan* 15:195-218.

Resink, G.J.
1949 'J. van Kan (18 juli 1877 – 6 juni 1944)', in: *Gedenkboek uitgegeven ter gelegenheid van het vijf en twintig jarig bestaan van het rechtswetenschappelijk hoger onderwijs in Indonesië op 28 october 1949*, pp. 250-7. Groningen/Djakarta: Wolters.
1974 'Rechtshoogeschool, jongereneed, "Stuw" en gestuwden', *Bijdragen tot de Taal-, Land- en Volkenkunde* 130:426-49.

*Resultaten Volkslectuur*
1925 *Resultaten van de Volkslectuur in het jaar 1924*. Weltevreden: Volkslectuur.

Ricklefs, M.C.
1988 *A history of modern Indonesia; c. 1300 to the present*. Reprint. London: Macmillan. [First published 1981.]
1993 *A history of modern Indonesia since c. 1300*. Second edition. Basingstoke: Macmillan.

Riggs, Fred W.
1961 'An ecological approach; The "sala" model'. [Lecture Annual Meeting American Political Science Association, St. Louis, Missouri, 6 September.]
1964 *Administration in developing countries; The theory of prismatic society*. Boston: Houghton Mifflin Company.

*R.I.J.B./H.I.R.*
1954 *R.I.J.B./H.I.R.* [Translated from the Dutch by] M. Karjadi. Bogor: Schenkenhuizen

Romaine, Suzanne
1982 (ed.) *Sociolinguistic variation in speech communities*. London: Edward Arnold.
1989 *Bilingualism*. Oxford: Blackwell.
2000 *Language in society; An introduction to sociolinguistics*. Second edition. New York: Oxford University Press. [First published 1994.]

Rutgers, D.
1911 *Het Inlandsch Reglement; Leiddraad voor studie en praktijk.* Amsterdam: De Bussy.

Sacks, Oliver
1991 *Seeing voices; A journey into the world of the deaf.* London: Picador.

Saleh, Ismail
1989 'Bahasa Indonesia sebagai sarana untuk menciptakan tertib hukum dalam masyarakat', *Varia Peradilan* 41:136-45.

Salim, Amarullah
1989 'Prof. Mahadi, S.H. dalam kenangan', *Varia Peradilan* 51:160-2.

Sastroamijoyo, Ali
1979 *Milestones on my journey; The memoirs of Ali Sastroamijoyo, Indonesian patriot and political leader.* Edited by C.L.M. Penders. St. Lucia: University of Queensland Press.

Scholten, Paul
1931 *Mr. C. Asser's handleiding tot de beoefening van het Nederlandsch burgerlijk recht; Algemeen deel.* Zwolle: Tjeenk Willink.

Schulte Nordholt, Nico
2001 'Indonesia; A nation-state in search of identity and structure', *Bijdragen tot de Taal-, Land- en Volkenkunde* 157:881-901.

Schut, G.H.A.
1985 *Onrechtmatige daad; Volgens BW en NBW.* Derde, geheel herziene druk. Zwolle: Tjeenk Willink.

*Seminar Evaluasi Pembaharuan Pendidikan Hukum*
1982 *Seminar Evaluasi Pelaksanaan Program Pembaharuan Pendidikan Hukum: [risalah]; Diselenggarakan oleh Badan Pembinaan Hukum Nasional bekerja sama dengan Konsorsium Ilmu Hukum, tanggal 17 s/d 19 Mei, 1978 di Bali.* [Jakarta]: BPHN, [Bandung]: Diedarkan oleh Bina Cipta.

Shen, Dan
1989 'Literalism; Non "formal-equivalence"', *Babel* 35:219-35.

Sibenius Trip, J.
1905 'Herinneringen uit de Inlandsche rechtspraak', *Indisch Weekblad van het Recht* 2168, 16 January.

Sidharta, Arief
2002 'Bahasa hukum Indonesia; Krisis bahasa di antara pakem dan frase', *Jentera* 01 (August):80-8.

Simandjuntak, I.P.
1972 'Peranan bahasa Indonesia dalam pendidikan', in: Djajanto Supra and Anton J. Lake (eds), *Seminar Bahasa Indonesia 1972; Puntjak Pass, 2-3 Maret*, pp. 22-38. Flores: Nusa Indah.

Simanjuntak, Marsillam
2002 'Marsillam: "Bahasa hukum sering memperkosa kaidah tata bahasa"', *Jentera* 01 (August):89-94.

Simorangkir, J.C.T. and B. Mang Reng Say
1975 *Tentang dan sekitar Undang-undang Dasar 1945.* Cetakan ke-8. Jakarta: Djambatan.

*Simposium Bahasa dan Hukum*
1976 *Simposium Bahasa dan Hukum; Diselenggarakan dalam rangka kerjasama BPHN dan FH USU pada tg. 25 s/d 27 Nop. 1974 di Medan/Prapat.* Cetakan kedua. Jakarta: Binacipta.

Sinninghe Damsté, J.S.
1999 *Advocaat/soldaat; Oorlogsherinneringen.* Amsterdam: Van Soeren.

Siregar, J.N.
1976 'Bahasa hukum dalam akta-akta/kontrak dan risalah rapat', in: *Simposium Bahasa dan Hukum; Diselenggarakan dalam rangka kerjasama BPHN dan FH USU pada tg. 25 s/d 27 Nop. 1974 di Medan/Prapat*, pp. 63-75. Jakarta: Binacipta.

Sjah, Soetan Mohamad
1960 'Undang-undang adalah karya kebudajaan; Pidato pelantikan Prof.mr Soetan Mohamad Sjah sebagai gurubesar pada Fakultas Hukum Universitas Hasanuddin di Makassar pada tanggal 17 Nopember 1959', *Hukum dan Masyarakat* 3/6:135-52.
1974 'Gaya dan bahasa peraturan', *Hukum Nasional* 24:13-22.
1976 'Pengumpulan istilah hukum; Beberapa sumbangan pikiran kepada usaha pembinaan istilah hukum Indonesia', in: *Simposium Bahasa dan Hukum; Diselenggarakan dalam rangka kerjasama BPHN dan FH USU pada tg. 25 s/d 27 Nop. 1974 di Medan/Prapat*, pp. 51-7. Jakarta: Binacipta.

Sjahrazad (pseudonym of Soetan Sjahrir)
1945 *Indonesische overpeinzingen.* Amsterdam: De Bezige Bij.

Sjahrir, Soetan *see* Sjahrazad

Soekarno
1931 *Indonesië klaagt aan! Pleitrede voor den landraad te Bandoeng op 2 december 1930 gehouden door Ir. Soekarno.* Amsterdam: De Arbeiderspers.
ca 1950 *Indonesia menggugat; Pidato pembelaan Bung Karno dimuka hakim kolonial.* Jakarta: Masco.
1959 'Res Publica, sekali lagi Res Publica!', in: Muhammad Yamin, *Naskah-persiapan Undang-undang Dasar 1945; Djilid I*, pp. 649-702. [Djakarta]: Jajasan Prapantja. [Redevoering 22-4-1959.]
[1964] *Lahirnja Pantja-Sila.* Djakarta: Departemen Penerangan R.I. [Speech 1-6-1945.]

Soemantri, Iwa Koesoema *see* Sumantri, Iwa Kusuma

Soeparto
1929 'De Bond van Oud-Rechtsscholieren', in: *Gedenkboek uitgegeven ter gelegenheid van de opheffing der Rechtsschool in 1928*, pp. 54-8. Weltevreden: Kolff.

Soepomo
1937 *Sedikit tentang hidoep hoekoem bangsa Indonesia (Indonesisch rechtsleven).* Mataram/Yogyakarta: Madjelis Peroesahaan Kitab Taman-Siswa. [Speech Rapat-Besar ke V, Persatoean Taman-Siswa, Mataram, 7-11 July.]
*see also* Supomo

Steiner, George
1975 *After Babel; Aspects of language and translation.* London: Oxford University Press.

Steinhauer, Hein
1981 *Standaard Indonesisch; Norm en ontwikkeling.* [Leiden]: n.n. [Typescript.]
2002 *Leerboek Indonesisch.* Tweede, herziene druk. Leiden: KITLV Uitgeverij.

Steinmetz, H.E.
1897 'Praktische aanteekeningen', *Tijdschrift voor het Binnenlandsch Bestuur* 14:47-66.

Stewart, Susan
1986 'Shouts on the street; Bakhtin's anti-linguistics', in: Gary Saul Morson (ed.), *Bakhtin; Essays and dialogues on his work,* pp. 41-57. Chicago: University of Chicago Press.

Sumantri, Iwa Kusuma
2002 *Sang pejuang dalam gejolak sejarah; Otobiografi Prof.Mr. R.H. Iwa Kusuma Sumantri.* Bandung: Pusat Penelitian Kemasyarakatan dan Kebudayaan, Lembaga Penelitian Universitas Padjadjaran.

Supomo
1949 'Prof.mr. B. ter Haar Bzn. (9 februari 1892 – 20 april 1941); Heroriëntatie op het gebied van adatrechtpolitiek', in: *Gedenkboek uitgegeven ter gelegenheid van het vijf en twintig jarig bestaan van het rechtswetenschappelijk hoger onderwijs in Indonesië op 28 october 1949,* pp. 38-52. Groningen/ Djakarta: Wolters.
1953 'Pidato [...] pada perajaan dies natalis Universitet pada tanggal 16 Pebruari 1953 di Bandung', in: [R. Supomo, Sumitro Djojohadikusumo and Soekarno,] *Tiga pidato pada dies natalis ketiga dari Universitet Indonesia pada tanggal 16 Pebruari 1953 di Bandung,* pp. 3-23. [Bandung]: n.n. [Foundation day speech President Universitet Indonesia.]
*see also* Soepomo

Supra, Djajanto and Anton J. Lake (eds)
1972 *Seminar Bahasa Indonesia 1972; Puntjak Pass, 2-3 Maret.* Flores: Nusa Indah.

Sutarso
[1996] 'Penggunaan bahasa hukum dalam pendidikan umum (buku dan kripsi)', in: J.S. Badudu (ed.), *Analisis dan evaluasi tentang perkembangan 25 tahun penggunaan bahasa hukum,* pp. 33-5. Jakarta: Badan Pembinaan Hukum Nasional, Departemen Kehakiman.

Tamanaha, Brian Z.
1993 *Understanding law in Micronesia; An interpretive approach to transplanted law.* Leiden: Brill.

Tasrif, S.
1975 'Tanggapan atas prasaran Prof. Dr. Mochtar Kusumaatmadja S.H.', in: Mochtar Kusumaatmadja, *Pembinaan hukum dalam rangka pembangunan nasional,* pp. 14-22. [Bandung]: Lembaga Penelitian Hukum dan Kriminologi, Fakultas Hukum, Universitas Padjadjaran.

Teeuw, A.
1955 *De bahasa Indonesia, de wereld en Nederland*. Amsterdam: Djambatan. [Inaugural speech Leiden University.]
1961 *A critical survey of studies on Malay and bahasa Indonesia*. With the assistance of H.W. Emanuels. 's-Gravenhage: Nijhoff.
1972 'The impact of Balai Pustaka on modern Indonesian literature', *BSOAS* 35:111-27.
1979 *Modern Indonesian literature. Volume I*. Second edition. The Hague: Nijhoff.

Termorshuizen-Arts, Marjanne
2003 *Juridische semantiek; Een bijdrage tot de methodologie van de rechtsvergelijking, de rechtsvinding en het juridisch vertalen*. Nijmegen: Wolf Legal Publishers. [PhD thesis Universiteit Leiden.]

Tirtoprodjo, Soesanto
1932 'Bezuinigings-suggesties', *Indisch Tijdschrift van het Recht* 136:497-9.

Tjokroaminoto, O.S.
1981 'Rechtspersoon; Lezing dalam vergadering C.S.I. 18 april 1914', in: A. Zainoel Ihsan and Pitut Soeharto, *Aku pemuda kemarin di hari esok; Kumpulan tulisan asli, lezing, pidato tokoh Pergerakan Kebangsaan, 1913-1938*, pp. 1-10. Jakarta: Jayasakti.

Uhlenbeck, E.M.
1980 *Taalwetenschap; Een eerste inleiding*. The Hague: Smits.

*Unificatie*
1921 'Unificatie', in: *Encyclopaedie van Nederlandsch-Indië; Vierde deel: Soemb – Z*, pp. 496-7. The Hague: Nijhoff; Leiden: Brill.

Utrecht, Elien
1991 *Twee zijden van een waterscheiding; Herinneringen aan Indonesië voor en na de onafhankelijkheid*. Amsterdam: Sua.

Van Niel, Robert
1984 *The emergence of the modern Indonesian elite*. Reprint. Dordrecht/Cinnaminson: Foris. [First published 1960.]

Velden, D. van
1977 *De Japanse interneringskampen voor burgers gedurende de Tweede Wereldoorlog/The Japanese civil internment camps during the Second World War*. Second, expanded edition. Franeker: Wever. [First published 1963.]

*Verslag Commissie hervorming Rechtsschool*
1920 *Verslag van de Commissie tot hervorming van de Inlandsche Rechtsschool (ingesteld bij G. B. van 4 Jan. 1919 no. 18)*. Batavia: Verwachting.

*Verslag Commissie opleiding rechterlijke ambtenaren*
1920 *Verslag van de commissie voor de hervorming van de opleiding van Indische rechterlijke ambtenaren*. The Hague: Algemeene Landsdrukkerij.

*Verslag Rechtshoogeschool*
1941 *Verslag van de lotgevallen der Rechtshoogeschool [...], uitgebracht door den Voorzitter van de Faculteit der Rechtsgeleerdheid [...] op 28 October 1941*.

Vollenhoven, C. van
1910 *Een adatwetboekje voor heel Indië*. Leiden: Brill.

1922 *Indonesische rechtstaal.* Amsterdam: Koninklijke Akademie van Wetenschappen.

1928 *De ontdekking van het adatrecht.* Leiden: Brill.

Voloshinov, V.N.

1973 *Marxism and the philosophy of language.* Translated [from the Russian and with appendices] by Ladislav Matejka and I.R. Titunik. New York: Seminar Press. [First (Russian) edition 1930.] [Generally attributed to M.M. Bakhtin.]

Vos, Pim de

1997 *Achter de blinddoek van Vrouwe Justitia.* Utrecht: Bruna Uitgevers.

Wageningen, H. van

1920 'Opleiding tot landraadsvoorzitter', *Indisch Tijdschrift van het Recht* 112:262-7.

Wahjono, Padmo

1983 'Beberapa permasalahan bahasa hukum di Indonesia', *Hukum dan Pembangunan* 13:201-13.

Wardhaugh, Ronald

1993 *An introduction to sociolinguistics.* Second edition. Oxford/Cambridge, Mass.: Blackwell. [First published 1986.]

Wertheim, W.F.

1956 *Indonesian society in transition; A study of social change.* The Hague/Bandung: Van Hoeve.

Wertheim, W.F. and Hetty Wertheim-Gijse Weenink

1991 *Vier wendingen in ons bestaan; Indië verloren – Indonesië geboren.* Breda: De Geus.

White, James Boyd

1984 *When words lose their meaning; Constitutions and reconstitutions of language, character, and community.* Chicago: University of Chicago Press.

1985 *Heracles' bow; Essays on the rhetoric and poetics of the law.* Madison: University of Wisconsin Press.

1990 *Justice as translation; An essay in cultural and legal criticism.* Chicago: University of Chicago Press.

Wiarda, J.

1988 'De taal van het BW; Over taalbronnen van het BW', in: W.M.J. Bekkers et al., *Meesterlijke taal: over taal en taalgebruik in het recht*, pp. 19-27. Zwolle: Tjeenk Willink.

Wignjosoebroto, Soetandyo

1977 'Keadaan dan masalah profesi hukum di Indonesia sekarang', in: *Seminar Pembinaan Profesi Hukum*, pp. 13-36. Bandung: Binacipta.

1994 *Dari hukum kolonial ke hukum nasional; Suatu kajian tentang dinamika sosial-politik dalam perkembangan hukum selama satu setengah abad di Indonesia (1849-1990).* Jakarta: Raja Grafindo Persada.

Wignyosoebroto, Sutandyo *see* Soetandyo Wignjosoebroto

Willems, Wim

2001 *De uittocht uit Indië, 1945-1995.* Amsterdam: Bert Bakker.

Winarta, Frans Hendra
2000 'Access to legal information; New information, new solution'. Paper, Seminar Access to Legal Information; Language, Dictionaries, Databases, Jakarta, 22-23 August.

Winch, Peter
1990 *The idea of a social science and its relation to philosophy.* Second edition, second printing. Atlantic Highlands, N.J.: Humanities Press International. [First published 1958.]

Winckel, W.A.P.F.L.
1920 *Rechtsbedeeling onder de Inlanders en daarmede gelijkgestelde personen in Ned.-Indië.* 's-Gravenhage: Nijhoff.
1927 'Onbevredigende rechtspraak', *De Indische Gids* 49, II:1007-12.

Wit, Augusta de
[1916] *De godin die wacht.* Second edition. Amsterdam: Van Kampen. [First published 1903.]

Witteveen, Willem Johannes
1988a *De retoriek in het recht; Over retorica en interpretatie, staatsrecht en democratie.* Zwolle: Tjeenk Willink.

Wiwiek, W. Liz
1989a 'Gajah Mada, Universitas', in: *Ensiklopedi Nasional Indonesia; Jilid 6*, pp. 16-7. Jakarta: Cipta Adi Pustaka.
1989b 'Indonesia, Universitas', in: *Ensiklopedi Nasional Indonesia; Jilid 7*, pp. 128-9. Jakarta: Cipta Adi Pustaka.

Wormser, C.W.
1946 *Adat of recht.* Leiden: Burgersdijk en Niermans.

Yamin, H. Muhammad
1959 *Naskah-persiapan Undang-undang Dasar 1945.* Edited by Muhammad Yamin. Vol. 1. [Djakarta]: Jajasan Prapantja.

Zaid, Nasr Hamid Aboe
[1996] *Vernieuwing in het islamitisch denken; Een wetenschappelijke benadering.* Amsterdam: Bulaaq.

*Zeven jaar Republik Indonesia*
[1952] *Zeven jaar Republik Indonesia.* [With a preface by Susanto Tirtoprodjo.] Den Haag: Information Service Indonesia.

Zorab, A.A.
1954 *De Japanse bezetting van Indonesië en haar volkenrechtelijke zijde.* Leiden: Universitaire Pers.

# Index

www.ingramcontent.com/pod-product-compliance
Lightning Source LLC
Chambersburg PA
CBHW061200240926
51846CB00006B/1068
*9789067182713*